Toward the Endless Day

OLGA LOSSKY

Translated by Jerry Ryan

Edited by Michael Plekon

Foreword by Olivier Clément

Toward the
Endless Day

The Life of Elisabeth Behr-Sigel

University of Notre Dame Press

Notre Dame, Indiana

Translated by Jerry Ryan from "Vers le jour sans déclin" by Olga Lossky, published
by Les Éditions du Cerf, Paris, France © 2007 Les Éditions de Cerf

Manufactured in the United States of America

Library of Congress Cataloging-in-Publication Data
Lossky, Olga.
    [Vers le jour sans déclin. English]
    Toward the endless day : The Life of Elisabeth Behr-Sigel / Olga Lossky ;
translated by Jerry Ryan ; edited by Michael Plekon ; foreword by Olivier Clément.
        p.   m.
    "Bibliography of works by Elisabeth Behr-Sigel"—P.
    Includes bibliographical references (p.   ) and index.
    ISBN-13: 978-0-268-03385-9 (pbk. : alk. paper)
    ISBN-10: 0-268-03385-4 (pbk. : alk. paper)
    1. Behr-Sigel, Elisabeth.   2. Orthodox (Orthodox Eastern Church)—France—
Biography.   I. Plekon, Michael, 1948–   II. Title.
    BX395.B44L6713   2010
    230'.19092—dc22
    [B]
                            2010001597

Contents

Foreword

When I was attempting to become a Christian, one of the first witnesses to the Gospel whom I met was Elisabeth Behr-Sigel. Despite our long friendship and work together on numerous initiatives, I never had fully realized the breadth of her life and work until I read this biography. Olga Lossky, who comes from a great and noble line (her great-grandfather Vladimir Lossky was himself a brilliant theologian and the son of a remarkable religious philosopher), despite or perhaps because of her own youth, was able to evoke with incomparable tenderness and humor the complexity of Elisabeth—her person, life, and accomplishments. Olga offers us this biography, born from an ongoing dialogue with Elisabeth and based on the discovery and use of her voluminous correspondence and papers.

Elisabeth Behr-Sigel appears in this biography as a modern saint of the Orthodox tradition, who, impassioned by God, became capable of witnessing here on earth the reality of the Resurrection and the Kingdom of Heaven. She confronted all the tragedies of the twentieth century, two world wars, and the weight of totalitarianism. In these encounters she never hesitated or wavered. In the face of one challenging situation after another, she was a woman with a fundamental vocation, responding to a call from God with complete faith. Through it all, she was a layperson. She was obliged to first teach German, then philosophy, in order to support her family. And in all of her positions she showed others how to live and to proclaim the Gospel, often in new, creative ways.

In the editing and publication of the journal *Contacts* and in the development of the Orthodox Fraternity, she was engaged with a number of friends in efforts to assure the encounter of Christians of the East with those of the West while the Church in Russia was undergoing persecution. Her spirit of openness and dialogue played an enormous role in the development of this work, enabling Christian traditions to meet and enrich each other.

Elisabeth was also a writer of great talent who enlivened a number of areas of theological work. Her first book dealt with the history of holiness in Russia, shaped by her attachment to that country's spiritual tradition. Later, she dedicated herself to the place and condition of women in Christianity, even asking for and receiving, from the patriarch of Constantinople, the promise to restore the diaconate to women, a sacred office that had existed since the eleventh century but that needed to be renewed and adapted to the present day.

All through her long life, this engagement of faith was sustained by a deep friendship with a French priest, Fr. Lev Gillet, who, under the pseudonym "a Monk of the Eastern Church," wrote a number of admirable books on spirituality. Their experience, at once chaste but of extraordinary depth, revealed a common ascent toward the Kingdom of God, a path particularly relevant and welcome in the chaotic world in which we live. So here is the story of a vocation of true holiness, a holiness rooted in eternity, in the Orthodox community of western Europe, and one that underlines the promise of an ecumenism that is no longer mere discussion but true friendship.

Olivier Clément

Acknowledgments

This biography was indeed a collective effort, with its origins coming from the urging of François Cousin. Many people have participated in its preparation, and I would like to mention here the most important of them.

First, I want to recognize Elisabeth's three children and their spouses: Nadine and the late Fr. Jean-M. Arnould, Mariane and Tony Greenan, and Nadia and Nicolas Behr. They made this biography possible by entrusting Elisabeth's archives to me. All welcomed me warmly, opening their doors as well as their memories and enriching the text and its revision by their careful reading and suggestions.

I also want to thank Olivier Clément, who advised me throughout my work and who was willing to do a detailed rereading as he crafted the Foreword. The care and help of Fr. Alexis Struve, who charged me with this project, was absolutely essential to its completion.

Those who agreed to read what I wrote have been a great source of support to me: Fr. Boris Bobrinskoy; Mother Éliane of the Carmelites of Saint Elias, who turned over to me her correspondence with Elisabeth; Fr. Michel Evdokimov; Emmanuel Hériard-Dubreuil, whose historical mastery and advice were very precious to me; Dom Emmanuel Lanne; Paul Ladouceur; Sophie Lossky; Véronique Lossky;

Gabriel Matzneff, who clarified my writing with his remarkable style; Fr. Michael Plekon, Elisabeth Sollogoub, Anne Struve, and Xénia and Jean Tchékan.

My thanks go also to those who were willing to share with me their familiarity with many aspects of Elisabeth's life and work: Lyn and Fr. John Breck, Fr. Jean Gueit, Kyriaki FitzGerald, Pastor Michel Freychet, Fr. Nicolas Lossky, Fr. Michael Plekon, Teva Regule, Michel Sollogoub, Philip Tamoush, and Jacqueline Westercamp. It was with the assistance of Jean-Jacques Laham that I was able to settle on the title, the final quotation, by Charles Péguy, and a number of bibliographic references. And finally, my gratitude goes to the family of Sophie and Fr. Nicolas Rehbinder, who, by their hospitality, made possible the organization of Elisabeth's archives.

Olga Lossky

Acknowledgments
to the English Translation

While Olga Lossky has expressed gratitude to many who made possible her work in writing this wonderful biography of Elisabeth Behr-Sigel, there are some others who deserve recognition and thanks for the appearance of this English language edition.

First, many thanks to Olga herself for writing this biography and for agreeing to this translation of her labor of love, the account of Elisabeth's life and accomplishments, so much of it drawn from Elisabeth's own writings, correspondence, and other archival material. Thanks also to Elisabeth's family for allowing all the photos to be used, and to Laurence Rondinet of Éditions du Cerf for agreeing to allow the University of Notre Dame Press to have the rights to translate. We want to thank Barbara Hanrahan, director of the University of Notre Dame Press, for her willingness to propose this project to the board and for her support. Thanks also to copy editor Ann Aydelotte for helping to iron out rough spots and make the English version flow as did the French and for painstaking attention to many other infelicities that required correction. Matt Dowd as always assisted in so many ways in this project. I also want to thank Fr. John and Lyn Breck for introducing me years ago to Elisabeth and her marvelous work in theology. Both of us thank God for the life, the work, and the witness of Elisabeth, whom we were privileged to have known. Her discerning of the signs of the times will endure for all the children of God.

Michael Plekon and Jerry Ryan

Introduction

"God writes straight with crooked lines." Elisabeth Behr-Sigel liked to cite this Portuguese proverb in her writings and conversations. The crooked lines of our lives sometimes trace meanderings that, from a human point of view, can be thoroughly disconcerting. Such is the case for the ninety-eight years of Elisabeth's life. The journey of the little Lutheran girl from Strasbourg, born German of a Jewish mother, to the Orthodox theologian who, hardly any taller, nearly a century later, would be considered an authority among religious thinkers, passed through several apparently astonishing changes and stages. But these twists and turns all led her in the same direction: the desire to know God. She invested her whole being in this desire, especially her intellectual gifts, through a theological commitment. Every choice that she made in the course of her life was the expression of a total confidence in God, of a faith in the Risen Christ, that sustained her throughout the great historical and religious events of the twentieth century.

I had already taken upon myself the task of unraveling the threads of such a rich life when, one Saturday in November 2004, I went to Elisabeth's little apartment in Épinay-sur-Seine for the first time. The "grande dame of Western Orthodoxy" was, at that time, ninety-seven years old, and many people had been hoping that she would write an autobiography. She had no such project in mind, but she had let it be known that she would have no objection to relating her past experiences to someone who would put them together in some sort of format. Thus it was that I presented myself, armed with a tape recorder and feeling very apprehensive, to this theologian whom I had previously only seen from afar, up on the stage, at a congress or at some important Orthodox assembly.

During this first interview, I had difficulty getting over my amazement at her longevity. I found it hard to believe that the fragile and energetic little woman sitting in front of me had heard the order of general mobilization at the beginning of the First World War or had socialized with the Russian émigrés of my great-great-grandparents' generation.

Little by little, in the course of our Saturday lunches, Elisabeth's personality became more familiar to me. I discovered a woman of strong character who, with the passage of time, had acquired an affability that in no way took the edge off her intellectual vivacity. While conserving an acute awareness of the needs of her times, she focused all her activity on the implantation of Orthodoxy in the West after having discovered it in the 1930s through her contacts with Russian émigrés in Paris. Having inherited the rigorous Protestant scriptural tradition and having served as a pastor in Alsace—one of the first women in France to be given such a post—she became one of the major voices in the ecumenical dialogue. Her desire to serve the Church played itself out within the context of an intense family life and a profession that had little to do with theology.

This living memory of the Orthodox Church in Western Europe did not, by any means, dwell in the past. Her readiness to take positions on today's controversies testified to her desire to find the answers to contemporary problems within the Tradition of the Church. She was fond of citing the Gospel passage where Christ speaks of the need to "discern the signs of the times" (Matt. 16:3), inviting us to sense in which direction the Holy Spirit is breathing so that we might be associated with its workings. With the audacity and freedom characteristic of her, Elisabeth never ceased to strive to make the Orthodox Church not just a simple religious identity but also a place where the Living God could be encountered.

✎ Our customary lunches came to an end a year after our first meeting in Epinay when, on a Saturday morning in November 2005, Elisabeth did not wake up. It was now up to me to give a voice to the pile of archives and letters that she had often casually pointed out to me as proof of her overwhelming work. Elisabeth's children entrusted these precious documents to me and shared their own memories, as did many of her friends. This led me to discover other aspects of this woman who, in spite of our age difference, treated me affectionately and as a friend: Liselotte, the restless adolescent, the young intellectual impassioned with Russian culture; the mother preoccupied with the challenge of providing for her family during the German occupation; the woman theologian who got on peoples' nerves by her determination to defend her ideas—I tried to put all these different images together, give them coherence, and connect them to this frail little lady who, with her kitchen cupboards as a backdrop, had said to me: "Actually, my life isn't all that interesting. I was just lucky enough to meet some extraordinary people."

When she retraced the long journey of her life for me in our conversations, Elisabeth never dwelt on events or acts but always on people. Her story was one of meeting the "other," the neighbor for whom she was always receptive, open, totally present in the given moment. Her personality was woven of all these destinies that intersected hers in the course of her life.

In addition to the stories related to me by Elisabeth and by those who knew her, I found a unique testimony of the evolution of her inner feelings in her archives. This evolution was sketched out through her letters and the notebooks in which she sporadically confided thoughts in moments of difficulty. The conservation of these intimate papers seems out of line with the personality of Elisabeth, who was reticent to speak about herself. But, in them, one can read the whole spiritual destiny of a life dominated by a single and permanent question: How do we live our faith in God at each instant through all the choices and events that we must confront?

No doubt, Elisabeth, by preserving these papers, was aware that the revelation of the very eloquent, crooked lines of her destiny could be useful to others. Indeed, this life-witness is given to us as a model. It is an example of a woman very much a part of the times in which she lived, who, in her successes as well as in her failures, in her great intellectual contributions as well as in her weaknesses, wanted to be the messenger of the Risen Christ, present in our midst.

From the angel at the tomb,

The holy women learned the joyous news.

Throwing off the curse that fell on Adam,

They ran in haste to tell the friends of the Lord.

Their hearts could not contain their joy as they cried aloud:

"Death is overthrown! Christ has risen,

Blessing all the world with His great mercy."

—Byzantine rite Sunday Resurrectional hymn, tone 4

chapter one

THE ENCOUNTERS OF THE FORMATIVE YEARS, 1907–1932

Eugene Sigel and a Strasbourg Childhood

It was in the heart of Alsace, in Schiltigheim, that Elisabeth was born on July 21, 1907. This village bordering on Strasbourg and affectionately called Schilick by its inhabitants, still conserves its rural charms, with its half-timbered peasant houses, its farms flanked by stables and barns. With the arrival of industrialization, the village little by little encroached on the surrounding countryside. There, in a new house on the outskirts, Charles Sigel and his second wife, Emma Altschul, set themselves up.

Elisabeth Charlotte Sigel was the eagerly awaited child of this couple who had married the previous year in Dresden. For the new household, her birth represented, for both Charles and Emma, the fulfillment of a dream. The first wife of Charles had sunk into dementia, a profound emotional pathology most likely genetic, while Emma, the youngest child of a large family, did not have the dowry that would enable her to marry within her circle.

Nothing seemed to predestine Charles, the Lutheran, and Emma, the Austrian Jew, to find one another. Emma Altschul, whose name means "old synagogue" in Yiddish and perhaps indicates that there were rabbis among her ancestors, saw her dowry and hopes for marriage dwindle as her five older sisters found themselves husbands. Rather than wait in vain for a hypothetical suitor, Emma, to the surprise of those around her, decided to earn her own living. She learned bookkeeping and honed her foreign-language skills in view of doing office work. It is with this in mind that she visited one of her sisters who lived in Strasbourg and whose husband was a businessman. Emma did find a job and met Charles Sigel, an Alsatian who was working in the offices of the Fischer brewery.

Elisabeth described her father thus: "He was typical of the people who lived close to the border, bilingual, a man of a double culture like so many Alsatians, with a heart sometimes divided between a twofold allegiance, but solidly rooted in the land and the region and at the same time open to the fullness of European culture."[1] Charles belonged to the Strasbourg bourgeoisie. His marriage to Emma was not to the liking of the Sigel family. In spite of the cosmopolitan character of the city, open to both France and Germany and, like Charles, shaped by both cultures, espousing an Austro-Hungarian Jewess was not part of the customs of the Alsatian bourgeoisie of those times.

The Sigel family had deep roots in Strasbourg and were descended from modest artisans who had enriched themselves in the nineteenth century through their painting and glazing business. Their rise to the middle class enabled them to acquire several houses in the old city, not far from the imposing cathedral, and also to construct a church there. Emma Altschul was therefore received very coldly by her in-laws. Fortunately, the untypical marriage of Charles had had a precedent, namely, that of his father, Eugene, to a German, Catherine.

✂ Elisabeth was well acquainted with the history of her grandfather, a familiar figure of whom she had legendary memories. The third of the Sigel sons, born in Strasbourg in 1836, Eugene wanted to become a pastor and thus moved toward the study of theology, to the great satisfaction of his parents. Eugene's religious education took place in the context of the Protestant liberalism of the end of the nineteenth century, marked by the development of scientific exegesis and, more specially, by the works of Ernest Renan. Under his influence as well as that of the German David Friedrich Strauss, Eugene questioned the historical certainty of the life of Christ. This rational questioning of the Gospel caused him to lose his faith. He then decided, in 1860, to end his theological studies. His father, disappointed by this choice, refused to pay for a substitute when the time for his military service came up, which he had done for Eugene's two older brothers.

When his number was drawn for mobilization, Eugene began a military career. He participated in the Mexican campaign under the orders of General Achille Bazaine, who had begun the fight against the Mexican government of Benito Juárez in 1861. In 1866, Napoleon III ordered the withdrawal of the French troops and Eugene returned to Europe with the rank of lieutenant. When the Franco-Prussian War broke out in 1870, Eugene again found himself serving under General Bazaine, who decided to shelter his army at Metz. Put under siege by the Prussians, the city surrendered on October 27, 1870, and Lieutenant Sigel was taken prisoner. He was imprisoned at Worms, in the Rhineland.

The conditions of detention were flexible, and the prisoner of war, who was well treated, was soon released after giving his word not to take up arms. He was now free to move around as he pleased in the German Empire. He became friendly with the Stressingers, a family of the Rhineland bourgeoisie, and fell in love with their daughter Catherine. In the middle of the war, Elisabeth's grandfather married this German woman who was fifteen years younger than he. The couple settled for a time at Worms, where their son Charles was born in 1873. The bankruptcy of Catherine's father forced Eugene and his family to return to Strasbourg, which was then under the German flag. Since its annexation in 1871 by the German Empire, the city had become the capital of Alsace-Lorraine.

After a chilly reception, the Sigels little by little accepted their German daughter-in-law. "Käthchen, a very sweet blonde, adapted to and

gained the affection of her new Alsatian family and became Francophile in the process," Elisabeth wrote in her autobiographical notes.
Eugene found work at the *Journal d'Alsace-Lorraine*, the only French
newspaper authorized by the Germans at that time. During the period
of German annexation, he became one of the rare Francophone Alsatian journalists. This native son, with deep ancestral roots in Strasbourg, remained very attached to France as did the rest of his family.
When he gave bread crumbs to the pigeons in Kléber Park, he even
spoke to them in French.

Thus, when Charles introduced his new wife, Emma, to his parents, Eugene and Catherine received her with understanding because
they too had suffered from the same family ostracism to which this
young couple had been exposed.

✻ Elisabeth came into the world during the first hours of a beautiful
Sunday morning after her mother's difficult labor. Her family gave her
the German name of Liselotte, and she would continue to go by that
name for the rest of her life. At the age of one she was baptized in the
Lutheran Church by a pastor who was a good friend of Charles and
who also became her godfather. The little girl, whose cosmopolitan
ancestry mirrored that of the city of her birth, an important center of
the Reformation marked by a multitude of diverse influences, spoke
her first words in German.

Young Elisabeth's infancy was very sheltered. For the well-to-do
of the bourgeoisie of which she was a part, the annexation of Alsace-
Lorraine by the Second Reich, from 1871 to 1918, was synonymous with
prosperity. Strasbourg, in fact, experienced an important industrial
surge because of its links with the extremely rich Ruhr region. Thanks
to his job with Fischer, Charles was well off, and this assured the child
of a life of ease. The Alsatian bourgeoisie did not consider the German presence an occupation by foreigners since it had always made it
a point of honor to affirm itself on the fringe of French identity. The
separation of Church and State proclaimed by the French Republic in
1905 turned the sympathies of the Alsatians, often monarchists, toward Germany. These years of annexation were thus a period of tran-
quility for the Sigels.

Everything was peaceful at Schilick as Elisabeth grew up. From an early age, the little girl became aware that she belonged to a dissident and somewhat eccentric branch of the Sigel family. Even though she was only three years old when her grandfather Eugene died, she knew his history well thanks to the many stories told about him. And she felt a special affinity with this ancestor whose scrambled destiny prefigured her own.

Elisabeth was soon able to set out to explore the empty lots and fallow gardens of the neighborhood in the company of her two friends, Herta and Jeanne:

> One [was] German, the other Alsatian. But we only became aware of this difference later on. They were our neighbors. One was the daughter of a notary, the other of a family doctor. We played together from morning till night. When the weather was nice, we played in the doctor's garden, which had a swing, but mostly in the "wild animal ditch," the low garden behind the notary's villa; when the weather was bad, we played in the big house with its nooks and crannies, its offices that we were not allowed to enter, its attic filled with old toys and mysteries.[2]

Elisabeth also remembered participating in the demanding farm work that mobilized the whole village according to the rhythms of the seasons: "As a child, I also helped at the bringing in of the hay and at the harvests. We would come home in big, sturdy wagons pulled with great solemnity by Brabançon horses, in the midst of sweet-smelling hay or sheaves of wheat. But I was only a guest at these important moments of rural life."[3] Among her first memories was the solemn sound of the great bell of Strasbourg's cathedral, which lulled her to sleep when she visited her paternal grandparents. It was a peaceful and reassuring sound, like a song from an idyllic childhood.

The Jewish Side of the Family and Summers in Bohemia

Elisabeth had a more sustained relationship with her mother's family than with her father's Francophone side, who always kept their distance from Emma. Elisabeth's mother, who spoke Alsatian badly and knew little French, felt like a stranger in Alsace, a sentiment that would become stronger when the region was returned to France after the World War, with the ensuing anti-German phobia. Emma kept very much in touch with her family, especially through her sister Olga, who lived in Strasbourg and whose daughter Gertrude was one of Elisabeth's playmates: "My cousin Trudel (the Alsatian diminutive for Gertrude) was ten years older than I and like a big sister. We amused ourselves by dressing up like dolls in Aunt Olga's dressmaking shop, whose clients included the actresses and singers of the Strasbourg Grand Theater."

Uncles, aunts, and cousins from Austria-Hungary had left their native village of Tcheska-Leipa in Bohemia to settle in Prague, Dresden, or Trieste. They often visited the Alsatian capital where they spent Christmas and Easter—pretexts for big family reunions—with the Sigels. Emma returned regularly to her childhood village in Bohemia at the foot of the Sudeten mountains where her father, Nathan Altschul, ran an upholstery business and where her mother, Sophie, still lived. It was there, in the house of her grandmother Sophie, that Liselotte spent most of her summers. The Altschul family was on the margins of the traditional bourgeoisie. They were not so rich, but they were more intellectual and owned a great deal of property. In her autobiographical fragments, Elisabeth gives a nostalgic description of these long-ago visits:

When I was small we would go to spend our vacations in Bohemia every other year. The journey was marvelous. We would leave in the evening. Mother would wrap me up in a plaid lap robe that cushioned the hard seat of the third-class coach, and I would fall asleep right away, lulled by the rhythmic movement of the train. When I woke up, we would have already gone very far, and everything seemed new and extraordinary to me. Sometimes we had some rather odd traveling companions, such as a woman who, to my amazement, opened a big black bag and took out a marmoset monkey who knew how to crack nuts. During the trip, we would usually stop at Dresden or Nuremberg, depending on the itinerary we had mapped out; and I recall, as if in a dream, glimpses of the old houses and the flower-filled ramparts of Nuremberg in that summer of 1913, which was the last summer of peace. We finally arrived at Prague where our cousins fell all over us, lifting me up, hugging me. Papa was speaking French. Nobody understood much of what he said, but that didn't matter. Like a magic charm, the language of the country synonymous with freedom provoked reactions of attentiveness and sympathy. Mama and her sisters spoke Czech—an impossible language, full of consonants—among themselves. But everyone knew German.

The little girl from Strasbourg, the youngest of all the cousins and the only Christian, was the idol of the Altschul family and especially of her grandmother Sophie. In spite of her Lutheran baptism, the child could be considered Jewish since this identity is inherited through the mother. Elisabeth had wonderful memories of the affectionate atmosphere that marked these vacations in Bohemia. She felt that she was deeply loved and badly spoiled.

✗ This childhood, so surrounded with affection, was not very marked by religious practices. Elisabeth went to church just once a year, on Good Friday, in the company of her father, who went as well to fulfill his "Easter duty." The Alsatian branch of the family had a special sentimental attachment to the new church building, which had been constructed, in part, by Elisabeth's great-grandparents.

Emma, her mother, was a believer but she did not attend the Alsatian synagogues, which were all Francophone. She was not very attached to the practices of her religion since she had married a Christian and had had her child baptized. All the same, she remained faithful to one Jewish Holy Day: once a year, on the Day of Atonement, she withdrew to her room to read the traditional prayers. Also, on the evening of the Sabbath, she went to sleep turned eastward toward the Temple of Jerusalem. Emma was not very ostentatious about her religious practices, and it was only later that Elisabeth even would realize that her mother was Jewish. If Emma never talked to her daughter about religion, however, she did teach her to pray every evening. Thus it was that, in spite of the absence of a religious setting, Elisabeth acquired at an early age the habit of turning to God each day.

This sensitivity to the divine was reinforced by the catechetical instruction that Elisabeth was given when she started going to school. When she was six years old, she began to attend a Protestant private boarding school as a nonresident student. The school was known for the quality of its education, especially in religious matters. From the start, Elisabeth was fascinated by the biblical heroes whose stories intrigued her. In the context of an open-minded family, where free thinking took the place of systematic religious education, she seized the initiative by exploring the religious topics that held a special attraction for her.

Her Schoolmates and the Liberation of Strasbourg

The peaceful harmony of Elisabeth's infancy and early childhood was shattered by the cannons of the World War. She had no way of knowing the scope of the drama that was taking place around her. Coming and going to school, she found the spectacle of the military drills at the army barracks amusing. But she was aware of the anguish in this atmosphere of combat around her and wrote in her autobiographical notes that the war was "the first shadow that fell across this happy childhood." On November 22, 1918, French troops entered Strasbourg, liberating a city with a mixed population and a complex national identity. The Alsatian Protestant bourgeoisie tended to be pro-French, while the common people and the villagers remained attached to their Alsatian heritage. Elisabeth saw her grandmother Catherine, a German, rejoice at the entry of the French troops among whom her husband Eugene had served.

The arrival of the French soldiers in the Alsatian capital was a traumatic experience for Elisabeth. The Germans who had settled in Strasbourg during the annexation period become the target of general contempt and were obliged to leave the city. At the age of eleven, Elisabeth personally experienced this eruption of nationalism and prejudice: the two charming German women who taught at her boarding school suddenly became the Boches and had to endure the sarcasm of those who previously had found them so kind.

The father of her best friend, Herta, had to abandon his grand villa in Schilick. Unable to face ruin, he committed suicide. Elisabeth and Herta, profoundly shocked by this tragedy, did not know where to turn for support and consolation. In the end they finally went to church, there to seek refuge in God. This brutal catastrophe was followed by the forced departure to Germany of other classmates. The cruelty that marked this change in national identity left its impression on young Elisabeth. She would keep a deep-rooted hatred for any form of nationalism whose absurdity she had so violently experienced. And the direct confrontation with death, in the suicide of Herta's father, opened within her an abyss of new questions.

❧ The year 1918 was also another turning point in Elisabeth's life, and this too was linked with the return of Alsace to France. She left the little private Protestant boarding school and entered the fifth-year class at the French-culture secondary school in conformity with her new nationality. The Treaty of Versalles, signed on June 28, 1919, integrated her totally into the French State.

Since Elisabeth had received some of her primary-school education in French, she was immediately placed in a Francophone class. The majority of her classmates were French young people from the interior of the country who had come to settle in Alsace at the end of the war. This meant a strenuous and difficult year for the German-speaking child. In this new setting, however, Elisabeth showed herself to be an assiduous student and quickly caught up with the others. By the end of the year she had completely mastered French. Her school-work, which had been judged unsatisfactory at the beginning, received high praise.

The French secondary school offered a multidisciplined education in an atmosphere of dialogue and freedom that opened new horizons for her and played a decisive role in her passion for her studies. It was also a time of deep friendships, which would greatly influence her. Elisabeth became especially close friends with Madeleine Charlety, the daughter of the dean of the University of Strasbourg.

Elisabeth now felt completely assimilated to French culture and was eager to discover its new riches, which aroused her curiosity. German would remain the language spoken within the family. This preference saddened Elisabeth's mother. Emma never took sides in the Franco-German conflicts and remained nostalgic for the Austria of her youth, even though the Treaty of Versailles gave her Czechoslo-vakian citizenship. Elisabeth's preference for French, coupled with her introverted personality, created a certain distance between mother and daughter.

After the return of Alsace to France, there was still a European climate in the Sigel household: one needed only to cross the Rhine to be in Germany, where Elisabeth felt as much at home as on the French side of the river. From this childhood, influenced by several converging cultures and peoples, she would retain a spirit of openness that enabled her to rise above any sentiment of nationalism, even though she chose French as her first language.

Suzanne de Dietrich and the Fédé

For Elisabeth, the transition from childhood to adolescence was marked by a growing spiritual search that led her to ask herself questions about her faith in God: "I was baptized in the Lutheran Church to which my father belonged. But I received hardly any religious education from my family. Like many children and adolescents who are spiritually left on their own, I asked myself a lot of metaphysical questions."[4] Freely, without any pressure from her family, she chose to make her profession of faith as a Lutheran, "a public act in which the young Protestant confirms his personal adherence to the faith confessed, on his behalf, by the godparents at the moment of his baptism and, at that time, unconsciously received by the infant."[5] By this profession, Elisabeth committed herself to an active life of faith.

"This confirmation was a moment of great fervor," she wrote in her autobiographical notes. The catechism classes given by the pastor in preparation for the event gave her the chance to freely ask the essential questions that haunted her. But a shadow fell over the joy of this new path on which she had set out. Elisabeth had the painful feeling that her faith commitment was not understood by her mother and only emphasized the distance between them—a process initiated by their linguistic differences. "After a turbulent adolescence, I experienced a personal conversion to Christ. This was a source of suffering for my mother, who saw it as the intrusion of an outside element between the two of us. But she said nothing."[6] Elisabeth made her solemn profession of faith on April 9, 1922, the year she completed secondary school. She received her certificate on July 10, just before she turned fifteen. Influenced by a schoolmate, she then joined the Strasbourg "Fédé," a branch of the World Federation of Christian Student Associations. To understand the decisive role that this movement would have in Elisabeth's life, one must outline its origins.

The World Federation was founded in 1895: a small group of Protestants engaged in missionary activity—among them John R. Mott, an American active in evangelization—decided to bring together the different youth movements to form a universal union of students.[7] At the time when Elisabeth joined the Fédé, the movement was enjoying a rapid expansion. It was already marked by an ecumenical and international openness inspired by its motto: "That all may be one, so that the world may believe." "The Fédé played an important role in the ecumenical movement that emerged after the World War . . . We wanted to dedicate ourselves to the service of Christ and to the task of restoring unity among Christians who had become separated in the course of history."[8]

This twofold objective—Christian unity, and renewal of the Gospel message so that it might become meaningful—had a significant influence on the orientation of Elisabeth's faith. The cell-group to which she belonged, and which met regularly, included several Roman Catholics among its members. Their activities were centered on Bible studies and reflection on contemporary social problems.

Participation in the Fédé would prove to be very important for this young adolescent preoccupied with existential questions. Elisabeth was most appreciative of the atmosphere of deep fraternity that characterized the circles of Bible studies and the meetings of the group. There she became aware of the reality of the presence of Christ in her life: "It is in this circle that I had the spiritual experiences that determined the direction my life would take: up to this time I considered the Gospel as, essentially, a code, or rather a moral atmosphere. For the first time I felt personally loved by God, called by Christ, as was the young rich man, to follow Him without worrying about the rest."[9]

During the different congresses of the World Federation, Elisabeth met a number of Protestants who would have a great influence on her. Foremost among them was Suzanne de Dietrich, the secretary of the French branch of the World Federation.

A militant Protestant, a theologian, and a descendant of the Alsatian aristocracy, Suzanne de Dietrich put her intelligence and faith at the service of the discussion groups she led. She was a woman of character, trained as an electrical engineer, and she became like an older sister to Elisabeth. The two women would meet again later in other ecumenical gatherings. Suzanne de Dietrich was also a mystic who radiated a spiritual strength acquired through a real relationship with God. During one of the summer camps sponsored by the Fédé, she wrote this phrase in Elisabeth's notebook: "My soul rests in God . . . in silence."

Elisabeth also met Pastor Marc Boegner. She already knew his brother, who was the pastor of the Reformed parish she attended in Strasbourg. Marc Boegner, a pioneer of ecumenism, would play a decisive role in the creation of the World Council of Churches while, at the same time, working actively in the social center of the CIMADE, or Comité Inter-Mouvements pour l'Accueil des Évacués [Inter-Movement Committee of Aid to Refugees], an ecumenical Protestant organization. Later on, she would be active in both these organizations. Moreover, she ran across Pastor Pierre Maury, who was at that time the secretary general of the World Federation. Maury would have a great influence on a whole generation of young pastors and laypeople in France by introducing them to the thought of Karl Barth.

The Fédé was, in addition, a place where Elisabeth served a literary and aesthetic apprenticeship. In the France of the years of madness, when the traumas of war led certain intellectuals and writers to seek spiritual answers, Liselotte discovered Paul Claudel through his play *Partage de Midi*. She was enthusiastic about the works of Charles Péguy, especially *Le Porche du Mystère de la deuxième vertu*, which Pastor Westphal would read aloud during the emotion-filled evening meetings of the Fédé.

These years full of meetings and apprenticeships forged Elisabeth's spirit. She acquired a rigorous knowledge of Holy Scripture as well as a freedom of conscience and of choice, all part of the Protestant legacy. The Fédé stimulated her questioning of the meaning of existence, gave her the opportunity to experience a faith both real and lived out, and made her responsive to ecumenical dialogue. "The Fédé has been a spiritual family, a place where I blossomed," she would later say. Henceforth, she was driven by the desire to have a more profound relationship with the Living God. This desire would have a significant affect on all her future decisions.

Russian Scholarship Students at the University of Strasbourg and the Encounter with the Eastern Church

Studies in Philosophy

In July 1925, Elisabeth was awarded her high-school diploma *cum laude* in liberal arts, and this marked the end of her courses at the French secondary school in Strasbourg. Since she was deeply interested in metaphysical questions, she quite naturally turned to philosophical studies. In September 1925 she entered the School of Fine Arts of the University of Strasbourg. One of her fellow students was Emmanuel Levinas, who was a year older than she. Elisabeth remembered this "little Lithuanian Jew" with affection, and they would maintain a correspondence until his death in 1995. Several years later, after he had left Strasbourg to continue his studies in Paris, Levinas took Liselotte into his confidence in a very personal way: "Even with the faithful friendship of the Blanchot brothers and the relationships that one has at the Sorbonne, I sometimes feel very much alone. It's not a physical solitude nor, still less, an intellectual solitude—it's quite simply that, like a little child, I miss my mother. This sentiment of the depth and the supreme value of the concrete, of the material and physical and palpably concrete, seems to me, more and more, to be the truth itself."[10]

At the University of Strasbourg, Levinas, Elisabeth, and a third student made up a friendly trio inspired by the same thirst for reflection. The small size of their class—some thirty students—aided their work. The philosophical approaches were varied: some of the professors were Thomists, others disciples of Emile Durkheim. With the discovery of Henri Bergson, Elisabeth felt that she could get out of the rut of scientism, which was very popular at that time. Together with

Levinas, she also became interested in the phenomenology of Edmund Husserl, a professor at Fribourg-en-Brisgau, on the other side of the Rhine.

But Elisabeth was not entirely satisfied with her philosophical studies. Her restless and constantly inquiring faith led her toward other fields: "The quest for a human wisdom left me unsatisfied, even though it provided me with great intellectual joys. I soon had the inner conviction that God was calling me to something else. When I was nineteen, I told my parents that I wanted to study theology. This upset my mother very much. But they gave me permission to go ahead on the condition that I first get my degree in philosophy."[11] Even though theological studies were, at that time, reserved for men, the innovative spirit that animated the Protestant Faculty of Theology at Strasbourg would enable Elisabeth to realize her desire when classes began in September 1927.

Before that, however, a tragic event threw a shadow over her life: Emma, her mother, had died on January 30, 1927, after running a high fever. This sudden death plunged the young woman into a period of depression and distress, intensified by the feeling that she had not sufficiently manifested her love for her mother. She mentioned this in her autobiographical fragments:

> I did not know my mother well—I mean, I didn't make the effort I needed to make to understand her as one understands a friend. When she died, at the age of forty-nine, I was only nineteen and just emerging from a prolonged adolescence, which was tormented and studious and which had left me wrapped up in myself. Mama certainly suffered from a certain coldness on my part, but beneath it there was a great deal of affection. I was extremely discreet and reserved and only showed my feelings in the letters I wrote to her during my vacations, when I was far away from her. I will always regret not having shown her enough tenderness—even though, in her final agony, she found the strength to murmur to my father and to myself that our love had made her happy. Actually, I'm afraid that I was more of a source of worry and concern for her, especially during the final years of her life. The war of 1914–1918 had created an abyss between her generation and mine.

Emma's agony, however, brought the mother and daughter closer together, and this relieved Elisabeth's sense of guilt: "During her long and terrible sickness our relationship deepened little by little. I had the consolation of feeling that there was an immense and silent tenderness between us."[12]

The wound of this premature loss left the scar of an emotional emptiness on Elisabeth. On her twentieth birthday, six months after the death of her mother, she wrote to a friend: "It seems to me as though these last few months have been a long, dusty road. I tried to pretend that I wasn't tired, but now weariness overcomes me." Emma's death marked the end of an era for Elisabeth. Her childhood and postwar carefree life now belonged to another time.

Admission to Theological Studies, September 1927

During the summer of 1927, Elisabeth stayed at the Fédé house at Mouterhouse, in the department of the Vosges. Suzanne de Dietrich was a familiar face there. On several occasions young Liselotte would spend time at Mouterhouse in the summer months. It was a peaceful place where she could absorb the spirit of the Fédé and find comfort. When she returned to the university, the fact of being admitted to the Faculty of Theology helped her to forget her sorrow a bit. The previous year a woman student had been allowed to sit in on the classes, but it was only in September 1927 that Elisabeth became one of the first women to start a course in theology while she continued to work toward her degree in philosophy. Such an innovation was not surprising at an institution very much influenced by the German mentality, which was open to change and used to an international mix.

Elisabeth recalled her first theology classes with a sense of humor. When the three ground-breaking female students entered the lecture hall, they were greeted with a thunderous stomping of feet underneath the benches. This somewhat derisive reception given to these pioneers by their male fellow students soon turned to friendship. Elisabeth, who had the advantage of her two years of philosophical studies and her aptitude for reflection, did very well and became totally assimilated into her class.

The Faculty of Strasbourg, faithful to its spirit of openness, also offered scholarships to foreign students. Elisabeth's class included three young Orthodox students—a Romanian and two Russians, all recent èmigrès, with whom the young woman sympathized. One of the two Russian scholars, Georges Serikoff, would become a priest. Elisabeth had more contact with the other, Paul Fidler. She described Fidler, almost ten years older than she, as "good-natured and, at the same time, a bit crazy and amoral." They shared a number of interests including music and theological reflection. He introduced her to an Alsatian couple who were artists—the Jaggis—and Elisabeth became a frequent visitor to their home, quite close to the Faculty. Madame Jaggi, who was a painter, did a portrait of Elisabeth with her head inclined, her eyes closed as if she were dozing off. Elisabeth explained this position by the fact that she was listening attentively to the music that the artist's husband was playing as a distraction during the long posing sessions.[13]

Through Paul Fidler, the young woman entered into contact with the world of the Russian èmigrès, which fascinated her right from the start. It was thanks to her classmate that Elisabeth first discovered Russian religious thought, and this would turn out to be of capital importance to her. The future theologian became enthusiastic about the works of the nineteenth-century Slavophile writer Alexis Khomiakov, especially his book *The Church Is One*. The reflections of this religious philosopher opened up for her a whole new vision of the Church, no longer envisaged as an institution but, above all, as a living community of faith and love: "The Church is a living organism, the organism of truth and of love, or, more exactly, truth and love as organism."[14] These were the definitions of the Church that the young Lutheran theology student assimilated and that counteracted the rather *a priori* negative and hierarchical conception she previously had held. Khomiakov wrote: "No one is saved alone. The person who is saved is saved in the Church, in union with all its other members. If a person believes, it is within a community of faith; if a person loves, it is within a community of love; if a person prays, it is within a community of prayer."[15]

An indication of the importance that Khomiakov attached to the quest for Christian unity can be found in the correspondence he maintained for ten years, from 1844 to 1854, with the Anglican William Palmer, a Fellow of Magdalen College, Oxford, who was engaged in the renewal of the Anglican Church. Khomiakov wrote to his friend: "I really believe that there are many cultivated Russians who recite the petition in the liturgy, to grant unity to all Christians, with all their heart and soul and not just with their lips."[16] Elisabeth was deeply moved by this desire for unity as well as by Khomiakov's idea of returning to the Tradition of the undivided Church—a return that would make it possible to "overcome the antagonism between Protestant individualism and the constraining and authoritarian unity of Roman Catholicism."[17]

The interdenominational friendship with Serikoff and Fidler, which put Elisabeth into contact with Russian religious thought, was not an isolated experience. It was in the context of the climate of openness that prevailed at the time. The budding ecumenical movement, rooted in a desire to know one another better, found concrete expression in the first Faith and Order conference in 1927. This meeting at Lausanne gathered members of the Protestant, Anglican, and Orthodox Churches—notably Fr. Sergius Bulgakov, one of the principal theologians of the Russian èmigrè community—and inaugurated an era of ecumenical reflection on the fundamental aspects of Christian faith in view of trying to find a way to bring the Churches closer to one another. The World Federation had, in fact, an ecumenical dimension insofar as its members were affiliated with associations of different denominations such as the Russian Christian Student Association, a movement of Orthodox young people founded in Czechoslovakia in 1923 by Russian exiles. Elisabeth wrote of these burgeoning interdenominational contacts: "Within the Fédé, the relations between the associations of Protestant inspiration and the Russian Christian Student Association (which defined itself as a movement within Orthodoxy) were frequent and warm, without any trace of proselytism on either side. We wanted to know one another better and love one another better. So I started studying Russian."[18]

Elisabeth participated actively in this overture to others and became president of the Strasbourg branch of the Fédé. The meetings she organized were the occasion for dynamic exchanges among the different denominations. Her three Orthodox friends were invited to these circles of reflection where each one could speak about the particularities of his or her Church. However, Elisabeth's enthusiastic discovery of Russian thought and of the émigré community through her friendship with Paul Fidler was not without its ambiguities. The relations between the two classmates became more complex as a sentimental dimension was added to the intellectual one. Fidler, who was already married, pretended to have fallen in love with Elisabeth. His attitude toward her caused her a painful emotional confusion.

The Experience of Easter Joy

In the spring of 1928, Elisabeth participated in the organization of a congress of the French Fédé for the feast day of Easter. This meeting brought all the regional Fédés to the Paris area and Elisabeth invited her three Orthodox friends. The gap between the Gregorian calendar, which Western Christians follow, and the Julian calendar, which was followed by the Orthodox, allowed her Russian friends to invite Liselotte to attend the Orthodox Easter Vigil celebrated at the St. Sergius Theological Institute. This school of theology, founded by Russian émigrés in 1925, sat on a little hill in the 19th arrondissement of Paris, on the site of a former Lutheran church.

This Easter Vigil at St. Sergius was an extremely moving experience for her, "a passage from darkness to light, symbolized by the church being first in darkness and then suddenly illuminated by hundreds of candles."[19] To describe her experience, Elisabeth made her own the words of the emissaries of Grand Prince Vladimir when, in the tenth century, they discovered the Christian religion in the basilica of Hagia Sophia in Constantinople: "I no longer knew if I was in heaven or on earth."[20]

After assisting at Matins, celebrated by Fr. Sergius Bulgakov and punctuated by the joyous acclamations of the Resurrection, the group of friends went to the nearby park of Buttes-Chaumont. Elisabeth felt carried away by a wave of exultation where all the sentimental difficulties and existential questions that had been plaguing her were swept aside. The painful situation created by Fidler's feelings about her was transcended at that moment: "That day was an extraordinary experience; I lived this liturgy steeped in Easter joy, as if it were an anticipation, *hic et nunc*, of the fullness of the kingdom of God. I felt cleansed of all the problems that were weighing on me."[21]

After the experience of this fiery Easter joy, Elisabeth felt a great desire to know better "this strange Orthodox Church, both so ancient, so archaic and yet so young and alive."[22] But at Strasbourg there was no Orthodox community where she could become familiar with Eastern tradition. This is the reason why, at the end of the academic year, the young woman, very determined, asked to continue her studies of theology at the Protestant Faculty of Paris.

Year of Study in Paris, September 1928–June 1929

Meeting Fr. Lev Gillet

After receiving permission to do her second year of theology in Paris, Elisabeth moved into an international students' residence near the Sorbonne, at 93, boulevard Saint Michel in September 1928. She continued her studies at the Faculty of Protestant Theology, on the boulevard Arago, where she had the occasion to become more familiar with French Protestant Calvinism, and also at the Sorbonne. Her Russian friends in Strasbourg, Fidler and Serikoff, gave her the address of a French priest recently converted to Orthodoxy and living in Paris, Fr. Lev Gillet. Accordingly, Elisabeth wrote to him explaining her situation: she was a young Protestant, a theology student, who wanted information on the Orthodox Church. Lev Gillet then went to see her in the reception room of the women's residence where she was lodging.

It was immediately obvious to Elisabeth that the priest understood her—and this was so, given the similarity of their journeys through life. Father Lev, who was fourteen years older than Elisabeth, had previously been a Benedictine monk. He had become fascinated with Russian spirituality to the point that he felt inwardly torn apart by the separation of the Eastern and Western Churches. This led him to embrace the Catholic Byzantine rite in the hope of healing the breaches between the Churches. In 1928 the papal encyclical *Mortalium animos* condemned attempts at ecumenism and declared that the only way to end divisions among Christians was by adherence to Roman Catholicism. Father Lev felt himself personally attacked by this warning against any type of ecumenism. This helped the Benedictine monk to decide to enter the Orthodox Church in the hope that this step would have a prophetic bearing on reconciliation among the Christian denominations. In the course of his career, Fr. Lev had acquired a spiritual openness, rational and without prejudices, toward the contemporary world. It was this openness that immediately impressed the young woman and inspired trust.

Their personal affinity was complemented by a spiritual resemblance on many points, and this helps to explain the closeness of Elisabeth and Fr. Lev: both had inherited the evolutions of the Western Church, both felt an immense attraction to Russian spirituality. They suffered from the divisions among the Churches that prevented them from living in full communion with the Eastern Tradition they loved so much. It was to the Orthodox Church that they both turned in their search for an authentic Christianity that would be meaningful in the modern world. Trying to define the reasons for such an attraction, Elisabeth asked herself: "Could it be that historical Orthodoxy, as heir of the ecclesiology of the undivided Church, purified and enlivened by suffering in the Russian Church, is called to become the matrix of the harmonious unity of the reconciled Church of the new era?"[23]

The former Benedictine assumed the role of intermediary for Elisabeth in her passage from Protestantism to Orthodoxy. When he had been studying psychoanalysis at Geneva, Fr. Lev had had the opportunity to enter into close contact with the Protestant Churches. He got to know them from within, and this inspired a desire to rediscover a Church that was stripped down to the essentials and free. Such a state of mind predisposed him to be most accessible to Elisabeth, and it allowed her, with him as intermediary, to open herself little by little to the Eastern Tradition.

For Elisabeth, her meeting with "the Monk of the Eastern Church"—the pseudonym he would later use for most of his writings—was providential: "I discovered a man with a very charismatic ability to listen and sympathize, along with a rigorous and lucid intelligence, who helped me to see myself clearly."[24] This first meeting in the reception room of the student residence was to be the point of departure for a friendship that, in the course of its development, would have a decisive impact on both of them. So that she might get a better look at this Church, which inspired her so much, and know it in its daily reality, Fr. Lev invited Elisabeth to the French-speaking Orthodox parish that he had started with the help of some Russian émigrés.

Young Russians of the First Francophone Parish

Metropolitan Evlogy, the bishop of the Russian émigrés in the Paris area, took the initiative for the first French-language parish in his diocese, which was to be for what he called "denaturalized Russian children," that is, the descendants of the first generation of émigrés who no longer understood Slavonic. When he explained the founding of this parish in his memoirs, the metropolitan wrote: "We must think of the future: even if the Russian language is lost, we must try to save the Orthodox faith and pass it on to these French-speaking Russians."[25]

The majority of the parishioners were young Russian intellectuals, most of them members of the Confraternity of Saint Photius. The goal of this brotherhood, founded in 1925, was to preserve the purity of the Orthodox faith in the context of the émigrés. At that moment it was trying to rediscover elements of the Tradition of the undivided Church that existed in the West and that would facilitate the implantation of an authentic local Orthodoxy. It was the members of the Confraternity, especially Evgraf Kovalevsky, who called the attention of the metropolitan to the need for a Francophone parish.[26]

The choice of Fr. Lev as its first rector was not accidental. His past experience in the Catholic Church and his recent decision to embrace Orthodoxy were representative of a desire to see the two traditions come together again in their common origin. In the first issue of his parish bulletin, Fr. Lev laid down the foundations of a local community: "Because Orthodoxy is not Byzantine or Slavic but universal, it is up to the Orthodox living in the West to create a type of Orthodoxy appropriate to Western culture. Since to do so would imply returning to local traditional sources, a Western Orthodoxy could differ notably, in certain aspects, from Eastern Orthodoxy." But it was more his great love for Russian spirituality that led Fr. Lev toward such a project among the Russian émigrés, rather than any desire to convert the French to Orthodoxy.

When she first took part in the liturgy at the little parish, dedicated to the Transfiguration and Saint Genevieve and initially located at the offices of ACER, the Russian Christian Students Association, Elisabeth was impressed by the intensity of the ceremony. Father Lev officiated without ostentation. He was the spokesman for the assembly and made the whole community participate in the liturgy by reciting the prayers aloud, even the Eucharistic prayers, which were usually heard only by the priest. When he offered the bread and the wine to God so that they might be consecrated and said, "We offer to You these gifts for all and on behalf of all," he represented the active participation of each person in the sacrifice of thanksgiving. The aesthetic element was not neglected: the parish choir, partly made up of members of the Kedroff family, who were all musicians, put itself at the service of the liturgy.

The liturgical texts had to be translated into French. Metropolitan Evlogy remembered how "a commission was set up for this. It included Fr. Deïbner, who was very skilled in literary French, and the Kovalevsky brothers. Our Eucharistic liturgy was eventually translated by Fr. Vladimir Guettée, a French Catholic priest who had converted to Orthodoxy."[27] This manner of celebrating the liturgy was extended into the simple and evangelical lifestyle of the parish. The little community was composed of about thirty persons, mostly from the Russian intelligentsia. There was a great deal of theological excitement within the group. The young intellectuals, such as Paul Evdokimov, Evgraf Kovalevsky, and Vladimir Lossky, sought to actualize Orthodox Tradition in a spirit of evangelical freedom. This intellectual elite, who saw the emigration following the Bolshevik Revolution as providential, wanted to bear witness to Orthodoxy in France. Khomiakov's writings also nourished Elisabeth's reflections on the Church and on the true meaning of community. In this little parish, she found an incarnation of "the communion in faith and in love" that had impressed her so much when she had read the Russian thinker.

There appeared at this first French-speaking parish future members of Orthodox Action, an organization of social assistance, such as Ilya Fondaminsky; and intellectuals such as the famous philosopher

Nicolas Berdiaev and the historian Georges Fedotov, with whom Elisabeth would collaborate for her master's degree. The parish also had the support of Lev Zander and Fr. Sergius Bulgakov, whose universalist outlook fully approved of this initiative of a Christianity lived beyond all national divisions.

The parishioners had in place an important social assistance program for émigrés in need. Marguerite Zagorovsky, a social worker linked with the university movement of mutual aid, became the head of this organization. She assumed the role of deaconess, visiting the needy and coordinating assistance through columns in the parish bulletin, *The Way*. Right beneath the Gospel meditations of Fr. Lev could be found appeals for food contributions or job offers.

Liselotte felt that she had become part of this Orthodox community, as its youngest member. The aura of Fr. Lev, the authentic charismatic atmosphere of the parish, the youth and also the poverty of its members made her feel at home. It was there that she forged a deep friendship with those whom she called "the three young Russians": Paul Evdokimov, Evgraf Kovalevsky, and Vladimir Lossky. Of the three, it was with Paul Evdokimov— or "Pavlik," as she called him—that she felt closest. At the Sorbonne, she and Vladimir took Etienne Gilson's courses on Thomism. These classes would have a decisive influence on both Lossky's and Elisabeth's thinking. They acted like a spur, goading her on to return to the Fathers of the Church and to her desire to be firmly rooted in the primitive Tradition. The rediscovery of the Church Fathers would lead to the neopatristic movement in which both Lossky and Fr. Georges Florovsky became important actors.

Elisabeth also became friends with the women of the community: the writer Nadezhda Gorodetsky, who translated the texts of Fr. Lev into Russian for *Put'* (The way) and *Novy Grad* (The new city), both reviews of the émigré community; Natalia Evdokimov, the wife of Paul, who had been a Protestant; and Marguerite Zagorovsky, whose husband was warden at Saint Alexander Nevsky, the rue Daru cathedral of the Russian diocese. The latter two women were among the French minority in the parish. This evangelical atmosphere, where the social was intimately linked with the spiritual, left Elisabeth with the impression of a community both rooted in its tradition and open to the world around it.

After having discovered Christ in the context of the Fédé, Elisabeth was now seeking a Church that would satisfy her thirst for an authentic Christianity, which also would provide the structure for a real communion with God. She found herself divided among the different communities with which she alternately prayed. In addition to the little Orthodox parish, she attended Lutheran services at the Passy church, where she met up again with Pastor Marc Boegner, whom she had already known from meetings of the Fédé. She was also attracted by a community of Benedictines on the rue de la Source.

One of her fellow students at the Faculty of Protestant Theology on the boulevard Arago was also in search of a church home. His name was Louis Bouyer, and he too attended at the little Orthodox parish, where he was entrusted with the reading of the Epistle. Such an ecumenical openness was frowned upon by the authorities of the Protestant Faculty, and Louis Bouyer's attraction to Orthodoxy caused difficulties insofar as he was studying to become a pastor. Elisabeth then counseled him to continue his studies at the University of Strasbourg, where the atmosphere was less narrow-minded. The future eminent Catholic theologian did so the following year.

In the course of this year so rich in discoveries, Elisabeth found herself immersed in the Paris intellectual circles where a growing ecumenism was lived spontaneously, without yet being institutionalized. Interdenominational connections were common, especially between Protestants and Orthodox. The post–World War political and social context aroused new excitement in the ranks of the young intellectuals.

Members of the Franco-Russian Studio

The traumas of the First World War, where two nations claiming the same God slaughtered one another, led a whole generation of intellectuals to try to establish the foundations of a world that would be peaceful and fraternal. In the religious dimension, this desire for unity, manifested by the emergence of ecumenical dialogue, coincided with the arrival in France of the Russian émigrés.

The historical context that brought together French intellectuals in quest of an authentic spirituality and émigré Russian intellectuals fascinated by the Western world was at the origin of a very fruitful dialogue. If some of the French thinkers opted for Communism, then Marcel Péguy (son of Charles), Emmanuel Mounier, and many others sought a Christianity that would fight for justice while remaining faithful to its message. Whereas the Catholicism of that time appeared to be focused on the institutional aspect of the Church, not hospitable to individual questioning and wary of any ecumenical overtures, the Russian intelligentsia, by its spirit of openness and freedom, was most attractive to the French thinkers.

This émigré circle, made up of an Orthodox elite, was heir to the Silver Age, that prerevolutionary period of Russian thought, so rich in its theological reflection, in which a fundamental renewal of the Tradition began. The group of Russian intellectuals whom Elisabeth met during her year in Paris—Bulgakov, Fedotov, Berdiaev—all had similar backgrounds. They had rejected the Church in the name of Positivism or Marxism before returning to the Orthodox Tradition, but with a spirit of creativity.

The Franco-Russian Studio represented a high point in the coming together of two intellectual worlds. This center of exchange and reflection, encouraged by Nadezhda Gorodetsky, one of the pillars of the Francophone parish, Vsevolod de Vogt, and Marcel Péguy, enabled French and Russian intellectuals to learn about one another and share their respective wealth of ideas. In the words of the historian Antoine Arjakovsky, "These meetings sought to reinforce the encounters between the East and the West . . . by a mutual discovery of the cultural treasures of Russia and France."[28]

The spirit of openness characteristic of the era, the general impression of renewal and change, favored the discovery of Orthodoxy such as it was presented by the émigrés: tradition and innovation seemed to coexist harmoniously. In the same spirit, Nicolas Berdiaev, along with the Catholic philosopher Jacques Maritain, organized Sunday afternoon meetings at his house in Clamart. Elisabeth occasionally took part in these ecumenical exchanges.

Immersed in this atmosphere of intellectual, ecumenical, and spiritual excitement, Elisabeth deepened her knowledge of Russian spirituality and the Orthodox Church. Even though she was fascinated by the Slavic world, she maintained her pluralistic outlook: the neo-Thomism of Maritain interested her, as did the neopatristic movement spearheaded by Florovsky. She felt very close to the group of the Veilleurs, a lay movement much like the Catholic third orders of the Franciscans and Dominicans, founded in 1923 by Pastor Wilfred Monod, one of her professors at the Protestant Faculty.

This community, born out of a desire for a spiritual and mystical life, defined itself by a twofold dynamic: the keeping of a rule of prayer made up of liturgical texts from the different Christian traditions, and the carrying out of social action in the spirit of the Beatitudes, which the members of the community recited at noon every day. Through this organization, Wilfred Monod wanted to propose a lifestyle that would reconcile the personal aspect of Christianity with its social dimension. The Veilleurs would later lead to the founding of the Protestant community of Pomeyrol, in the south of France, by members of Monod's third order. Thus, going from one community to another, Elisabeth was enriched by new encounters that witnessed to a Christianity lived and rooted in the life of Christ. It was through them that she sought her own path.

Turning Point at Strasbourg, September 1929–September 1931

Reception into the Orthodox Church

By the end of this year of studies in Paris—a year rich in fruitful encounters and reflections—Elisabeth was sure of having found a Church within which she could realize her desire to live in Christ. Her contact, both intellectual and spiritual, with the Tradition of the Eastern Church and her budding friendship with Fr. Lev and the young Russians of the first Francophile parish played a decisive role in her choice. When she left the capital, Elisabeth decided to join the Orthodox Church as soon as circumstances would permit.

After a summer tour of the Austrian mountains in the company of a roommate from the Paris residence for women students and a stay with her father at Menton, Elisabeth returned to Strasbourg in September 1929. There, she continued with her courses at the Protestant Faculty of Theology. At the end of the calendar year, her Russian friends invited Fr. Lev to celebrate the liturgy at the church of Saint Paul, which Pastor André Boegner put at their disposal. It was during this visit of Fr. Lev that Elisabeth received the sacrament of Chrismation—also called Confirmation—which sealed her reception into the Orthodox Church. Since Fr. Lev, out of respect for the Lutherans, did not want to administer the sacrament within their church, he did so in the room of a student by the name of André Behr, a cousin of Evgraf Kovalevsky. It was there that Elisabeth was confirmed on December 13, 1929, on the feast day of Saint Odile, the patron of Alsace. The young theologian was henceforth "united" to the Orthodox Church as attested by a certificate of the act, signed by Fr. Lev.

When she analyzed the motives that had led her to such a decision, Elisabeth discerned two principal causes. First, the discovery, made possible by the new ecumenical context, of a Tradition incarnate in everyday life in which Christ could be found. She felt drawn toward Orthodox ecclesiology as Khomiakov had defined it—as going beyond the mere institution to take root in a lived community of faith and love. It seemed to her that such a concept abolished the antagonism between Roman centralism and Protestant individualism that she herself had experienced.

Her quest for a theology that was more mystical and more lived out went hand in hand with a reflection on rites and practices, which might be partially explained, perhaps, by her Jewish ancestry. Her attendance at the Francophone Orthodox parish of the Transfiguration-Saint Genevieve answered these questions by putting her in contact with a liturgical practice that was both dense and theological. Liselotte discovered an Orthodox Church in rich, fruitful tension between tradition and freedom. Each believer, in a communion of love with the whole community, tried to live a creative tradition in a personal way, in a constant renewal through the liberating breath of the Holy Spirit.

Many years afterward, Elisabeth, made wiser by her later confrontation with the lived reality of the Orthodox faith, would see, in retrospect, the young idealist that she had been then in a more critical light. Along with this intellectual discovery there was the existential experience: the shock of the Easter Vigil at the St. Sergius Institute. This experience of faith, in which she sensed the reality of a new life bestowed by Christ, gave birth to a very profound hope that would not cease to sustain her later in moments of difficulty. The presence of Fr. Lev was the catalyst in her progressive discovery of a lived Orthodoxy. Unhesitatingly, Elisabeth affirmed that without the mediation of the Monk of the Eastern Church, she would never have embraced the Orthodox tradition because it would have remained too foreign for her.

Moreover, this young woman with a critical spirit, always on the alert, was astonished, right from the beginning of her conversion, by the intransigent position of Orthodoxy regarding women and was perplexed as to what form her personal journey would take:

> This Church into whose communion I felt myself, in conscience, called to enter, in which I discerned the sacramental fullness of the life of Christ through the Holy Spirit, this same Church, it seemed to me, would not know what to do with a woman theologian. After excluding women from any form of public ministry, the Church offered them, as a means of sanctification, either the monastic life or marriage, but it did not foresee that women could be entrusted with any official responsibilities.[29]

Many years later, this reflection on the place of women in the Orthodox Church would take on greater importance for her.

✂ The young woman's decision to enter the Orthodox Church was not an isolated case. It took place in the context of a general movement of reconciliation between Protestant minorities and the Orthodox, notably within the Fédé. The Protestant aspiration to return to the roots of the undivided Church was at the source of a new attention to the origins of Christianity, before it became institutionally organized. In this respect, Suzanne de Dietrich had a profound influence on the young student and thus prepared her for her encounter with the Orthodox Tradition in which Elisabeth hoped to find the atmosphere of the primitive Christian community penetrated by the Holy Spirit. Other Protestants, such as Natalia Brunel, the wife of Paul Evdokimov, also turned to the Orthodox tradition. Louis Bouyer was equally attracted by the Eastern Church, but the jurisdictional rupture that shattered the Russian Orthodox émigré community in 1931 contradicted his ideal of catholicity, and he turned away from Orthodoxy to enter the Catholic Church.

Elisabeth's road toward Orthodoxy was marked by personal encounters facilitated by the historical context, which served as bridges to a tradition alien to her Lutheran mentality. Because of their ethnic and religious mixture, the Sigels were not shocked by their daughter's choice, even though her father told her that he was sorry she would never become the pastor that he dreamed she would be. So it was that, at the age of twenty-two, Elisabeth entered the Orthodox Church with great hopes that there she would be able to live an evangelical Christianity, both open to the world and anchored in a tradition enriched through centuries of experience: "I went toward the Orthodox Church because I saw in it the Mother Church, where everyone could come together, in mutual recognition, without losing their own charisma. There I discovered an evangelical Catholicism where the freedom of each person was respected."[30]

Meeting André Behr

There was another important event that marked Elisabeth's return to Strasbourg for two more years of studies. She met her future husband, André Behr. This coincided with the moment when she took the official step that united her to the Orthodox Church. At the beginning Elisabeth only considered this chemistry student, in whose apartment she was confirmed—thanks to the mediation of Evgraf Kovalevsky, André's cousin—as a younger friend of whom she was protective.

André belonged to the circle of Russian émigrés who had so fascinated the young woman. Two years younger than she, he had known the turmoil of the Russian Revolution, which forced him into exile. The youngest of three sons, André was born in 1909, in the Russian city of Luga. His father, Michel Alexeevitch Behr, a very cultured man descended from a family of high-ranking civil servants, was a colonel in the Imperial Cavalry. He married his cousin, Nadezhda Nicolaievna, who also belonged to an aristocratic family. When the couple divorced, André first lived with his mother, on the large estate of his maternal grandmother, Maria Alexandrovna Behr (née Lanceray), sister of the sculptor Eugene Lanceray. For his whole life, André would have idyllic memories of this estate called Protassiev Ougol, situated in the province of Ryazan.

When the Russian Revolution erupted in 1917, Nadezhda Nicolaievna took refuge in the forest with her youngest son to escape the soldiers of the Red Army. Her terror provoked a fatal heart attack. Now motherless, André was forced to leave for Moscow to rejoin his father, with the approval of his mother's family and his older brother Viktor. Michel Alexeevitch had married again, to Mariana Borissovna Soukhanoff-Podkolzine, a descendant of a family of the Russian high aristocracy. Mariana Borissovna would raise André as though he were her own child.

The continual raids by the Tcheka, the Soviet police, become more and more harassing, and the family decided to leave Russia. Mariana Borissovna, with André, was the first to depart in December 1922. In a family album, Mariana wrote: "This was a relief I can hardly describe, but it was, at the same time, a heart-rending separation. I knew that it was forever."

Mariana and André got as far as Nice. This resort city, which had always been a vacation spot for Russian aristocrats, was now filled with a large minority of émigrés fleeing the Bolshevik Revolution. The Behrs settled in the Villa Paskevitch, in the Imperial Park, where Mariana Borissovna's mother already lived, after a second marriage, to Boris Ivanovitch Paskevitch. Michel Behr would rejoin them there the following year.

After the traumas of the flight from Russia, André enjoyed a peaceful adolescence. He quickly mastered French, became a Boy Scout, and attended the Catholic school of Massena, where the Jesuits provided him with a very good education. His ties to the Russian émigrés remained strong: André was an altar boy at the Nice cathedral, and his distant cousins, Maxime and Evgraf Kolalevsky, spent their summer vacations at the Paskevitch villa. At his cathedral parish, André was the student of Fr. Alexandre Elchaninov, one of the great spiritual leaders of the Russian émigrés, who, at that time, was serving as a priest at Nice.

The young man showed a predisposition for painting, as evidenced by a watercolor he did during the journey to exile, a work that depicted the border train station where he and Mariana Borissovna were forced to spend several days. But in spite of his artistic talents, André opted for a scientific vocation, which he hoped would provide him with financial stability. This is why he turned to chemistry and, in 1928, left for Strasbourg to continue his studies at the Faculty of Chemistry. There he met Elisabeth, when she was confirmed in André's *turne*, as the university dormitory rooms were called in the slang of the period.

When André told Elisabeth of his feelings for her, she was at first surprised. Then, as they got to know each other better, a special relationship began to grow and seemed to develop into a mutual love. Elisabeth accompanied André on his visits to his parents at their home on the rue de la Glacière in Paris. She also met Mariana Borissovna, André's stepmother.

Mariana was a dynamic and vivacious woman, with a strong character, very intelligent, who would like to have studied medicine had such a thing not been frowned upon. She had dreamed of becoming a specialist in eye infections and organizing a traveling clinic that would go from village to village in the Russian countryside to treat the many children suffering from ocular diseases. A rich and complex relationship developed between these two women because of their intellectual affinity and their strong personalities, which were not always in harmony. As she became part of the Behr family, Elisabeth grew better acquainted with the world of the Russian émigrés of which she was so fond.

✄ While the relationship between André and Elisabeth was becoming more intimate, the Orthodox circles in Paris were being shaken by a grave crisis. Metropolitan Evlogy felt that he had to break with the Moscow patriarchate, which appeared to be under the control of the Soviet government, and place his diocese under the temporary jurisdiction of Constantinople.[31] This rupture, which occurred in February 1931, led most of the communities formed by the Russian émigrés to submit to the Ecumenical Patriarchate, and it affected the small Francophone parish where Fr. Lev was rector. Several of its founding members, the Kovalevsky brothers and Vladimir Lossky among them, decided to remain obedient to the Moscow patriarchate regardless of the situation of the Church in the Soviet Union. Father Lev was brokenhearted to see his close colleagues and friends abandon the parish, which now was under the Ecumenical Patriarchate. This separation, however, did not affect the deep mutual friendships that still bound them together.

Father Lev wrote of his inner suffering, caused by all this, in a letter he sent to Elisabeth in June 1931: "I am surrounded by almost desperate personal difficulties."[32] This letter revealed the closeness of the two friends and the role of confidante assumed by Liselotte. She had gone beyond the timid student's admiration that had characterized their first meetings. Indeed, Fr. Lev proved to be an attentive guide for the young woman. When she wondered what to do with her life, he wrote:

> Let me just remind you of two things. First, the *infinite* value of *each* person, whoever that might be: this makes all our pretensions of *giving* something appear as illusions. And this too, concerning the problems you have with your studies and projects. Don't preoccupy yourself with *doing* and *acting* but rather with *being*. The important thing, the only necessary thing, is to arrive at a certain way of being. Seek and ask, first of all, what is the best way to be; what you should do will then follow naturally. We make a mistake by asking ourselves whether we should do this or do that. The real question is: Should I be this or that? What we will do is the result of what we are. Let your action be the *necessary* expression of who you are! Can you find the image of Christ that you seek in this or that? Let Christ Himself tell you! I pray that you might receive *now* the gift of Easter, the light of Easter, the joy of Easter![33]

The friendship between Elisabeth and Fr. Lev became stronger during a short stay at Menton, in September 1931, at the home of Paul and Natalia Evdokimov, where they attended at the baptism of their friends' son, Michel. Elisabeth held the child at the baptismal font as proxy for the godmother, Marguerite Zagorovsky.

In her biography of the Monk of the Eastern Church, Liselotte described these "times when a lasting friendship was born" in a series of simple images.[34] Their affinity was particularly manifest on the intellectual level. The erudition of Fr. Lev was able to satisfy the curiosity of the young woman, who consulted him on numerous theological points, notably in the field of Russian spirituality, which she wanted to explore for her master's thesis. The Monk of the Eastern Church provided her with the theme and the material she would work with: "A personal suggestion: do something on the Russian ideal of holiness as found in the saints canonized by the Russian Church. This would be original and could lead to something very profound. I offer my services to guide you and document you in this task—humble services, to be sure, but services I wouldn't permit myself to offer if I didn't have positive resources on this subject matter."[35] Thanks to Fr. Lev, the intellectual and spiritual orientation of the young woman began to take shape.

Her emotional life also took a decisive turn. Near the end of the summer of 1931, after a stay in Paris where she visited the Behrs frequently, Elisabeth wrote to André's stepmother: "I'm leaving Paris a very different person from the one who visited you this morning and had so many scruples. André had decided to leave me entirely free, but I myself felt that I had to make a decision to go ahead, confiding in the grace of God. It's true that André and I still quarrel a lot, even about *blinis* (Russian crêpes), but deep down, where our souls touch God, we are in harmony."[36]

From this moment on, André and Elisabeth considered themselves engaged. But their marriage would have to wait. André, who had earned his diploma as a chemical engineer, now had to do his military service, while Elisabeth had chosen to go to Berlin to work on her master's degree. Thus, in the autumn of 1931, the couple decided on a temporary separation. André headed for Nice, then Corsica, for his military service; Elisabeth left France to settle in the German capital.

The Stay in Berlin, October 1931–March 1932

Thanks to Marguerite Zagorovsky, whom she had met at Fr. Lev's parish and who had contacts with a student-aid program, Elisabeth received a scholarship from the National Bureau of Schools and Universities to go to Germany for a semester of her year of studies for her master's degree. This choice was indicative of the young woman's cosmopolitanism as well as of her fondness for the German language and culture, which she had never renounced. When the school year began in October 1931, she boarded with a Berlin family during a winter that she hoped to dedicate to her studies.

Fedotov and Russian Holiness

The theme of the young theologian's research for her master's thesis was shaped by her interest in Russian spirituality, as it had been passed on to her by the counsel of her friend, Fr. Lev, in whom she discovered the echo of her own love for Russia. During Elisabeth's year of study in Paris, the Monk of the Eastern Church introduced her to Georges Fedotov, a professor at the St. Sergius Institute and an occasional parishioner of the little Francophone community.

Professor Fedotov, a historian, was a member of the émigré community and a specialist in Russian holiness, whose writings provoked a lively interest on the part of the young theologian—in particular his article entitled "The Tragedy of Russian Holiness." Fedotov used the conflict that in the sixteenth century had opposed Joseph of Volokohlamsk, the defender of a powerful Church with an official position that enabled it to bring help to the needy, and the monk Nil of Sora, who favored evangelical poverty, to illustrate the break between a purified mystical spirituality and the social work made possible through the Church's institutional structures.

Influenced by such writings and the advice of Fr. Lev, Elisabeth settled on the subject of her master's thesis in the autumn of 1931. In one of her many letters to André, she told him of the progress she was making in Berlin:

> I'm beginning to figure out the very complicated system of this immense university. I've definitely decided on the subject of my thesis, which was suggested to me by Fr. Gillet and which will interest you also. It's "The Russian Concept of Holiness." By a historical study of Russian saints down through the ages, I will try to define the meaning of the ideal they pursued, the profound concept that forged the unity of their lives. I think this work will have the advantage of acquainting the West with an unknown aspect of Orthodox piety as

well as a practical aspect, which could help us all to live the Christian life more perfectly.[37]

In these lines one can already detect a major concern that will penetrate her work throughout her life: to make the spirituality of the Eastern Church meaningful for her contemporaries.

During the 1929–1930 school year, Elisabeth had already started to study Russian, taking advantage of an intensive course given at the Strasbourg Faculty. This enabled her to use the sources that would help her to determine the characteristic traits of Russian holiness through an analysis of the lives of its principal saints. The correspondence that she continued to maintain with Fr. Lev helped her greatly in understanding the elaboration of the plan of her thesis according to his guidance. He wrote:

> The study of the Russian saints would show how far Russian Christianity is from being stylistic, hierarchical, and ritualistic, as is commonly thought. In my opinion, a work of this type could be organized as follows—General orientation into the world of Russian hagiography: the ancient sources and modern critique. Canonization in the Russian Church: its history, its meaning, its conditions (what exterior criteria of holiness are required). The legendary element and the historical element in Russian hagiography: does the relationship between these two elements lead to a real notion of holiness? The traditional types of hagiography (apostles, martyrs, confessors, princes, et al.): relationships between the Russian model and the Byzantine and Roman models. Rapid view of the development of holiness in the history of the Russian Church. How Russian piety tends to substitute specifically Russian *essential* models for the *formal* hagiographical models mentioned above. Historical analysis of some representative Russian models: the "passion-bearer," the "starets," and the "fool for Christ" (*iourodiv*). The Russian concept of holiness: conclusions. What do you think about that?[38]

Thus it was that, using the plan proposed by Fr. Lev in his letter, Elisabeth completed "Notes on the Russian Idea of Holiness as Exemplified by the Saints Canonized by the Russian Church," her first extensive study.

The philosophical approach made itself felt right from the start in this work. In the introduction, she tried to define the object of her study: "It is a question of a problem of religious phenomenology and not historical criticism."[39] Elisabeth was not concerned with questioning the historicity of the hagiographic sources, but rather with analyzing them as they have come down to us in order to develop a typology of Russian holiness and to "understand the religious essence of the Russian people."[40]

With this perspective, she first described the lives of the great saints who have sprung from Russian soil in the course of centuries, following an analysis of the hagiographic documents she had at her disposal. This historical overview enabled her to sketch a global typology, which she divided into three categories: the passion-bearers, the fools for Christ, and the startsy, or elders. She had no intention of conducting a systematic and exhaustive analysis and stated that her approach was subjective: "We chose . . . those traits that seemed to us to illustrate the ideal of Russian holiness."[41] Elisabeth then described, as criteria she made her own, the nature and meaning of the process of canonization in the Orthodox Church, a process based on the spontaneous veneration of the people.

Choosing a thesis topic relative to hagiography was significant for a Lutheran who had just embraced Orthodoxy. It showed Elisabeth's determination to immerse herself in this new tradition, which she had made her own, notably in the cult of the saints, which was foreign to her Protestant sensitivity. As her research in Berlin progressed, she became aware of the vital bond that linked her to the great spiritual figures of the Church. She wrote about this to André:

> I understood that this fearful asceticism was their way of struggling against everything that separated them from God. Their goal— which is also ours, even though the means may be different—was *to arrive at feeling and really being in the presence of God always.* It is the perpetual state of inner prayer that they were seeking with so much fervor. You understand, I already knew all that intellectually but today, for the first time, I think, I felt with my heart what a transfiguration that must be of a whole life, if someone arrives at feeling and being in the presence of God always. That is perhaps the whole mys-

tery of Christ—that He was the Man who lived His whole human life in the presence of God and in a communion of prayer with Him. This insight filled me with joy![42]

Through her research, Elisabeth dedicated herself to defining models of Christian life where the Holy Spirit was revealed in a personal and original manner. Separated from her origins by her religious choice, an innovator in theological reflection at a time when the discipline included very few women, she took an interest in particular lives as frameworks within which the desire of being in the presence of God could find its fulfillment. Beneath the surface of this reflection on "The Russian Idea of Holiness" was her own inquiry about what form her life was going to take, now that her search in faith had led her to choose the Orthodox Church.

Elisabeth asked herself where the theological studies she had undertaken were bringing her because, logically, they should have led to a pastoral responsibility within the Church of the Reformation. Her conversion to Orthodoxy had not modified her desire to serve the Church, but it placed her in a complex situation that she hesitated to reveal to her superiors. She explained this to André:

> Since I have to choose the tradition to which I consciously wish to belong, don't you think that I should make things clearer and simpler by revealing my convictions to the president of the Reformed Synod on whose administration I depend? It is possible that I might be asked to do social or religious work in a Protestant parish all the same. But my collaboration will be more frank and I will also be dispensed from certain pastoral actions which, as an Orthodox, I could not carry out (distribution of Holy Communion, for example).[43]

This time in Berlin was a period of inner growth for Elisabeth during which she reflected more in depth on the reasons that had caused her to change her ecclesial allegiance. Her work on the concept of holiness led her to meditate on the catholicity of the Church, one of the elements that had brought her to Orthodoxy:

> I agree with you that religion is something very personal and should be free from outside pressures. On the other hand, however, we

need guides if we are to arrive at a greater fullness of spiritual life, and it cannot be a question of each of us inventing his own particular way. It would take a lot of arrogance to believe ourselves capable of that. In this field, religion is not something purely personal but rather an ecclesial reality,[44] because it is within the communion of the Church, in the communion of our brothers, and, above all, in the communion of the saints who are our older brothers, that we should try to go to God. And the goal is not our solitary communion with Him, but the union of everyone in the love of God, through the Holy Spirit. This is the Church in its mystical reality.[45]

In this way, Elisabeth arrived at the experience of Orthodox ecclesiology, such as she had discovered it, theoretically, through Khomiakov. She began to regard Protestantism with a critical eye, without, however, denying all that she had gotten from it:

> Protestantism, which makes religion something entirely free (and I like this about it), does not, on the other hand, recognize this principle of love in the spiritual life. It is individualistic. Every Protestant is ready to break with the whole ecclesiastical tradition because he thinks that he can come to God all by himself, without the communion of saints and that of his brothers. That, in my mind, is its heresy. The *Eastern* and *Roman* Catholic Church, on the other hand, affirm that each one of us is only pardoned and transfigured through the intercession of all and in the communion of the whole Church. You understand that I'm not reproaching Protestantism for a purely intellectual error but for something false in its fundamental attitude, an attitude of the heart. The intellectual and practical manifestations of this error of the heart are the reformers' rejection of prayers addressed to the saints, of prayers for the dead, of veneration for the Mother of God as she who, above all, intercedes for us. Each individual Protestant, of course, is not responsible for these errors, and, fortunately, there are many humble and loving souls among them. But it is the Protestant-type attitude that I see as vitiated by individualism; and, as a theologian, I believe that I should openly position myself on the side where I think and feel there is more *spiritual* truth . . . ; even though I have chosen the spiritual path of Orthodoxy,

nothing prevents me from loving what I find good in Protestantism.[46]

Elisabeth seemed to want to dedicate her life to the pursuit of this
"spiritual truth" and saw theological reflection as the function that she
was called upon to exercise in the Church, given her interests and her
intellectual capacities.

First Engagements in the Struggle against Social Injustice

Elisabeth's stay in Berlin was not confined to the muffled atmosphere
of libraries. Plunged into the heart of a Germany whose lifeblood had
been drained by the provisions of the Treaty of Versailles after the
First World War, the young woman could not remain insensitive to the
misery that she saw around her. Even the relatively comfortable bour-
geois family who lodged her suffered from shortages. In a report written at the beginning of 1932, Elisabeth gave a detailed description of
the situation in Berlin:

> By sharing the life of a family, I'm able to get a firsthand idea of the
> repercussions of the economic situation on the German middle class.
> Life is very hard for the bourgeoisie. My host, who is part of the upper
> echelon of an industrial firm and who once had a rather large in-
> come, now receives a salary that just barely supports his family. They
> can't allow themselves any luxuries—no plays, no concerts—they
> don't even have enough to buy books. In the spring they will have to
> dismiss their maid and move from a seven-room apartment to a more
> modest one of four rooms. Almost all the bourgeois families I know
> have been hit with the same lowering of their standard of living. In
> addition to all that, there is the fear of a future even more somber, the
> anticipation of social and political troubles in Germany, the humili-
> ating sentiment of belonging to what they call "a ruined people," at
> the mercy of their former war enemies. All of this creates an atmos-
> phere of despair manifested, on the one hand, by the increasing
> number of suicides and, on the other, by a political radicalism.[47]

On her own, Elisabeth tried to do something about the destitution
around her by getting involved in a soup kitchen set up by a group of

students to feed the unemployed in the eastern neighborhoods of Berlin. There she rubbed shoulders with jobless workers who had been reduced to misery, and she was exposed to the ideological propaganda of political agitators who were trying to rally the desperate masses to their ideas. She related to André:

> Last night, a distant relative, an eighteen-year-old boy, took me to a meeting where a young Communist agitator tried to indoctrinate about twenty youngsters between the ages of twelve and sixteen! But there too, where, on the outside, life goes on beneath the bourgeois label, I felt that it was anti-Christian. It's the affirmation of mankind, the exaltation of its needs and appetites. What a difference there is between the contemplative life of the saints and the useless agitation of these millions of people![48]

The profound crisis in which Germany was plunged did not seem to have any solution other than an extreme political engagement, nourished by the resentment of the Germans against the victors of the World War, who were held responsible for creating the situation. In her report on Berlin, she noted:

> It seems to me that this sentiment of being the victim of an unjust and merciless oppression is characteristic of the overall mood in Germany. The most common reaction, above all among the young people, is revolt. But the name of the oppressor whom one is revolting against changes according to one's political party: for the nationalists, France is the oppressor; for the Communists, it's international capitalism . . . The brawls between nationalist and Communist students, which temporarily shut down the university twice in recent weeks, although insignificant in themselves, are a sign of the tensions among them. The main building of the university is like a well-guarded fortress where security guards strictly bar entry to anyone who does not have a student identity card.[49]

In this context of stress, misery, and hatred, Elisabeth wanted to do something, not only through her practical involvement with the soup kitchen but also through the search for a political response that she might be able to articulate. She felt that, by virtue of her cosmopolitan identity as both French and German, she might be able to understand the position of both sides, and she was torn between her double heritage. She evoked this in a letter to André: "I am very sensitive, almost physically so, to the insanity of politicians who try to pit against one another two peoples who have no reason to hate each other, who resemble each other in many ways, whose culture and spiritual life, although distinct, have more similarities than differences. Indeed, 'Woe to those who take advantage of the ignorance and stupidity of the masses in order to create artificial hatreds.'"[50]

The young woman felt herself called to establish channels of communication between the two mentalities in order to help abolish the tragic misunderstandings fomented by governments and to overcome the fear of the "other," a fear rooted in ignorance of the "other." Again, to André:

> I think that our own little task consists in fighting against the prejudices, the lies, the fatalism in accepting the present state of hatred, all of which are the cause of wars. This cannot be just sentimental gushing. We have to systematically work among our circles of friends to dissipate the lies that people believe about one another. That demands as much courage as does war. For example, I believe that, right now, it is very difficult in France to state this truth, more and more recognized in other countries, that the Treaty of Versailles is unjust because it was imposed on the vanquished by the victor, and it provokes a sentiment of humiliation in the people of Germany that will explode, one day or another, in the form of hatred and war. I think this must be said.[51]

Elisabeth tried to make the French public aware of the situation in Germany, notably by publishing an article entitled "Student Life in Berlin: Impressions of Germany." The article appeared in December 1931 in the Alsace-Lorraine newspaper *Les Dernières Nouvelles* as well as in the political daily *Le Petit Marseillais*. She depicted a Germany that wanted to live, in spite of its chaotic economy and the fact that there did not seem to be any alternative to political fanaticism. Her earlier report from Germany had underlined the extreme nature of the situation as it was lived by the Germans whom she had come to know. Pushed to the limits of their patience, people were showing signs that they were ready for anything:

> You would have to experience physically, so to speak, the unhealthy agitation caused by several years of unemployment to understand how much level-headedness can be expected from those who live in such an atmosphere. This is what the French, who live in a state of relative security, often do not understand. They still don't realize that, where despair reigns, violent and irrational instincts fatally prevail over sound judgment. It is natural that the most dynamic among the young workers, whose energies cannot find an outlet in a productive job, become fanatic Communists. For them, the Fatherland and the German people are only "phantoms." Many of them have told me that they would prefer to die rather than take up arms in another Franco-German war. But these same people are ready to participate in any bloody coup d'état. It is the danger that this "Red army" represents for the German State that explains the surge of the Nazis of Hitler, whose program, at present, is focused on domestic policy; from a patriotic point of view, this is not surprising. In east and north Berlin, there is a constant guerrilla war going on between the two parties, and it is only the *Shupo*[52] that keeps them from openly jumping at one another's throats, like wolves.[53]

This stay in Berlin left Elisabeth with the anguished feeling that "the world was rolling toward an abyss."[54] More than seventy years later she could still recall the hysterical accents of Hitler's voice, which she had heard on the radio. She had a premonition of an inevitable war in the future and shared her thoughts with André: "All of a sudden, I understood that something diabolic, a clashing of peoples with one another, was inevitable. This terrible sin and this terrible trial cannot be avoided, and, surely, it will be the German people who will suffer the most."[55]

With her weak pair of arms breaking through the waves of misery that flowed through the soup kitchen, with her small voice crying for peace drowned out by the bellowing of nationalist ravings, Elisabeth, in the course of her stay in Berlin, experienced her own powerlessness in the face of History's tragedies. She had the feeling that the real answer could only be spiritual rather than social or political. But how was one to convey a living testimony to this truth in a world where, from the human viewpoint, Christianity seemed to have failed to implant its message of peace and love?

But in the darkest night of human distress, she saw that the presence of Christ continued to shine forth:

> I am struck by the fact that many [of the workers] who despise "official" Christians admire Christ. Today, for example, a young man eighteen years old, defending his point of view against a Communist, exclaimed: "and yet I believe all the same that Christ did not live in vain." I don't know if you can imagine the courage and faith that is needed to say something like that in the midst of all this misery, in the midst of this chaos of hate, errors, and fanaticism, in the midst of all these people who think that there is no hope and that everything will end up a complete disaster. It's like a little light that shines in the darkness and that you want to protect so that the night does not envelop everything . . . All that doesn't make me blind . . . the threat of Communism, the threat of Hitler . . . but it does break my heart to read articles full of hatred in the French newspapers. They are like blasts of a glacial wind that extinguishes all our little glimmers of hope. I think that we Christians should be among those who believe and hope in the brotherhood of people, even if we sometimes appear to be vanquished, like Christ seemed to have been vanquished on the cross. If we believe only in brute force, is that not a proof of much less faith than that of that young man with no money, with no job, who still cries out: "Something better will come; Christ has not lived in vain"?[56]

In the midst of a hell that she embraced out of compassion for those beings crushed by a merciless History, Elisabeth drew, from the depths of her faith, the courage to hope for something better beyond the difficult reality of Berlin in 1933, even though everything pointed towards a very bleak future. This was a lesson in hope that she would soon have to put into practice in her own life.

During her winter in Berlin, Elisabeth had the opportunity to make some new friends in the Orthodox community formed by the Russian émigrés. Father Sergius Bulgakov had given her the address of the religious philosopher Simon Ludvigovitch Frank, who was teaching at the university. Elisabeth visited the Franks often and became close friends with their daughter Natasha, who was several years her junior and for whom she played the role of a protective older sister. Liselotte talked with Simon Ludvigovitch about her master's thesis and absorbed the philosopher's perspectives on Russian religious thought.

She got to know other members of the German-Russian circle, especially at the little parish of Tegel, on the outskirts of Berlin, which she attended. It was there that she had a decisive meeting with the rector of the parish, Fr. John Shahovskoy. She told André about her first meeting with the priest:

> As I wrote you, this Saturday evening I went to the Russian church where there's a new priest, just arrived from Paris, Ioan Shahovskoy [*sic*]. Mariana had already written me about him, saying that your uncle [Fr. Nicolas Behr], who knows him, considers him a saint and, in fact, I've seldom seen a person so otherworldly. It was as if his purity was shining upon all of us who were in the church, and that a prayer went out from him and took our prayers toward heaven. When I try to figure out the source of his beauty, I think it comes from his humility. When he speaks, there is nothing forced, no attempt at making an impression. When he prays, you sense that he no longer thinks of himself at all and that he is in the presence of God alone. I'd like to share my joy with you that such a person exists. Maybe I will never see him again. But when you see so many mediocre lives, when you feel yourself so small and filled with sin, there is the risk of losing sight of the meaning of life. But if such a person [as Fr. John] exists, that proves that holiness is possible and that it is the divine goal proposed to us all.[57]

In the context in which the young woman found herself, with her uncertainty about the future intensified by the instability surrounding her, the meeting with Fr. John seemed to bring an answer to her questions and doubts:

> Last Friday I talked more at length with the Priest-monk Ioan . . . He understands very well my situation as a Protestant Orthodox. He thinks that marriage shouldn't prevent me from continuing in the same line of work and that I shouldn't worry about what form this work will take but pray to God to do with me what He wishes, with the wholehearted and joyful confidence that He will give me a way to serve Him. It wasn't so much the exact content of his words that filled me with spiritual joy as the radiance of faith that went out from him. When you are with him, you understand that the Christian message is a joyous shout of victory over the world, over the sin in us and around us, and that we cannot keep the secret of this victory to ourselves but must transmit it to all those who thirst for consolation and true life. This conversation made me understand the aura of Orthodox holiness—not an aura of superficial optimism that ignores what is somber in life and the struggle we must undergo with the demons within us and around us, but an aura of love and gratitude toward God that lightens the weight of the cross each one of us has to carry. When I try to describe my impression, I feel very inadequate. It's that the holiness of a person isn't something simply rational and moral that can be defined with a few laudatory epithets; rather, it is a veritable perfume, the good odor of the Holy Spirit emanating from a person.[58]

As a luminous incarnation of this holiness whose outlines the young theologian was trying to define in her master's thesis, Fr. John impressed Elisabeth by his evangelical way of being: "He's really an extraordinary person, radiant with light and love. After the service he had us all sit down, and he spoke to us very simply, asking us to pose questions to him about the spiritual life. He resembled Jesus, sitting among simple folk and talking with them very casually, like family."[59] What Elisabeth glimpsed in the life of Fr. John, a man shining with the love of God yet in a modest and discreet manner, seemed to be the only authentic attitude of resistance to the hate and despair with which she found herself face to face during her stay in Germany.

The Parishioners of Villé-Climont

Her experience in Berlin came to an end at the same time as winter drew to a close. In March 1932, Elisabeth began the journey home. There she found André after long months of separation. His two weeks of leave allowed them to announce their engagement at Strasbourg. The young lieutenant then returned to Bastia to continue his military service.

For her part, Elisabeth, who had graduated first in her baccalaureate class of theology, presented herself to the inspector of the Reformed Church, who asked her: "Mademoiselle, what are we going to do with you?" Whereas most of the male students who had pursued the courses at the Protestant Faculty of Theology were destined to be pastors, the admission of women to theological studies had not faced up to the problem of what they would do afterward. The women had benefited, however, from exactly the same classes as those male students who were called to carry out a pastoral ministry. The training included preaching and liturgy, with the instruction given in tandem, each of the two students specializing in one or the other. Liselotte's partner was her friend Pastor Mathiot, who specialized in liturgy while she concentrated more on homiletics. She also had an opportunity to do a first practical internship at a parish in the Vosges. On the completion of her theological studies, she was graduated and theoretically prepared to assume the duties of pastor.

The First World War deprived many parishes of their male spiritual leaders. This is why the inspector proposed to Liselotte that she take the post of auxiliary pastor at Villé-Climont, a small community in the Vosges, which had been without a pastor for three years. She went to Fr. Lev for advice. With his usual openmindedness, he told her that she should give it a try. She also consulted Fr. Sergius Bulgakov, who likewise was in favor of her taking on pastoral work. Thus, Elisabeth accepted this pastoral charge. She would later explain her decision: "In the name of the royal priesthood of all the baptized, being called in the specific context of the lack of a pastor within the Reformed Church of Alsace-Lorraine (ERAL), I thought that I could and should assume the ministry."[60]

After the inspector convinced the parish council to accept a woman pastor, the inhabitants of Villé-Climont gave a warm welcome to the young lady who would preside over their parish, a first-of-its-kind experience. The community consisted of two small towns: Villé, in the valley, was made up of working-class houses, while Climont was located higher up in the Vosges Mountains, which meant an uphill ride on her bicycle for Elisabeth. After years of a spiritual vacuum, the parishioners were delighted to again have a pastor, now in the person of this dynamic and athletic young woman who had no fear of venturing into the mountains to visit the more isolated farms:

> Yesterday I was at Ranrupt, a small village lost in the mountains, where I have several parishioners. They live on farms scattered over the mountain slopes. Tourists never come into this neck of the woods where all the trails simply disappear into the forest. The good farmers received me very kindly, and I sensed that they were moved by the fact that I made the effort to climb all the way up there. After my visits I climbed still higher until I reached a solitary spot with a view of the whole Vosges mountain chain, which spread out in front of me like a petrified sea. That is where I had my modest breakfast (a piece of bread and some wild strawberries that I had run across). Then I prepared my sermon for next Sunday. The descent, at full speed on my bike, with the wind in my hair, was splendid, and I returned home delighted with my day.[61]

This was a very happy period in the life of Elisabeth, who appreciated the outdoor life and her simple contacts with her parishioners. She stayed in a spacious rectory that had been built with a whole family in mind. Mariana Borisnova, her future mother-in-law, visited her during the summer. An accomplished musician, she agreed to play the harmonium during the services.

The pastor's duties were twofold: the celebration of the liturgy of the Reformed Church, which included hymns, Confession according to the formula of Theodore de Beza, and Bible readings; and the sermon, whose rules Elisabeth had mastered. The young Orthodox woman, who had not been ordained since she was serving as an auxiliary, would never preside at the Eucharist, which, moreover, was rarely celebrated in the Reformed Church. Her liturgical service was mainly in the transmission of the Word of God, which she believed she could offer, as an Orthodox Christian, in order to respond to a need. Another important aspect of her ministry was visiting families, the sick, and the children, and giving them material as well as spiritual support. Being a woman, she inspired confidence, and many people opened themselves up to her.

Elisabeth was also one of the first official women pastors, paid by the State, as attested to on her marriage certificate, which listed her profession as "auxiliary pastor." In spite of her initial misgivings about accepting such a post, she would retain fond memories of this experience. But she continued to question the legitimacy of her ministry and was troubled by its singularity. At the beginning of August 1932, Suzanne de Dietrich organized an ecumenical retreat of the Fédé at Mouterhouse. There, Liselotte again was with the Evdokimovs, Nicolas Berdiaev, and Fr. John Schakovskoy. The souvenir photograph of this retreat shows her in pastor's garb, near Natalia Evdokimov.

During the retreat at Mouterhouse, Liselotte had an opportunity to discuss her situation with her friends. She wrote to André:

> Paul Evdokimov thinks that I should ask Bishop Vladimir [the auxiliary bishop of Metropolitan Evlogy] for permission to continue my ministry in the Reformed Church. What do you think about that? It seems to me that he's right, and that would put an end to the ambiguity of my present situation. As for the Protestants of the Fédé—the fact that I have openly declared myself Orthodox, far from prejudicing me, has, on the contrary, enhanced me in their eyes.[62]

Although she was torn between the two, Elisabeth felt the urgent need to definitively choose either Protestantism or Orthodoxy; and through her own heartbreak, she saw herself experiencing the whole drama of the Christian schism: "I can't help feeling, as a personal suffering, the division among Christian Churches and the need to separate myself from one in order to belong to the other. That causes me the same pain as a quarrel in the family. For we all belong to Christ's family—all of us who, 'having been baptized into Christ, have again put on Christ.'"[63]

Elisabeth progressed in her reflections on the causes of her journey toward the Eastern Church by relying on the riches that she had received from Protestantism. In a letter to her fiancé, she gave a very exacting definition of the Orthodoxy on which she wanted to model her life:

> For me, the Orthodox Church is not an administrative subdivision of Christianity. It is the fullness of life in Christ—a life in which all Christians should one day participate. This is why I am willing, if God so asks me, to sacrifice my material interests for it, but it is also why I'm so opposed to the conception of certain Orthodox persons who only see the Church as an institution, as a society with rules that must be obeyed in the same way in which you outwardly conform yourself to the customs of the country in which you find yourself . . . Tomorrow, in my sermon on the Church, I'm going to talk about the Church, the Body of Christ, one and holy—a mystery that Protestantism has lost sight of. Now that my Sundays are perhaps numbered, I use them, not to indulge in proselytism, but to awaken a sense of the Church in my parishioners. God and the Holy Spirit can do the rest.[64]

Elisabeth's work on Russian holiness, which she had nearly finished, continued to guide her in her ardent search for an authentic faith:

> What I don't like at all is this business of making religion a kind of poetic and sentimental framework for our own feelings, a sort of comic-opera accessory. That's why I believe that, when we talk of our own spiritual life, we should do so with sobriety, without fancy phrases. We're so spiritual in our talk and much less so in our actions. These thoughts came to me as I was working on the final chapter of my thesis, the chapter on Saint Seraphim. Almost all his life was a silent, hidden, spiritual action. What blabbermouths we are compared to him![65]

At the end of the summer, the young pastor, animated by the desire to adhere to Orthodoxy as authentically as possible, resolved to take a painful but necessary step: to inform the ecclesial authorities. She knew that, in all probability, this meant the end of her pastorate at

Villé-Climont and, more generally, the impossibility of any post within the church. She told André about this interview:

> The most important event of these two days [at Strasbourg] was my visit to Mr. Knutz, the president of the Consistory of the Reformed Church. I told him . . . that I had been received into the Orthodox Church and understood that this could oblige him to strip me of my post. His reply went something like this: he had pretty much guessed my opinions and he had also been forewarned, but he didn't see any reason from one day to the next why he should sack me. As far as he was concerned, I could stay in my parish as long as I did not get married, provided the situation doesn't drag on too long . . . but I understood that public opinion would make it difficult for him to continue to employ me, even though my duties were exclusively visits and religious instruction, once the marriage took place . . . I must do what I can to find a job outside of a career in theology. This doesn't make things easier and there's a bit of sadness to realize that all those studies are of absolutely no practical use . . . I'll try to find a teaching job on the basis of my diploma.[66]

Liselotte's worries were complicated by the financial situation of the household she hoped to establish with André. She had to resign herself to the fact that she would not be able to find work along the lines of her theological studies. For his part, André, who had finished his studies in chemistry, could hope for work as an engineer. The economic situation, however, made it difficult to find employment. Thus, while Andre was still tied up in Corsica until the end of his military service, Charles Sigel was sounding out the industries in the Alsace region, trying to find a position for his future son-in-law. Liselotte and André's marriage could not be imagined until at least one of them was able to assure financial stability for the couple.

The young theologian profited from her final weeks at Villé-Climont to finish writing her master's thesis. The month of September 1932 was taken up by the urgency of this task and was colored by her impatience to finally settle down with her husband:

> I'm supposed to present my thesis on October 1 and, as usual, I have to end it with a big flourish. On top of that I've another worry: pre-

serves! Can you imagine that we're drowning in plums? There are so many in our garden that I don't know what to do with them. We are giving them to all the parish children and to all our friends. And when we think we've gotten rid of them all, more appear! There is only one solution: make preserves. So my heart is going back and forth between the saints and the preserves. At any rate, you'll have plum jam to put on your toast come winter! Since we now have all this jam, we really have to get married. Your uncle seems to think the same,[67] though for other reasons, according to a letter he just sent me.

At the end of October, André's military service came to an end and he returned from Corsica. He spent a few days in his fiancé's parish and then went to his parents' house in Paris, where he began to look for a job.

On December 3, Elisabeth, after completing and defending her master's thesis, received her bachelor's degree in theology. At the end of the year she had the painful obligation of relinquishing her pastorate at Villé-Climont. She would remain in contact with the parish and later visit it with her children. Now, however, she had to return to Strasbourg and the family home. But this family home was no longer the peaceful refuge of her youth. She had a difficult relationship with her new stepmother, Anne Marie, whom Charles had married when Elisabeth left to study in Paris. Thus, Elisabeth was especially eager to start her own household with her husband.

The student years came to an end at the same time as her pastorate, her final service within the Protestant Church. But a new and important task was beginning for Elisabeth, a task for which Fr. Lev had encouraged and strengthened her—to become, in her turn, like her priest friend and other intellectuals among the Russian émigrés, a bridge between the East and the West, a point of contact between the two traditions that would enable them to know one another better and to rediscover, beyond all the differences accumulated down through the centuries, the essential truth of the undivided Church.

chapter two

THE YEARS IN NANCY, 1933–1969

The Behr Family's Installation in Nancy, May 1933–August 1939

While to the east of the Rhine, Hitler became chancellor of the Reich, André and Elisabeth were married on February 19, 1933, at Plessis-Robinson on the outskirts of Paris. Father Lev officiated, assisted by André's uncle, Fr. Nicolas Behr, a former diplomat then living in London. The Behr family, still mourning the recent death of André's grandmother, who had passed away on January 29, decided that there would be no photographs made of the ceremony. Disappointed that there would be no visual souvenir, Elisabeth would later ask André to take a picture of her in her wedding dress.

Shortly thereafter André found work in the metallurgical industry, which, at that time, was prospering. He obtained a position as chemical engineer at the Pompey steelworks in Meurthe-et-Moselle. Thus it was that in May the couple settled in Nancy, several kilometers from Pompey. They moved into an old house at 21, rue d'Auxonne, where they rented four rooms on the ground floor. This would be Elisabeth's home base for forty years.

Although originally built for a single family, the house was occupied by three families of tenants. The arrangement of the Behr's new ground-floor lodgings was not very convenient. The common stairwell, which led to the upstairs apartments, divided their rooms in two. To the left of the stairwell was the bedroom, whose furniture was a wedding present from Charles Sigel; it was next to the bathroom, and then there was the dining room, the center of the household.

To the right of the stairwell was Elisabeth's "studio," as she called it, with furniture her father had made for her and which she would keep for the rest of her life: a big desk lined with drawers, a long shelf, a small bed over which hung a bookshelf. It was there that she worked and received her guests. Next to that was a narrow room that would be the children's, and then the kitchen—freezing cold in winter—that overlooked the garden.

The front windows had a view of a large weeping willow, which hid the street. Behind the house, a few steps led to the garden, which was shared by the three families of tenants. The Josts, who would quickly become good friends of the Behrs, lived on the second floor. Madame Vivin and her daughter lived on the third.

In Nancy, Elisabeth was relatively cut off from her family in Alsace and her Orthodox friends in Paris. The only Orthodox parish in Nancy celebrated the liturgy in Slavonic once a month. The priest accepted the young Frenchwoman, recently converted to Orthodoxy, into the community thanks to a written recommendation from Fr. Sergius Bulgakov. The parishioners were Russian workers, most of them employed in the metallurgical plants scattered throughout the region. André made friends among the other immigrant engineers at the steel mill, while Elisabeth, in Nancy, was reunited with her friend Pastor Mathiot, with whom she had been teamed during her pastoral studies.

The Behrs also became friends with a physician, Pierre Châtelain, who owned a large property several blocks away. Châtelain was a gifted radiologist who lived with his aged mother and a maid in their spacious family house. He had a great love for Russia, spoke the language fluently, and sheltered families of refugees in buildings he owned. This brilliant man of science had a strange, capricious personality. His colleagues had to lock him up to force him to write his thesis.

A confirmed bachelor, Châtelain got into the habit of stopping by to see the Behrs every evening after work since their house was a convenient stop halfway up the hill to his own place. The radiologist installed himself in the studio to read the newspaper and chat with Elisabeth or André about current events in Russia or to dispute questions in theology. The discussions could become stormy, and often Elisabeth, fed up with him, declared categorically, "Châtelain, it's time for you to go home!" During the years in Nancy, the relations between the Behrs and their neighbors, especially Pierre Châtelain, would become solid friendships that would sustain the family in difficult moments.

First Publications

In Nancy, Elisabeth, although separated from the intellectual ferment she was accustomed to, remained intensely active: she read, in Russian, the many books her mother-in-law sent to her from Paris, and she wrote articles for the local newspapers and also important pieces for religious publications. In 1933 one of her articles appeared in *Revue d'histoire et de philosophie religieuses*, a Strasbourg periodical. It drew on her master's thesis and was entitled "Notes on the Russian Idea of Holiness as Exemplified by the Saints Canonized by the Russian Church."

La Quinzaine protestante, a regional religious journal, published an article dated May 16, 1935, "Easter in the Eastern Orthodox Church," in which Elisabeth explained the meanings of the different liturgical rites proper to the period of Great Lent and Holy Week, which precede the celebration of Easter. She attested to her own experience of the importance of the feast day of the Resurrection as it was celebrated in the Byzantine tradition:

> "To go out to meet the feast of Easter," according to the picturesque Russian expression, signifies, for Orthodox Christians, not simply

commemorating the Resurrection of Christ but also reliving it, personally participating in it, as a reality that is still going on, in which each Christian is called to take part even in this life. This is the source of that unique atmosphere of joy and spiritual lightness that permeates Orthodox worship during Eastertide.

It was through this kind of analysis, which tried to make the Byzantine rite known to the Western reader and to explain its meaning, that she continued to exercise what she felt was her role of mediator between the traditions of the East and the West.

That same year saw the beginning of the publication, in installments, of her master's thesis, *Prayer and Holiness in the Russian Church*, in the review *Irénikon*, published by the monks of Chevetogne. This was made possible through the intervention of Fr. Lev, who was a close friend of Dom Lambert Beauduin, the principal founder of the community. This first really important publication, which would extend through three issues of the review, established the young Elisabeth as a specialist in Russian hagiography and contributed, as she had hoped it would, to making this spirituality known in the West.

But in her desire to initiate the Western believer into the Orthodox Tradition, Elisabeth did not renounce her Lutheran roots. She submitted her contributions to reviews that were open to ecumenism, such as *La Vie Intellectuelle*, and she wanted to establish a dialogue between Catholics and Protestants. This Catholic publication, put out by the publishing house Cerf, showed, in its section dedicated to religious questions, a desire to make the Protestant Church better known to its Catholic readership.

Elisabeth's article, "Life and Thought of Protestant Youth," dated October 10, 1935, presented the point of view of a former active member of the Fédé. She described the aspirations of Protestant youths concerned about "the Church, its nature, and the vocation of each Christian within it."[1] The ecumenical openness shown by the Fédé, which wanted to be detached from any specific denominational membership, was very much in harmony with Elisabeth's quest: "Rather than seeing it as doing away with confessional differences, [the universalism of the Fédé] is now becoming interpreted as a collaboration among different confessional groups where each brings its own specific spiritual riches."[2]

The description of the spiritual searching by young Protestants in the 1930s could be read as a direct autobiographical testimony by Elisabeth: "It was a time when you could find young Protestants who would attend the Sunday Mass of the Benedictines at Passy before going to listen to their own pastor's sermon. It was the beauty of the liturgy and the solidity and internal logic of the Catholic dogma that attracted them."[3]

The spirit of freedom and ecumenical openness that, according to her article, characterized the Fédé was rooted in a reality lived out profoundly by the author herself and that she would continue to proclaim as an Orthodox Christian. Elisabeth's confessional change did not prevent her from continuing to engage herself in the dialogue between Catholics and Protestants. Her reception into the Orthodox Church did not imply any abandonment of her Lutheran origins but rather accentuated her quest for unity in Christ. Elisabeth showed herself most attentive to the theological development of other Christian denominations, as was evidenced by her analysis of neo-Calvinism, which she hoped would be synonymous with a convergence among the Churches: "One thing that must be objectively noted is this new-found love of the Christian community, which neo-Calvinism has revived in a segment of young intellectuals."[4]

The hope of an ecumenical reconciliation, which Elisabeth shared with many other theologians of her generation, would take a concrete and very significant form several years later when, in 1937, the Ecumenical Council of Churches was founded. This international organization, which would only take its definitive form after the Second World War, brought together members of the Protestant, Anglican, and Orthodox Churches to consider the great questions of their faiths.

Elisabeth's intellectual activity was not limited to the strictly theological. The young woman met Henri-Irénée Marrou, a colleague of Emmanuel Mounier and also a member of the personalist movement. To offset the powerful influence of the extremist movement Action française, Marrou organized a gathering in Nancy in order to make known the views of personalism and the review *Esprit* as well as the groups linked to the review, scattered throughout the provinces of

France. As soon as the first issue of *Esprit* came out in 1932—with an important text of Nicolas Berdiaev cited in the table of contents—Elisabeth, who was in Germany at that time, was very eager to see the review and asked André to send her a copy. When she returned to France, she became a faithful subscriber. Moreover, at Marrou's request, she agreed to represent *Esprit* in eastern France. In this capacity, she contributed to the intellectual life of Nancy by participating in conferences and debates organized under the auspices of the review. Her theological reflections, centered on the reconciliation of the different Christian traditions, as well as her other occupations were in the context of her family life, which would soon consume most of her time.

Expansion of the Family Circle

During the years prior to the war, the life of the young couple was organized around the birth of their children. The family expanded with the birth of Nadine on January 21, 1934. She came into the world after a difficult labor during which the physician recommended that Elisabeth offer up her suffering to God. The rebellious patient fired back, "No way!" She was against any form of dolorism that saw the suffering of childbirth as a punishment especially reserved for the descendants of Eve. Father Lev later wrote to the Behr family about their first-born: "I pray that your Nadezhda lives up to her name and is a bearer of hope."[5]

But the happy young parents had not been delivered from financial worries: due to the difficult economic situation, André's meager pay barely supported the household. Elisabeth tried to find a way to earn a bit of money to buoy up the couple's income. She wrote to her mother-in-law: "We're not very rich this month . . . If only I could give some lessons! Or if I had the talent to write one of these best-selling novels instead of theological treatises!"[6]

While she was pregnant with her second child, Elisabeth found a position as substitute teacher in a primary school. The job lasted from November 3 to December 3, 1936, when she left to give birth to Mariane, born on December 17. The two children were now Elisabeth's principal occupation. She wanted to ensure that they had the best environment possible during those times of economic hardship when growing international tensions foretold the approach of war.

Father Sergius Bulgakov and the Paris Friends

Although she had settled in Nancy with her family, Elisabeth continued to return to the capital as often as she could, where she stayed with her parents-in-law on the rue de la Glacière. During these visits, she saw her Paris friends and especially Fr. Lev Gillet, with whom she corresponded on a regular basis. These letters reflected the concerns of both theologians during that period. Father Lev, deeply saddened by the 1931 crisis that had obliged Metropolitan Evlogy to separate himself and his diocese from the Moscow patriarchate, confided to Elisabeth the hopes and disappointments caused by his ministry in Paris. The Monk of the Eastern Church was assisting in the social outreach work undertaken by Mother Maria Skobtsova, the poet and former Socialist revolutionary, twice married and the mother of three children, who had emigrated in the 1920s and had received the monastic tonsure in Paris at the hands of Metropolitan Evlogy: "Mother Marie Skoptsoff [*sic*] has far-reaching plans, a little fantastic yet very real—an extensive mission to all the Russians dispersed in the various departments of France, itinerant teams, a sort of Orthodox Salvation Army. It's to begin a year from now, after systematic preparations. I support the idea with enthusiasm mixed in with a bit of irony, but with more faith than irony."[7]

After having gone throughout France to give support to Russian émigrés in difficulty in her capacity as secretary of the Russian Christian Student Association, this out-of-the-ordinary nun founded Orthodox Action, an agency formed to help anyone in need. She decided to establish a home for single women first; then, in 1934, she opened a shelter for the destitute at 77, rue de Lourmel in Paris. In the autumn of 1935, Fr. Lev, who, at his own request, had been relieved of his duties as rector of the Francophone parish, settled in at the center on the rue de Lourmel as its chaplain.[8] It was there that Liselotte went to see him when she visited Paris.

She was greatly impressed by the evangelical atmosphere at the Lourmel shelter. The homeless, who had come for a bowl of soup, found themselves sharing the premises with the meetings of Berdiaev's Society of Religious Philosophy. This center of social assistance was led by the radiant personality of its founder, Mother Maria, whom Elisabeth now had a chance to get to know better. Mother Maria's unusual character—a woman of action who, on becoming a nun, had decided to put her whole life at the disposal of the poor—had a profound effect on Elisabeth. She saw in the founder of Lourmel the model of a woman of faith, immersed at the heart of people's everyday misery, performing an authentic diaconal ministry there, without waiting for any official recognition. However, she did have the enthusiastic support of Metropolitan Evlogy, who encouraged her efforts and contributed toward the purchase of the first building for the shelter. At Lourmel, Elisabeth found other Russian friends whom she had met in the Francophone parish during her year of studies in Paris: Georges Fedotov, Ilya Fondaminsky, and Fr. Sergius Bulgakov.

The young woman also attended the new parish, Our Lady Joy of the Afflicted Saint Genevieve, founded in 1936 and located at 36, rue de la Montagne Sainte-Geneviève with Fr. Michel Belsky as its rector. Its core membership was made up of former members of the Francophone parish who had decided to remain with the patriarchate of Moscow: Vladimir and Madeleine Lossky and the Kovalevsky brothers, along with others who were part of the Confraternity of Saint Photius, such as Leonid Ouspensky. Although most of the services in this parish were in Slavonic, the main objective of the community was to render the Byzantine rite accessible to French speakers.

At first, the liturgy was celebrated in French once a month; then, after the completion of the difficult task of translating the liturgical texts—an undertaking directed by Madeleine Lossky—the Francophone celebrations become more frequent. In this cramped and poorly installed parish situated in the rear of a courtyard, Elisabeth rediscovered the liturgical riches of the Byzantine Tradition expressed in her own language, and she was reunited with her Russian friends, notably Vladimir and Madeleine Lossky, who would be her friends for life. During the summer of 1935, the Behrs and the Losskys spent some time together at Mouterhouse, in the Fédé building.

At the beginning of 1938, Fr. Lev decided to leave Paris for London. By so doing, he hoped to escape from the ecclesiastical bounds that he found stifling, in order to be free to pursue a more open type of evangelization, especially among those who were cut off from the Church. He entrusted his friend Elisabeth to Fr. Sergius Bulgakov as the person most suited to respond to her intellectual and spiritual expectations and needs.

Elisabeth struck up a very friendly relationship, based on their intellectual dialogue, with Fr. Sergius, whom she had seen for the first time at the St. Sergius Institute, during that memorable Easter Vigil of 1929. Her visits to the Lourmel shelter became the occasion of long conversations, in German, with the great theologian, whose French was hesitant and shaky. She remembered Fr. Sergius as a man with a charisma for pastoral care, a person who was kind and simple in his relations with others.

Even though she admired his theological breadth, Elisabeth was critical of his ideas about the figure of Holy Wisdom, one of the cornerstones of Fr. Sergius's thinking. When this part of his work stirred up considerable and serious controversies, to the point of its being condemned by the Moscow patriarchate and the Synod of the Russian Church Outside of Russia, Elisabeth came to his defense. She wrote an article on his theological efforts, her first critical and analytical effort of this kind. It was published in 1939 in the *Revue d'histoire et de philosophie religieuses* and would remain an important first piece of Bulgakov scholarship over a half-century later.[9]

In this first study published in French on the sophiology of Bulgakov, Elisabeth defined Bulgakov's effort as "one person's theological opinion, interesting and characteristic of the spiritual concerns of a part of the Russian intelligentsia, but it is in no way expressive of the unanimous faith of the Orthodox Church nor does it represent a general conviction among its members."[10] She did not pretend to summarize Fr. Sergius's theological conception of Wisdom in a few pages, but she tried to present a global vision of his theological project. She recalled the traditional foundations on which Bulgakov constructed his work: the Bible, especially the Wisdom literature, and sacred art, which attested to a very ancient veneration of Holy Wisdom, notably in iconography and in the number of churches dedicated to Wisdom.

The concept of Divine Wisdom is rooted in the dogma of the Trinity. It is the very life of the Three Persons of the Trinity, their common substance, which is hypostasized in each one of them. Elisabeth thus described Bulgakov's thought: "If the essence of trinitarian life is love, 'ecstatic love,' by which each of the Three Persons, in self-renouncement for the sake of the other, 'goes out' from its metaphysical egoism, then it is Wisdom that constitutes this sacrificial love."[11] Wisdom is at the foundation of all creation, as the divine seal on all things, particularly on humanity. Wisdom gives humanity its divine potential, which it is free to develop by its creative activity and, by so doing, reveals the true vocation of the world.

Elisabeth insisted on the continuity between Bulgakov's Wisdom theology and the thought of the religious philosopher Vladimir Soloviev. His insights inspired Fr. Sergius, who reformulated them in patristic language. Although she felt the "unquestionable aesthetic attraction" of Bulgakov's Wisdom doctrine, Elisabeth offered three major criticisms: the weakness of its roots in Scripture; the priority given to the speculative dimension over the evangelical dimension; and the displacement of the center of gravity of Revelation toward Wisdom at the expense of Christ, who becomes only a step in the process of the reunification of the Created and Uncreated brought about by Wisdom. In spite of her criticism of some of the positions of Fr. Sergius, Elisabeth had enormous respect for the theologian and admired the breadth and depth of his intellectual and spiritual gifts. He was quite aware that she did not share certain of his ideas.

The regular meetings with her Paris friends, whom Elisabeth visited as often as possible, and her correspondence with Fr. Lev, now living in England, shaped her reflections. Father Lev continued to encourage her in her mission of mediating between the Eastern and Western Traditions:

> I think you can play an important role in explaining Russian spiritual values to the West. I don't think you should take on [Nikolai] Gogol (the question of Gogol is very complex and far from being clear), but you are singularly appointed to write either a series of sketches on the most original Russian religious thinkers or even an overview of the evolution of Russian religious thought. In brief, better than anyone else, you can lead Western Europeans into the Russian vision of Christianity . . . I don't think that theology takes you

away from your family. I think with admiration on the way Pavlik [Paul Evdokimov] reconciled Bukharev and his family life.[12]

But Elisabeth was only able to dedicate a fraction of her time to "leading Western Europeans into the Russian vision of Christianity," as Fr. Lev had encouraged her to do.

In 1938, Elisabeth was forced to resume her professional activities in order to bring in more money to the household. From May 1 to July 12, she taught literature at the Jeanne d'Arc secondary school in Nancy. This was only a temporary position with no assurance of tenure. This first assignment in the public school system was the beginning of a long, itinerant teaching career that would occupy most of her time right up to her retirement. But the peaceful domestic and intellectual equilibrium that characterized Elisabeth's life in Nancy, in spite of her worries about money, would soon be shattered by the outbreak of the Second World War.

The Second World War and the Ecumenical Group in Nancy

Hitler's objective, when he became chancellor in 1933, was to conquer the "vital space" needed for the demographic expansion of the Third Reich. After remilitarizing the Rhineland in 1936, he annexed Austria at the beginning of 1938 and then, in December, he partitioned Czechoslovakia and made it a German protectorate. During the summer of 1939, international tensions reached their peak, and the imminence of war with Germany had everyone on edge. When a partial mobilization was announced, the Behrs, who were in Paris for a congress of the Fédé, returned in haste to Nancy. It was around this time that Elisabeth began to mark down in a black notebook the historic events she witnessed and their repercussions on her personal life.

At the end of August, the family was still able to travel to Strasbourg for the seventy-fifth birthday of Elisabeth's aunt and to be reunited with Charles Sigel and her cousin Gertrude. She left her native city very preoccupied: its inhabitants were in the grip of an unspoken anxiety. But in Nancy the climate of uncertainty was becoming even more palpable. The city was on the route taken by the mobilized soldiers who were massing on the German border:

> The threat is becoming more sure. I'm reacting against André, who, every day, comes back from the factory with alarmist news. But I too feel anguish. At night, especially, when I can't sleep, when I hear the trains go by, one after the other, ceaselessly, bringing soldiers to the border. I feel as though the wheels of the trains were rolling over my heart. Partial mobilization. The city is strangely empty. Some people leave. Others put off their return. In the evening we anxiously listen to the news on the radio.[13]

But on August 28, the mobilization had a direct impact on the Behr family:

> André has been called up to active duty. A difficult day. André is acting as if he were crazy. I wind up crying. That makes him pull himself together. We talk cheerfully at the station while waiting for the train. We are all sad but we know how to hide our pain by joking. I'm torn apart as André's figure disappears from my sight. But I have to go home, put the children to bed, remain calm, smile.
>
> When we left the train station, the evening was mild and beautiful. I chatted gaily with Ch[âtelain] but tears were streaming down my face, tears that no one could see, for night had fallen.[14]

André's precipitous departure left Elisabeth feeling helpless, alone with her two daughters whom she had to protect against the battles that now seemed imminent. The following day she decided to flee Nancy and seek refuge on the outskirts of Paris:

> Now that André is gone, I have to calmly envisage what has to be done for the security of the little ones. M. Jost [the upstairs neighbor] is optimistic but he advises me to leave. I send a telegram to my parents-in-law telling them that I am leaving for Drocourt. All my friends have been very kind and help me as best they can.
>
> In the evening we get together in my studio one last time: Châtelain, the Walters. The suitcases on the floor remind us of this reality so mind-boggling that we'd be tempted to forget it. War is at

our door. But it seems to me that we will only be separated for the space of a short journey. All the same, there is anguish behind our laughter. And our conversation continually returns to the respective chances of war and peace.[15]

When the moment of departure arrived, Elisabeth, who did not know if she would ever see her apartment on the rue d'Auxonne again, summoned up a resigned determination:

The departure is very calm. M. Jost and M. Le Hire [one of André's colleagues] put us on the train. The children are proud of their little knapsacks and consider this evacuation a pleasure trip. They are very funny with their little bags and their air of determination.

Châtelain gets a bit sentimental. I send him away. As it often happens to me in difficult moments, I experience a sort of intoxication that makes me appear calm and happy. For one last time, I show the children their street and their house—the house of their infancy, where they had slept, played, and lived almost all their little lives— beneath the tall elm trees.

[On the train] we share a compartment with an Alsatian woman who is fleeing Strasbourg with her two children. She is a simple woman who speaks with a thick accent. She offers me some peaches from her garden. She explains to me that she preferred to take this train rather than the preceding one because she wanted to put a bit of order in the house, make the beds, etc. When she says this, her eyes fill with tears and her voice suddenly breaks: . . . "even though it's probably not worth the while to make the beds if you're never going to return."[16]

Elisabeth and the children reached a farm in Drocourt, on the outskirts of Paris, and known to them through André's parents. Several families of Russian refugees were already living there, and Elisabeth, with Nadine and Mariane, installed themselves as best they could. On September 1 the news of the German invasion of Poland threw the country into consternation. When the government declared a general mobilization, hordes of Parisians invaded the roads to escape from the capital. Some of them arrived at the farm in Drocourt, which now had a very diverse population, yet they were all united, anxiously awaiting the unfolding of events:

A feverish evening. The same anguish unites all of us in spite of extreme differences of character and origins. Old Ivanoff, a former Russian officer, looks like some aged servant of a rundown farm. Only his clear eyes, bulging out from under bushy eyebrows and reflecting goodness and mischief, reveal something of his soul. His wife is a plump Greco-Russian grandmother type: a chatterbox, loud, dirty, and continually sighing. His daughter, Valia, is a blonde nightclub dancer. She has nothing between the ears and hardly even looks at her son, little Ioura, who is, however, very handsome and alert. Two sisters, Marietta and Sachenka, both in a state of panic. This evening a common anxiety lurks around the hearts of us all.[17]

In this climate of unbearable waiting, where she was without any news of André, in the midst of the painful crowding at the farm where tensions were vented in petty quarrels, Elisabeth could only entrust herself to God's hands:

After Mass, the village priest says goodbye to his parishioners. He does so very simply, like a father of a family taking leave of his own, and imparts his final recommendations to them . . .

But all the sorrow that has been accumulating over these last few days, which I've been hiding from the children, now gushes forth. I start crying, almost shamelessly, in the middle of the church. Many women are crying as I am.

The words of the Gospel reading for that day fall into my heart and embed themselves deeply there: "Do not worry about your life . . . nor about your body. Seek first the kingdom of God and His justice and all the rest will be given you as well.

"Do not worry about tomorrow, for tomorrow will worry about itself. Each day has enough trouble of its own."

I prayed at length for everyone, our government, our enemies, even for that man whose Satanic pride has led us to the edge of the abyss. May God open his heart and fill it with grace. I give everything over to Our Lord, the Lord and Master of my life . . .

A tense afternoon. We have no news. There are no more news-papers, no more letters. The wireless radio is quiet. Somebody says that the French ultimatum expires at five o'clock. A thought tortures me: these people will perhaps begin to kill one another after five o'clock. My dear old Strasbourg. Luckily my parents are at Plombières.[18]

In Eastern Europe, Germany and the Soviet Union partitioned Poland after it had been conquered by the Wehrmacht in a couple of weeks. Then the "phony war" began on the Western front: the Allied soldiers, camped behind the Maginot Line, awaited a German attack that did not materialize. In this context of widespread uncertainty, Elisabeth, who had run out of money, applied to the National Education Board for a teaching position. At the beginning of October, she was appointed to Saint-Cast, a small Breton port town near Saint-Malo, where the college of Dinan had opened an annex for the refugees.

Saint-Cast, October 1939–September 1940

Once the family was installed in Saint-Cast, communications were partially reestablished and Elisabeth finally received news of André; he had been mobilized as a munitions engineer at Sorgues, in the south of France. A gall bladder infection, however, had led to his hospitalization at Avignon. Charles Sigel had gone to Plombières with his second wife, while Elisabeth's aunt and her cousin Gertrude had taken refuge at Périgueux, in the Dordogne.

Now reassured about her husband and relatives, Elisabeth began to organize her new life, dividing her time between her teaching job and taking care of the children. At the end of the autumn of 1939, which was still very warm after a scorching summer, the rhythmic sounds of the sea dominated life at Saint-Cast and brought respite to the family after all their recent difficulties. Elisabeth, who was a good swimmer, and her daughters took advantage of the beach. In spite of the absence of André and the anxiety around her, Elisabeth succeeded in restoring the balance of a peaceful household. She wrote in her notebook:

After Drocourt, Saint-Cast seems like a paradise. I have a little house with a garden where the children can run around. I'm finally "at home" again and don't have to put up with that interminable and incomprehensible chatter, all those stupid and prejudiced discussions. The little ones are happy. The sea is nearby and allows me to refresh my soul by contemplating its unending horizon. My job leaves me very tired. The [school]children are pretty undisciplined. But I love almost all of them and want to be something more than just a teacher for them.

God has been merciful to us. Glory to the Father and to the Son and to the Holy Spirit. Amen . . .

Mathiot said somewhere that war, for us, is a sort of general rehearsal for death, when everything must be left behind.[19]

During the winter, André, whose gall bladder infection was healing slowly, obtained a convalescent pass to spend the Christmas of 1939 at Saint-Cast. But the family reunion was not what the couple had hoped for due to his poor health, which made him nervous and irritable. Elisabeth described to her mother-in-law the changes in her husband:

The least variation in his regime makes him sick . . . But you have to feel sorry for him in his constant discomfort, which contrasts notably with his strong build and outward appearance as a healthy and vigorous man.[20] . . .

It seems to me that, in the last two days, André is doing much better . . . He has again realized that the least little excess, especially with wine, makes him physically sick and, morally, totally deprives him of his common sense . . . It's a shame that even a ridiculously small amount of alcohol brings about such really disastrous consequences . . . On the other hand, André always needs a certain amount of time to get used to a new place and to recover from his emotions, even the joyous ones he felt when he arrived here.[21]

Those five days of leave at Saint-Cast were overshadowed by André's chronic illness. Elisabeth sensed that her husband's poor health was the manifestation of a profound discontent from which he sought to escape through alcohol. She could only accept this fact and ask herself what she could do to help him:

> I've searched and searched trying to discover the cause of his horrible nervousness. I think that part of it is due to his illness. When you suffer, you're nervous. But that doesn't explain everything. André should go to Paris to see a good specialist, not only for his gall bladder but also for his nerves . . .[22]
>
> Today, Saint-Cast is all white under a bright sun. A landscape that makes you think of those of the Dutch painters. We're all intoxicated by the sun and the snow. Why can't André just simply enjoy all that?[23]

In the spring of 1940, critical international events pushed Elisabeth's worries about her husband into the background. On May 10, German troops launched a sudden attack, penetrated the Allies' lines, and overran French territory. The local populations flooded the roads, trying to escape from the invading armies. Once again, there was the uncertainty of not knowing what to do, the impression of being constantly threatened with catastrophe:

> Since May 10, our peacefulness has been changed into an ever-increasing anguish, which, in my opinion, reached its height today. We've witnessed the arrival of a crowd of refugees from Belgium and the North of France. We were nourishing the illusion that the invasion would spare our little corner . . .
>
> And here is how things stand today: the Germans are in Paris and beyond, up to Chartres to the southwest: they have arrived to the southeast and the east of Reims and have pushed as far as the outskirts of Dijon. They bypassed the Maginot Line, which appears to be broken at Sarre and on the Rhine. The Italians are bombing the Midi of France.
>
> I have no news of André or my parents. The problem is knowing whether to leave or go back. The Germans could be here the day after tomorrow.[24]

Hour by hour, Elisabeth followed on the radio the advance of the German troops and the French surrender. On June 17 she listened to the address of Marshal Philippe Pétain announcing the forthcoming armistice between France and Germany:

> The French cabinet has been deliberating all day this Sunday, June 16th. At 11:30 PM, the French radio announced the resignation of the Reynaud cabinet and the formation of a new ministry under the presidency of Field Marshal Pétain and including several generals.[25] What is the meaning of this ministry? All-out struggle or a surrender whose responsibility can only be assumed by Pétain himself? The radio cleared that up for us on Monday, June 17th, at 1:30 PM. In a clear and monotonous voice, which made for more drama and emotion than if he had sought oratorical flourishes, the marshal announced that he had requested an armistice: "I have been with you in days of glory, I will be with you in days of disaster. I have given my life to France." In spite of the crushing defeat it announced, his voice maintained a great deal of grandeur. I can't fight back my tears.
>
> We await the armistice whose conditions depend on the pleasure of Hitler and Mussolini, who are deliberating in Munich. What is certain is that the advancing German armies will occupy Brittany within the next few days or at least cut it off from the southwest of France where the government will sit.[26]

A new exodus began: the populations in the North of France started to flee before the advance of the *Wehrmacht*. At Saint-Cast it seemed that the arrival of the Germans was imminent, and its inhabitants, not knowing what to do, witnessed the rout of the French soldiers:

> A lot of people want to leave. But that is becoming more and more difficult. There's hardly any gasoline to be had, the roads are packed, and the word is that the authorities no longer allow anyone to use the bridges over the Loire. This catastrophe has fallen upon us so quickly that we still can't believe it's real.
>
> In the distance, explosions can be heard or the firing of artillery . . . airplanes are buzzing over the bay, adding to our fears.
>
> At 6:30 PM, while we are eating our dessert, Odette [the maid] runs into the room, shouting: "Look! The sailors are leaving!" And,

in fact, the sailors at the nearby semaphore station are running with their rifles and gear toward the road leading out of our town. It is a beautiful day with a blue sky, and everything is calm. Just these men running. I approach them, and they yell out in passing that they have been ordered to leave immediately. The Germans are at Saint-Malo or at least drawing near to it. These good sailors are beside themselves and running as if the devil himself was at their heels. A short red-headed sailor who exchanged a few words with me yesterday evening shouts to me, "Don't come near, they are going to bomb the semaphore and Cape Fréhel at any minute." Nothing happens, of course.

Mme. Chauvel and I go down to the beach by car; then we go into town and to the post office. There is no way to make a telephone call or send a telegram. We are cut off from the rest of the world.

I realize that we have to stock up on provisions. All the grocery stores are already crowded with people grabbing up whatever is available. From the beach, an immense plume of smoke can be seen rising above Saint-Malo and Saint-Servan. These are the gas tanks, which are on fire. The noise of explosions is now closer and makes the houses shake. It seems as though the locks of the port of Saint-Malo have been blown up. The most absurd rumors are circulating. All the same, the people, aside from a few exceptions, keep calm. Everyone thinks that the *feldgrau* are going to appear at any minute.[27]

Foreseeing the invasion of Paris, Elisabeth had brought her parents-in-law to Saint-Cast for their safety. In the midst of the collapse of everything, she was able to keep a climate of peace around the children thanks to the presence of Mariana and Michel Behr:

The children too sense that something terrible threatens them even though we try to keep smiling. Mariane cuddles up in the arms of her grandmother. Nadine is mostly interested in the little boats that transport the refugees from Saint-Malo. These are the people from Paimpol, who, in spite of a raging sea beneath the blue sky, continue their rather dangerous voyage in little fishing boats. Night falls. The

Germans have not come. They are not interested in our little hole. A somewhat terrifying silence, a silence of death, hovers around the abandoned semaphore station.

[June] 18–21: we are getting used to our new situation. The only painful thing is that we have no news and are anxious about our husbands. We also have to find something to eat and that is not easy. Unarmed soldiers are arriving from Lamballe Plancoët and even from Caen, seeking either to escape to England or to return to their homes or just not die of hunger. They are disgusted, totally demoralized. Their officers took away their guns and then left them, saying, "Every man for himself!"

People who had been very afraid of the Germans start to be reassured. It seems as though they don't hurt anyone and socialize with the French troops. We can only wait.[28]

During these days, which were decisive for France, Elisabeth took advantage of a low tide to bring along Nadine to the beach in search of mussels at the foot of a cliff. Surprised by the rising tide, the mother and her child were no longer able to find the little path leading to the summit. The current tugged at their feet, and they could not get a grip on the steep cliff. They had to climb up a rocky crag, clinging to tufts of grass. At the top of the cliff, Mariana Borissovna was astonished to see two small haggard silhouettes still hanging on to their mussels and nets. She sharply reproached Elisabeth for being so careless as to take such an unnecessary risk with her six-year-old. Once again, Elisabeth, whose rashness often bordered on imprudence, felt that she had been protected in the midst of danger.

It was also on the cliffs of Saint-Cast that Elisabeth had her first encounter with the Occupation army, and this gave her a chance to affirm her twofold cultural identity. She crossed by some German officers, who, noting her dark complexion and very black hair, remarked in German, "These French are really a mixed race!" She let them know, in their own language, that she was one of them. The arrival of these troops, which put an end to the anguished wait, was almost a relief. Elisabeth reassuringly noted that the German soldiers, whose language and culture she shared, were greeted like human beings by the local people:

It's been several days now since the Germans have really invaded Saint-Cast. They have been received with more curiosity than fear. Although the common folk suffer morally from the Occupation, they don't feel any hatred toward these soldiers. The soldiers, moreover, are generally rather friendly: tall and well built, they appear to be enjoying this extraordinary adventure that has led them to the confines of Brittany. And the young girls are already beginning to flirt.

Yesterday, along with two colleagues, I went on my bicycle to Saint-Brieuc. We passed an interminable stream of cars, trucks, cyclists, and people on foot going toward the east and the north. The indescribable, tragic, and comic spectacle of these cars, interspersed with bikes and baby carriages, padded with mattresses, crammed with human beings and a collection of strange items—brooms, pitchers, sacks of food. And the poor people on their bikes, heavily loaded, some with a child on the handlebars.[29]

In this climate of exodus, where it seemed as though the end of the world was at hand, Elisabeth found a certain comfort in the natural beauty around her. The unwavering beauty of the sunsets over the sea rekindled her hope in the future:

Still no news of André, of my parents, of Aunt Olga. I cannot think of the future without anxiety because this armistice *cannot be the final word*. All the same, I can't help rejoicing in this extraordinary summer. With this anxiety, it seems to me that my joy in living becomes stronger than ever. To be at one with the sea, to let one's self be cradled by it, to let one's eyes absorb the infinite luminosity of the sunsets behind the dark towers of the Latte and the crags of Cape Fréhel while hearing, at the same time and as if it were a warning, the thunder of the guns of some distant ship. The sunsets, above all, are unparalleled.

I lean against the side of the cliff among the ferns and the honeysuckle. In the pale sky over my head the first bats cross the last of the swallows. Little by little the golden disc sinks behind the high cliffs of Cape Fréhel, casting a track of light over the bay, which leads to the open sea. I want this moment to last forever, but it is impossible for me to retain this vision of the harmony of mauve, purple, golden yellow, and pale green where only the frail grid of the silver on the waves separates the sea from the sky.[30]

Summer brought reassuring news of André, who was still in the south, untouched by the German invasion. The June 22 armistice, which divided France in two, seemed to have stabilized the situation. Elisabeth thought about the possibility of returning to Nancy in the upcoming months so that the family might be reunited. Then, at the end of August, she took stock of this whole year, which she had spent far from her home—terrible months of despair and uncertainty, but also a time of wonder with the beauty of nature and the growth of her children:

> It was a year ago today that we left Nancy. We left in anguish and yet in an atmosphere full of hope and the promise of heroism.
>
> Those train stations at the beginning of the war, during the days of mobilization: dimly lit with a bluish light, full of sobs and crying but without disorder. Vibrant, above all, with tears suppressed by a smile. No singing, no patriotic fanaticism, but a steady resolve to do one's duty, to be calm, to be brave, to be good for the sake of others. During the last days of peace and the first days of war, the French people harbored no hatred toward the German people but were convinced that they had to defend the last bastion of freedom left in Europe. Even I, who hate war, who doesn't believe that spiritual values can be defended by the sword, I myself was seized and caught up in this atmosphere.
>
> And now . . . what material and, above all, what moral devastation! We are already afraid, we already listen for the heavy steps approaching our door to meddle in our private affairs.
>
> All the same—praise God for the manner in which He spared us. We are all in good health, the children are coming along wonderfully, and, in spite of all my anxieties, I've derived an infinite joy from the luminous sea, from the wind, from the sun. The guns pointed away, the sea washing the bodies away, and . . . we are alive![31]

At the beginning of the new school year of 1940, her situation remained very precarious. While her father tried to arrange for André to return to the Pompey steel mill, Elisabeth awaited her assignment for the school year. The survival of the family depended on it:

> The war continues. The financial problem is very serious. I'm alone and I have to feed my little family. The humiliation, perhaps salutary, of feeling the weight of this task. Nights crisscrossed by the flashes of the searchlights, which cut the sky in geometric segments, clear and obscure.
>
> The murderous buzzing of airplanes. Pillars of smoke.
>
> The diabolical beauty of this scene. I'm going to Paris to try to get authorization to return to Nancy.[32]

Leaving the children at Saint-Cast with their grandparents, Elisabeth went to Paris, where she obtained an unhoped-for laissez-passer for Nancy, which was within a "forbidden zone." While she was in Paris, she was able to see Fr. Sergius, who was greatly incapacitated by throat cancer, which had necessitated the removal of his larynx: "A conversation with Fr. Sergius Bulgakov. Very impressed by this voiceless man who calls upon his last resources to say to me, 'I feel responsible for you before God.'"[33]

Elisabeth then took the train to Nancy in order to size up, on the spot, the possibilities of returning. As she was walking along the aisle outside the compartments, she had an encounter that she considered providential. She noticed a well-built and familiar figure leaning on a windowsill: it was André. He had been taken prisoner in the south, had escaped easily, and was also going to Nancy in the hope of finding some trace of his family there. They decided that the whole family would return. In September 1940 the Behr family was reunited at the house on the rue d'Auxonne after a year of separation.

Nancy and the Members of the Ecumenical Group

The ground floor of their house at Nancy showed traces of its occupation by German soldiers, who had, as propaganda, left behind a copy of *Mein Kampf* on the living-room table. Charles Sigel's birth certificate, hanging on a wall and written in German, seemed to have made a favorable impression on the soldiers, who had not made off with anything.

At the beginning of October, Elisabeth was appointed a philosophy teacher at Neufchâteau, some sixty kilometers from Nancy. She
had to live in a hotel during the week while André, who was still unable to get back his old job at the Pompey steel mill, remained at
Nancy and looked after the children. This new separation from her
family, after the joy of being together again and the relief of getting a
position, worried Elisabeth. She went back and forth between confidence and anxiety during her stay at Neufchâteau:

> Here I am alone in an ugly little hotel room, which is dirty and sad,
> yet I find myself calm and confident.
>
> These last few weeks have been full of providential signs and in-
> dications, of miracles. I've never felt the power of prayer as palpably
> as I do now . . .
>
> The return to Nancy. The sadness of the city, of this frigid apart-
> ment that smells of abandonment. Difficulties, despair, and hell.
> This unexpected arrival of André, which, at any rate, resolves the
> problem of the children for now and lets me leave for Neufchâteau
> with fewer scruples. How long will I stay there? I enjoy teaching phi-
> losophy. The ingenuousness and purity of my students. They are
> without guile, they expect something from me—but my anguish at
> leaving André alone.
>
> May God help me to make a wise decision![34]

A few days after she wrote these lines, Elisabeth decided to resign.
It was too far from Nancy and kept her separated from her family for
too long a time. For his part, André, after two months of inactivity that
he found difficult to bear, finally was able to get back his job at the
steel mill.

A new period began for the family—a period marked by the
dreadful conditions of wartime. Daily life was made up of a mountain
of details caused by the Occupation, especially in regard to provisions.
Elisabeth and her mother-in-law kept up an intense correspondence
in which they discussed ration coupons, jars of food, boxes of cherry
plums, etc. In spite of the cruel lack of essentials, the Behrs were
privileged thanks to André's job in the steel mill, which supplied them
with coal: "They aren't too strict about the ration cards except for meat

and coal. As for the latter, we just received some from the mill delivered by a German military truck."[35]

Coal served as currency on the black market. Friday, after the end of his work week, André went around to the farms to exchange coal for eggs, milk, potatoes, etc. For her part, Elisabeth scoured the countryside in search of food: "I put in my fifty kilometers of bicycling on a regular basis just to find eggs and butter."[36] But a supply of coal was not the only advantage of André's job at the steel mill: "We've been given a garden of two hundred square meters by the Pompey factory. I'm kind of proud of that because I was the one who extorted it from M. Fort. With the help of a gardener, we'll plant potatoes and vegetables. We have the use of *four plum trees* and two apple trees!"[37]

André devoted himself to the cultivation of this little garden. The constant struggle for survival as well as the wartime deprivations were, paradoxically, healthy for him: obliged to stay sober, he showed a great deal of courage in providing for his family. Along their garden wall, the Behrs had hutches for raising rabbits, to which Nadine and Mariane became attached. When the tasty animals disappeared, Elisabeth told the children that they had been stolen. A few days later, the children were delighted by the aroma of the meat on the dining-room table.

Elisabeth's days were now centered principally on finding provisions, as she explained in a letter to her mother-in-law: "If we run errands and stand in line all day, we keep our heads above water. Sometimes I get discouraged when I realize that this is all I do every day and don't have the time to do anything interesting."[38] Thus, the everyday life of the family fluctuated according to the overall situation, the packages from Paris, the harvests, the black market. Elisabeth sewed some Russian sarafanes for the children, which made them look like little Bavarians. She braided their hair and sent them to the German telephone center across the street. The young telephone operators felt sorry for these blonde children and gave them something to eat.

Another worry was soon added to the list: Nadine was stricken with tuberculosis and needed an extremely varied diet. Thanks to Mlle. Godard, the director of the Devaley private school where Elisabeth taught, Nadine was able to go regularly to a place overlooking

Lake Gérardmer where she could breathe cleaner air. Godard gave free lodgings on her farm there to several students.

On May 25, 1941, Fr. Sergius Bulgakov wrote to Elisabeth: "Your daily life, like everyone else's nowadays, is an exhausting effort, but it is still more important than ever to preserve one's soul and spiritual resources." As the financial situation of the Behrs became worse during the autumn of that year, Fr. Sergius's letters were a great comfort to Elisabeth. She wrote in her notebook:

> No letters arrived today. André's salary isn't enough. We have to sell papers and there is just about nothing to sell. And there are other concerns: the impossibility of visiting Papa at Strasbourg . . . and then the other worry, which is becoming more and more depressing: the war and the suppression of free peoples. On this glacial morning of November 18, 1941, thousands, hundreds of thousands of people, suffer, die, above all in Russia, prisoners packed like animals in open freight cars in the frigid cold, homeless refugees, German and Russian soldiers dying on the frozen plains of the Northeast. And our prisoners who are in Germany working, working to help Hitler continue his war. And these mindless Frenchmen who pledge loyalty to a German general."[39]

During the war years, Elisabeth, with her Alsatian background, passed herself off as a German in the eyes of the occupying troops. There were times when she went to the police station with certain Jews who were so naïve that they turned themselves in. More than once, her impeccable German got her out of difficult situations or helped her to obtain privileges. At Christmas time in 1941, thanks to her German descent, Elisabeth succeeded in getting a laissez-passer to go to Strasbourg to visit her family. She wrote to Mariana Borissovna: "Can you imagine that I unexpectedly received a pass to go to Strasbourg? My father requested it at Strasbourg. It's valid until January 10. I'll leave on January 2 with the children since I don't want André to be alone during the holidays. How happy my dear old Papa is going to be to see us again after two years of separation!"[40] But the reunion in Alsace was a mixture of joy and sadness: "After two years I was finally able to see my father again and the city of my ancestors, *die Vaterstadt*. The ravages of old age on his beloved countenance."[41]

With her characteristic recklessness, Liselotte took some valuable pieces of porcelain from the apartment of her cousin Gertrude, who was still taking refuge in Périgueux, rolled them up in her daughters' pajamas, and put them in their knapsacks. When they returned to Nancy, they arrived after the curfew. Elisabeth, with her daughters and a suitcase full of forbidden provisions, managed to get a ride from the train station to the rue d'Auxonne in a car belonging to the German army.

In February 1942, Elisabeth once again got a job for several months teaching German at the Jeanne d'Arc secondary school in Nancy. The climate of anxiety and suspicion was intensifying. The walls of the Gestapo headquarters could be seen from the Behrs' garden, at the end of the fields. Soldiers came regularly to visit the ground-floor apartment on the rue d'Auxonne without noticing the little French flag that Liselotte had pinned beneath an engraving of Strasbourg.

The measures taken against the Jews were soon felt, even in Elisabeth's class. Some of her students were forced to wear the yellow star. One of them was arrested in the middle of a class, and Elisabeth, who could do nothing to stop it, returned home in tears. Another evening, when she was going home after classes, she spotted a crowd near her house, in front of a little grocery store. German soldiers were taking people out of the house and herding them onto a truck. Among them was an elderly gentleman who especially caught Elisabeth's attention. As the truck started off, she desperately asked herself whether she should throw herself under the wheels. The futility of such an act only accentuated her feeling of powerlessness.

The roundups she witnessed heightened Elisabeth's fears for her own Jewish family members who were still in Bohemia and of whom she had no news. Another reason for anxiety added itself to the others: the review *Esprit*, for which she was the local representative, had been banned in the East, and the names of its subscribers were in the hands of the Gestapo. The Germans began to systematically investigate the racial descent of public functionaries, and Elisabeth, fearing that her Jewish origins might be discovered, chose to quit her teaching job. This life of permanent fear affected her deeply and forced her to suppress her sensitivity in order to bear all these difficulties without caving in:

How our hearts are hardened against the sweetness of this spring of 1942! I remember how, in the past, my eyes drank in the hazy beauty of the orchards in bloom, how I would throw myself upon the re-born earth to inhale its warm and intoxicating odor and let myself be penetrated by its fragrance. Now we cast a cold, dry, and distracted glance at the gardens in flower; all our attention is focused on the struggle to survive and in expectation of I know not what anguish.[42]

During the summer of 1942, the Behrs were able to take a few days of vacation on the shores of Lake Gérardmer, in the Vosges, not far from the farm where Nadine had stayed in order to breathe the healthy mountain air for her tuberculosis cure. During this brief mo-ment of peace, Elisabeth jotted down her impressions in her black notebook:

A little respite in our mind-numbing life. Four days of camping above Lake Gérardmer, near the house where Nadine spent her vacations.

My soul is dry and I can no longer find my old spark. Getting old. All the same, it is nice to lie down on the warm, moss-covered stones in the middle of the afternoon and be cradled by the shivering and murmuring silence of the pine forest.

And then . . . you have to return to everyday life with the errands for provisions, the lines, the tickets, whatever has to be done to stave off hunger.

The black market here. Mlle. M. swaps some eggs and a bird for a pair of stockings. She gave two pairs of sandals for a ham.

Persecution of the Jews. For me, this is like a wound I carry on my body. The yellow star. But this is still nothing. One day, at 6 AM, they came to round up all the Polish Jews. They tore children from their parents and sent them to different concentration camps, the children to one and the parents (men and women separated) to an-other. They will go to work in Poland or the Ukraine. These are real modern slaves.

What if they took *my* children from me!

And not to be able to do anything. To be a powerless witness to this unleashing of barbarianism. The world has plunged into hatred. The world suffocates in hatred and in blood.

More than ever, we Christians are strangers and pilgrims on earth.

How I understand the words of Fr. Lev: "I'm a stranger to every-thing that is said or done around me. It is time to remain at the foot of the Cross."

"The rest is silence," as Fr. Sergius [Bulgakov] writes.

What stands is the communion of prayer and charity by the grace of the Holy Spirit in the Church.[43]

Elisabeth continued to hear from her friends in Paris thanks to her correspondence with Fr. Sergius, who wrote to her every month, usually in French, sometimes in Russian when he was pressed for time. The professor of dogmatic theology reassured her about the Frank family, who had taken refuge in Lavandou; told her about the status of his own theological publications; and replied to Elisabeth's questions and gave her his opinion on what to read: "Someday I'll be able to loan you Florovsky's book.[44] He's an exceptional scholar but on the level of intuitions and intentions we totally disagree with him. In particular, he is hostile to my Wisdom theology and, in general, he has an 'evil mind' in the sense that he sees heresies everywhere and thinks he has to refute them. You'll see this very clearly in his book. This is why his opinions should be taken with reservations."[45]

In the midst of her daily worries, Elisabeth was still able to devote a few rare moments to her theological work, thanks to the advice of Fr. Sergius and the books her mother-in-law enclosed in her packages of provisions. This intellectual activity helped her keep up her morale: "As for myself . . . I'm not really sad in spite of hours of weariness. There are joys to compensate for the rest, above all the joy of seeing my children grow and bloom . . . I also have the joy of friends who share my interests, even the joy of being able to do a bit of theological work."[46] The barbarities that filled this period with uncertainty and deprivation accentuated the need for an authentic solidarity. So it was that, in Nancy, an ecumenical group of friends met informally. Since this initiative was opposed by the local Catholic bishop, it took on a clandestine character.

The group ended up by coming together fairly regularly on the ground floor of the house on the rue d'Auxonne. The meetings were held in the studio, where chairs were arranged in a circle for the discussions. Some immediate neighbors took part: the Josts, fervent Protestants; the faithful Châtelain, who was a Catholic. Among the others could be found Fr. Châtillon, and Fr. Berthélemy of Lunéville, who would later become chaplain at the Carmelite convent of Nancy, as well as a Dominican friend from a nearby community. Pastor Mathiot was part of the group, along with Jean Schneider, a professor of history at the University of Nancy. The Orthodox were represented by the Mojaïskys—the husband, an engineer, was a colleague of André. In 1943, Fr. Elie Mélia, who had come from Belfort to replace Fr. Sylvester for the monthly liturgy at the parish in Nancy, was added to the group. Each one brought something to eat. In spite of their fear, there were some profound theological discussions. A very strong friendship grew up among the members, who felt deeply united in their rejection of the Nazi barbarities and in their desire to act according to their Christian convictions. The camaraderie that linked them was cemented by observations, good laughs, and hopes. Elisabeth described them in a letter to her mother-in-law:

> A small but truly luminous sign in our life is the little ecumenical group that meets at our place once a month and where we have made real and deep progress in our mutual understanding. These are not superficial, chatterbox meetings. We go frankly, and sometimes almost cruelly, to the heart of the problems and yet, at the same time, we have already attained an authentic reconciliation on the level of faith and charity. Orthodoxy's role as the representative of patristic thought seems to me to be full of promise for the future. Do you know if *The Lamb of God*, the first volume of Fr. Bulgakov's trilogy, is going to come out soon in French?[47]

The resistance to the Germans was not just intellectual: most of the members were engaged in some sort of concrete action against the forces of the Occupation, even if each one was ignorant of what, exactly, the other was doing. Their cooperation was discreet and tacit, at the service of the person in danger; "I know a youngster that I'd like to send to the countryside for a bit of fresh air." The network of friends organized itself to help those who were most threatened, without asking unnecessary questions. When Schneider was arrested and deported for his activities in the Resistance, his wife was questioned extensively. She owed her freedom to the fact that she was sincerely unaware of what her husband was doing.

A Jewish colleague of André, a prisoner of war, was able to warn his wife in time to change their last name from Rabbinovitch to Rabey. Periodically, when it was thought that roundups were imminent, Mme. Rabey would entrust her daughter Yvonne to the Behrs while she hid in the countryside. Little blonde Yvonne was passed off as a cousin of Nadine and Mariane. The three girls invented all sorts of games in the garden behind the house, the only place where they were allowed to go.

In spite of the danger of wiretapping, Elisabeth made telephone contact with Mother Maria Skobtsova in Paris at the shelter on the rue de Lourmel, and this enabled her to pass Mme. Rabey and her daughter into the Free Zone. For her part, Mother Maria had put together a vast network to help the Jews and was able to give them false baptismal certificates thanks to the complicity of Fr. Dimitri Klepinine, the chaplain at Lourmel during the war years.[48] Both Fr. Châtillon and Pastor Mathiot were chaplains for the partisans and brought spiritual support to those people of the Resistance hidden in the deep forests that surrounded the city. When Schneider was deported to Dachau for his activities in the Resistance, the Mojaïskys took in the rest of his family.

This time of Nazi Occupation was marked by the need for a practical and intensely lived ecumenism to help overcome the constant fear. The cohesion of the group gave it the courage to triumph over anxiety and conserve the essential values of the Gospel, an act that could lead to martyrdom during the Occupation. United in the same absolute conviction and feeling the presence of God's grace upon them, they kept up their hopes. Their friendship gave them the strength to resist by sharing the risks they were taking. During this period, Elisabeth was in communion in a special way with André.

Fr. Sergius Bulgakov was an ardent supporter of the initiative of an ecumenical group: "I'm following the work of your circle with great joy. It is of no importance that this isn't representative of what the main ecclesiastical bodies are doing. The history of the Church is not just what appears in official acts; and the seed, sown in souls, can eventually have a much greater importance than we might imagine."[49]

Elisabeth kept Fr. Sergius updated on the discussions of the group by sending him the minutes of the meetings. He gave his impressions:

> Thanks for sending me the account of your ecumenical exchanges . . . the very fact that such exchanges take place is a spiritual event. I beg you to convey my fraternal and Christian affection to all the participants. As far as I can judge from the account you sent me, I find the atmosphere and spirit of your exchanges very much to my liking: this is the only way Christians can understand and listen to one another—all united in Christ even if each one differs from the others . . . As I see things, basing myself on your notes, you are representing the Orthodox point of view very well and I admire your energy, which, in spite of your domestic worries, is able to integrate theological interests and works.[50]

The group's solidarity manifested itself in the details of everyday life. When someone stole Elisabeth's bicycle, which she rode to scour the countryside in search of food, a Protestant friend presented her with her own, saying that she had hopes of getting another one through her brother, who worked at the Peugeot factory.

Pierre Châtelain generously shared the vegetables from his plot, and, when the water was shut off, he let the whole neighborhood use the spring in his garden, which contained a certain amount of arsenic. This did no harm to the neighbors, who became used to it little by little, but when the Germans began to retreat in 1944, the soldiers who drank from this source became sick.

The Behrs' impractical apartment made their activities dangerous. To go from the studio to the dining room, one had to pass by the staircase shared with the other tenants. If the Josts had any doubts about the identity of little Yvonne, they kept it to themselves. On the third floor, Mme. Vivin received regular visits from a German officer but never caused the Behrs any problems.

There was very little news concerning developments on the international scene. The English radio station, listened to in secret, was the only trustworthy link with the outside world, since all official information was subject to censorship. Near the end of the summer of 1942, the bombardments intensified. The proximity of the German telephone center, just across the street from 21, rue d'Auxonne, put the

Behrs' house in the middle of a target area. On September 23, 1942, Elisabeth related in her notebook that a bomb had landed in the garden of the house next door, an event she witnessed thanks to her recklessness:

On the night of September 19–20, we had a serious bombardment for the first time. This is what happened. It was around midnight. I was reading when I heard the noise of planes flying very low. At the same time the air-raid siren went off far away—surely at Maxéville or Champigneulles. Since that happens very frequently, I wasn't worried and went out through the door leading to the garden. The night was clear and full of stars, the threatening roar of an airplane was just over our house. All of a sudden, something that looked like a little comet crossed the sky and, at once, the glow of immense fires—doubtless rockets—arose from the vicinity of the train station platform. I wake up André to show him the spectacle. Mme. Vivin comes down from the third floor with Liliane. Our children are sleeping like angels. This time things are getting serious. The explosions are getting nearer, shaking the house, and we start trembling in spite of ourselves. André wants to go out at any price and help with the passive resistance. He empties a half bottle of wine. This is clearly a matter of nerves. I already sense that he no longer really knows what he is doing and saying. I have to let him go out. He had hardly left when a terrible whistling noise causes us to crouch on the ground. With a deafening crash like a cyclone and an impression of the end of the world, a bomb had just fallen on us, raising a dust of sand, plaster, and broken glass. It would only be the next day that we would realize that it fell in the garden next door, at fifty meters from us. Then there is a silence, a supernatural silence, barely troubled by the noise of the planes. My first thought: the children. In total darkness (the electricity is out) I grope my way into their bedroom, stumbling among the debris all over the floor. But the explosion has left the door jammed, and I can't open it. I go around through the garden, tumbling over broken branches, and am able to get into the bedroom through the window. Fortunately, they haven't had time to be very afraid. They are lying quietly in their beds, awakened by the noise but, all in all, very calm. Mariane hides under her blankets. Nadine is more excited but very brave. We're expecting another explosion. Happily, there aren't any more. André returns. Together we thank God for having so miraculously saved us. André goes out again to give first aid to the wounded. There are four people dead in the neighborhood. I inspect the apartment with the light of a candle. The windowpanes are broken, some plates have been shattered, the shutters are in ruins. But there is no major damage.

Only on the next day will we realize that there are holes in the roof and pieces of shrapnel in the walls. The little room next to the kitchen is the most picturesque: the linen armoire is knocked over and its contents are all over the floor, its door is broken, and also, of course, the windowpanes.

The damages in the neighborhood are much more severe. The bomb that fell in the garden next door dug out a crater where you could fit two houses the size of ours. Another bomb fell near Boudonville, on the house of Mlle. Chassigné, killing four people who were coming home from a movie . . . Firebombs the whole length of the road. A bomb that didn't explode lying on the train station platform.

It's curious to realize how it takes but an instant to pass from one world to another—from the world of security, where death is something distant, to the world of danger, where death is near at hand, possible at any moment, where everything comes down on top of you. Only one desire remains: that God give me the grace to die *with* my little ones.

"To look death in the face." I now know what that is, thanks be to God. Amid the collapse of everything, faith endures. What is terrible is that the children also felt the brush with death. And how touching was their courage in the face of death, their confident abandonment to their destiny . . . as long as their mother was there for them.

Today, André has a nervous crisis. This is a natural consequence of what we went through but it is very painful for the children . . . "worse than a bombing," they say.[51]

When the bomb tore apart the garden next to the Behrs, it scattered all the vegetables that the owner was cultivating for the Germans. The Behrs benefited from this horn of plenty, which wound up on their property and enabled them to eat a bit better.

In 1943, Fr. Sergius Bulgakov informed Elisabeth of the arrest of Mother Maria and her companions at the shelter on the rue de Lourmel. There had been no news of her since her deportation: "As for Mother Maria, the only thing that is known is that she is not here, that she has been taken to Germany. Nobody knows what happened after that."[52] It was only after the war that she would learn of the death of Mother Maria, who had been sent to the camp at Ravensbrücke and gassed there, as well as that of her son Yuri, Fr. Dimitri Klepinine, and Ilya Fondaminsky.

During this period, to overcome her anxiety, Elisabeth found comfort in reciting the Jesus Prayer. She had often come across this simple formula of invoking the name of Jesus in her research on Russian spirituality. Saint Nil of Sora, whom she had discovered through Fedotov and of whom she was very fond, based his contemplative life on this prayer. Father Lev, who put into practice this prayer from the heart and wrote a small book about it after the war, also introduced Elisabeth to this way of praying.

When she was pedaling in the countryside, going from farm to farm in search of butter and eggs, Elisabeth had recourse to this invocation of the name of Jesus based on the repetition of the formula, "Lord Jesus Christ, Son of God, have mercy on me, a sinner," in order to quiet her worries and fears. The want of sacramental life in Nancy, where the liturgy was celebrated in Slavonic just once a month, made a sustained personal prayer life all the more necessary.

The years of German occupation were one of the most significant periods in Elisabeth's life. It was a time when one lived intensely, in true communion among the members of the ecumenical group, who abolished the very real social barriers characteristic of Nancy; and it was also a time of profound harmony with André. Above all, the certainty of a transcendental Presence, acquired by the repetition of a sincere prayer, gave Elisabeth the courage to go beyond her suffering due to fear and deprivations.

The Liberation

By 1943, the progress of the Allied troops gave reason to hope that the war would soon be over. In the brief annotations in her black notebook, Elisabeth charted the positions of the British and Americans and the German defeats, especially on the Eastern Front, notably at the battle of Stalingrad on February 2. During that summer, her vacations at Gérardmer were, once again, an occasion for her to take stock of her life. Her assessment of these stormy months ended in an act of thanksgiving:

> It's been a long time since I last made an entry in this notebook. My life has been literally devoured by worries and politics. Nadine's illness, the lack of money (by the 15th of the month, we are wondering what can be sold or who will give us a loan in order to survive), the lack of food. And always glued to the radio, hoping for news indicating that the end of the war is at hand. Lack of will power, spiritual paralysis. My only excuse: my energies are absorbed by the simple struggle to survive. But that's not an excuse.
>
> All the same, today, August 8, I praise God for what is, for this beautiful summer day, for this spiritual peace that He has given me and that I do not deserve, for the harmony between A[ndré] and myself over these last few months, which is a miracle of His grace. I praise Him for these luminous days, free of cares, that I've been able to spend with my children at Gérardmer. I praise Him for the grace of knowing that the children are pretty, strong, even Nadine, and secure; and for this maturity that rises within me like a calm summer's day. Blessed be You for all this, and grant that I might never lose the spiritual sense of Life . . .
>
> I believe that the war will be over in Europe by next spring. The prisons, the concentration camps will be thrown open. We will be able to think of something else once again. May God heed our hopes![53]

On Christmas Day, faithful to her German heritage, Elisabeth invited the young German telephone operators to celebrate the birth of Christ with the Behrs:

> Christmas, in spite of the war . . .
>
> Two German women spent the evening with us. The children sang some old French carols, then the German women sang "*Stille Nacht, Heilige Nacht*" in two-part harmony . . . as well as other songs,

including a Christmas carol composed by one of them. We all felt like crying.

Silent communion, beyond all words and yet what an insurmountable wall of misunderstanding and distress separates us . . . Poor Germany. Berlin totally destroyed by the air raids.[54]

Thanks to the ecumenical group, Elisabeth entered into contact with a Dominican community on the rue Lacordaire and visited them often. It is certainly through them that she was introduced into the circle of the Dominicans of the Istina Center and the Cerf publishing house when she went to Paris in 1944. A plan to publish her master's thesis on Russian holiness in the review *Russie et chrétienté* (whose name would be changed to *Istina* in 1954) began to take shape. In a letter to her mother-in-law, Elisabeth explained how she was revising it chapter by chapter and adding appendices:

All these days, I have been very busy drafing the first appendix to my work on holiness, something my editor asked me to do. I just finished with it and am satisfied. It's a twenty-page study, "Eastern Monasticism and Its Role as Guardian of the Essence of the Orthodox Spiritual Tradition." As you can see, my trip to Paris was an intellectual stimulant for me. During these difficult times, it is good to be able to think about other things . . .

Can you also *send me the two volumes of Chetvericoff on the Jesus Prayer? This would be extremely helpful* . . . If you can't send these books, it will be almost impossible for me to write my second appendix on the Jesus Prayer as a type of Orthodox mysticism.[55]

In spite of the uncertainty of the situation, Elisabeth made progress with Mariana's help:

My editor just informed me that my manuscript has been in the hands of the censor since the beginning of the month. I just sent him the first appendix and am now working on the second. I find this work very interesting even though, quite naturally, I'm having some difficulties. Could you, by any chance, send me the dates of the birth and death of Bishops Theophane the Recluse and Ignatius

Briantchaninoff? But if you don't have this information, don't worry. I think I can find it in the *Dictionary of Catholic Theology*.

Did you know that Fr. Bulgakov is seriously ill? He had some sort of stroke and I wonder if he will recover. His death would be a great loss to me. He wasn't just an intellectual but also a man of prayer who had a deep inner life. I'm impressed by the influence he has had on the three young priests we have had here—Fr. Sylvester, Fr. Paul Golycheff, and Fr. Mélia. All three of them hold him in veneration.[56]

Father Sergius died, after lying in a coma for over a month following an apparent stroke, on July 12, 1944, less than a month after this letter was written.

The approach of the Liberation was marked by an intensification of the bombing raids in the Northeast and the resumption of ground battles. Once again there was a climate of uncertainty as to how the situation would unfold: "For several weeks now, our life in Nancy . . . has taken on some new and disagreeable aspects, especially the air-raid warnings, which we are taking more seriously since the airport and its surroundings were severely damaged. Certain parts of the city have been declared 'danger zones' and the children are being evacuated from these sectors. Our house is not within a danger zone."[57]

The hope of the Liberation was accompanied by another happy anticipation by the Behrs: Elisabeth was pregnant again and wishing with all her heart that a son would be born to them, in the autumn of 1944. But first came the news of the invasion of Normandy in June, followed by the liberation of Paris; the people in Nancy were expecting the imminent arrival of the Allied troops. "The Americans are at Vitry-le-François, when will they be in Nancy?" Elisabeth asked.[58] She witnessed the departure of the German troops, then of the Gestapo, in the midst of a climate of feverish anticipation:

The evening and the night have seen a flurry of activity. Trains, trucks—the last ones—were taking off in the direction of Strasbourg. It seems as though the road to Metz has been cut off or become too dangerous. Explosions. At first we thought that the bridges were being blown up, but then learned that it was the munitions depot. The young girls in uniform, our neighbors, have departed: the first half left around four o'clock in a comfortable car; the rest left at dusk and at night in trucks. These were in a hurry. There is no milk this morning. Those who usually go to fetch it are afraid go out.

The French observe all this hustle and bustle with mockery and satisfaction. But I'm pleased to find myself at one with the crowd on this point.

The usual phenomenon: all the cars the Germans left behind are being systematically stripped. The old rapacious instinct.

Will there be any resistance in the area around Nancy? Very little, I think! All the same, there are some trucks installed up on the heights.

In the reaction of the people there is satisfaction, the hope of being able to return to the good life of previous times. But the best people are certainly not speaking and are not here . . .

The children are taking all this very well and are getting their little flags ready.

May this truly be the triumph of an order that is more humane and more just and not one of simple revenge.[59] . . .

The Allies have arrived at Thionville, at Namur, several kilometers from the Siegfried Line. There is no doubt that this is the end of the Great Germany. The inhabitants of Nancy are complaining because the Americans are slow in arriving at their city.

What will happen to the new émigrés? Yesterday I saw a distinguished-looking man about fifty years old with a young lad about seventeen, French, certainly, but in German uniforms. They seemed to be totally disillusioned. They left in the Gestapo's convoy of automobiles. In the same convoy there were two young Frenchmen who were tied up, surely members of the FFI [French Forces of the Interior]. The brutal gestures of the Gestapo as they pushed them into the car. Will any of these men see their native land again?[60]

The atmosphere of uncertainty became more intense, especially after the Swiss radio announced that General George Patton's army was already in Nancy. There was contradictory information as to the whereabouts of the American and German troops. At a distance the sound of artillery kept echoing. There was fighting going on around Nancy, but the inhabitants did not know exactly what was happening:

> Pessimism and boredom. Although the English and Swiss radios are saying that Nancy has been occupied by the Allies, nothing has really happened and "they" are still not here.
>
> The sound of cannon. Very loud throughout the night. Where are they fighting?
>
> The laughter of the children mingles with the roaring of the cannon.
>
> The acquired habit of a joyful indifference. For us adults, the worst is the uncertainty. It is as if we were cloistered within the city limits. We know very little of what is happening at Maxéville. We are almost completely in the dark as to the situation at Champigneulles. To say nothing of Pompey, Varangéville, Dombasle.[61]

The wait became all that more anxious due to the fear of running out of bread and water. On the evening of September 8, the cannon-fire worsened and the Behrs set up their cellar as a refuge in case of a violent bombardment. But Elisabeth refused to panic and continued with her daily tasks in spite of the threat: "This morning the bombers are nosediving. There's a rumor that the barracks in Nancy have been hit again. Violent bombardments around Nancy all morning. You get used to it. I gave a dictation lesson to the children in the garden with the roar of combat on just about all sides. We still have bread. André has given up his daily walk."[62]

The Behrs heard that the Pompey mill had been severely bombed and there were many victims. Every night the roar of cannonfire became more intense, indicating that fighting was drawing closer to the city:

> Another night filled with noise. A large part of the inhabitants of Nancy are sleeping outside or in their cellars. It's like living in the catacombs. I can't get used to it. We still sleep in our beds, but uneasily. It's hard to see God in all this terrible disorder. What can be seen are pathetic human beings and demons. May Your Kingdom come . . .

I feel tired, worn out, empty.

No, ordeals do not make us stronger. They use us up, they gnaw away at us. Lord, have mercy. I don't have the strength for any other prayer.

The Americans have entered Germany, in the region of Trèves and Aix-la-Chapelle.

Anguish for my parents. Will they be evacuated to Germany?[63]

Rather than hide in the cellar, Liselotte took Nadine and Mariane to the hills surrounding Nancy. From Haut-du-Lièvre, an abandoned field overgrown with weeds, where the still-summer sun brought out the colors in the vegetation, they watched the spectacle of the bombardments. The young girls learned to distinguish among the different artillery pieces by the noise they made.

On September 15 the Americans finally appeared:

Yesterday evening, after the last explosions at around 9 PM, we had a night that was calm and dark (the gas and electricity have been cut off since 1 PM).

This morning there were FFI patrols in the streets. Maurice J. is also wearing an armband with the Cross of Lorraine [symbol of the Free French]. I suspected as much.

At eleven o'clock there are shouts from the corner of the place Aimé Morot: "There they are, there they are!" And indeed, the first American motorized patrols come out onto the boulevard Albert 1er. Like magic, flags appear in all the windows. There are bravos and hurrahs from all sides while troops with submachine guns branch out into the surrounding streets. Everyone is crazy with joy, congratulating and embracing one another. I'm not cut out for this sort of display, but I feel like crying . . . What we believed in and hoped for has finally happened and we still can't quite believe it.

The children put little flags in their hair. I don't think they'll ever forget their impressions of this day. May Peace finally descend upon the earth. And may the Germans lay down their arms and understand that we will respect them when they prove that they are capable of working for peace.[64]

In the midst of the joy of the Liberation, however, the cannon continued to thunder: the Germans had taken up positions on the hills surrounding Nancy and were shelling the city. General Patton had set up his headquarters across the street from the Behrs, in the house that had been used by the German telephone operators. A V-2 rocket aimed at the American headquarters hit a house on the rue d'Auxonne, a hundred meters from the Behrs. Mariane found the fragment of a shell in the garden, a heavy piece of metal with sharp points. Elisabeth kept this souvenir until her death and used it as a paper weight in her study. On September 18, for the feast day of Saint Elisabeth, Nadine gave her mother a new notebook on which she had painted the crossing of the Meurthe by the Americans. This became the "second wartime journal," where Elisabeth jotted down her thoughts well beyond 1945.

It was in the middle of the violence of the final battles that Elisabeth prepared for the birth of her third child. Thanks to the black-market sale of some coal by André, Elisabeth was given first-class treatment in the maternity hospital. She gave birth to Nicolas on October 8, 1944, amid the noises of an artillery duel. Several hours after his birth, there was another bombardment and, for their safety, the new mothers were sent to the cellar. The babies were placed in niches in the walls. In spite of the climate of tension and the tears of those around her, Elisabeth felt a profound happiness, as if she had been released from the anxiety that had been weighing on her these last few months.

In the following weeks she was absorbed in taking care of her son, and this made her forget the rationing (which was still in effect) and the continuation of the fighting. The end of the war seemed to be at hand: "The Allied Armies are on the outskirts of Strasbourg! This news pierces the fog of our little daily miseries like a bright ray of the sun. Strasbourg will be liberated tomorrow and doubtless without too much damage. What an almost unexpected miracle of Providence. Papa will get to know his grandson!"[65]

At the beginning of 1945, when Mariane was returning home from school, she saw the figure of a man whose beard was flaked with frost, walking a bicycle and turning into the rue d'Auxonne. It was Fr. Elie Mélia, whose wife had also just given birth to a son, and who had come from Belfort, crossing the German and American lines, in order to baptize Nicolas. Furthermore, Mariane had bragged about the charms of her newborn little brother to an American officer who lived across the street, in General Patton's headquarters, and the officer gave his Christmas parcel to the Behrs. The parcel was filled with delicious and mysterious foodstuffs, such as cans of sliced pineapples, which were opened to celebrate the baptism.

Elisabeth went to the local photographer to have a picture taken with the new baby in her arms to send to her mother-in-law. Mariana Borissovna reproached her for not waiting until the child was a little bigger before spending so much money. Elisabeth defended herself: "I had this crazy urge to have a picture taken of me with my 'little one.' When I'm an old lady, this will be a souvenir of an incomparable moment of happiness!"[66] Indeed, the photograph shows a laughing baby and a radiant young woman for whom the joys of motherhood seem to have swept away all the old anxieties of wartime.

Later, in May 1945, Jean Schneider returned from deportation. Marie Mojaïsky went to wait for him at the train station. After a year in the camps of Struthof and Dachau, the future dean of the Faculty of Letters was unrecognizable.

The members of the ecumenical group maintained the close relationships that had been forged among them during the times of trial: "Our little ecumenical circle keeps meeting in spite of—or even because of—the difficult times in which we are living. Our relationships have become very frank, very simple, and on a level that is not merely intellectual."[67] The circle also expanded: Dom Clément Lialine, a Benedictine monk from Chevetogne, who was staying with the Schneiders, joined the group. This extraordinary man, a descendant of the Romanov dynasty on his mother's side, enriched the meetings with his culture and erudition. He was the director of the review *Irénikon* for a long time.

Although the ecumenical group was not well regarded when it was formed, it gained a certain reputation in Nancy, thanks in large part to the testimony of the Dominicans. All of them felt that it was their unity that gave them the strength to resist the Germans. The bonds that were formed during the war were lasting ones: years later, Fr. Châtillon would officiate at the wedding of Mariane Behr and would testify on behalf of Pastor Mathiot when the latter went on trial for opposing the use of torture during the Algerian War. The Schneiders and the Mojaïskys also remained close friends.

After four terrible years of oppression and deprivation, the city progressively recovered its former peace. In October 1946, Elisabeth was named delegate of the rector at a technical school for young girls in Nancy. This did not prevent her from pursuing her theological research. She had, in fact, written an essay on inner prayer entitled "The Jesus Prayer, or the Mystery of Orthodox Monastic Spirituality." Through Vladimir Lossky, she entered into contract with the review *Dieu Vivant*, with which she collaborated right from its founding in 1945. This ecumenical journal included well-known religious thinkers such as Fr. Jean Daniélou and Maurice de Gandillac.

Near the end of June 1946, Elisabeth wrote to her mother-in-law: "I might come to Paris in the beginning of July. This could be very helpful since the director of *Dieu Vivant* wants to meet me and there are 'relationships' that have to be kept up. He wrote me that my essay on Inner Prayer will appear in one of the next issues (but they only come out once every three months)."[68] In fact, the article would only be published a year later: "I just learned that my essay on the Jesus Prayer will come out in the next issue of *Dieu Vivant* but in an abridged version. Do you know that the director of the review had submitted the essay to your professor, M. Pascal,[69] who spoke very highly of it to him? I'd like to get to know this Pascal."[70]

Elisabeth's essay, published in *Dieu Vivant* in 1947, dealt with the spirituality of the Jesus Prayer, which had been put into practice in the East since the first centuries of monasticism. She used a rigorous historical analysis that evoked the biblical basis of this prayer and its full flourishing in the hesychastic milieus in order to arrive at its finality: thanks to a prayer "so simple that one need not learn it to be able to use it," as Nadezhda Gorodetsky put it,[71] a person could find, little by little, the path to a real communication with Christ, through the joint action of one's own efforts and Divine Grace.

Elisabeth explained that all our moral and spiritual efforts, all our ascetic exploits, which are manifestations [of prayer], are only life-giving if they lead to humility—an active humility that does not gaze complacently on the spectacle of human misery but rather brings us back to our essential task, which includes both the avowal of our powerlessness and the sign of our hope, the prayer of every moment: "Lord Jesus Christ, Son of God have mercy on me, a sinner." For the person aware of his own misery, this prayer was no longer a "merit-earning work" agreeable to God but rather a cry of the heart, a cry of despair and of hope, an irresistible and never-ending need to call upon Christ to help us in our powerlessness in our struggle against the forces of Satan and against our own evil inclinations, which make us accomplices of the devil.[72]

Using the ascetic writings of the great spiritual masters of the Eastern Church, Elisabeth described the different stages of this prayer: at first it is hard and painful, but then it becomes charismatic when the Holy Spirit itself comes to pray in our heart in response to our avowal of weakness. The presence of Divine Grace is manifested by the peace and joy that take hold of the one who prays.

Elisabeth reminded us that this prayer, even though it began in the monastic solitude of the deserts, can be adapted to any way of life, and she founded this claim on such recent authors as Seraphim of Sarov and Nadezhda Gorodetzky. Anyone searching for God can use this prayer in the context of contemporary life:

> This prayer can be said by a factory worker in his plant, by a miner in the depths of the earth, as well as by a professor of theology. In this new historical context, the Jesus Prayer is stripped of concepts inherited from the past and recovers its original spontaneity and simplicity. By so doing it reveals what it has always been essentially: not a belief in the magical power of a formula, but an attentiveness to the presence of God whose Divine Name is the sacrament; not an alienation in an obsessing mechanism, but a spiritual art, which prepares the heart to accept pardon, peace, and illumination by bringing the intelligence of the world of phenomena into the depths of the heart, that is, of the person; not the abolition of thought and of personal awareness, but a communicating and lucid meeting with the human-divine person of Jesus.[73]

The tone of Elisabeth's article came from the context in which it had been written. It was during the darkest moments of the

Occupation, when the invocation of the Name of Jesus became a last recourse for her, that she composed this essay. Although the article was based on a very exact knowledge of the history of Eastern spirituality, it bore testimony, above all, to a deeply lived practice of the Jesus Prayer as a support in hours of anguish. On many later occasions, Elisabeth would reiterate her special attachment to this prayer. The article "The Jesus Prayer, or the Mystery of Orthodox Monastic Spirituality" was published in *Dieu vivant* in 1947 and was reprinted four times, including in a collective work on the prayer of the Eastern Church entitled *La Douloureuse Joie,* published in 1974 by the Abbey of Bellefontaine.

✖ After the war, Elisabeth remained without news of the maternal branch of her family, who had remained in Bohemia. It was only more than forty years later, in 1988, when she was in Prague for a conference of the World Council of Churches, that she had any confirmation of what had happened to them. At the Museum of Deportation in Prague, where the archives of the war were stored, Elisabeth found written proof that they had all been deported and died in concentration camps. The only survivor of the Holocaust was her cousin Gertrude, who took refuge at Périgueux and then returned to Strasbourg.

Reunion with Fr. Lev at the Fellowship of St. Alban and St. Sergius, Summer 1947

Contact with Great Britain became possible again after the Liberation: the correspondence between Elisabeth and Fr. Lev, cut off since the summer of 1940, was able to resume. On a postcard dated June 21, 1945, Fr. Lev wrote to Elisabeth and André: "You have never been far from my thoughts or far from my heart. I embrace you both with all my affection!" Once again the two friends were able to exchange ideas and advice. Father Lev encouraged Elisabeth in her theological work: "Your article in *Dieu Vivant* was brought to my attention a week ago through a letter I received from the continent. Last Thursday, I was able to read it at Dacre Press. You've done an excellent job."[74] Thanks to Fr. Lev, Elisabeth's article was translated into English and would appear in the *Eastern Churches Quarterly* in September 1947.

After arriving in London in 1938, the Monk of the Eastern Church participated actively in the Fellowship of St. Alban and St. Sergius. This confraternity, the result of meetings between Orthodox and Anglicans in the context of the World Christian Student Movement, had been organizing summer conferences since 1927.[75] During these conferences, participants of both denominations shared ideas and prayers in the hope of advancing mutual reconciliation. The Fellowship also published a review, *Sobornost*, with the goal of furthering understanding between the two Christian confessions. Metropolitan Evlogy held the post of Orthodox president of the Fellowship and, since the 1930s, Fr. Lev had been invited to take part in their conferences: as soon as he took up residence in England, he became the representative of Metropolitan Evlogy. The metropolitan had complete confidence in Fr. Lev's efforts to advance the dialogue between the two confessions. When, after the end of the Second World War, communications with the Continent were reestablished, Fr. Lev invited his French friends to attend the conference held in August 1947 at Abingdon.

Elisabeth made her plans for the trip. Mariane would remain in France with her grandparents while Nicolas and Nadine would accompany their mother. Nadine would stay with an English family recommended by Fr. Lev. This first trip outside France after the war was a breath of fresh air for Elisabeth. After spending the night in Paris with her friends Vladimir and Madeleine Lossky, they all set out for London. The food in the dining car of the train seemed fabulous, like the symbol of newly recovered freedom after so many years of deprivation.

On July 18, Elisabeth and the children arrived in London and from there went to Aylesbury to spend a few days with the English branch of the Behr family. This first stay in England was an occasion for Elisabeth to get to know better Tatiana and Alexis Behr, a cousin of André and the son of Fr. Nicolas Behr, the priest who had married them. Toward the end of the war, Tatiana and Alexis had been able to send food and clothing to Nancy for little Nicolas.

In London, Elisabeth had the great joy of being reunited with Fr. Lev. In spite of the years of separation, their friendship had remained intact; their mutual understanding had in no way diminished, a fact they became aware of during their long walks through the streets of the capital. Elisabeth found him to still be the exceptional person she had so admired. She wrote about this first stay in England to Mariana Borissovna: "All in all, I'm fascinated by England and the English, very happy to see Fr. Lev again—so kind, so radiant, and still as intellectually brilliant."[76]

On August 4 they left for Wistow, where there was a first theological colloquium, and from there to Abingdon. Her participation in the camp-conference of the Fellowship of St. Alban and St. Sergius, which had attracted a number of Orthodox theologians from among the Russian émigrés, opened Elisabeth to new horizons. These real vacations, where there was also an emphasis on sports, set the stage for high-quality theological reflection. Morning prayer alternated between the Byzantine liturgy and the Anglican rite. The communal life encouraged the forming of strong bonds between the Orthodox and the Anglicans, which often developed into personal friendships. Liselotte described her participation in the Fellowship to her mother-in-law:

> I thoroughly enjoyed my stay at Abingdon and Wistow. At the Fellowship conference I met Professor Arseniev and we immediately became good friends, mostly because of Kiki [Nicolas], whom the professor found adorable. As planned, Fr. Séménoff Tian-Chansky, Fr. Schmemann, and Fr. Evgraf were there. I got to know the first one a little and hardly saw the second, who only arrived at the end of my stay. The Anglicans were pretty diversified but, generally, very High Church. Some of them had a profound knowledge of Orthodoxy. Among the Orthodox there were many young people who were almost ignorant from a religious point of view but very friendly. There were some Greeks and two nice Syrian women who were full of enthusiasm. My lecture had me worried because of my difficulty in speaking English, but thanks to Alexis [Behr] it went off well and I acquired an unfounded reputation for being able to write a very literary English. I also led a so-called seminar on Orthodox mysticism. In fact, we spoke about a bit of everything and I had to fend for myself in English; that certainly contributed

to the reevaluation of my false reputation for language skills. But the atmosphere was very friendly and everyone spoke with simplicity and frankness. The daily morning prayer service, whether it was the [Orthodox] Liturgy or the Anglican Eucharist, set the tone for the rest of the day. Usually the liturgy was celebrated in English, but on the day of the feast of Saint Seraphim, the chant was in Slavonic and almost everyone took communion. Fortunately, the Russians had enough tact to not put their jurisdictional quarrels on display.[77]

Father Lev was one of the central figures in the Fellowship conferences. He put his preaching gifts at the service of the participants for their edification: every day he would select a Gospel passage and, for about twenty minutes, improvise a commentary. All felt personally touched by these brief daily sermons. At Abingdon, moreover, Elisabeth found other former members of the first Francophone parish: Nadezhda Gorodetsky, who was now teaching at Oxford; Nicolas Zernov, one of the founders of the Fellowship; and Vladimir Lossky, who had had a great deal of influence on English Orthodoxy and its dialogue with the Anglicans.

The following year, Elisabeth had the opportunity get better acquainted with André Bloom, a young physician. The former student whom she had noticed in the little parish on the rue de la Montagne Sainte-Geneviève had settled in England in January 1949. He would become Fr. Anthony, a priest at the cathedral in London along with Nicolas Behr, before accepting the responsibility of bishop in 1957. In the course of these summer conferences, a deep friendship developed between Elisabeth and André Bloom, and it continued to grow with the passage of time. She also made new contacts at Abingdon, such as her meeting with the young Anglican student, Timothy Ware, who, years later, in 1982, would become the Orthodox bishop Kallistos as well as her close friend.

In the context of the Fellowship, Elisabeth rediscovered the intellectual, prayerful, and family-like atmosphere that had so marked her time with the Fédé. Henceforth she would try to return with her family each summer to profit from this simple community life where she found so many intellectual, social, and spiritual resources.

Family Problems during the Postwar Years, 1947–1952

Deterioration in André's Health

After the terrible but exciting war years, when the constant danger stripped life of any pretensions, the return to a calmer daily routine brought new problems. André and Elisabeth felt very close to one another while they were devoting all their efforts to the spiritual and material resistance against the Nazi regime, but when peacetime returned, their personal differences resurfaced.

André seemed unable to find stability in his profession. His choice of chemistry as a way to have a steady job did not diminish his love for painting. Intellectual and urban life did not suit this man of the countryside, who liked the soil, musical comedies, and the simple life, whereas his wife preferred classical music and abstract questions. The courage shown by André during the war years, growing vegetables in the garden and devoting himself to the Resistance, ebbed away once life returned to normal. At the Pompey steel mill, his job as a chemist did not help. He was doing the work of an engineer yet retained only the status and salary of a technician. In addition to lowering his self-esteem, this injustice was also the cause of the Behr family's financial woes. It was André's miserable salary that had led Elisabeth to seek work as a teacher in order to make ends meet.

In search of a more gratifying and better-paid job, André took a position in Paris for a while in 1945 and then returned to the Pompey steel mill. In the autumn of 1946 some new job possibilities opened up for him: he negotiated with several factories, one at Clermont-Ferrand, the other at Paris, with Peugeot. For her part, Elisabeth was relieved to see her provisional position as rector's delegate at the technical school in Nancy renewed from year to year. Teaching commercial German was not very intellectually stimulating, and it was only because of her family's dire financial situation that she accepted such a job, as she wrote to Mariana Borissovna:

> Even though I don't like my job very much, I want to get tenure so as to have more security in the future. It seems as though this would

perhaps be possible in technical education. But the thought of teaching commercial German for years fills me with horror. Brrrrrh! I'd really have to have a whole lot of love for the children to resign myself to such a prospect. Meanwhile, we'll see, and, to tell the truth, eighteen hours of boredom a week is not a terrible price to pay for a certain material security![78]

Elisabeth's professional activity caused new problems in the household: Nadine and Mariane took care of their little brother when they returned home from school, but during the rest of the day, when his mother was away, Nicolas was entrusted to the care of the housemaid. Elisabeth was at the mercy of the maid, who left at the beginning of 1947. The over-burdened mother asked her mother-in-law to look after Kiki for a couple of weeks. But Mariana Borissovna had just found a new job herself at that moment and could not take care of her grandson. Elisabeth finally sent Nicolas to stay with some friends at Dombasle. The Behrs often had to resort to these types of arrangements in order to reconcile everybody's schedules. In June, André apparently found a new job, both important and interesting, at Simca, in Paris. He left for the capital and stayed with his parents on the rue de la Glacière. In the meanwhile, Liselotte's position at Nancy was renewed.

Elisabeth sought to swap her rooms on the rue d'Auxonne for an apartment in Paris, which would enable the family to reunite with André. She confided her daily worries to Fr. Lev, who reassured her, especially in regard to the demoralizing nature of her teaching job: "I hope you will soon be able to move your household to Paris. Don't have any regrets about having to pound German into rebellious heads, for it is through such a painful effort that one heart can speak to another, and that's what is essential."[79]

But André, separated from his family and obliged to settle in his parents' living room, did not find stability in his new job. His fragile health deteriorated and he started drinking again, which his body could not handle. André's worrisome state put on hold the Behrs' plan to move to Paris. During the summer of 1948, Elisabeth sent her husband, who was on sick leave at the time, to Strasbourg for a period of rest with his father-in-law, Charles, with whom he got along well.

Elisabeth, for her part, went to the annual meeting of the Fellowship, which, that year, was held at Eastbourne on August 5–25.

September was marked, as had become the custom, by the anxious wait to see if Elisabeth's job would be renewed. She was determined to continue teaching in the hope of one day getting a permanent post. This she explained in a letter to Mariana Borissovna:

> If I get a good recommendation from the inspector general, I will doubtless be named ministerial delegate, perhaps even in the course of the year. By making all these efforts to get into technical teaching, I sometimes feel like I'm digging my own grave. But I'm sure that, for now, my duties toward André and the children require that I do this. So let's die merrily and with the hope that the ground grain of wheat will be used. All my morality and philosophy consist in that.[80]

To everyone's relief, Elisabeth's position at the technical school was renewed for another year, and André returned to work in Nancy. As it turned out, this stability proved to be fragile, compromised as it was by the worsening of André's nervous attacks and his chronic illness. Father Lev was consulted but he could only offer spiritual support: "All that is very painful. I can't write to André since I really don't know what he has: words of sympathy are cheap. I can't even find the right words for you. All I can do is to ask Our Lord to open His arms, more than ever, to embrace you and André, 'you who are afflicted and burdened.'"[81]

During the winter of 1949–1950, a "terrible winter," as Elisabeth described it in her letters, André's health continued to fail. His dependence on alcohol affected his work and soon led to his dismissal:

> André lost his job in the laboratory, without warning, from one day to another; and the other possibility—that of finding work at Pont-à-Mouson—fell through. No need to tell you that, from a financial standpoint, this is a catastrophe. On top of that, or rather along with that, André is going through a grave moral crisis. Maybe this is my fault? Maybe I could have prevented things from going this far if I had acted better, been less desperate.[82]

At the beginning of March, André was admitted to a psychiatric hospital for a period of observation with the view to control his crises of alcoholism. Elisabeth now found herself alone in providing for her family.

In the autumn of 1949, her teaching duties became more diversified. She now had eighteen hours of classes divided between literature and history, still at the same technical school in Nancy. This was the beginning of a painful period when she was overcome by financial worries and by her anxiety over her husband's condition—all this made worse by her feelings of guilt for not having been sufficiently attentive to André.

André then started on a detoxification program. Elisabeth consulted Fr. Anthony Bloom, a physician as well as a priest, and he proved to be a great support for the family. He especially recommended Esperal, a drug used in England to combat alcoholism, which induced vomiting when so much as a drop of alcohol was ingested. Thanks to this medication, André's condition improved somewhat and he was able to leave the hospital in the summer of 1951. He then went job hunting, but his morale was seriously affected.

By autumn, André felt ill again. On October 25 he was operated on for appendicitis and found himself hospitalized once more, this time for the long term, throughout the autumn of 1951. Elisabeth considered the possibility of finding a room for him where he could live once released from the hospital, so that he might gradually readjust to an active life without having to put up with the hustle and bustle that characterized the family routine on the rue d'Auxonne, and which could wear on his fragile nerves.

This period was the darkest in Elisabeth's life. These were years of tension, of violent disputes with André, who became deranged when he drank, of the struggle to satisfy minimal needs, of constant efforts to give priority to establishing a climate of peace around the children. On March 16, she wrote to her mother-in-law: "I'm sick and tired of being enslaved, absorbed, alienated in tasks that have nothing to do with my true self. But this is what God wants, and I must hand myself over to Him, like iron to a blacksmith."

Until his death, André only very occasionally enjoyed good health and held a steady job. Elisabeth was forced to endure this new situation, which constantly pushed her to her limits. From this point on, her life revolved around the ups and downs of her husband's health, which required frequent periods of hospitalization. André was subject to extreme mood swings, but when his nerves left him in peace, he could be really charming. On these occasions, Elisabeth found again, if only for fleeting moments, the man whom she loved so much.

Her notebook has very few entries during this tormented period. At the end of what seemed to be the paroxysm of the ordeal she lived with André, she explained this long muteness: "Silence concerning the terrible years 1947–1952. It's better like that. Forget everything . . . suffering, folly, despair . . . everything except the Grace of God, which has saved us. Never forget that, never be proud."[83]

The Support of Friends

Elisabeth did not find much friendly support in the life of the local parish in Nancy. She was accustomed to the Orthodox circle in Paris, where there was an active reflection on the meaning of the liturgical offices, and she was unable to get used to a liturgy that was entirely in Slavonic. The new priest, Fr. Eugene Popov, spoke little French and had had hardly any theological training. Liselotte did not have enough contact with the parishioners, who were, for the most part, from the Russian working class, to feel that she was part of a community. Yet the parish allowed her to have a regular sacramental life and to receive Communion, a practice that would always be at the very heart of her existence. During these painful years, Elisabeth's principal support came from the ecumenical group, which continued to meet on a regular basis. After its almost clandestine existence during the war years, the circle began to become more visible among the religious milieus of Nancy, thanks, in large part, to its connections with the Dominicans. After his return from deportation, Jean Schneider became chairman of the Department of Medieval History at the Faculty of Letters of Nancy (he became dean of this Faculty in 1962). This position helped give the group a good reputation. The new postwar ecumenical climate also contributed to making these interdenominational meetings better known and more acceptable. Through Fr. Berthélemy, their chaplain, Elisabeth got to know the Carmelite community in Nancy, which later, following the lead of the call of Vatican II to return to the Eastern Fathers, would become interested in Eastern spirituality. It was at the Carmelite convent that Elisabeth met the prioress, Mother Elisabeth, who would later found the Eastern Carmelite convent of Saint-Rémy, with which Elisabeth herself would have a very special relationship.

The ecumenical circle now began to organize lectures and discussion groups in Nancy that went far beyond the confines of the original small group. Elisabeth played an active role in setting up these events. And the bonds among the members remained very strong: Olga Mojaïsky became Nicolas's godmother, while his godfather was a Russian engineer who used to work with André. Through the intermediation of the Mojaïskys, the group of Russian émigrés in Nancy increased. Young Boris Bobrinskoy spent his vacations with them and became very friendly with the Behrs' daughters.

In addition to her friends in Nancy—especially Pierre Châtelain, whose daily presence was always a big help—Elisabeth was able to renew herself through her visits to Paris, when André's health allowed her to make such trips, as well as through her summer vacations. Each year, a part of her month of August was reserved for the Fellowship of St. Alban and St. Sergius meeting at Abingdon, Broadstairs, or Oxford. She usually brought along Nicolas while Nadine and Mariane attended the Russian scout camps at Saint-Jean-de-Monts and Ronce-les-Bains.

Elisabeth also spent a part of her summers at Gassin, in the south of France, a place she had known in her adolescence and loved very much. Her first vacation at Gassin went back to 1927. Charles Sigel, then recently widowed, and his daughter went there along with some Alsatian friends, the Volkringers, who owned a house in Cavalère, not far from Saint-Tropez. The Volkringers fell in love with the abandoned village of Gassin, perched on a mountaintop and surrounded by vineyards, and decided to buy a house there, to which they moved when the war broke out.

Elisabeth was enchanted with this village close to the sea, where the constant sunshine and intense heat of summer suited her, and she wanted her father to also buy a summer house at Gassin. When this did not happen, the people of the village lent them a house where the Behrs would go almost every summer, from 1952 onward. There, Elisabeth could soak up the bright sun of the south, and this gave her the courage to confront the dreary winters in Nancy.

It was on Mariana Borissovna's insistence that her grandchildren learn to speak Russian that had led Elisabeth to send her daughters to the Russian scout camps. There, Nadine and Mariane mingled with the young Orthodox children from the Paris circles of the Russian émigrés. In 1957, when Nicolas had grown up a bit, Elisabeth would send him to the Russian Christian Student Movement's summer camp in Isère, overlooking Lake Laffrey. For several years in a row, she herself would camp out for two weeks near the vacation colony. Every day she went to the Daily Office celebrated under the tent by Fr. Alexis Kniazieff and took long walks in the mountains with Madeleine Lossky, who lodged with some local farmers. These summers gave her a break during the school year.

Continuation of Theological Activities

During these years of financial instability, all of Elisabeth's energies went into her job and the care of her family. Nonetheless, as soon as it was possible, she went back to her theological work. Thanks to the contact she had established with the Cerf publishing house, her research work on Russian spirituality appeared and brought her a certain fame. Although the contract for the publication of *Prayer and Holiness in the Russian Church* was signed in May 1947, it would not appear until 1950.

Elisabeth wrote an introduction explaining her choice of the approach she had used in this study and why she preferred it to a more theoretical theological methodology. The saints manifest the incarnation of the dogmas of the Church, she said. They bear witness to a lived-out theology made fertile by the relationship they have established with God: "Hagiography appears as one of the ways of entering into the mystery of the Church and into the vision of its Unity in the diversity of the persons and human families who compose it."[84] Elisabeth put the object of her study into relationship with the cause of Christian unity, which was so important for her, by affirming that the knowledge of the types of holiness specific to each Church enabled one to intuit their basic identity: "The life of 'its' saints expresses the vision of Christ specific to each [of the separated Christian Churches] perhaps better than their learned theological works."[85]

The original text of her university thesis was augmented by two appendices that she wrote at the end of the war. The first explained the method and the hagiographical sources used by the author. In the second appendix, entitled "An Essay on the Role of Monasticism in the Spiritual Life of the Russian People," the author affirmed the decisive influence of the monks on the life of the Church through their spiritual radiance. With academic rigor, she painted a historical panorama of the development of monasticism in Russia through the lives of the persons who marked this development. She concluded: "Monasticism seems to us to be the great religious educator, along with the Gospel and the Liturgy, of the Russian people."[86] This reflection on the essence of monasticism continued to interest her for many years; she wrote a number of articles on the subject.

In 1957, Elisabeth, who apparently had intended to give a talk on Orthodox monasticism to the ecumenical circle in Nancy, posed some questions on this subject to Mother Eudoxie, the superior of the Monastery of the Protection of the Mother of God at Bussy-en-Othe, in the Yonne. Mother Eudoxie had been a colleague of Mother Maria Skobtsova at the Lourmel shelter in Paris when Elisabeth met her. The two nuns had very different concepts of the monastic life: Mother Eudoxie wanted one that was traditional and well-regulated, whereas Mother Maria lived out her vocation in her own way, outside of any predetermined framework. When Metropolitan Evlogy received Mother Maria as an enclosed nun, he told her: "Your monastery will be the desert of human hearts."

For her part, Mother Eudoxie wanted to found a community in the spirit of monasticism such as had existed since the fourth century, a life structured by rhythms of prayer and work. In a long letter, which seems to have been a reply to some of Elisabeth's questions, the founder of the Monastery of the Protection of the Mother of God came back to her personal vocation, the origins of her community, and the spirit that she wanted to infuse in it. The following text reproduces this letter almost in its entirety because it is a unique witness to the implantation of Russian monasticism in France. On January 14,

Mother Eudoxie wrote to Elisabeth from a convalescent home in Switzerland where she was recovering from pleurisy:

> I just received your letter, which was forwarded to me here, in Switzerland, where I arrived more than four months ago. I remember you very well and our meeting at M[other] Maria's place [the Lourmel shelter, prior to the war]. I've read your book on Russian holiness.
>
> I'm sorry not to be able to attend the meeting of your ecumenical group [in Nancy] since meetings of this sort interest me very much. I can reply to the questions you ask but, given the time limits imposed by circumstances, I can't meditate sufficiently on my answers or formulate them as well as I would like.
>
> I left Russia in 1932, where I had made my monastic profession in a small convent—clandestinely, since this was already prohibited by law. I began to wear the habit only when I came to France. At the beginning, I lived with M[other] Maria [Skobtsova], who was dreaming of a new vocation for monasticism, and since there was nothing else, I began to collaborate with her. Her ideal was the active life and social advocacy. Unfortunately, she didn't have any fondness for the liturgical offices or any knowledge of the Orthodox monastic tradition, and yet it is *tradition* that links us to the principal goal of monasticism: the transformation of the carnal being into a spiritual being, the purification of the heart by every means—self-denial, obedience, in brief, life according to the Gospel. Activity should be based on this fundamental premise. M[other] Maria practiced a lot of authentic denial herself, but she refused to believe that the traditional means for attaining it were efficacious. This gave our life with her an aspect of disorder, of arbitrariness. In the end, I wasn't able to continue. I went to England where I had good relations with Anglican convents and, with their help, I got enough money to found a community in France. The beginnings were very difficult. Finally, a friend gave us her property in the Yonne: a big country house, a large garden, and two fields outside of the village. We have been there for ten years. At this moment, we are fourteen sisters, a chaplain, and several persons whom we lodge and who help us with our work. During the summer we have boarders; in winter there are a few old

women who stay with us on a permanent basis and whom we take care of. They pay us, and it is our only income, which enables us to receive all sorts of exceptional cases: a mother with two small children, abandoned by her husband; sick people without any means; old women who do not yet have their papers to be able to enter rest homes, . . . sometimes abnormal persons. People know we are there and that they can send someone to us only if we have enough room. As you can see, we do not have a defined activity.

Now, as for the convent itself. We are, of course, faithful to tradition. Orthodox monasticism is perhaps closer, in the way it is organized, to the Benedictines of old, in the times when they cleared the land, when they formed cultural centers in an uncivilized Europe, when you couldn't be a specialist, when you had to take care of all the needs of the neighbors. The inner structure is also similar. A convent is an independent *family,* under the protection of the bishop. The abbess is the indisputable head until her death, and it is her personal inspiration that forms the spirit of the community. But only the spirit, because there are fixed rules. The origin of these rules goes back to the Stoudion monastery of Constantinople. There are fundamental rules that have been laid down by the ecumenical councils. But in all that, there are varieties in the details and they form the body of the traditions of a given monastery. We had to begin with everything up in the air and in very difficult conditions. I adopted the rule of a convent in western Russia along with another rule from a Carpathian convent, modifying both of them according to the circumstances. These circumstances were, above all, the psychology of the novices, who were women no longer young and with whom you couldn't be too rigorous about matters of fasting, vigils, etc. All that is very flexible, and I take advantage of the leeway offered by tradition. Our sisters do everything themselves. They tend the garden and the two fields, which give us our vegetables; we have two cows and some chickens. We have to take care of the old women, do the housework, sing the Daily Office. All that requires a lot of physical strength—and it also has a spiritual goal that is called "the obediences," which should be carried out with prayer in one's heart . . .

The inner life of the sisters develops under the inspiration given by the Daily Office and the spiritual direction they receive from their superiors and confessors. Since our chaplain is a member of the "white" clergy who is unfamiliar with the monastic tradition, I occasionally invite a priest-monk for spiritual direction, and it is he who professes the sisters.

According to the canons, the age for profession is forty, so the primitive and regular (*rassophor*) novitiates last a long time. There are exceptions, but these depend on the judgment of the abbess.

Sometimes, Western Christians do not understand that, in our concept of monasticism, which is that of a perfect Christianity, a single monastery embraces all sorts of different lifestyles within its walls: from those active in projects on the outside to contemplatives, and all the intermediary states. All that is individual, as are all human souls. Everything should be dominated by love, which is the true goal of the Christian life; monasticism is just one of the paths toward this goal.

Obviously, in our times there are many areas of activity where we could deploy our talents: the translation of the Daily Office into French (one of our sisters is Greek but culturally French), into English (we have a former Anglican who used to be a journalist and the literary editor of a publishing house on the Continent)—all that is very interesting but, unfortunately, there aren't enough of us; we have all the manual work that needs to be done just to subsist, and we don't have young people willing to commit themselves to the religious life. We feel useful, people seek us for different reasons, but what do you want us to do?

Let's go back to the essential: Tradition is steadfast; the goal of monasticism is to give a new birth from the old self in us, and that is why a new name is given us when we make our profession. The goal is to purify the heart by fighting against the passions; the means are the vows of chastity, obedience, and poverty and the task of imitating the model given us in the life of the Lord; and the true shaping of the soul comes about through the life of the Community, where we all share the heaviest and most disagreeable tasks—all the novices go through that. Later a place, an obedience, is found for each according to her talents. I hope you understand my French, which is far from perfect, even though my father was French. If you need more particulars, please let me know; this letter is more like a rough draft. Pray for me . . .

P.S. The oral recitation of the Jesus Prayer enters into all of that, obviously. But we still don't feel able to attain the summit.

This testimony of a monasticism lived out authentically enabled Elisabeth to grasp better the particular nature of this vocation, of whose permanence down through the ages Mother Eudoxie's monastery—still flourishing—bears testimony: its adaptability to different historical contexts. The vitality of the Orthodox monasteries of both Russian and Greek tradition, which grew up in Western Europe in the course of time, contributed to the enrichment of the Orthodox Church by becoming centers of prayer and places of renewal for the laity.

Elisabeth's special interest in the monastic life at the heart of the Orthodox tradition went hand in hand with her fascination with marginal figures such as Mother Maria, whose audacious and innovative faith she greatly admired. Right after the war, Elisabeth felt the need to make known this uncommon personality, venerated by those who knew her, such as Fr. Lev, as soon as they learned of her death.

Elisabeth continued to collaborate with *Dieu Vivant*, to which she contributed two critical reviews during this period: one on the book by Archimandrite Spiridon, *My Missions in Siberia*, published in 1951; and the other, written in 1952, on the English text of her friend Nadezhda Gorodetsky on Saint Tikhon of Zadonsk. Thanks to these publications, the name of Elisabeth Behr-Sigel began to spread among Orthodox theologians and Russian teachers. This growing fame gave a new impetus to her research and enabled her to make some stimulating contacts, of which one was with the Slavic expert, Pierre Pascal.

Pierre Pascal and the Study on Bukharev, 1952–1959

It was through the review *Dieu Vivant*, to which both contributed, that Elisabeth first met Professor Pierre Pascal in the course of one of her visits to Paris. This extraordinary person was a military attaché at the French embassy in St. Petersburg at the time of the Russian Revolution. After having collaborated with Lenin for a while, he narrowly escaped prison thanks to his repatriation to France. Married to a Russian, he became one of the foremost specialists on the teaching of colloquial Russian as well as an authority on Slavic literature and religious thought.

Aware of Elisabeth's difficult financial and emotional situation, he wanted to see her return to her reflections on Russian spirituality. At the end of a discussion he prodded her: "Let's go—you're going to do a doctoral thesis." It was due to his urging that, on May 7, 1952, Elisabeth was enrolled on the register of theses at the Sorbonne with the goal of obtaining a State-recognized doctorate. Even though the greater part of her time was already taken up with caring for her husband and children and with her teaching job, Elisabeth threw herself wholeheartedly into her research work, which she carried on late at night.

Thanks to Pierre Pascal, Elisabeth was compensated for her research. On September 24, 1954, she was assigned as an intern research assistant to the director of scientific research in the field of Russian religious thought. This provisional position at the Centre National de la Recherche Scientifique (CNRS) lasted until the autumn of 1956, when she was obliged to rejoin the technical college in Nancy. The two years she spent at the CNRS enabled her to dedicate herself exclusively to theology. She still had to choose a subject broad enough for a doctoral research project in which she would be able to continue to make the theology of the Orthodox Church accessible to the West.

Bukharev, the "Monk in the City"[87]

Elisabeth's lively spirit was continually seeking new subjects to study. In her letters to Fr. Lev, Fr. Anthony Bloom, and her Paris friends, she kept asking for ideas. She was still fascinated by Orthodox spirituality as it was made incarnate in the lives of the Russian saints, and she was looking for an outstanding hagiographical personality as the centerpiece of her study. She consulted the future bishop, Fr. Anthony, who gave her his opinion:

> There is a need for a serious and impartial study on Joseph of Volokolamsk and the Josephite tradition. There is a task of personal rehabilitation waiting to be done, a spirituality to be analyzed and

understood, and a philosophy of the State, which needs to be situated and pursued. Joseph of Volokolamsk is a true saint and a tragic historical personage. This is the subject I'm most interested in.

The same tradition of Paissius Velitchkovsky is expressed in an astonishingly different way in the schools of Optino and Valaam.

You suggest Theophane the Recluse; he is more one-sided than Ignatius Briantchaninoff and, in a way, less promising, but I think that Ignatius would disappoint those who want to know the Tradition, that he represents a spirituality that is only given by Theophane, who, in ways sometimes surprising, rejoins and unites both Optino and Valaam. But I like him too much to take it upon myself to advise you to make him the object of your research. I'm afraid I can't think about him without a prejudice in his favor.[88]

Outside of the great ascetic figures evoked by Fr. Anthony, Elisabeth's attention was drawn, from many different angles, toward a little-known personage unrecognized by Russian religious history, Alexander Bukharev. Paul Evdokimov had already introduced her to this tormented nineteenth-century monk who returned to the world in order to follow, as a layman, what Evdokimov called the way of "interiorized monasticism,"[89] that is, an authentic spiritual search in the midst of a secularized society. Evdokimov was careful not to compromise the universal character of his witness and did not insist on the personal veneration he harbored for this man, who had been disowned by the Church of his time and who had always had a multitude of critics.

For his part, Fr. Lev wrote: "I still think that Bukharev should be your topic."[90] It was Pierre Pascal who determined the final choice: the professor put his considerable documentation on Alexander Bukharev, which he had gathered when he was thinking of doing a book about him, at Elisabeth's disposal. Henceforth, this monk and theologian would be the essential subject of her reflections until she defended her thesis, twenty years after beginning her research. She never missed a chance to evoke, everywhere and anywhere, her interest in her subject, to the extent that Nadine embroidered the name of Bukharev on a cushion for her, and Nicolas developed an intense dislike for the former monk who, he felt, was stealing his mother's time away from him. He kept asking his mother whether Bukharev, in her history, would soon be dispatched to the next world.

The rediscovery of this forgotten personage took place in the context of the theological climate of the postwar years, which itself was the result of the intellectual excitement that had characterized Orthodox circles in Paris during the 1930s. In the line of the religious renewal set in motion by the intellectuals of the Silver Age at the beginning of the century, the guiding theme was the "churching" of life, a neologism incorporated into the charter of the Russian Christian Student Movement. The idea was to put each instant of one's existence into continuity with the Sunday Eucharist and no longer consider participation in the liturgy as a ritual separated from daily life and detached from the contemporary world.

Bukharev wanted to fully take on this concern for putting the Gospel at the center of one's being in the very different context of the Russian society of the mid-nineteenth century. It was a time of rupture between the Slavophile intellectuals and the official Church, whose ever-increasing institutionalization emphasized the formal aspects of religious practice, often at the expense of its spiritual components. The man who took the monastic name of Theodore, gifted with a lively intelligence and sensitivity, wanted to affirm that the Church was not just a collection of rituals to be observed, but the place where the whole person, the secularized person marked by his time, was to be transfigured: "An effort must be made to *Christify*—that is, to *humanize*—this culture, not from outside, by constraint, but from within, by the energies of the Holy Spirit."[91]

Bukharev's evangelical outlook clashed with the rigidity of the ecclesiastical mentality of his times, which considered his ideas dangerous. His writings were violently criticized. His commentary on the Apocalypse was denied publication. This opposition, along with the monk's reflections on the need to bear witness to Christ beyond the monastery walls, led him to ask to be relieved of his monastic vows in order to continue his quest for God in the world; and he dedicated himself to this search as a layman, but with the same integrity as he had when a monk. At the moment of being reduced to the lay state, he wrote to two close friends: "Can I not also try, *with the help of God*, to seek only the things of God, His Grace, and His Truth, in the terrestrial and visible reality?"[92]

Shortly after he had left the monastery, Bukharev's change of status was sealed by his marriage to a young woman who had supported him in his search. He wanted to show that marriage could be an authentic path to sanctification, as authentic as monasticism: "God had ordained . . . that I meet a woman, a young girl, who understood what I was doing. She shares my aspirations and is willing to stand by me in my spiritual struggle . . . It seems to me that it is important to be able to affirm, someday, not only in theory and speculation, but, based on my own experience, that *Divine Grace is given to us—and truly given—also in marriage* and in all that concerns it."[93]

The reaction of the official Church did not take long: it barred any possibility of his publishing in religious reviews, which amounted to condemning Bukharev to poverty. The ideas of the former archimandrite, who wanted to open the message of Christ to the realities of the contemporary world, represented a threat to the ecclesiastical institutions of that time, which wanted to avoid any hint of scandal. Bukharev paid for his unwavering faithfulness to an ideal by living the latter part of his life in misery, supported only by his wife and a handful of friends.

As a former Lutheran, Elisabeth was deeply moved by this marginal person, who both accepted unjustified calumnies—a trait characteristic of Russian spirituality—and intended to live an evangelical Orthodoxy freed from the institutional straitjacket that distorted its message. She enthusiastically plunged into the documents given her by Pierre Pascal, which consisted, essentially, in the theological writings of Bukharev as well as his correspondence. She undertook a painstaking task of translation, sorting, and analysis. Father Lev encouraged her: "I'm glad to see that you are persevering with Bukharev. This is the type of project that constitutes, in a deep sense, 'French Orthodoxy.'"[94] Father Basil Zenkovsky, the author of a famous book that came out in 1953, *Histoire de la philosophie russe*, also supported Elisabeth and took a keen interest in her research. He summed up Bukharev's ideas concerning the relationship between the Church and the world: "The most remarkable thing about Bukharev is that he both firmly confesses the profound difference between the realm of the divine and that of the 'world' (in its fallen state) and yet has a strong sense of the Divine Light penetrating *the whole life of the world*. The opposition between the Church and culture is thus put aside.

This opposition is an illusion or intentionally exaggerated. In the measure in which the artisans of culture are Christians, there cannot be any real contradiction."[95]

Because of her professional and family obligations, Elisabeth changed her State doctorate into a secondary thesis that exacted less advanced research and was more in line with her desire to edit texts of Bukharev conjointly with her study. It would only be in 1976, after she retired from her teaching job, that she would defend her thesis for the doctorate at the University of Nancy-II. Elisabeth's study was published the following year by the Beauchesne publishing house under the title *Alexander Bukharev: A Theologian of the Russian Orthodox Church in Dialogue with the Modern World*. In its time, it was the only serious study undertaken in French about this misunderstood theologian.[96] With the very controversial gesture of the monk renouncing his monastic vows as a focal point, Elisabeth looked for the causes and the theological implications. She traced a biography of Bukharev according to Pascal's documentation.

The life story of the man whom his contemporaries denounced as a new Martin Luther, was entirely placed under the sign of Christ's self-emptying. This choice of taking on, with all its consequences, a life immersed in the tempests of the world rather than pursuing a career in the monastic state—which, at that time, meant more belonging to a superior class than renouncing the world for the sake of God—converted the very existence of Bukharev into a theological message. Since Bukharev's writings were complex, clumsy, and hence not easily accessible, Elisabeth painted his themes with broad brushstrokes. It is for this reason that, in her conclusion, she spoke of his "destiny" rather than his "thought." Bukharev affirmed that "to unite ourselves to Christ today, we must follow His *descent* into this hell with only the weapons of faith, hope, and compassionate love."[97]

This lived-out kenotic[98] theology shines through in the letters published at the end of the study. Elisabeth translated long sections of letters that Bukharev had written to his close friends Fr. Valerian and Alexandra Lavrski. Their chronological order enables the reader to read the biographical material, but this time, as seen from within, as signed by the pen of Bukharev himself. In these letters one can follow the evolution of the former monk's convictions and see how he made these incarnate in his own life.

In this study, Elisabeth gave us a picture of an inspired and tormented person who unceasingly placed his weaknesses in the hands of God and accepted, right to the very end, his destiny as a disgraced failure in order to take part in the transcendence that Christ opens in the depths of death. Elisabeth's admiration and compassion for this complex man was obvious on every page.

Father Lev was delighted when this work was published, thinking that it would propagate the message of this unrecognized theologian: "I'm really overjoyed that, thanks to you, a life filled with humiliations and inspirations can become known to those who were unaware of it and, for at least some people, give light and stimulation."[99] Nonetheless, Elisabeth's book had hardly any more success than did the writings of Bukharev himself. For the Orthodox world, the personality of a defrocked monk still retained the wift of scandal. Without consulting the author, the publishing house quickly withdrew the book—something rare at that time.

This important work, which consumed Elisabeth's leisure time, was not a mere intellectual game for her. Alongside the prophetic dimension of Bukharev, which she hoped would have an impact on the contemporary situation of the Church by challenging it to be open to questions of the present day, Elisabeth's interest in this suffering figure seemed to be a way of giving meaning to her own difficult situation with André due to his chronic depression. The study of Bukharev helped her to transcend her own daily suffering at seeing André sick by transposing it to another level of existence, using the example of people who were able to escape despair by putting themselves entirely in the hands of Christ, as had Bukharev.

Far from being the simple object of a study, the *kenosis* theme, the emptying of the person, to which Elisabeth constantly returned in her writings, especially as it found expression in the "fools for Christ" dear to the Russian Church, was echoed in her daily life. She had to suppress her pastoral talents and did not have the leisure to develop her theological reflections as she would have liked due to her teaching job; in all this she experienced a certain measure of self-renunciation, a renouncement of her aspirations and capabilities.

The repeated choice of concentrating on such kenotic figures also showed a particular sensitivity on Elisabeth's part to human weakness, which led her to want to bear, as much as possible, the sufferings of those close to her. Her privileged friendship for Fr. Lev was a case in point, a friendship not without clashes and storms due to the monk's difficult character and Elisabeth's stubbornness in trying to promote his charisma, sometimes against his will.

Father Lev, a New "Monk in the City"

In certain aspects, Fr. Lev's life journey resembled that of Bukharev. In his determination to appear as a symbol for his contemporaries, he put himself outside of any recognized categories in order to bring the Gospel message to as many people as possible. Elisabeth wrote that Fr. Lev, "in Beirut, as in London and Paris, is a monk in the city. If he summons people to the contemplation of the Divine Mystery, it is always with the concern that this mystery might illumine the daily personal life of each and every Christian as well as their social and political life."[100]

This concern of Fr. Lev with making incarnate the Gospel message in daily life was very much in continuity with Bukharev when he wrote: "The truth of the Lord remains forever and ever. It is one and immutable; but our relationship to this Divine Truth varies according to the particularities and needs of each time period."[101] This singular vocation was the cause of Fr. Lev's permanent instability—a monk without a monastery, a priest without a parish, who preached in Hyde Park in London as well as at the ecumenical institute in Bossey. Even though he had chosen it, this original type of ministry was a crucifying burden for the Monk of the Eastern Church, whose restless and sensitive soul suffered from such a perpetual vagabond existence.

The unflagging correspondence maintained by the two theologians over a long period was a source of comfort and support for both of them in the midst of their respective trials. Elisabeth, caught up in the worries of her daily life, received each of Fr. Lev's letters as a blessing, as a way of participating in the life of her friend. Even though his difficulties were scarcely less than hers, he reaffirmed her in her own vocation by guiding her toward Christ in all things, a path that he himself followed.

After the war, a new ministry opened up for Fr. Lev Gillet: showing the young Christians in Lebanon that Orthodoxy could be vibrant and liberating. The founders of the Orthodox Youth Movement of the Middle East (MJO), who were trying to bring about a spiritual renewal in the Church of Antioch, discovered in Fr. Lev the kind of preacher who could help them carry out their project. As of February 1948, Lebanon became the new center of the monk's spiritual influence, and he would go there almost every year for the rest of his life. Elisabeth followed the itinerary of his frequent trips to the Near East through his letters, thus sharing the impressions, joys, and sorrows of her friend.

Among the places where he stayed regularly when he was in the Near East, Jerusalem held a special fascination for Fr. Lev:

> I think of you. I pray for you in this cruel, exhausting, anguishing city where one feels crushed, as if under a winepress, in an atmosphere of desolation and sometimes of hatred, but where one also senses strange forces and promises. May the power of the Passion and Resurrection, which go forth from this place, be given to you in abundance! . . . The 800,000 people whom Israel has chased from their homes, without clothing, without bread . . . the crime of the Arabs' immense suffering cries out to heaven. These almost naked children who cry because they are hungry. This makes me weep.[102]

Several years later, the city of Christ, so full of painful paradoxes, would lead him to invoke some lines from the Rhineland mystic Thomas à Kempis in his *Imitation of Christ*: "Once again, Jerusalem has moved me deeply by its grandfatherly and humble tenderness, by its bloody spasms, its human misery, and its pentecostal power . . . O God of truth, my sole desire, unite me to Yourself with strong and sweet bonds; I'm tired of listening, tired of reading, but not of saying to You that You are my sole desire."[103] In between these trips, which inspired him and nourished his intense spiritual life, Fr. Lev returned to the haven of his simple routine in London. He now lived at Saint Basil's House, the headquarters of the Fellowship of St. Alban and

St. Sergius. He had moved there in the autumn of 1948 and would remain there until his death in 1980.

Being very taken up by his new ministry in the Near East, he seemed to distance himself from the Orthodox circles in Paris where Elisabeth had known him as a very active participant. In her biography of Fr. Lev, she wrote: "In the 1950s, when Lev Gillet's life was divided between London and Oxford, on the one hand, and Beirut and Jerusalem, on the other, the problems of Orthodoxy in France—those of the insertion of the Orthodox Church into both the cultural fabric of an ancient Western Christian country and its contemporary Western modernity, about which he had formerly felt so passionately— now seemed very far from the concerns of the Monk of the Eastern Church."[104]

In Paris, the little Francophone parish of the Transfiguration Saint Genevieve, where Fr. Lev had focused his enthusiasm in the 1930s, had disappeared among the upheavals of the war, after having had for rectors Fr. Jouanny and then Fr. Valentin de Bachst. The parishioners were scattered but, in their hearts, continued with their desire for a Francophone Orthodoxy. Father Lev's stays in Paris were now reduced to short visits on his way to the port of Marseille, where he embarked for the Near East. He would meet a few friends from his early years in Paris: Paul Evdokimov, Vladimir and Madeleine Lossky, Marguerite Zagorovsky. He would run across Elisabeth when she was staying in the capital with her parents-in-law. But little by little a series of events once again placed him in the midst of the life of the Paris Church and involved him in the problem of the implantation of the Orthodox Church in France. This had become a burning issue that both Elisabeth and Fr. Lev wanted to advance and on which they collaborated closely.

In January 1956, Paul Evdokimov asked Fr. Lev to give a series of lectures at the Center for Orthodox Studies, which had been founded by Evdokimov and Lev Zander in September of the previous year for the purpose of teaching a theological course in the French language. It was during this 1956 sojourn in Paris that the Monk of the Eastern Church found himself closely involved in the search for a canonical status undertaken by the community of Fr. Evgraf Kovalevsky. Father Lev and Elisabeth assiduously followed the development of their friend's thorny situation and remained very attached to him.

Evgraf Kovalevsky's story was strange and complex. When he returned home from the war after having been a prisoner in Germany, where he discovered that he had a great deal in common with the French, Fr. Evgraf launched a new ecclesial project. In the spirit of the Confraternity of Saint Photius, of which he was a member, this intellectual, full of ideas, wanted to advance a French Orthodox Church that would take the heritage of the Western tradition into consideration. He was supported in this initiative by other members of the confraternity, notably by his brother Maxime and Vladimir Lossky.

The French Orthodox Mission, which Fr. Evgraf founded after the war, was in continuity with an Old Catholic Francophile community of the Western rite, formerly centered around Bishop Irénée Winnaert. This community, which had originally been Roman Catholic but had since marginalized itself, wanted to become Orthodox. In 1936 it was received into communion by the patriarchate of Moscow, after Fr. Lev's attempts to obtain the approval of Constantinople were met by a stony silence.[105] When Bishop Winnaert died in 1937, Fr. Evgraf, who had been ordained a priest that same year by Bishop Eleutherius of the Moscow patriarchate, became the leader of the community. After the war, the group founded the parish of Saint Irenaeus, on the boulevard Blanqui in the 13th arrondissement in Paris. Maxime Kovalevsky then left the parish of Our Lady Joy of the Afflicted, where he was choir director—a post he turned over to young Nicolas Lossky—to take up the same position in his brother's community.

The French Orthodox Mission founded the St. Denys Institute, which, like the Center for Orthodox Studies, imparted theological instruction in French. Vladimir Lossky, the dean of the institute, taught dogmatic theology and Church history, Fr. Evgraf taught canon law, and Fr. Alexis Van den Mensbrugghe,[106] a former Benedictine with ties to the convent of Amay-sur-Meuse, taught liturgy.

Later, the French Orthodox Mission would change its name to the Orthodox Catholic Church of France (Eglise catholique orthodoxe de France, or ECOF). Historical research resulted in a liturgy of the Western rite inspired by ancient forms once used in Gaul. The special situation of the ECOF community caused certain tensions. Father Evgraf, a very charismatic person, felt that he was called to evangelize among the most marginal people and was not afraid to take risky initiatives that he thought were in line with his vocation. Complaints about his behavior, notably his contacts with certain esoteric circles, came to the attention of his bishop. Thus, in 1953, the patriarchate of Moscow ordered him to leave his position as rector of the Saint Irenaeus parish for a year and to serve at Nice until the situation was clarified.

At the instigation of his parishioners, Fr. Evgraf refused to accept this ecclesiastical penance; he sent a letter to the patriarchate of Moscow stating that he no longer wanted to be under its jurisdiction. This pre-dated letter, which made it seem as though his departure had taken place prior to the disciplinary measures, enabled him to ignore the conditions that the patriarchate wanted to impose.

Vladimir Lossky then tried to reason with his friend, hoping to dissuade him from putting himself in an untenable canonical situation. Nicolas Lossky remembered witnessing, in the family kitchen, the painful discussion between his father and Fr. Evgraf, his professor of canon law at the St. Denys Institute. His father had pleaded with the future Bishop Jean not to take off on a "canonical adventure" that would shatter the conciliar dimension of their undertaking. But Fr. Evgraf believed that it was his duty to seek a jurisdiction that would accept the ecclesial autonomy of the French Orthodox Mission, the Western-rite celebration of the Gallican liturgy, which he had introduced, and his ordination as bishop. The break between the ECOF and the patriarchate of Moscow was confirmed. Vladimir Lossky left his teaching post at the St. Denys Institute, feeling obliged to distance himself from the initiatives of his friend, who had now placed himself outside of Church bounds.

In 1954, in search of a new canonical legitimacy, Fr. Evgraf approached the patriarch of Constantinople. Patriarch Athenagoras then consulted Fr. Lev Gillet on the matter and proposed that he become a bishop and assume responsibility for Fr. Evgraf's group. Father Lev turned down the offer because he doubted that this arrangement would be accepted by the concerned parties and also because he did not think that he had a bishop's vocation.

In his letters to Elisabeth, the Monk of the Eastern Church had much to say about the development of the "Evgraf question." In her biography of Fr. Lev, Elisabeth included long extracts from these letters.[107] Father Evgraf's adventures with the Church led Fr. Lev to ask himself how an Orthodoxy with a local angle was going to take shape in France. Such a process seemed to him to be hardly compatible with the audacious road taken by Fr. Evgraf but rather called for a more discreet and patient approach:

> I think (and Fr. Anthony Bloom agrees with me) that what the French Orthodox need is a priest (no matter what his jurisdiction) who celebrates the liturgy in French on a regular basis, every Sunday, saying a few words at each service and holding a weekly meeting of Bible studies, without mentioning the jurisdiction controversies, without publicity, without propaganda, without any pretension of founding a French Orthodoxy, without anything spectacular. There would be a lot of difficulties, but I'm sure that after three years of such a modest undertaking, without much ado and with perseverance, this priest would see a serious nucleus forming around him. In this Russian community in Paris, where people talk too much and too loud, and where words almost always go beyond what the speaker thinks and always go beyond reality, only a sustained, humble, and charitable effort, as unpretentious as the life of the Holy Family at Nazareth, can bring about some good.[108]

All the same, Fr. Lev used to go to the parish of Saint Irenaeus to visit his friend, and he remained sensitive to Fr. Evgraf's initiatives and to the openness of his community, which accepted anyone who sought God without any sort of discrimination:

> If there existed a parish (and it would be an exaggeration to attribute this to Fr. Evgraf's group) that was open to divorced people, to those living in concubinage, to homosexuals, to alcoholics, to drug addicts, even to murderers and thieves, I would rejoice in Christ. That doesn't mean that you can tell them: "Go in peace, keep it up." But it means that, before their eyes, especially for those people, the image of the Crucified One, with His arms extended, is displayed: "He who comes to Me, I will not cast out." Salvation is offered to them, if they choose to accept the Savior, but how can they choose Him if nobody tries to put them in contact with Him? Evgraf's gift is that he is able to reach these souls. Don't ask him to organize ordinary, edifying parishes—and this is why I persist in thinking that what he does

shouldn't affect or trouble the majority of the Orthodox who are seeking a Western expression of their faith and who need the structure of these ordinary, edifying parishes—but let him lead a rescue mission, let him be an Abbé Pierre on the spiritual level, offering hospitality and nourishment to the spiritually homeless, a task that will have its chaotic aspects, but so what?[109]

In her biography of Fr. Lev, Elisabeth was careful to tone down her friend's idealized vision of Evgraf's work: she reminded the reader of the somewhat nationalistic dimension of this enterprise.[110]

When he returned to London in the spring of 1956, Fr. Lev went to the bishop representing the Ecumenical Patriarchate to once again plead the cause of the French Orthodox Mission, which was still without a canonical connection. And once again he was urged to assume the leadership of the group as bishop. This time, in spite of his reservations about being ordained a bishop, Fr. Lev declared himself ready to accept this responsibility in view of implanting a local church, but Fr. Evgraf's community refused this arrangement. They were finally received into the communion of the Russian Church Outside of Russia, and Bishop John Maximovitch, the future Saint John of San Francisco, consecrated Fr. Evgraf to the episcopacy in 1964. Father Lev's involvement in the affairs of the French Orthodox Mission during the years 1955–56 put him back into the midst of the ecclesiastical debates of that time and led him to multiply his trips to France and his contacts with the theologians of the émigré community. Whereas a few years previously Fr. Lev had aspired to nothing other than his ministry in Lebanon, he now once again found himself involved in the Russian circles in Paris from whom he thought he had finally distanced himself.

When he stayed in Paris, whether for lectures at the Center for Orthodox Studies or for his contacts with Fr. Evgraf's group, Fr. Lev lodged at the CIMADE center at Sèvres, where Paul Evdokimov was the director. During the war, Evdokimov had joined the CIMADE, a Protestant organization assisting displaced persons.[111] In 1945 he had decided to open a home for refugees at Bièvres under the auspices of the CIMADE. Several years later, he founded a hostel for students at Sèvres. About fifty students, both French and foreign and of all denominations, shared a community life there.

When he went to Sèvres, Fr. Lev celebrated the liturgy in the hostel's chapel and often took part in the interdenominational discussions sponsored there. This group attracted a number of theologians from the older generation, including those who had shared the adventure of the first Francophone parish with Fr. Lev, but also some younger people, descendants of the Russian émigré intelligentsia. In that context, he gradually reestablished contact with the Paris Orthodox.

During that period, the discussions in Paris about the problems of jurisdiction were in full swing among the participants in the CIMADE circle. The question of the realization of a Francophone Orthodoxy was always on the agenda, encouraged by the complex development of the Evgraf group. Elisabeth had great hopes for the role that Fr. Lev could play in this project. By so doing, she created a climate of expectation around her friend, who became more and more in demand among the different groups in Paris.

Father Lev, in fact, came to ask himself whether his ordination as a bishop would not resolve the aberrant historical situation in which the Western Orthodox Church found itself, where several bishops, representing different patriarchates and dioceses, presided over the same territory. His letters to Elisabeth at this time brought to light his dilemma. He wanted to put his experience at the service of the implantation of Orthodoxy in France, but he felt himself unworthy and incapable of taking on the duties of bishop. Elisabeth frankly encouraged him to go ahead, to become this bishop who could realize an Orthodox federation above and beyond ethnic distinctions. Her correspondence with Fr. John Meyendorff revealed her dream of a new situation for Francophone Orthodox centered around the person of Fr. Lev.

With Fr. Lev's consent and with the help of her Paris friends, Elisabeth sent a letter to Metropolitan Vladimir who, in 1946, had succeeded Metropolitan Evlogy as head of the diocese of the Russian Orthodox Churches in Western Europe. She set forth the situation of the Church in France through the prism of her own experience:

> I have always loved the Russian Church with filial love since, through it, I was received into the universal Orthodox Church. I have devoted several articles to the study of Orthodox spirituality in its

specifically Russian expression, and I am doing my doctoral thesis on a nineteenth-century Russian theologian.

And yet, in spite of my attachment to Russian Orthodoxy, I have always hoped that, someday, a French Orthodox Church would become a beacon from which the universal Orthodox Truth would shine forth on the West. This hope now seems to me to have become a necessity. In the majority of our Orthodox centers, even those of Russian origin, a generation of young people has come of age and their culture is almost entirely French. Since they do not understand the liturgical language, many of these young people have distanced themselves from the Church and, at the same time, from Christ. But those who have remained faithful to the faith of their fathers constitute lively and enthusiastic groups, desirous of incorporating their Orthodox spiritual life into the context of Western culture. Yet they suffer from the divisions of the Orthodox Churches in the West and look upon these divisions as meaningless. They aspire, more or less consciously, to make incarnate their unity of faith in one single ecclesiastical organization. It can be argued that it is too soon to envisage the total autonomy of French Orthodoxy. But it is incontestable that these young people need both a certain freedom and, at the same time, a guide who can advise them, moderate their impatience, bring them closer together, and, above all, help them to deepen their spiritual life and their ecclesiastical awareness.[112]

Elisabeth went so far as to propose the person she deemed most qualified to take on such a responsibility:

Such a task is delicate. Several of us, however, think that the Church has a person capable of carrying it out: I dare to propose Archimandrite Lev Gillet. Whereas other names will only provoke discussion and more division and, due to their lack of prudence, feed the suspicions of the very idea of French Orthodoxy in the case of some people, Fr. Lev Gillet could play the role of peacemaker. By his profound faith and luminous intelligence, by his charity and unquestionable disinterest, he would seem to be the spiritual father who could guide a new Western Orthodoxy by paths both original and traditional and give it a decisive spiritual impulse.

This panegyric did not provoke any concrete reaction on the part of the hierarchs, even though Metropolitan Vladimir seemed to have, at one point, considered making Fr. Lev his vicar-bishop. Nonetheless, the group of friends who gathered around the monk when he came to Paris continued to reflect actively on how to respond to the challenge posed by a Francophone Orthodoxy. Father Lev wrote to Elisabeth: "I understand quite well the desire of young people to make incarnate French Orthodoxy in a clearly visible and clearly defined structure. I'm also in entire agreement with the idea that the Russian episcopate at Paris should lead the way in this and even be the center of gravity."[113]

Gillet's reflections on the situation of the Church found a practical application in concrete propositions whose execution he entrusted to Elisabeth: "I will be in Paris in August to take part in a more or less ecumenical conference of the CIMADE (from the 11th to the 20th). This would be an opportunity to meet French Orthodox members of Metropolitan Vladimir's diocese, perhaps organize a liturgy in French, etc."[114] During his conferences in Paris, Fr. Lev had the chance to measure the strength of the expectations of a Francophone Orthodoxy on the part of the new generation: "Could it be that these young people [he had just mentioned Meyendorff] will realize what another generation of young people—Evgraf, Lossky, Khroll, the 'French parish' of those days—hoped for in 1928? . . . to bring about with these youngsters of 1956 what the young people desired twenty-eight years ago? . . . How that makes us feel old! Will something happen? Everything is in the hands of this new generation."[115]

The tensions of all these ecclesiastical negotiations as well as his constant state of overwork had repercussions on the health of the Monk of the Eastern Church. In June 1956 he suffered a coronary thrombosis. This sudden setback, at the age of sixty-three, resulted in a loss of vitality. Nonetheless, he would continue to play a central role during the years to come, years that would be decisive for the development of a local Church in France.

On the other side of the Channel, Fr. Anthony was trying to implant Orthodoxy in Great Britain. In 1957 he accepted the office of bishop, which had been offered to him by the patriarchate of Moscow. As can be seen from a letter sent to Elisabeth, he saw this role as an act of obedience to God's will, which put him at the service of the laity:

What can I say about my nomination? For the third time, God has spoken to me at a moment when I had already decided to follow another path, and it is precisely in this conflict between my intention and what events dictate that I see a Sign that it is God's, and not human, will that has determined this choice and this decision.

And what can I say about my feelings as I prepare myself to be consecrated bishop? I think that every Grace draws us more deeply toward the Foundation and Cornerstone of the Church, deeper *down*, and exacts from the one who receives it a fuller communion with the humiliation and humility of Christ as well as with His charity and sacrificial compassion. I don't ask God for the strength to fulfill my ministry but rather for the weakness of which Saint Paul speaks and in which the Power of God deploys itself freely and becomes manifest; I *want* to diminish to the point of being nothing more than a window through which the light of God enters, something whose only value is its absence, whose most precious characteristic is to be imperceptible, which only fulfills its role by being invisible and forgotten.[116]

Elisabeth was very attached to Metropolitan Anthony and Fr. Lev. Both of them continued to work, each according to the mission he had been given, for the rooting of the Orthodox Church in the West.

Contributions of the Paris Group toward the Development of the Local Church

During these years of intense professional and family concerns, Elisabeth was continually shuttling between Nancy and Paris. Her stays in Paris represented times of intellectual and spiritual enrichment. She would go to the parish of Our Lady Joy of the Afflicted Saint Genevieve, which was still the only Francophone canonical community in postwar Paris.

Elisabeth recalled how, during one of her visits to the parish, Vladimir Lossky had given her a copy of his book, *The Mystical Theology of the Eastern Church*, published after the end of the war, which presented the theological foundations of Orthodoxy to a Western public. When she was reading the book during her return trip, she had to shield her copy from the interest of the vicar general of the bishopric of Nancy, who was sharing her compartment on the train and who wanted to borrow it. This incident indicates the degree of attention that Orthodoxy still aroused in Western circles.

The Orthodox scene in postwar France was undergoing significant changes, as can be seen from the activity of Fr. Evgraf's French Orthodox Mission. These years were also marked by a period of movement within the émigré community: some Russians, settled in France since the 1920s, had heeded Stalin's 1947 invitation to return to the Soviet Union. From the opposite direction, new immigrants from the East arrived and diversified the Paris parishes. This new wave of Russian-speaking émigrés made it necessary to maintain the Slavonic-speaking parishes at a moment when there was a growing desire to promote French as the liturgical language. Within this context, Elisabeth took an active role in two projects that were of capital importance for the evolution of a local Church: the refounding of the review *Contacts*, and the emergence of the Orthodox Fraternity.

Olivier Clément and the Contacts *Group*

Elisabeth was one of the instigators of the renaissance, in 1959, of *Contacts*. This review had originally been founded in 1949 by Jean Balzon, a member of the French Orthodox Mission and a colleague of Fr. Evgraf. It was through Fr. Evgraf that she met Balzon.

Father Evgraf did not restrict his activities to Paris. He wanted to set up French-speaking parishes in the provinces. With this plan in mind, he organized regular celebrations of the Mass in Nancy, which Elisabeth sometimes attended. Father Evgraf wanted the Nancy community to have an official status and thought that Elisabeth could help to have it recognized by the local prefecture. He sent his colleague Jean Balzon to talk with the Behrs about this procedure.

Balzon, who had discovered Orthodoxy in Lebanon, was a lawyer by profession with considerable administrative talents. Although he was more a man of action than an intellectual, he was interested in theology and wanted Orthodoxy to have a review in French. With this goal, he had founded the *Contacts* ten years previously as an organ of the Orthodox Mission. In 1956 he acquired commercial space at 30, rue Madame, in Paris, where he set up a small Orthodox bookshop as well as the Enotikon Center, which served as a publishing house for brochures on Orthodoxy. Several of Elisabeth's articles were published by the Enotikon Center, notably, the one on the Jesus Prayer that had appeared in a brochure entitled *Pages of Orthodox Spirituality*.

During his visits to the Behrs with the aim of setting up an Orthodox Mission parish in Nancy, Balzon confided his ambitions for the review to Elisabeth: *Contacts* would be an organ for theological reflection in French, over and above all the jurisdictional divisions of the Orthodox Church in the West. But Elisabeth, who considered Fr. Evgraf's group a marginal minority, gave her opinion: "If you want to reach out to everyone and play a role within Orthodoxy in France, you have to open up the review." Moreover, she refused to be the agent for negotiating the legal status of the Francophone parish of the ECOF with the prefecture, as Balzon had requested. She thought that there were not enough Orthodox faithful in Nancy to warrant the opening of a second parish, which, moreover, would disperse the few forces they had.

Elisabeth would serve as a link between the little review of Evgraf's marginal group and the Orthodox intellectuals of the Russian émigré community. First of all, she put Balzon in contact with Fr. John Meyendorff, who had become the Mojaïskys' son-in-law when he married their daughter, Marie. Father John enthusiastically supported the project and helped to persuade Balzon to change the orientation of his review so that the whole of Orthodoxy might find expression in a publication that would appear on a regular basis.

Balzon also met Fr. Lev through Elisabeth on the occasion of one of the periodic visits that the Monk of the Eastern Church made to Paris from 1956 onward. However, Fr. Lev was initially very mistrustful of Balzon and his review. He even told Elisabeth to not get involved in any way:

> I advise you to not submit this study on Bukharev to *Contacts*. On the one hand, intellectual courtesy, if not the regulations themselves, would be violated by an anticipation of this sort. On the other hand, it would be better if, in general, you don't collaborate with *Contacts*. The very names of Fr. Evgraf and M. Balzon have aroused wide-

spread suspicion about this publication. Is this justified, or not? I won't enter into this question here. But one thing is certain: Fr. Evgraf has assured me that *Contacts* does not depend upon him in any way. All the same, it has been his mouthpiece. And M. Balzon doesn't inspire confidence. For my part, I find inadmissible the way that he reproduces, without prior consultation or authorization, already published fragments of such-and-such a writer; I wrote to him very clearly and have forbidden him to associate my name with his undertakings in any way whatsoever . . . A "French Orthodox" publication where neither V. Lossky, nor Olivier Clément, nor Mgr. Cassien [Bezobrazov], nor Mgr. Anthony Bloom collaborates, nor would agree to collaborate, and which presents itself as more or less associated with Fr. E[vgraf], cannot be taken seriously.[117]

This very categorical judgment of Fr. Lev bore witness to his critical view of Fr. Evgraf's activities and his suffering at seeing his friend put himself outside of canonical bounds and seek to become a bishop: "I'm afraid of this—that in the more-or-less near future, he'll be consecrated a bishop by some *episcopus vagans*. That would be the final catastrophe."[118]

All the same, thanks in part to the mediation of Elisabeth, Fr. Lev finally let himself be seduced by the project of a review addressed to the whole of Francophone Orthodoxy. Little by little he became more involved in the brainstorming about how to broaden the review's appeal, although he maintained a critical distance:

As for *Contacts*, I feel strongly that a committee of laypeople would be better. As for myself, given the distances, I can't be very helpful. And I also have some difficulties of principle. The title, "The French Review of Orthodoxy," strikes me as both pretentious and ambiguous. And the spirit of the project seems to me to be unfortunately narrow and polemical . . . Yes, something like *Dieu Vivant* but less intellectual, in a smaller format, but providing spiritual nourishment rather than ecclesiastic debates and avoiding any controversial subject. "Hear what the Spirit says to the Churches," as the author of the Apocalypse admonishes. The review should be attentive to the practical problems of our times—social, international problems.

There are things that are more urgent, needs that are more pressing than all this Orthodox provincialism.[119]

From the tone of his letters to Elisabeth, Fr. Lev, at the time, seemed deeply hurt by the tension between the different jurisdictions, which contradicted his ideal of what catholicity should mean for Orthodoxy. Torn between his desire to work for the birth of a Francophone Orthodoxy and his wish to stay out of ecclesiastical quarrels, he maintained an ambiguous relationship, both close and yet distant, with the editorial board of *Contacts*.

In his project for the founding of an Orthodox review, Jean Balzon had an associate and close friend, Germaine Revault d'Allones, a woman whom he had met on a train and who discovered the Eastern Tradition through him. Father Lev then guided her spiritual search and received her into the Orthodox Church in 1959. He wanted to protect her from the messy situation of the Orthodox dioceses in the West: "I think that the moment has come for Mme. R[evault] d'A[llones]. I will tell her that I am opposed to any abjuration or 'reception.' To facilitate matters, I'll temporarily attach her to the chapel of St. Basil's House—my jurisdiction, and thus that of the Ecum[enical] Patr[iarchate]—and give her a letter attesting that she belongs to the Orth[odox] Ch[urch] and can be admitted to its sacraments on a regular basis. I don't want to 'pin her down' in a confessional institution."[120] Germaine, a physician, came from a wealthy family and would be a great help both in financing the review and in putting her intelligence and enthusiasm at its service.

But if *Contacts* was to have a fresh beginning, a unifying personality was needed to ensure the cohesion of the editorial staff. During one of the preparatory sessions, Fr. Lev suggested calling upon a young French intellectual, converted to Orthodoxy in 1953, whom he had encountered at the meetings of the Cimade: Olivier Clément. "He's your man," Fr. Lev declared.

The incorporation of Olivier Clément as secretary into the editorial staff enabled *Contacts* to take on a whole new dimension. Clément, born in the south of France and raised in an atheist environment, was a historian who had discovered Christ after an intellectual and spiritual journey. Clément would later describe this journey in his autobiography, *L'Autre Soleil*.

Elisabeth was won over from the start by the new editor's charismatic and radiant personality. The gift of friendship, spontaneously emanating from Clément, immediately created a climate of camaraderie among the editorial staff of *Contacts*. By affirming the indispensable link between reflection and experience, he helped to make the review the expression of an ecclesial research that was deeply rooted in the living Tradition as its inspiration for solutions, in a contemporary language, to the problems of the times.

At the beginning, the core group consisted of Jean Balzon, Germaine Revault d'Allones, Elisabeth Behr-Sigel, and Olivier Clément; they would be joined by Fr. Boris Bobrinskoy and Nicolas Lossky. Elisabeth knew Fr. Boris well, since he had spent part of his youth with his cousins the Mojaïskys at Varengeville, near Nancy. He was a good friend of her daughter Nadine. Nicolas Lossky, the son of the philosopher Vladimir Lossky, who died in 1958, was also known to her. Frs. Lev Gillet and John Meyendorff, though not part of the editorial staff, played the role of consultants. Later on, Elisabeth would describe the committee of *Contacts* as "a collaboration, marked by mutual trust, among Orthodox of different ethnic origins and jurisdictions."[121]

Contacts initiated its "rebirth" at the beginning of 1958 with issue no. 25. The foreword stated the goal of the review: to provide a space where its contributors could "witness to the fullness that we discover in the Orthodox Church."[122] Such a witness should lead to a threefold dialogue: with other Christian confessions, with other religions, and with nonbelievers. The collaborators were aware of the "duty to inform"[123] as a necessary condition for such a task, and this would translate in practice into a certain openness, a continual lookout for articles by new authors. Each issue would have a foreword describing its principal themes, in-depth articles on important points of the Orthodox Tradition, a narrative of current events, and an annotated bibliography on the latest publications concerning religious questions. As a forum for discussion, *Contacts* periodically published the reactions of its readers regarding current religious events. In this way, the review contributed to making Orthodoxy known in the West as well as being a means for the Orthodox believer to deepen his faith. The review's ecumenical openness was affirmed from the beginning and became more pronounced as time went on. Elisabeth insisted that it publish articles by her friend Louis Bouyer, a former Lutheran pastor who had converted to Catholicism in 1939.

Elisabeth traveled to Paris several times each year to experience the stimulating meetings of the editorial board. She found the climate of these sessions very amiable, thanks to the deep friendships among the members, similar to the atmosphere of the ecumenical group in Nancy. She became especially close to Germaine Revault d'Allones inasmuch as they shared the same questions and had a similar intellectual vivacity.

At the beginning, the group met in the back room of the Balzon bookshop. Later on, when Germaine purchased a small apartment at 43, rue du Fer-à-Moulin, the committee got together there and discussed things over a meal. Most of the members had connections outside of the review, but they knew one another well and treated each other with a great deal of familiarity. The articles were chosen in a climate of freedom and dialogue, where each member could make his own proposal, which would then be discussed by the rest of the committee. Germaine, who was a strong-willed woman, often stood up to Olivier, who had an assertive personality.

Elisabeth was fond of repeating that "the refounding of *Contacts* was an important moment in my life and in the life of French Orthodoxy." The impact of this event on her own life, where the board meetings nourished her spiritually and emotionally as well as intellectually, cannot be disassociated from its consequences for the evolution of Orthodoxy in France. Through her collaboration with *Contacts*, Elisabeth was able to fulfill her goal of mediator between the traditions of the East and the West and contribute to the implantation of a local Church. Right up until her death, Elisabeth would play an active role in *Contacts*. In addition to her role on the editorial board, she contributed an impressive number of theological articles and book reviews that reflected the evolution of her thinking. Rare were the tables of contents that did not include her name.

These articles were of three types. The first was in-depth theological contributions where she exposed a question, the thinking of an author, always with the same systematic rigor that led her to examine every aspect of a problem. She would then evoke the repercussions of the topic in the actual life of the Church. Through articles of this type, she would interrogate Tradition to find answers to contemporary questions. It was along these lines that she proposed "Reflections on the Doctrine of Gregory Palamas" in issue no. 30 of *Contacts* (1960). After presenting the thought of the great fourteenth-century theologian, as it had appeared in the recently published thesis of Fr. John Meyendorff,[124] Elisabeth demonstrated how Bukharev and Gogol were the successors to Palamas by bringing his teachings into the very heart of a secularized world and thus opening the way to an "interiorized monasticism," as Paul Evdokimov described it. Evdokimov insisted that it was possible for a layperson engaged in society to become a full participant in the divine life in the same way as a monk. The layperson, through asceticism and a habit of prayer adapted to daily life, could be reborn and transfigured by the divine energy emanating from God.

A second type of article took a position on contemporary issues—whether within Orthodoxy, such as the "Perspectives of Orthodoxy in France" (1964), or along ecumenical lines as, for example, when she reacted to the letter, published in *Le Monde*, of Paul VI to Cardinal Villot concerning the celibacy of Catholic priests (1970). In addition, Elisabeth provided the readers with a narrative of Church events that she had attended: meetings of the Paris Fraternity, the great congresses of the Orthodox Fraternity, the trips organized by Syndesmos, the colloquies, the ecumenical circles, and then, after 1976, meetings on the place of women in the Church. Through these articles, she gave a picture of current realities, each time stressing the heated issues. And third, her vision of her times was completed through her numerous book reviews.

Appearance of an Orthodox Fraternity within Contacts

The camaraderie among the *Contacts* team was a powerful force in the complex situation experienced by Orthodox in the West. The members of the committee, conscious of any impact that they might have, wanted to use their friendship to bring the different jurisdictions closer together. In the course of a meeting in 1959, when the committee was asking itself what it could do to promote Christian unity, Fr. Lev gave them this advice: "Form a fraternity." In his view, such gatherings of laypeople had kept the faith alive down through the ages: "On many occasions, [the fraternities] have been the instrument used by the Holy Spirit to preserve and enliven the faith of the Orthodox people. This could also be the vocation of a group of consecrated lay-people within the Orthodox dispersion throughout Western Europe."[125]

Father Lev suggested that this fraternity be directly dependent on the Ecumenical Patriarchate so that it might be free of jurisdictional conflict. In August 1959, at his urgings and those of Paul Evdokimov, Elisabeth wrote a letter to the permanent representative of the patriarch of Constantinople at the World Council of Churches, Metropolitan Emilianos Timiadis, about the group's aspirations:

I am writing to you in the name of a certain number of Western Orthodox communicants grouped around the review *Contacts* . . . Most of us are French . . . in general, we belong to Russian Orthodox parishes of different patriarchal affiliations, whether the Ecumenical Patriarchate through the Russian European exarchate, or the patriarchate of Moscow or the synod of "Anastasian" bishops. We are very grateful to these parishes that have received us into Orthodoxy. But, at the same time, we suffer from the present situation, from our divisions, from this dispersion that is harmful both to our spiritual life and to the image of Orthodoxy in the Western world.

As we pray for the Lord to show us a way out of our present difficulties, we believe that we have discovered, in the ancient and recent Tradition of the Church, an institution that the Holy Spirit has often used to preserve and vitalize the faith of the Orthodox people: we are referring to the idea of a Stavropegial[126] [word added by Fr. Lev] *Confraternity* whose aim would be to unite those Western Orthodox faithful who desire both to deepen their spiritual life through common prayer and to witness, in their own milieu, to the Light of Christ received in the Orthodox Church.

The framework for such an association already exists. It seems to correspond to real needs. We have an office in Paris and we believe that Archimandrite Lev Gillet would agree to be our chaplain if he were authorized to do so by his hierarchical superiors. Other ecclesiastics are ready to assist him in a ministry that would be, in great part, itinerant.

However, in order to be able to unite all the Western Orthodox faithful in common prayer, whatever their nationality or jurisdictional affiliation (for it would not be a question of abandoning the jurisdiction to which they belong) [parentheses added by Fr. Lev], the confraternity envisaged should depend on the Ecumenical Patriarchate, either directly or through its exarchate in London or the bishop residing in Geneva. We are about to make a request of this latter, humbly asking him to deign to take us under his *omophor*[127] [bishop's stole, word added by Fr. Lev] and give us his blessing . . . We would be very grateful if you would agree to grant an audience to one of us who could travel to Geneva at the end of the month or at the beginning of September to speak to you on behalf of our group.[128]

This correspondence helped make the patriarch aware of the aspirations of the postwar generation concerning the unity of the Church. In *Contacts*, Elisabeth wrote: "We were trying to unite in a lay fraternity that would be open to all the Orthodox on the sole basis of our common faith, and, in general, to all forms of culture, including that of the West."[129]

Metropolitan Emilianos replied enthusiastically and assured them of "the full approbation" of Patriarch Athenagoras in regard to the founding of such a confraternity. The little group then thought of sending Fr. Lev directly to Constantinople to plead the cause of a lay fraternity to the patriarch and raise money for this project. But Metropolitan Emilianos pointed out that such a trip would be futile because he had already told the patriarch of the group's aspirations:

When I was in Istanbul, I spoke at length with His Holiness, Patriarch Athenagoras, about the confraternity. I told him about your plans, and when I returned here I wrote a detailed report that I immediately sent to the patriarchate and the Holy Synod, so that they might be able to do an in-depth study and make an appropriate decision concerning this case. So I don't think that it is necessary or urgent for Fr. Lev Gillet to go to Istambul because, for the moment, we know nothing about the patriarch's frame of mind.[130]

Although the correspondence with Metropolitan Emilianos assured the group of the blessing of Patriarch Athenagoras, it did not lead to a final verdict. Given the absence of a more concrete reaction from the patriarch, Emilianos advised Elisabeth to contact Bishop Athenagoras of Thyatira, the exarchate of the Ecumenical Patriarchate in London, to enlist his help. In spite of the absence of structure, the members of the committee were already living as a fraternity, coming together regularly to pray and to share their reflections in the course of a meal.

A first draft of the by-laws entitled "Friendship for Orthodoxy in France" was dated June 15, 1960. There, Fr. Boris Bobrinskoy summed up what had to be done to put a structure in place, pointing out especially the need for "spiritual direction," which could be assured by Fr. Lev. Another text, written around the same time, presumably by Elisabeth, presented the outline for the by-laws of a "confraternity. . . that brings together Orthodox belonging to different jurisdictions but united in the same Orthodox faith . . . and with a common desire to witness to Orthodox in the West, in the countries in which they live."

In the face of these attempts to create an official framework, Fr. Lev once again expressed his mistrust of any form of institution and was careful to keep his distance from the team that was organizing the project. He said so in a letter to Elisabeth:

> In Orthodox ecclesiastical language, the term "confraternity" necessarily implies a canonical status within the institutional community, and experience has shown that, at this moment, it is useless to expect any kind of official sanction. Having said this, I unreservedly endorse the points defined by you and those defined by Fr. Boris. Between now and autumn, I think that many practical questions will have matured through inner reflection and been enlightened by the Holy Spirit. For my part, I insist that the idea and the word "spiritual director" be thrown out. I am opposed to any kind of "spiritual direction" except in very exceptional cases. Since you have a confidence in me of which I feel completely unworthy, I'm willing to be a sort of spiritual assistant, a counselor, a Servant (I can't find the exact word for what I want to say), but never a sort of director or chaplain. Moreover, it would be more especially the role of Fr. Boris and the young people to "serve" in the sense that I have in mind, rather than someone entering into the evening of his life.[131]

Father Lev continued to have a complex relationship with the group as he both encouraged them and wanted to remain on the sidelines. Up to what point would he have been willing to assume the function of itinerant chaplain, which Elisabeth had asked of the patriarch on his behalf? What part did Elisabeth have in this initiative, since she was always eager to play up her friend, felt that his capabilities were not being used for all they were worth, and wanted to see him take on a ministry in France?

Although he wanted to be detached from the project, Fr. Lev still gave advice to his friends. He counseled Elisabeth to work only within the limits of the Church and to take special care to always inform the bishops of what the group was doing in regard to the confraternity project: "If I venture to give you a bit of advice, it is to postpone any founding of a fraternity, any redaction of by-laws, even provisional ones, as long as you have not made a serious examination of all these questions with Bishop Alexis [van den Mensbrugghe]."[132]

In 1961 the first by-laws fixed the aims of this little group. They were co-authored by Elisabeth and Olivier Clément using outlines of earlier "confraternities" and "friendship groups." The project thus continued to fine-tune what it wanted to be, clarify the spirit in which it wanted to function, and specify the structure best suited to it. It focused on reflections on the local Church, which were already generating initiatives, such as the first Francophone parish served by Fr. Lev. The fourth article of the by-laws stated that "the members of the Fraternity believe that the meeting between Orthodoxy and Western Europe is not an accident of history, but rather the realization of God's plan."

The Fraternity defined itself as responding to four exigencies specific to Western Orthodoxy: "an expression (of the Orthodox Church) in the local language" (Article 2), respect for the original traditions through maximum contacts with the countries of origin, openness toward the Western Christians already living in these lands, and reflection on the juridical status of the Orthodox Church in Western Europe with a view toward discovering a solution to the problem of the superposition of jurisdictions. The Fraternity, which at its beginning was a spontaneous movement of a modest group of laypeople awkwardly seeking points of reference in an ecclesiastical jungle, underwent a first expansion from the core group of *Contacts* in the framework of the assemblies put together by Paul Evdokimov at the CIMADE headquarters.

Paul Evdokimov and the CIMADE Sundays

The CIMADE hostel, which Paul Evdokimov ran in Sèvres, took in foreign Christian students who had come to Paris to study. Paul organized meetings so that these young Orthodox students, whatever their origins, might be able to speak of their faith in their common language, French. It was among this group that Fr. Lev, during his stays at the hostel, celebrated the liturgy, preached, and occasionally gave lectures. When the hostel moved to Massy in 1963, there was much more space for these gatherings and more people participated.

The "Massy Sundays,"[133] originally intended for theology students, attracted, in fact, a much larger number of people who were interested in the Church and their faith. They found cohesion by participating in the Eucharist: Sunday began with the celebration of the liturgy in French. Father Lev was one of the privileged celebrants, and he made time for these assemblies when he visited Paris.

The Monk of the Eastern Church marked the liturgy with his own simple and austere style, just as he had at the first Francophone parish, where everyone felt as though they were participating in the service. The sermons, brief and intense, would center on a few passages of the Gospel, which, speaking without notes, Fr. Lev would highlight to point out their relevance here and now. During the afternoon, there was a conference where the burning questions of the moment would be debated.

Father Lev was the central figure in these assemblies even though he did not always seem disposed to respond to the appeals of Elisabeth, who could not imagine the Massy Sundays without him. When she wrote him about a meeting she was trying to organize on November 1, 1963, he replied: "In the case I am able to come, I suppose that the 'evangelical' contribution you speak of would be at the homily, in the course of the liturgy . . . But, once again, it is inconceivable that you can't find a young priest or layperson who would say something inspirational, in its 'pristine originality.'"[134] His presence and the simple pastoral language with which he transmitted the Gospel created an intense spiritual climate. Although a theologian of great intellectual rigor, he also knew how to be a humble and caring confessor who never tried to impose his views since he, also, had his own doubts and torments.

Soon these informal gatherings attracted a great number of young people descended from the Russian émigrés, the same generation as Elisabeth's children. Here, people who were looking for a Francophone expression of Orthodoxy shared their concerns in an unequaled climate of openness. Catholics who were seeking spiritually also participated in the Massy Sundays and came away strengthened. A group of believers who shared the same hopes quickly materialized: they, too, wanted to create a Francophone Orthodox milieu free of the restrictions raised by the different jurisdictions.

The first era of the Massy meetings, from 1963 to 1970—the year of Paul Evdokimov's death—was profoundly charismatic: their spontaneity, which had a deeply spiritual dimension, did not follow any formal structure. The respective bishops gave their blessing to this initiative without involving themselves in it. During a brief period the meetings were held at the Istina Center on the rue de la Glacière, thanks to the hospitality of the Dominicans, but in 1972 they were transferred to Montgeron, where Princess Andronikov ran a Russian orphanage. The chaplain of the orphanage at that time was the future bishop, Paul Aldersen. However, the basic idea remained the same. Invitations were sent out by the secretary, Nina Evdokimov, Paul's daughter, and notices appeared in the bulletin "Orthodox Youth Activities," the newsletter of the Coordinating Committee, of which more will be said later, with the date of the next gathering.

Along with the "regulars"—among them, Elisabeth—there were strangers who came from all sorts of places and backgrounds. Some were from marginal parishes or found themselves in awkward situations, and these people were able to express themselves frankly at this neutral site where a climate of attentiveness and dialogue reigned. A whole group of enthusiastic young people felt that they could speak freely in these meetings.

The Massy Sundays began with the celebration of the Eucharist. The rest of the day, aside from a meal in common, was spent in lectures and information sessions followed by exchanges of ideas. There was a central theme, such as *The Unity of the Church,* or *The Orthodox Church and the Renewal Movement in the Roman Catholic Church,* just to mention the final two. Elisabeth wrote about these meetings in *Contacts.*[135]

But the euphoria that marked these assemblies always ran up against the painful fact of the divisions among the jurisdictions. The Orthodox Fraternity, which was now the official organizer of these meetings, provided a unique setting for discussions on matters of faith outside of all the ecclesiastical quarrels. Father Lev gave his opinion on the movement to Elisabeth and warned her that it could turn into an isolated group of people who were searching at the margins of the Church. For him, the mission of the Fraternity within Francophone Orthodoxy should, on the contrary, be a bond among the parishes and jurisdictions and bring people together:

> Since the liturgy is now being celebrated in French at the rue Daru, Montagne Sainte-Geneviève, Saint Denys, Massy, why not open up? Why couldn't the Fraternity go to *each* of these parishes (including that of Evgraf) one after the other, not to celebrate a service of the Fraternity, but to take part in the services of the priests of these churches, and leaving the responsibility and direction of the service up to them? Without intercommunion—or with intercommunion. It would be dangerous to allow the Orthodox Fraternity to identify itself with the CIMADE, with a group, with a certain manner of thinking. A little band of intellectuals going around in circles. I know better than anyone how much Massy has helped, and continues to help, and with what sincerity and disinterest, yet I want (like the patriarch) to open all the doors that are now closed. For my part, I see more clearly than ever that my vocation is not within French Orthodoxy. I can be nothing more than a visitor there, a guest.[136]

This spirit of openness was very much in accord with what Fr. Lev wanted to inculcate. He unceasingly insisted that the narrow straitjacket of discussions about the canonical status of the Church should be loosened so as to rediscover the true sense of Christian existence:

> All this [the eventual founding of a metropolis of the Ecumenical Patriarchate in France] is of little importance when placed alongside the concrete, urgent, immediate, and personal exigencies of the Kingdom of God in daily life. "It is I who should be coming to you, and you who come to me!" These words of John to Jesus, "You come to me . . . ," and the crises and decisions that this implies—like the flour in the parable, which "rises" after the slow and invisible action of the leaven yeast—obsess me during this beginning of Lent.[137]

The advice of her friend influenced Elisabeth's ecclesiological positions and strengthened her hope for a local expression of Orthodoxy as well as her desire for a maximal openness to dialogue. She contributed actively to this search for a local Church by working within the Orthodox Fraternity. The Fraternity would be an essential part of her life until the very end, as shall be seen further on.

Daily Life on the Rue d'Auxonne

If Elisabeth multiplied her visits to Paris during this period when so many things were stirring in the capital, then these were only parentheses in her teaching job. In spite of the importance she attached to ecclesial questions, daily life continued in Nancy, with André and the children.

Job and Family Changes

André's job situation improved in 1953 when he obtained a new, more stable position: he was appointed head of the laboratory of the Center for Petrographic and Geochemical Research at the National Geology School of Nancy. Although worn out by his sickness, André took his job very seriously. When he came home from work at 6 PM, he was so exhausted that he went straight to bed. Thanks to the voluntary detoxification treatments he imposed upon himself at that time and the Esperal that Bishop Anthony sent him, André ceased drinking little by little. His health, however, remained very fragile. His new, more prestigious position, which enabled him to use all his skills and earn a very good salary, made this the most successful period of his career. In 1960, along with two of his colleagues, he published an article in the review *Analytical Chemistry* with the results of his research on methods of measuring rocks. But in 1965, André had to leave his job due to his physical weakness.

For her part, Elisabeth also succeeded in finding more job stability. In 1957, after more than ten years of uncertainty about the annual renewal of her contract, she finally obtained a permanent position. A sympathetic inspector was astonished by the status of replacement teacher in which Elisabeth had been stuck, partly because she had not been very good at career planning and making pragmatic decisions. "We have to think about your retirement," he warned her.

Thanks to the inspector's help, Elisabeth began the paperwork that would allow her to be certified without having to pass the competitive teachers' examination. After several inspections, she was put on the top of the list of candidates. Her appointment took place on September 27, 1957, when she had just been named rectoral delegate in philosophy at the college of Mirecourt. This promotion finally ensured her a stable job and a higher salary. But this change of status meant that Elisabeth was assigned to Verdun, 135 kilometers from home. To be able to teach at the lycée Marguerite, she was obliged to rent a hotel room near the school during the week.

Thus began another period of separation for the Behrs. Nadine was no longer living at the rue d'Auxonne. In 1954 she had married Jean-Marie Arnould, a young Frenchman recently converted to Orthodoxy through Fr. Valentin de Bachst. At that time the couple were living in Paris, in the apartment of Elisabeth's mother-in-law. Therefore, it was Mariane, a student of modern literature at Nancy, who took care of her father and little brother when Elisabeth was in Verdun. Mariane took on the role of mistress of the house; she would bring his meals to her father when he returned, exhausted, from the laboratory. This difficult situation, which kept the couple separated during the week, led the director of the Center for Petrographic and Geochemical Research to write to the inspector general of Secondary Education to explain his colleague's case:

> [André Behr] has been very sick for several years . . . and tries to fulfill his duties in conditions that I can say, without exaggerating, in-

spire admiration in those who work with him . . . He has already been operated on several times for a stomach ulcer and was operated on again recently for a bone infection in his leg from which he has barely recovered . . . It happens that Mme. Behr has a certification in philosophy but received it with a great deal of delay at the end of a somewhat abnormal career; she would desire, for reasons closely linked to the health of her husband, to have an appointment in Nancy; this past year she was a professor at the lycée in Verdun, and this made her situation terribly difficult given her husband's state of health.[138]

This request supported the petition of a change of assignment made by Elisabeth herself. In September 1959, she obtained her transfer but it was not to Nancy, as André's director had asked; it was to a teachers' college in Metz. The fact that Metz was much closer—50 kilometers from Nancy—enabled her to live at the rue d'Auxonne. She made the daily trips in her Citroën "deux chevaux" to give her classes in literature and educational psychology. This assignment, however tiring because of the distances, gave her the chance to establish new friendships with her colleagues, with whom she remained in contact all of her life. Finally, in 1960, she obtained the post of a substitute teacher at the lycée Chopin in Nancy. In September 1962 she had to accept another transfer to the teachers' college of Maxéville, on the outskirts of Nancy.

Family life suffered from these continual job changes. The separation between Elisabeth and André, due to the latter's sickness, was exacerbated, while the children, as they grew up, detached themselves from their mother. In one of his letters, Fr. Lev referred to this situation: "Yes, your job is a major problem with its distance and the separations this implies. You should find someone to help you out with your daily tasks."[139]

In 1957, Elisabeth's life was darkened by the death of her father. In her notebook she wrote: "The death of my best friend: Papa. The invisible presence of his love."[140] Charles Sigel was her last link with her childhood, with Emma, her mother, who had left her so early in her life, with Strasbourg and Alsace, which were so close to her heart. In her native city there remained only her cousin Gertrude and her stepmother, Anne-Marie, with whom she had never gotten along. As for André, he lost his father, Michel Alexeevitch, in 1953. His step-mother, Mariana Borissovna, left for Cannes to found an old-age home for Russians there.

After Nadine's departure in 1954, Mariane married in 1959. She had met her husband at a Russian Christian Student Movement summer camp, which accepted, alongside Orthodox youth of the émigré community, people of any other nationality who wanted to speak Russian and who could not go to the Soviet Union. Thus it was that Mariane met Anthony Greenan, an Englishman of Irish origin, who was studying Russian language and literature. Mariane and Tony were married in Nancy in 1959 and then, in June 1960, moved to Liverpool, where Tony taught Russian at the university while Mariane taught French.

The rue d'Auxonne no longer housed the two older children. As of 1960, only Nicolas and his mother lived permanently in the apartment. André was hospitalized for long periods, and Elisabeth's life was determined by the fluctuations in his health. In addition to the emotional problems linked to his alcoholism, André suffered from nephritic and gastric infections that required several more operations.

During a voluntary detoxification cure in a hospital on the outskirts of Nancy, André was able to work in a nearby laboratory. It was there that he met Madeleine Arnold, a nurse from Lorraine who came from a wealthy family and owned a large house in Laxou. She offered to lodge André during the weekdays and take care of him, since Elisabeth, who at that time was teaching at Metz, was seldom at home. Elisabeth accepted this arrangement, which provided André with the calm and attention that he needed. This odd situation, which worked to the benefit of all concerned, was, notwithstanding, painful, and it increased the distance between André and Elisabeth, whose time was taken up by her teaching and theological research.

Although he had to stay in bed most of the time, André still found a hobby. This passionate philatelist expressed his artistic talent in a magnificent stamp collection, which he had patiently put together over the years. The collection, which was an outlet for his meticulous and scientific mind, received several awards during the 1950s and made him a recognized philatelist.

A new period of trial now began for Elisabeth, a combat more inward and more bitter than her struggles with financial misery or with André's health. The entries in her notebook show how hard it was for her to see André sick, her perception that their relationship was falling apart, and her sadness at watching their children leave home. Once again, it was in the depths of darkness that she experienced the reality of the presence of God, as she wrote in a letter to Fr. Lev. While she was sitting alone, having lunch, and brooding over the bitterness of her situation, a verse of a psalm came to her spontaneously and chased away the despondency that had paralyzed her for months: "Today, if you hear My Voice, harden not your hearts."[141]

Elisabeth realized that she was passing through the crucifying experience of *kenosis*, the emptying of one's self, which she admired so much in the Russian saints who accepted humiliations to be like Christ, He who had voluntarily divested Himself of His divine omnipotence out of love for humanity:

God can only fill those hearts that recognize that they are empty.

Turn my spirit toward this truth.

Such is, perhaps, the meaning of this awful sensation of nothingness. The void of despairing illusions. Know one's self for what one is: vain and empty. The awful void of the world when the Lord withdraws Himself from me. But to suffer this void is also grace. The divine call. All food has become bitter. Lord, give me the Bread of Life. "My nourishment is to do the will of my Father."

Here is the Paschal Lamb. Here is the mystical banquet. Lord, I dare not draw near. My lamp is without oil, my garment stained. Something repugnant and ridiculous: a Christian, that is to say, a saint, who has failed. Come, Lord. *Kyrie eleison.*

Of all the virtues, the only necessary one, the only one that is totally inaccessible unless the Lord gives it: humility, not its mask but its reality.[142]

Elisabeth placed this state of emptiness, which she so acutely experienced, in the context of her day where the prevailing philosophical climate, profoundly marked several years earlier by existentialism, tended to negate any element of transcendence:

I don't think that any Christian of our times, unless he be a saint, has not flirted with absolute atheism, experienced as an abyss at his side. But, at the same time, there are no longer possibilities of idolatry. All the idols—Reason, Progress, etc.—have been thrown down from their pedestals. It is all or nothing. And perhaps the only proof for God in our day and age is that one cannot live if God is a void. God as a void is suffocation. Look at Sartre, at Simone de Beauvoir.[143]

Elisabeth was going through the mystical night, an abyss well known by those who embark on the path of faith, as attested by Saint Teresa of Avila or Saint Silouan of Mount Athos. At the heart of the impression of failure that Elisabeth sensed within herself, when the voices of ambition and of human projects, constantly thwarted, fell silent, there echoed the voice of a sincere faith:

To believe means to abandon myself, to no longer let myself be twisted up in doubt, refusal, revolt, to leave all that behind. The presence of hope that calls to us from the bottom of our heart.

To believe also means to want to refuse to abandon myself to passions, to despair, to sin. It means rooting myself in the Presence through obedience, through the sacrifice of a heart set up against the Evil One, through a heart that seizes by faith (a faith purified of all sentimentality and exalting imagery) Christ, suffering and victorious.[144]

Prayer then became a fine thread that connected her to Life, a thread of hope in tension toward the true life in Christ, which allowed her to rise above her suffering:

Lord, I abandon myself to You, I lose myself in You, I lose my little, insignificant suffering in the immense suffering of the world, which You took upon Yourself. As long as we can pray, we don't walk in total darkness, even in the middle of the night.

Pray for André. The mystery of freedom and of the communion of the saints and of prayer.[145]

For Elisabeth, the participation in the life of the Church, in its liturgical celebrations and its Eucharist, was the ultimate means of overcoming the bitterness that she felt during these years of trial. In

THE SIGEL FAMILY

Emma Altshul and Charles Sigel, Elisabeth's parents, in 1906

Eugène Sigel, Elisabeth's grandfather, as a theology student at Strasbourg

Elisabeth, one year old, in her mother's arms

THE YOUNG LISELOTTE

Elisabeth at age 15

In 1931

Elisabeth as a student, painted by
M. Jaggi

ANDRÉ BEHR

The Behr and Kovalesky families in Nice, 1925. André Behr is third from the left, Maxime Kovalesky is furthest to the right, and Fr. Evgraf in the front, on the right.

André in 1931

Leaving the cathedral in Nice. In the middle, Metropolitan Evolgy, to his left in altar server's vestment is Michel Behr, vested to his right is the young André Behr.

ELISABETH AND ANDRÉ

Elisabeth as a lay pastor in
Villé-Climont, March 1931

André in military uniform, on leave
in Villé-Climont, March 1931

André and Elisabeth in 1931

CHILD-REARING YEARS

The Behrs and their first child, Nadine, in 1935

Elisabeth and her two daughters, Nadine and Mariane, on the beach at Saint-Cast, 1940

Before the house of hospitality in Rue de Lourmel. From the left, Sophie Pilenko (mother of Mother Maria), Fr. Lev Gillet, unidentified, and Mother Maria Skobtsova.

Elisabeth and her son Nicolas in 1945

The Fellowship of St. Alban and St. Sergius, 1947. In the first row, fourth from the left, is Elisabeth Behr-Sigel, and in the same row, second from the right, Vladimir Lossky. In the second row, Veronica Lossky is fourth from the right, and in the third row, fourth from the right, is Nicolas Lossky.

The Behr family without Nadine, 1948

Elisabeth and André in 1950

On the steps at rue d'Auxonne in 1950, Charles Sigel with his grandchildren, from the left, Mariane, Nadine, and Nicolas.

ELISABETH THE GRANDMOTHER

Fr. Lev Gillet with Nadia Vorontsov-Veliaminov and her fiancée Nicolas Behr

Elisabeth and her grandson Marc Greenan, August 1961, in Liverpool

ELISABETH THE GRANDMOTHER

In 1964,
at Pépiniè (Nancy),
André and Elisabeth
with their grandsons
Andrew and
Marc Greenan

Elisabeth in Strasbourg in 1966, surrounded by the six Arnould grand-children

Elisabeth on the faculty as professor of philosophy at the lycée Chopin in Nancy, 1960–61. She is in the first row, fourth from the right.

The Syndesmos pilgrimage to Jerusalem in 1965. Elisabeth is in the first row, second from the right, Fr. Lev Gillet is the eighth from the right.

The *Contacts* editorial group in 1967. From the left, in profile, Nicolas Lossky, Jean Blazon, Germaine Revault-d'Allones, Olivier Clément, Elisabeth, and Fr. Boris Bobrinskoy.

Elisabeth in her new apartment in Épinay in 1976

Fr. Lev Gillet at Épinay in 1976

Fr. Lev and Elisabeth in 1975

Pope John Paul II receives the delegation from ACAT in 1986. From the left, Fr. Pierre Toulat, Jacqueline Westercamp, the pope, Guy Aurenche, and Elisabeth.

Elisabeth at Épinay in 1995   Elisabeth at Vézelay in 2000

On the island of Kos in 1999

At the Carmelite monastery of Saint-Elie, Fr. Boris Bobrinskoy is second from the right

Elisabeth surrounded by her children, grand-children, and great grand-children, at the baptism of one of them in January 2004

In her living room at Épinay in 2005

this way, she was able to contemplate, above and beyond the rather drab reality of her parish, life in its true perspective, shining forth from the Risen Christ:

This morning I attended the Sunday Liturgy and received Communion. Without much fervor, at first, with the same despairing feeling of barrenness. Our poor choir sang as badly as ever. The chapel with its ridiculous "transparent" curtain over the altar, the reading in Slavonic, incomprehensible, the new altar boy who acted like a big, frightened bird—all this conspired to make any real meditation impossible. But suddenly it was as though everything became concentrated in an exclusive and intense spiritual contemplation of the victorious Christ (while the choir once again sang the Easter hymn ["Christ is risen from the dead, trampling down death by death, and bestowing life upon those in the tombs"]).

Christ, Victim and Vanquisher, the prototype of the procession of vanquishers, of those who have washed their robes in the blood of the great tribulation. This awful history of Humanity, a history of suffering and of blood, recapitulated in Christ to become, in Him, the Eucharist. In this poor church, through these poor people who were singing *Христос Воскресе* (Christ Is Risen), I thought I saw, in a purely spiritual vision, the icon of the Risen Christ, triumphant over death, pulling Adam and Eve from limbo with His powerful grip.

Certainty, peace, and joy (painful) beyond all words.

Not any death, but the death, the agony in faith, of the whole Christ is victory over the ancient Serpent, the crushing of its head. The least, the most pitiful (in appearance) of our Eucharists announces this death and this victory over death until the return of Christ.

Believe that Love is stronger than death. Not human love, but the Love of God. And it shines in the darkness and enlightens everyone who comes into the world. It opens the way, it shows the way, it is the way. Think of the Christ of the Descent into Hell as depicted in the fresco at Kariche Cami [Holy Savior in Chora, in Constantinople].

Open myself to the strength, to the energy coming forth from Death Triumphant to a suffering taken in hand by faith, to the love and the Hope of the God-Man. *Experience* all its *reality.*[146]

This period of inner struggle was alleviated by the experience of a kind of joy new to Elisabeth: the birth of her first grandchildren. Michel, the eldest son of Nadine and Jean-Marie, was born in 1955. Four other boys and a girl followed until 1964. Elisabeth was a proud grandmother, attentive to her new descendants. Whenever she could, she went to Strasbourg, where the Arnoulds lived, to see her grandchildren. When Mariane and Tony came to Nancy in 1960 along with André, their son born a few months previously, Elisabeth took them on a grand tour of their Alsatian family in her little car.

Elisabeth delighted in taking care of her grandchildren. When three of the Arnould children came down with meningitis, she had no qualms about taking in the only healthy one, Etienne, who wound up spending three weeks with her on the rue d'Auxonne. She was also on the scene for Mariane and Tony when they found out that their second son, Marc, had neurotic problems. The attention she gave to her loved ones helped this young and energetic grandmother to cross over the abyss of her personal distress.

Tensions and Solace in Her Friendship with Fr. Lev

In moments of darkness, Fr. Lev's support was very important. If, during these troubled years, Elisabeth's attention was focused on events in Paris, then it was, above all, because these events enabled her to remain in contact with the Monk of the Eastern Church. As often as she could, she would go to the Massy Sundays to seek fresh courage from her friend. Father Lev expressed his concern and compassion for André whom he had known for many years; he constantly supported Elisabeth through his letters and spiritual counsel:

> André: I realize the gravity of the situation—of your anxiety for one another. I am praying with you. Throw yourself into God's hands—and also André. Entrust yourself to His will, whatever it might be, with confidence, faith, and obedience. Once you are on this *rock, which will never be destroyed*, the onslaught of the waves becomes insignificant—this word "insignificant" might seem cynical, painful, when it is a question of moral agonies or of the worst physical danger—but I'm speaking as someone who has received wonderful

pentecostal graces and who sees *everything that could happen* in the light of a dazzling sun. Yes, *see everything in the sunlight.* But let us pray and hope. Keep me posted. Don't allow yourself to be overwhelmed. "The fool says in his heart: there is no God." The believer who allows himself to become depressed—whatever the sorrow that weighs upon him—says in his heart that there is no God. Faith is an "even though."[147] . . .

I'm anxious about André's health and the moral tension that imposes on you. When I pray for him—something I try to do every day—I simply repeat the phrase of the Gospel: "Lord, he whom you love is sick."[148]

The "pentecostal graces" Fr. Lev mentioned refer to a religious experience he had had in June 1959 during a retreat of the Fellowship. The visitation of the Holy Spirit that he felt on that occasion brought him joy and a total confidence in God that he wanted to share with Elisabeth, while being aware that she had to make her own personal journey:

I didn't reply sooner to the spiritual questions you posed to me. I feel the greatest repugnance in giving advice on such matters or even making suggestions. Each person has his own way. God never leads two souls in the same manner. All I can do is to tell you something in confidence. Last June, it was clearly and imperatively shown to me that I should never worry about tomorrow, but *concentrate only* on what each day brings. It is someone I meet or some event during a given day that communicates to me the Divine Message for that day. It is a matter of *receiving* the person or the event as a gift sent by God—and of *giving* one's self without reserve to this person or to this event as if, at that moment, nothing else existed. This banishes all anxiety, unifies and simplifies everything.[149]

Father Lev's role as a friend and spiritual guide was not without emotional complications. Although he wholeheartedly wanted to support the couple during the troubles caused by André's sickness, he also seemed to want to keep his distance. He enjoined Elisabeth to remain in Nancy, with André, rather than come to Paris to participate in a congress that, according to Fr. Lev, would not do her any good. But Elisabeth, in her distress, had great hopes that he would come to help André. She continually begged him to come to Nancy, so that she might be comforted by his luminous presence. But Fr. Lev was cautious: "If André's condition was very grave and if he wanted to see me very badly, I would do all that I could to come to his side. I don't think that there is such an urgency right now according to what you tell me . . . and what I fear most is this: that André expects too much of me, and if he is spiritually disappointed (and, alas, it seems to me that this would be the case), then this disappointment could create a very dangerous and deplorable backlash."[150]

This reserved attitude of Fr. Lev saddened Elisabeth, who reproached him for not carrying out his spiritual responsibilities toward André and herself by his repeated refusals to visit them:

> I wasn't surprised by your refusal to come. But, to my astonishment, this was much worse than a disappointment for André. It was a scandal. You are a man of God, and the man of God passed by the person lying by the side of the road.
>
> I don't think that he [André] is right. But this is what he feels: bitterness and disappointment. I guess it is too late and that your plans are already made. But have you perchance left a margin of flexibility for charity? Or, at least, will you consider doing so in the future?
>
> André's pain overwhelmed me. Sometimes I don't understand you. But I still have confidence in you and consider you a friend. For André, it's much more serious. Try to understand him, put yourself in his place, or, rather, see him with the eyes of Jesus. Do I have to tell you this: you once accepted responsibility for a soul. And that is *forever*.[151]

Elisabeth was expecting solace from the "man of God" in the unhappy situation of André's sickness, even if Fr. Lev continually warned her of his own limits: "I still feel that you attach too much importance to physical presence and even to moral possibilities. What can I say? What can I give?"[152]

Her insistent expectations vis-à-vis Fr. Lev showed the importance of the bond that had built up between them over the years through their meetings and their regular correspondence. Father Lev was not just a spiritual guide for Elisabeth, as though she were just one of his flock. Their intellectual and emotional complicity, their similar viewpoints, and the mutual support they gave one another in the search for a common goal created a very close relationship between them. The monk appeared as a person with whom Elisabeth had a close affinity, and thus as someone who could best respond to her intellectual and spiritual interrogations.

This relationship sometimes included conflicts: Fr. Lev did not give the same importance to the human element in their friendship as did Elisabeth, and he did not feel the need to see her on a regular basis. Accustomed as he was to a solitary life and tormented by the feeling that he did not know how to give anything to others, he disapproved of his friend's insistence on wanting to meet him:

> You are making light of all the good reasons I can give you for not going to Nancy . . . I don't do what I want. I never take vacations. I only go somewhere when I'm called for a specific task and, in conscience, I give my time to those who have summoned me . . . We shouldn't have illusions about the need for a physical presence. This would be an error and a weakness . . . Everything that is essential can be put into writing. I see less and less what I can give to others. Let me "weep my poor life" (as the Curé d'Ars put it) in solitude and humility.[153]

In spite of these regular misunderstandings, due to the different lifestyles of the two friends and the difficulty in finding a balanced relationship between the monk and the mother of a family, Elisabeth remained Fr. Lev's confidante, his favorite correspondent, to whom he revealed his moods and inner feelings. In a letter written around this time, he evoked an episode of his life that he saw as an example of his singular destiny: "This year, on Easter morning, in front of the Mosque of Omar, within the court of the ancient Jewish Temple, I, a Frenchman, a Roman Catholic priest in communion with Greek Orthodoxy, read, in English, the passages of the Koran concerning Jesus to a group of European Protestants. This is a *sign* of my life."[154]

His universalistic spirit was exasperated by the canonical narrowmindedness of certain of his co-religionists, and he reminded

Elisabeth, not without provocation, how much his own situation broke free from the norms of the Church:

> I was never technically "received" into the Orthodox Church. I never went through the rituals of abjuration and reception as prescribed and practiced. I never, in writing or orally, defined anything. All that happened was that, one Sunday morning, Metropolitan Evlogy had me concelebrate with him in the church at Clamart. I was never asked to sign the agreements that future Russian priests sign before being ordained. According to the strict terms of Roman canonical law, I'm a monk-priest of the Byzantine rite, attached to the eparchy of Lviv in the Ukraine, who practices *communio in sacris* with the Orthodox. But who would understand that?[155]

His polemical tone was another indication of how angry he was about the jurisdictional disputes that were tearing the Church apart.

The correspondence between the two friends mixed together accounts about activities and events in their lives, spiritual or theological advice, comments on what they were reading, their viewpoints on the evolution of the local Church, and the progress of projects in which, moved by the same ideal, they were both involved: *Contacts*, the Massy Sundays, the Confraternity. The fate of Fr. Evgraf and the ECOF continued to be one of their major concerns. Thus, Fr. Lev wrote:

> As for our poor and dear friend Evgraf, my opinion is the same as that of Bishop Anthony [Bloom]: he should be "recognized," declared Orthodox but independent, a bishop if that is what he wants, without trying to integrate him into any of the jurisdictions existing in France and without trying to put too many limits on his ritual and other fantasies. What matters is that he brings many people to Christ—he knows how to console, he knows how to "wash the feet" of others. Does Daru [the archdiocese of the Russian Orthodox Churches in Western Europe] know how to do this?[156]
>
> Twenty-five years of priesthood for Fr. Evgraf! He has made many mistakes. But maybe that isn't so important when you look at the help he has given to so many souls who were asking for bread and receiving nothing but stones from the Orthodox.[157]

Through Fr. Lev's letters, one can sense more and more the bitterness he felt because of his disappointment with French Orthodoxy: his ideal of evangelical simplicity, of communion, had been torn to shreds by jurisdictional quarrels and by the rigidity of certain trends he had run up against.

By his life and his ideals, Fr. Lev took a position that was, at the same time, both audacious yet respectful of Tradition. Although he was averse to any institutional framework that confined a person, he professed a dogged obedience to his bishop, as the guarantor of apostolic succession, and never undertook any ecclesial activity without episcopal permission. In regard to the innovations of Fr. Evgraf—especially concerning the liturgy, when he introduced a reconstructed Western Gallican rite into the Orthodox Church—Fr. Lev had his reservations and, once again, stressed the unique importance of transmitting the Christian message: "I don't know what to think about the approbation given to the 'Gallican rite.' I would have liked to read the original text. Nothing indicates that this 'approbation' implies or foresees an institutional integration. But that is, after all, possible. The weeds and the good seed are growing together pell-mell in this field and are difficult to distinguish. The Divine Harvester will sort them out. If Jesus Christ can be better known, better loved through E[vgraf], then praise be to God!"[158]

For Fr. Lev, the unique criterion of ecclesial activity was the priority of the Gospel, of the Good News communicated to the greatest number of people. He constantly reaffirmed this, especially in the case of the focus of *Contacts*:

> Orthodoxy, its structures and its rites, are of little importance. Only the Gospel matters. I see more of the Gospel in what Vinoba Bhave and Danilo Dolci[159] are now doing than in all the pontifical liturgies in the world. I would have liked *Contacts* to really be a point of contact with all the great spiritual movements of the modern world rather than simply a point of contact between Orthodoxy and the West.[160] . . .
>
> All that needs to settle for a while so that the lasting and essential element might rise to the surface. No format, no institution is indispensable. Only the Gospel will endure.[161]

Concerning the later developments of the jurisdictional negotiations over the ECOF, Fr. Lev wrote: "These are all intermolecular movements. Let's look rather at the sun and the galaxies!"[162]

He also continued to encourage Elisabeth in her theological work. He reacted to her contributions in *Contacts*: "This morning I read the end of your study of Gogol in *Contacts*. I think that if you could translate and publish extracts from the best pages of Gogol and use your articles as an introduction, you would find that there are people interested and you could do a lot of good."[163]

Although Fr. Lev was a spiritual and theological counselor for Elisabeth, he was, first and foremost, a friend who gave comfort, who knew how to find the right words to relieve her distress when daily life in Nancy became too much of a burden: "What you are offering is more than a 'little suffering.' It is the greatest of sufferings—on the moral level. I don't dare say anything else. But such an offering will bear its fruits."[164]

The theme of suffering was a constant with Fr. Lev, who, in his ministry as confessor and pastor, was continually led to support people in distress. This caused him to reflect theologically on the attitude that a Christian should have when immersed in this suffering, which God Himself carries when a believer abandons himself to Him: "I myself came to reject the idea of God suffering—because the only attitude that has a basis in Scripture is putting one's self into the hands of the Father, without questions, without discussions, with the confidence of a little child and with the assurance that more excellent graces will compensate all one's griefs."[165]

In 1964 the relationship between the two friends started to become more affectionate. Father Lev gently warned Elisabeth that her friendship prevented her from seeing his works with the distance necessary for a critical appraisal: "I'm very grateful for the review you did of *Be My Priest*. But this review belongs to what I would call a 'sympathetic criticism,' whereas the useful thing would be to point out, without indulgence, weaknesses and gaps. You shouldn't review anything I write because your friendship makes you blind (or perhaps prevents you from saying what you want to say). But I'm moved by your good intentions."[166]

Although, in the past, Fr. Lev had sometimes reacted very curtly and coldly to Elisabeth's displays of affection, he seemed to have mellowed and come to realize what this thirty-five-year-old friendship meant to him. Elisabeth, for her part, had long been aware of the vital importance of her ties to him and rejoiced to see them become mutual ones.

At one of the Sunday meetings of the Fraternity at Massy, in the spring of 1964, she once again had an opportunity to see how essential this relationship was for her. She wrote in her notebook:

> This weekend in Paris (April 11–13) might be the start of a new beginning. It seems ridiculous to say something like that when you're fifty-six years old! But, in God, there is always the possibility of beginning again. Liturgy and Communion. Saw Fr. L. at Massy. Whereas a month ago he seemed tense and tormented, a bit sour, this time our exchanges were marked by light, clarity, and infinite gentleness. Other souls, more heroic, fly to God directly like a dove soaring into the heavens. I should humbly recognize that I'm not able to advance on my own, without the assurance of this very special friendship, irreplaceable and perfectly pure. Were I to refuse it, I would become paralyzed, hardened in an attitude that is both false and proud. There is nothing possessive in my feelings. But always the desire that Christ be with us, that the gift of the Holy Spirit will transform our impure lives into a gift, an offering, mixing them together as the *zeon* [hot water added to the Communion chalice in the Byzantine rite] is mixed with the wine in the Unique Sacrifice.[167]

Father Lev, obviously in one of those periods when he was more open to others, seemed to be more attentive to Elisabeth and sensitive to what she had been suffering during these last few years. He was astonished to see that she was already a grandmother several times over because he still had an image of her as the young student seeking her way whom he had met in the hostel on the boulevard Saint-Michel: "A grandmother! I can't get used to the idea. For me, you are still the young girl Liselotte, a restless child, seeking and questioning, sometimes stubborn and irritating, always ardent and intelligent and full of good will, always a Liselotte tenderly loved."[168]

Memories of moments of privileged communion shared during the prewar years began to come back. This allowed him to measure how far they had come and how great was the affection between the two of them, now that they had matured through suffering: "I remember very well, my poor beloved child, of that day we spent under the lemon and fig trees at Grimaldi. Do not think that I love you less now than then. I even believe that I love you better, now that life has wounded you."[169]

Although for Elisabeth, this bond with the Monk of the Eastern Church had, for a long time, taken a preponderant place in her life, stimulating her intellect and comforting her amid her family problems, it seemed that it was only all of a sudden that Fr. Lev realized to what degree she was attached to him. This discovery moved him deeply, for he was so focused on his personal suffering that he often had the overwhelming sentiment that he could not ease the pain of others:

> Dear, dear Liselotte, what you tell me—that "for so many years" I have been the "best part" of your life—touched me profoundly, and plunges me in my abyss of unworthiness, an unworthiness I can measure. What have I done for you? What can I do? Tender and ardent Liselotte, I can only come to you with empty hands—you are closer to God than I am—I can only listen to you, love you. Remember the kiss I planted on your forehead at the train station in Paris, before the war? I give this kiss again; take it with you forever. I was intentionally rude to you because I was afraid of attracting you by mirages and disappointing you cruelly. You say that you want to always remain my "little child." Yes, you are my child, dear Liselotte, forever.[170]

The two friends met again at another Massy Sunday at the end of December 1964. On that occasion, they told one another how much the bond that united them was privileged and unique. The display of this mutual affection was the source of great joy. Father Lev wrote: "I'm glad that all this is clear, transparent, pure, and luminous."[171]

From this point on, the tone of their letters changed. They addressed one another familiarly and were not afraid of revealing their most intimate thoughts. The absolute sincerity that each used with the other allowed them to live their relationship authentically, in God's presence: "You write: 'You have given me a moment of *perfect* happiness, such as I have never known.' Do you realize how deeply moving this phrase is? If I have given you that, then, because of that minute, my life will not have been entirely wasted. Would that it were true! That it were always true!"[172]

The singularity of their relationship was founded on their intense attention to one another, on Fr. Lev's care to be a help to Elisabeth and not an obstacle: "If you feel that I am making—that I am going to make—your life more difficult, if I am or become the occasion of trouble for your soul, then let us cut this emotional and spiritual bond at its root—or rather, leave only the spiritual bond—and put some distance between us."[173] This same sentiment was repeated by Fr. Lev several years later: "Do I represent an element of truth, of authenticity and peace in your life, or do I cause anxiety and trouble? I would like to be a help."[174]

The recognition of a shared love became a new source of strength for both of them, as Fr. Lev testified when he spoke of his ministry. The difficulty of being totally attentive to Elisabeth in a given moment was transformed into a natural outpouring toward everyone, thanks to the love he found in their relationship and the power of the renunciation it exacted:

And yet, I don't forget that there are moments when I should kill you within me—and kill myself at the same time—and that, every time a man or woman comes to me to open their soul to God, it is that person to whom I should give myself totally, to the utmost, exclusively, and become capable of reciting within myself the marvelous poem of Walt Whitman: "Whoever you are, I place my hand upon you, that you be my poem . . . Many men and many women are dear to me, but nobody is dearer than you."[175]

I should tell you—with gratitude—the marvelous thing that has happened to me because of you. I think that I needed this. Otherwise there would have been a lot of fog in our relationship. But now all is very clear. There is no source of obscurity, no cause of misunderstanding. But here is where the marvelous element comes in. Since the precise moment when the walls between us came down, I received a sort of charisma of openness and passionate attention to each person, to every man and woman, which envelops them in a network of loving compassion, whoever they may be, whatever they might do. And so it is that young people come to me in ways that are beyond my comprehension. But this demands a continual inner suicide on my part. This charisma diminishes or disappears as soon as there is a *finite* desire, as soon as I reach out for a satisfaction that is egotistical or mixed with egoism.[176]

The discovery of this reciprocal sentiment implied a great deal of vigilance to ensure that it was lived as God willed it to be, in a permanent movement of giving of the self without any attempt to possess the other for one's own emotional satisfaction. It was only under these conditions that this friendship could become a continual reflection of God's love. But Fr. Lev was worried about the unbalanced relationship that could result from Elisabeth's expectations: "You must be free of me. . . . I'm very much afraid of becoming a fleeting mirage in the desert for you and of leading you far from what could be your own way, your true vocation. . . . What I fear is that you become 'dependent' on me—but I'm not afraid of a total confidence that is possible and blessed."[177]

Father Lev's fear of "dependence" brought to light Elisabeth's spiritual state at the end of the postwar decade, when the struggle for survival was so exhausting that she was often on the verge of despair. Her wounded sensitivity found an immense comfort, both emotional and spiritual, in Fr. Lev. In the draft of a letter to her friend, she justified the vital need for their relationship by the peace that it brought her: "Forgive my exigencies and anxieties. You know . . . when I was a student, my companions nicknamed me 'Her Serenity.' It is life that has made me fragile and anxious. And yet, deeper than the anxiety, there is an immense peace, bathed in sweetness and tenderness.'[178] Father Lev tried to counter this tendency to worry by showing her how to get past these feelings:

> Twice this morning, speaking of yourself, you used the word "anxiety." This moved me and troubled me . . . Anxiety? Why? In the face of what? "*Angst*" = feeling hemmed in, restrained, without any liberating escape. Anguish can only exist if there is no possibility of "giving," of "giving one's self." But you—who are not alone, who have so

many occasions to give and give of yourself, whether to those who are near and dear to you, whether to those for whom you have a professional responsibility—how can you be a prisoner of anguish? "Open up your hearts," says Saint Paul.

Your danger, my dear, is this perpetual restlessness and agitation, your desire to change and to explore—the lack of an inner peace. This is not your fault. It is your danger. But I believe and hope that you will one day reach a calm haven.[179]

At the heart of this privileged relationship, Fr. Lev remained, above all, a man of God, a pastor who wanted to show his friend the way so that she might always be on the road toward Christ. He exhorted Elisabeth to overcome her desire to be emotionally possessive in order to use this love given to them as a force that would enable her to open herself to those around her, to relieve their pain and to create a climate of peace, especially in regard to André: "You should continue your tender and loving ministry to him. This is a high form of gift."[180]

Father Lev had a very objective vision of the nature of the relationship that linked him to Elisabeth and was aware of its amorous character. Rather than suppress this fact and risk a questionable situation, he appealed to his friend to take upon themselves the love between them, not in some sentimental way but from the perspective of the Kingdom of God, where all are called to experience a perfect love for one another in response to the love of Christ.

He continually urged Elisabeth to go beyond the human categories of love, according to which their relationship could be nothing other than a tortured impasse, and consider the sentiment that united them in its true dimension, in the light of Christ: "I don't think it's good for you to mull over the wound you speak of. Cast out from yourself all the dark nights, all the fog. Set yourself up in a sun-filled landscape, the landscape of the light of limitless Love."[181] In reality, this reciprocal love, which blossomed when Fr. Lev was seventy-two and Elisabeth fifty-seven, escaped any sentimental definition. Based on a common nostalgia for an idealized past and yet deeply anchored in the present, it was an intimate communion between two beings in the presence of God.

Father Lev and Elisabeth, by being faithful to their respective commitments—the one to the monastic life, the other to marriage— succeeded in avoiding the trap of becoming a couple, which would have made them betray their resolve to follow Christ. Although Fr. Lev unceasingly called on Elisabeth to sublimate her love for him, he was not insensitive to the situation. Since he thought of himself as a decrepit old man, he was amazed at the depth of her feelings for him:

> You insinuate that our relationship was, in a way, a discovery for you and a high point. Is this possible? How can I—a walking ruin who has nothing attractive left in him—how could I be that? You, who have had the experience of conjugal intimacy, of the union of flesh and spirit, do you not find that our rapport of proximity and tenderness is something pale and bloodless? . . . I can't understand why I mean so much to you.[82] . . .
>
> I feel so unworthy of this sentiment that I'd like to crawl into a hole. I think that when your eyes are opened, you will discover that I am *nothing*.[83]

Lest their relationship of "proximity and tenderness" be misinterpreted and become a scandal, Fr. Lev and Elisabeth were very discreet. Their meetings were rare: in London, when Elisabeth attended the assemblies of the Fellowship; or, more frequently, in Paris, at the meetings in Massy or those of the group at *Contacts*. It was in their voluminous correspondence that they expressed their mutual affection.

In spite of Fr. Lev's instructions, Elisabeth saved all of his letters, carefully dated them and classified them. It is probable that, aside from the emotional support she found in rereading them, she kept these letters with the idea that they might someday be useful in writing a biography of her friend. She was well aware of the historical, theological, and spiritual value of this correspondence, and it did, in fact, serve as the documentary basis for *Lev Gillet, "A Monk of the Eastern Church,"* where she cited many extracts.

When she finished her biography, Elisabeth decided to keep the letters in her archives in spite of their intimate nature, which could leave them open to ambiguous interpretations. Such a choice was indicative of her honesty. She felt that since the nature of her relationship with Fr. Lev had nothing that needed to be hidden or that was contrary to the Gospel, she could leave these precious letters to posterity, hoping that they would be useful.

Reading these letters today, after the deaths of the two protagonists, one can retrace an atypical love story. It could be interpreted, primarily, as an emotional link that, due to circumstances, would only find expression a long time after their initial meeting. Such an interpretation from a purely human viewpoint is not very convincing when one considers overall Elisabeth's destiny: her life was a series of impasses that, thanks to the intervention of God in response to her always well-anchored faith, became so many steps leading her to the Kingdom. It was in the midst of apparently desperate situations that she renewed her total commitment to follow Christ.

The encounter with Fr. Lev doubtless constituted the foundation for this ascent to the Kingdom; the impossibility of an exclusive bond between them, due to their respective life choices, which, through their love for God, they did not want to betray, translated into an experience of true love. By God's grace, they knew how to choose "the better part" of their love and live their shared sentiments in the communion of the Persons in the Trinity. In this respect, these two extraordinary people appeared as models for a life in Christ, and this was all the more touching because they bore witness to the power of God working within human weakness.

The First Long Trips

The short stays in Paris for the meetings of the *Contacts* team and the Massy Sundays were not the only displacements that punctuated Elisabeth's daily routine in Nancy during the postwar years. Aside from the summer conferences of the Fellowship of St. Alban and St. Sergius, Elisabeth made three long trips, preludes to a very mobile period of her life. She discovered countries where the Orthodox faith had been implanted for many centuries: Greece, Lebanon and Israel, and the Soviet Union.

Discovery of Greece, August 1963

In 1963, Elisabeth was officially invited to participate in the summer camp near Athens organized by Zoi [literally "Life"], a renewal movement in the Greek Orthodox Church, which was trying to promote a kind of evangelical spontaneity in Christian life. A few days before she left Nancy, Fr. Lev wrote her: "So here you are about to leave for Greece. I won't say anything about the scenery, which is thrilling and luminous (although other landscapes are fixed in my heart). I suppose you will find a great contrast between the groups of young people you will be meeting, in which there is, as far as I know, a great deal of purity, generosity, and inspiration, and official Orthodoxy, which is narrow, frozen, and almost lifeless. I hope that this trip will be profitable."[184]

Elisabeth experienced this paradox even within the Greek fraternity that had invited her. The invitation proffered by Zoi was a chance for her to embark on a somewhat incredible journey. She left the rue d'Auxonne behind the wheel of her "deux-chevaux," taking along her son Nicolas, who had just finished his first year at the university. They drove the little car through Germany, Austria, and Yugoslavia, where Skopje had just been shaken by a violent earthquake, before arriving in Greece. After having visited the Meteora monastery, Elisabeth and Nicolas reached Athens. That was where the Zoi congress was being held. Elisabeth gave a lecture and participated in the meetings.

The fraternity struck her as both sympathetic and archaic. She was especially shocked by the barriers between men and women even within a community that prided itself on being very open. The young peoples' camp enforced a strict segregation between the boys, who were at the seashore, and the girls, who were installed more inland. This inequality grated on Elisabeth both as a theologian sensitive to the status of women and as someone who liked to swim. The event gave rise to new friendships, notably with the Zombouli family, with whom the Behrs would have a very warm relationship.

After the congress, Elisabeth got behind the wheel of her little car and drove with Nicolas to visit Delphi, then the Peloponnesus. One of the Zombouli girls went along with them and served as their interpreter. The trip was an adventure: they camped out in a small tent and put their trust in Greek hospitality, which was never found wanting. Elisabeth was happy to go swimming and free to strike out into the open sea. She had mixed impressions of the country, which, at that time, was opening up to Western society; she was moved by the kind-

ness and the admirable devotion of the people under clerical domina-
tion and certain traditional customs that seemed to be from another
age. During this trip, Elisabeth was received by Patriarch Athenagoras.
Leaving Nicolas in Athens, she took a plane to Istanbul.

This improvised little trip had its moments of anxiety: while Elisabeth was in Istanbul, the tension between the Greeks and the Turks
over Cyprus came to a boiling point. The Turks refused to let her go
back to Athens, and, for a while, she thought she would have to return
directly to France. She was finally able to get back to Greece where
Nicolas was waiting for her, and the two of them set out for Nancy in
her little car. This summer tour through southern Europe gave her a
sense of freedom and openness. It marked the onset of a long series
of trips to Greece. Near the end of her life, Elisabeth would return
regularly in September in the company of Mariane and Tony Greenan.

Pilgrimage to the Holy Land, August 1965

Two summers later, Elisabeth, accompanied by a group of Orthodox
young people, embarked on a more distant voyage: the Near East. The
three-week pilgrimage, organized by Syndesmos, was the first of its
kind. Syndesmos was a federation of Orthodox youth movements
born from contacts among Orthodox of different countries—contacts
that had become frequent since 1930, especially on the occasion of
ecumenical assemblies. It was founded in 1953, spurred by such personalities as Lev Zander, Paul Evdokimov, and Fr. John Meyendorff,
in order to establish a link among young Orthodox the world over. To
this end, the federation organized, on a worldwide scale, events, pilgrimages, or days of reflection that brought together believers from all
horizons.

Fr. Lev Gillet was very much involved in the Lebanese Orthodox
youth movement, which had played a role in the founding of Syndesmos, and he had been named the movement's official spiritual
guide by Patriarch Athenagoras in 1965. It was in this capacity that he
led a pilgrimage to the Holy Land in August of that same year.[185]

Elisabeth had hesitated a bit before deciding to join the group.
Her desire to join Fr. Lev in the Near East and discover the Holy
Land, which attracted her both because of her Jewish roots and her

Christian faith, was tempered by her fear of again being separated from André for a long period as well as by the financial problems that still persisted for the Behrs. Nonetheless, she resolved to participate, with great expectations, especially for her relations with Fr. Lev, who wrote her: "Pray that all will become clear for you in Jerusalem."[186]

The core of the group, essentially young members of the ACER, embarked from Marseille on August 12, under the direction of Fr. Pierre Struve and his wife Tatiana. Once on board ship, Elisabeth became acquainted with her fellow travelers, who, aside from the Struves and a few others, were people she did not know. She had some reservations about them, which she noted in her travel diary:

> I met the ACER group from Paris . . . They sing a Te Deum for the departure. The sweetness of Slavic chants. All the same, I feel somewhat isolated in this group where the younger ones speak French, but the leaders "want to preserve Russian culture." I don't like their ambiguous attitude, which is perhaps due to the nature of things. Neither Russian nor French.
>
> Beautiful scenery. The harbor of Toulon. We pass very close to the Levant islands around 7 PM. Comfortable ship, a moderate number of passengers . . .
>
> The boat sails eastward leaving a wake of liquid gold.[187]

Life aboard was marked by the Daily Office celebrated by Fr. Pierre "amid the clanking of chains and winches." Elisabeth, who had a cabin, let the younger members, who slept on the deck, use her shower. In her diary, she noted the long days at sea where time seemed to have stopped:

> Sunday, August 15: Morning liturgy with the ship rolling with the waves. We are still following the current. Suddenly, Stromboli appears, its summit covered with gray smoke. To the left is the famous rock jutting out of the sea, massive, monumental. During the afternoon we pass through the Strait of Messina and follow the Calabrian coast. Poor villages, deserted beaches, bald mountains. Then the open sea once again. Most of the passengers are bored to death. They dance to kill time. A very sexy Armenian woman has the men

all excited. Indignation, mixed, perhaps, with a bit of jealousy on the part of the "proper" girls. A flock of little English geese. In the evening, long conversations with a Greek anticlerical propagandist, Fr. Pierre, and Tania.[188]

During the crossing, Elisabeth got to know better Fr. Pierre Struve, the priest of Holy Trinity parish, which had just been founded in the crypt of the Saint Alexander Nevsky cathedral. She also became friends with his wife Tania and appreciated her forceful personality. The long days at sea gave the two women the chance to have lengthy, impassioned discussions. After a stopover at Genoa, the ship arrived at Athens on August 17. There the group was joined by Greek and Finnish young people, and they were able to do some sightseeing. On August 19 the Egyptian coast came into view:

A sunrise of gold and rose. Arrival at Alexandria . . .

Alexandria: warehouses, domes, some minarets by the waterfront, some palm trees on the horizon.

Lengthy formalities with the police and customs. Customs officers and policemen: robust guys in rowboats. A handsome old man standing up in one of the rowboats looked like an image from the Bible. Alexandria: harassment by the police, sordid vacant lots, apartment buildings under construction. Alongside, the swarming, picturesque, and miserable crowds one finds in the Near East: watersellers, breadcarriers, a pack of kids following us. There is no way of being alone here.

Return to the ship. A long wait while the cargo is loaded. Meanwhile, we haggle with small-time merchants over knick-knacks, toys, suitcases, and leather bags. It's a real sport: the chivalric spirit of the little jewelry merchant who makes the gift of a bracelet to console a young Frenchman whose eyeglasses had fallen into the water.[189]

Finally, on August 21, they arrived in Lebanon. In Beirut, the group met Fr. Lev and members of the MJO, among them, the future bishop, Georges Khodr. The next day, they all left for the Holy City: "An epic voyage from Beirut to Jerusalem. A thirteen-hour car ride. It is difficult to go up to Jerusalem. Camels in the desert. Frontier posts.

The Damascus oasis."¹⁹⁰ Elisabeth's description of her discovery of the Holy Land, with the charismatic guidance of Fr. Lev, is limited to succinct notations, in which a sober emotion, stamped with spiritual joy, shows through:

> August 23: Visit to the Holy City. The Holy Sepulcher. Saint Anne. The Church of the Dormition. The Russian convent of Gethsemane. Sunset over the city walls.
>
> 24: Bethlehem. Silence. Visit to the Russian convent of the Mount of Olives. Formal dinner with a bishop, a real despot.
>
> Beautiful view of the City.
>
> Reception of the delegates of Syndesmos as all the church bells ring.
>
> Unforgettable night at the Holy Sepulcher. Procession to Gethsemane . . .
>
> 26: Visit to the Temple, to the Mosques, to the Church of Saint Peter Gallicante. The remains of a paleo-Christian church on the site of the house of Caiaphas. The ancient road that could be the one that Jesus followed when he was taken to the high priest. This is perhaps hypothetical from an archaeological point of view, but it left a profound impression. It enables one to imagine (= make present) what happened on that great night.
>
> Descent to the Cedron [Kidron] valley under a blazing sun.
>
> Reception at the patriarchate.
>
> Afternoon with Fr. L. Holy Sepulcher. Saint Veronica. The Biblical Institute. Garden Tomb.
>
> Purchase of souvenirs. Returned alone to the Holy Sepulcher. Great peace . . .
>
> 28: Departure at sunrise, at dawn, to the singing of "Christ is Risen." Crossing of the Judean desert. Stops at the Jordan and Dead Sea—torrid. Ascent to S. where the patriarch of Antioch resides. Descent toward Damascus at sunset, in the golden light of dusk.¹⁹¹

After this pilgrimage in the footsteps of Christ, the group returned to Lebanon to participate in a Syndesmos conference in the city of Broumana.

This meeting, led by Fr. Lev, had for its theme "The New Man" and brought together eighty participants from eleven different countries. At the end of his talk, he reaffirmed the reality of the pentecostal grace he had experienced: "I ask you to believe what the Holy Spirit can accomplish in each one of you during this conference of Broumana. I ask you to believe that the Holy Spirit can descend on you, not visibly, but you can receive the baptism of the invisible Spirit that is mentioned several times in the Acts of the Apostles. You can be changed, transformed . . . The new man is created by the Holy Spirit."[192] Elisabeth never ceased to aspire to this renewal by grace throughout the complex paths of her life—a path in the image of this pilgrimage to the Holy Land, where discomforts and difficulties mingled with moments of completeness, in the constant company of Fr. Lev, whose duty was to all people and who seldom saw her alone.

First Trip to the USSR, Summer 1967

Another type of journey led Elisabeth to the USSR. Whereas her trips to Greece and the Near East were officially ecclesial insofar as she had been invited as a theologian, her discovery of faith in the Soviet Union was made possible thanks to a more clandestine channel, under the veneer of an academic exchange program. Her first trip there was through the teachers' college at Maxéville, where she had been teaching since 1962.

It was in the context of a trip organized by the Franco-Soviet Association, and thus outside of any ecclesial context, that Elisabeth discovered this country that was both unknown to her and yet very familiar, and to which she felt linked in so many ways. Before her departure, Elisabeth consulted her friend Bishop Anthony Bloom, who was subordinate to the patriarchate of Moscow and was well acquainted with the situation of the Church in Soviet Russia. In her notebook she wrote:

> This long-desired voyage really began in London, in the office of Mgr. A[nthony]. A long conversation with him on the situation of the Russian Church. A complex situation where different tendencies clash, where the same people, according to the circumstances and the moment, speak different languages and present different public personas. The impossibility of having a frank discussion; long-entrenched habits of submission and hypocrisy nourish mutual suspicion. Nobody trusts his neighbor.[193]

It was with such expectations in mind that Elisabeth embarked on the Gulf of Finland to sail to Leningrad: "First contact with Soviet reality: the ship is clean and comfortable. The crew are well intentioned and well dressed. A long evening on deck. A cloudy sky, a sea of silver. In the West a vague sunset, rose-colored clouds buried in the mists. Infinite clarity."[194]

Elisabeth had lined the bottom of her suitcase with books on theology, which she was to hand over to Bishop Paul Golycheff of Novossibirsk, a first-generation Russian émigré who had been a priest in Nancy and who had returned to the Soviet Union after the Second World War. At customs, a young soldier, not particularly zealous, leafed through the books half-heartedly and declared, "*Nietchevo.*"[195]

The group of teachers was taken from one official site to another. During these visits the surveillance was irritating; it was difficult to get away from the guides and interpreters who made their presence felt anytime anyone in the French group made a move. But in the museums, Elisabeth's knowledge of religious themes made her a sort of specialist in Byzantine art, and the guides were happy to have her explain the symbolism of the icons, something they seemed to know nothing about. At Iaroslav, Elisabeth met Fr. Boris Stark, a former student at the St. Sergius Institute in Paris, who had known Fr. Lev when the latter was a French teacher there.

At Leningrad, Elisabeth succeeded in contacting Bishop Paul, to whom she was to deliver the theology books, which had crossed the border without any problem. And she had the chance to experience the permanent ambiguity of the status of the Russian Church of which Bishop Anthony had spoken. Bishop Paul appeared in a cassock and very freely met with Elisabeth in the lobby of the hotel where he lived. But it was only several days later that she was able to give him the theology books, and this was done in a dark alleyway. When the group returned to Moscow, after having visited the towns of the Golden Ring, Elisabeth was invited to a lavish suite in a hotel that seemed to be Bishop Paul's official residence. A while later, Bishop Paul was arrested because of his extensive pastoral activity. It took the pressure of his friends in the West, notably Constantin Andronikov, to get him released and brought back to France.

During this trip, Elisabeth found herself face to face with all the ambivalence of the Soviet system, where situations often seesawed between the comic and the dramatic, where the luxurious hotel in which Bishop Paul received Elisabeth was not too far, for him, from the sordid reality of the *goulag*. Afterward, Elisabeth summed up in her notebook her impressions of the places she had visited, notably Leningrad, which, for her, was bathed in the light of so many illustrious ancestors:

> Return from this pilgrimage through the monastic cities of Holy Russia carried out, paradoxically, under the aegis of France-USSR.
>
> The City of Peter with its noble perspectives so dear to the heart of Archimandrite Theodore [Bukharev]. I believed that I was following in his footsteps in strolling alongside the Neva, under the lime trees of Decembrist Square and all along the Admiralty, following the procession from Saint Isaak to Our Lady of Kazan, such as he described it. Then Moscow, Zagorsk, Iaroslav, Rostov, Pereiaslav.[196]
>
> Delight in meeting, in the flesh and in the spirit, Eternal Russia. Overwhelmed with emotion at Compline admirably and soberly sung at the monastery of Saint Alexander Nevsky. The pathetic, radiant faces of the old women whose features seemed to be sculpted in wood under the traditional white kerchiefs wrapped around their heads The Kremlin at sunset, an immense chandelier set before the royal sky. At a few hours from Moscow, the Russia of old: *isbas* [cabins] of smoke-darkened wood with pretty painted and sculpted doorways, forests of silver birch and pine as far as the eye can see. Here and there a clearing; then, in the distance, a lake or some immense river (the Volga at Iaroslav) and, floating between heaven and earth, the gold or jade or turquoise cupolas of a monastery. Bulldozers everywhere, crews of workers cleaning and restoring sanctuaries. This is for tourism. But, at the same time, the Soviets are also consciously retrieving this past that has fashioned them. Crowds of scouts, accompanied by teachers, marvel at the icons they see in the cathedrals. Here and there one finds an antireligious note, but it seems that only the foreign tourists pay attention to that.[197]

This edifying vision was moderated, however, by what Elisabeth could glimpse of the delicate situation of the Church in the USSR insofar as it had been marked by denunciations and infiltrations by the KGB:

And yet the Russian Church is oppressed. Conversation with Mgr. Paul Golicheff, Fr. Vsevolod Spiller, and Boris Stark.

The incident at Iaroslav. The crisis of the Russian Church, . . .

Depressing climate of mutual suspicion that poisons all human relations. What to make of Genia???? The opulence of Mgr. Paul. The drab and oppressing Soviet reality. The crowds . . . the feeling that one is being watched. Genia: "we're banging our heads against the wall. How can we get out of this?"

But I won't forget the bright faces of some young Christians and the intelligent beauty of Lydia Brodskaya, so cruelly battered and yet so generous.

Send them some books [underlined twice].[198]

Elisabeth would return to the Soviet Union under other circumstances, notably with Cyrille Eltchaninoff, director of Aid for Russian Believers, one of the branches of the ACER, in order to bring religious books clandestinely to the Russian Orthodox. In 1991 she would go to Russia accompanied by Mariane and Tony, where she was given an emotional welcome by her husband's family, who had remained in Russia.

Final Years in Nancy

In 1965, Fr. Lev wrote to Elisabeth: "You are doing the right thing by letting yourself become absorbed in your daily duties. That can bring a great peace. The simple, simple things . . ."[199] In fact, her life, although punctuated by her brief encounters with Fr. Lev in London and Paris and by the meetings of the *Contacts* team and the Fraternity, remained, on the whole, always dominated by the tension caused by André's worrisome health. She found escape from this tension in her teaching job, which occupied her mind, in her children and new grandchildren, as well as in her theological work. Nicolas returned to Paris for his studies, and Elisabeth now lived alone in the house on the rue d'Auxonne. André, at this time, usually lived at Madeleine Arnold's when he was not hospitalized. Father Lev, from afar, was worried: "Has André's state become alarming? One would think so on reading your letter. It looks to me as if the situation is becoming more difficult, both physically and morally. It is a fact that the distance between you is growing. That doesn't mean that you still can't do a great deal for him."[200]

Elisabeth briefly considered moving to Paris, where nearly all of her children now lived and where she had so many friends and activities awaiting her. Yet André and Elisabeth both wanted to keep making a real effort to understand each other, in spite of the complexities of their relationship, and this effort bore fruit: "How wonderful it is that you have arrived at such a simple, confident, and friendly relationship with André," Fr. Lev wrote.[201] Elisabeth and André succeeded in remaining on amicable terms until the very end.

Elisabeth continued to give classes at the teachers' college and accommodated herself to her painful and emotional family situation. But in November 1967, a health crisis interrupted her daily routine: Elisabeth had an operation to remove a cancerous tumor on her breast. The cancer was discovered in time, the operation went well, and there were no complications. When she was released from the hospital, she resumed her busy life.

In the spring of 1968, she followed the revolt of the students in Paris with keen interest; she saw the outbreak of violence as an expression of great disorder, as she wrote in her notebook: "Night of May 10–11. Revolt of the students. David armed with a stone against Goliath. Since then we are on a downhill slide *more or less* controlled by the trade unions and political parties. But the 'kids' want to destroy *all* the structures . . . Those who are revolting are among the best. A revolt that springs from the institution, from the emptiness of a society of consumption. Anarchy? Dictatorship? Is there a third alternative?"[202]

Always concerned about understanding the events of her times, Elisabeth went to a meeting of the Faculty of Letters at the University of Nancy. This led her to form her own opinion of the revolt:

June 6, 1968. Big meeting in the packed amphitheater (people forced their way in) of the Fac[ulty] of Letters.

A speaker from Nanterre traced the history of the movement. Interesting and enlightening. Small groups at the beginning: intelligent minorities, well organized, revolutionaries, armed with an elaborate dialectic and a subversive technique. The crowd of students—like a pile of compost. A flock of sheep, disoriented, vagabond, restless, generous, romantic, sometimes nihilist. The coming together of the two produces a massive surge. The young people of France, in a sort of tragic, heroic, fluid delirium, wipe out their common Oedipus. This explains the protests from all the parties, from the PCT and the CGT as well as the Gaullists. An iconoclastic and patricidal rage not without a certain naiveté . . .

Chance and a series of blunders and the worrisome economic situation give this minority its opportunity . . . Will the lecture rooms be the Montségur of the students, as P[ierre] Emmanuel predicts? This would be a tremendous disappointment, a real catastrophe in every sense of the word . . .

A girl said that the revolution means being "honest and sincere." And nobody laughed.[203]

The events of 1968 led Elisabeth to a critical judgment, which tried to be as nuanced as possible and brought her to take a clear political stand:

6/8/68. Not to be an accomplice of the established disorder . . . refuse to docilely recite the catechism of Madame the Left.

Opportunism of the Communist Party, but which is also realism and a sense of responsibility. The tragic utopianism and the violence of the students, but also purity, a surge of faith even when it is garbed in Marxist-Leninist ideology—and revolutionary tactics.

"The Christian and the Revolution." A theme hammered out by certain progressive Catholics and Protestants. But *what* revolution are we talking about?[204]

Several days after she wrote these lines, Elisabeth was suddenly brought back to everyday life. Nicolas had come to Nancy to present to his parents his fiancée, Nadia Varantsov-Veliaminov, whom he had met at the ACER summer camp. On June 21, 1968, while the young couple was staying with them, André, who at that time was residing at the rue d'Auxonne, died. His sudden death marked the end of an era in Elisabeth's life. It had been a dreadful period marked by fighting against illness, working hard to survive financially, but these were also years marked by the great joys brought to her life by André and her children, then her grandchildren, in spite of all the difficulties in her relationship with her husband. According to his wishes, André was buried in Schiltigheim, in the same tomb as his father-in-law, Charles Sigel, who had been his great friend.

The loss of André overturned Elisabeth's plans for the future, now that she found herself permanently alone on the ground floor of the house on the rue d'Auxonne. There were very few ties binding her to Nancy, where her husband had several acquaintances among his former colleagues at work. Her three children lived around Paris or in Great Britain; the members of the ecumenical group had partially dispersed.

She was then confronted with the delicate question of choosing a new context for her life. Should she return to Strasbourg, the city of her childhood and family, for which she still nourished a great affection? Or should she go to the capital, where the essential part of her theological work was centered, where her children lived, and where she could profit from the frequent visits of Fr. Lev? The latter encouraged her to choose this path: "I think it would be better to get yourself appointed in Paris, if this is possible. It seems to me that it was only the presence of André that was keeping you in Nancy."[205] It took a certain time for Elisabeth to decide.

Her decision hinged on two possible directions for her life that were profoundly different; Strasbourg would be the framework for a peaceful retirement, whereas Paris would immerse her in the middle of ecclesial agitation. The opinion of Mariane and Tony, who would find it much easier to visit her in the capital, was decisive. Father Lev continued to push her in the same direction, seeing this as a means for her to actively exercise her vocation as a theologian: "I believe that you're making the right move in leaning toward Paris. Aside from my personal sentiments, I think that it is there that you can receive the most and give the most."[206]

At this crucial moment, Fr. Lev's objectivity was essential to her in deciding which direction she should take: "I sense, more than your children themselves, what you might be feeling at this moment. Your children know segments of your life. I see the whole curve. I follow your sufferings, your anxieties, your hopes. I remember your marriage. I think that you still have a lot to do, a lot to give, a lot to receive."[207]

Thus it was that Elisabeth decided to move to the capital. She asked to be transferred to the academy in Paris and was helped in this step by a very positive evaluation of her previous work. In the autumn of 1969, she was named to a position at the Center for Pedagogical Research at Beaumont-sur-Oise. The hour had come for her to leave Nancy and the ground-floor apartment on the rue d'Auxonne, where she had lived through so many domestic dramas but also so many domestic joys.

chapter three

PARIS AS A TURNING POINT, 1969–1980

The choice of settling in Paris was to prove decisive for Elisabeth. By getting closer to the Orthodox circles there, she was be able to dedicate herself more fully to the planting of a local Church through the different initiatives in which she was already involved. This last period of her life, during which, as Fr. Lev had said, she "still had a lot to give, a lot to receive" was marked by an ever-increasing fame that, little by little, made her a point of reference in contemporary theological thought.

Center for Pedagogical Research in Beaumont-sur-Oise

In the autumn of 1969, Elisabeth took over the room that had been assigned to her at the Center for Pedagogical Research in Beaumont-sur-Oise. This institution was used on a voluntary basis by public-school teachers who were interested in pedagogical problems. Elisabeth was designated to give classes in psychology focused on maladjusted children in an effort to develop teaching methods suited to such students.

Her departure from Nancy was gradual: Elisabeth continued to rent her apartment on the rue d'Auxonne, leaving her books and furniture there, while living in her room at the research center. After the shock of André's death and the radical changes that this brought about in her life, a happy period began at Beaumont. Elisabeth appreciated the friendly, communitarian atmosphere of the center and the excellent relations she had with her colleagues. She enthusiastically renewed her studies of psychoanalysis, and she worked in collaboration with psychologists who were specialists and who stimulated her reflections on pedagogy.

In this new setting, Fr. Lev's letters were a great support. They always tried to point out the positive aspects of her situation: "I wonder if your role at Beaumont is not to be a ray of affection and light—certainly among the Communist teachers, perhaps in some hideous public housing project—but don't take this as a recommendation to go live in one!"[1] Elisabeth was, in fact, looking for an apartment in Paris where she could bring all her belongings—a difficult search because she was not very good at it. Father Lev wrote her: "I think that you are doing well by interrupting your campaign to find an apartment. I have the impression that you need daily moments of rest and silence in your life."[2]

This advice was indicative of Fr. Lev's general spiritual outlook, that of an eternal pilgrim with little care for earthly dwellings. During these years when Elisabeth was getting settled in Paris, Fr. Lev, on his part, seemed preoccupied by the idea of his own imminent departure. In January 1969 he wrote: "Various signs make me feel that the hour is approaching for me to pass over to the other side. This should be welcomed with joy and simplicity." And, at the conclusion of that same year: "I have the feeling that I'm approaching the end, and I accept that with lucidity and peace, as I see many things now that I did not see before."

In 1970 two great friends from her first Paris period died within a few months of one another: Paul Evdokimov and Evgraf Kovalevsky, who had become Bishop Jean. Father Lev, feeling the effects of old age on his body, was also preparing himself to "pass over to the other side," as he liked to put it:

I don't have any personal belongings, no book other than the Bible, no pictures, no icons. I'm not attached to houses and things. All my papers are destroyed by me every day. I could leave you the French Bible of Segond, very worn, and put this legacy in writing. I don't have any literary heritage. . . . I don't have any particular symptoms indicating an imminent demise, but I feel old age creeping over me from all sides. The most painful of these signs is the physical difficulty in writing; my hand shakes. My voluminous correspondence has become a torture. I am, after all, seventy-seven years old.[3]

These lines, written almost exactly ten years prior to his death, indicate the state of simplicity and detachment in which he was striving to live. All the same, he continued to carry out his ministry with lucidity and charisma during the final decade of his life.

During this period when his strength was declining, Elisabeth continued to manifest her great affection for him, which continually astonished him: "And you too, you are an enigma, what is there about me that attracts you? It certainly isn't anything physical. Everything— my temperament, many of my reactions, my age—should drive you away from me. I sometimes feel that you are making a mistake and will only suffer from it! Tell me the truth: What is it that I give you? Do I bring you something authentic, something profound, something that *helps*? . . . Do you have any regrets?"[4]

Although there were clashes due to their strong personalities, the transparent relationship between Elisabeth and Fr. Lev continued to grow in purity and depth. His loving support enabled her to make the transition to her new lifestyle. She could have chosen a quiet retirement at Strasbourg, the city of her childhood, rather than confront all the unknowns of a completely different kind of life in Paris.

Elisabeth's search for an apartment finally bore fruit. One day, when she was behind the steering wheel of her little car, returning from Saint-Leu-la-Forêt where the Arnoulds lived, she noticed a sign on a bloc of recently built apartment houses in Épinay-sur-Seine announcing units for sale. From her very first visit, she was completely taken with the cozy two-room apartment on the tenth floor, overlooking a shipyard and the banks of the Seine. Thanks to the financial help of Pierre Châtelain, who gave her part of the legacy he had intended for her, Elisabeth was able to purchase it.

After so many years of financial insecurity, the fact of becoming a property owner changed Elisabeth's situation considerably. The two rooms, with all the modern comforts—hot water and central heating—seemed a luxury to her. She found it wonderful to have a space to herself where she could have all her books and papers; it also gave her a sense of security.

After a final visit to Nancy near the end of the school year, Elisabeth moved into her new apartment at the end of July 1970. There she set up her furniture, books, family pictures, and porcelain, as well as her archives, which already took up a considerable amount of space. She lived in this apartment until her death but always with the idea that it was temporary. The original rural setting, criss-crossed by power lines, gave way, little by little, to blocs of high-rises. It was from here that she drove daily to her job at Beaumont.

In January 1972, Elisabeth asked the Board of Education to waive the age limit so that she could work an additional year in order to pay off her new apartment. It was only in June 1973, after teaching at Beaumont for three years, that she finally retired, thus bringing to a close a very active and atypical professional career that spanned thirty-five years. She was now able to devote herself to theological research and to her activities in Orthodox and ecumenical circles. A new period of commitment began, which put all her lively energy at the service of the Church.

A New Francophone Parish in the Crypt of the Saint Alexander Nevsky Cathedral

Now that she was a full-time Parisian, Elisabeth was able to participate actively in one of the French-speaking parishes that were beginning to spring up in the capital. Even when she was still living in Nancy, she had carefully followed the founding of a new Francophone community, installed in the crypt of the Saint Alexander Nevsky cathedral on the rue Daru.

Liturgies in French had been celebrated there from time to time since 1956, thanks to the urging of Paul Evdokimov, who had been very sensitive to the need for celebrations in the local language for his children's generation, who had become French-speaking. With the blessing of Metropolitan Vladimir, Fr. Lev officiated in the crypt when he came to Paris for the Sunday meetings of CIMADE. After Fr. Lev, other priests became involved in this young community, which mainly consisted of students and still had a somewhat sporadic character: Fr. Valentin de Bachst, and then, after Fr. Valentin's death in February 1963, Fr. Pierre Koppel.

Father Pierre Struve was also an advocate for the development of a francophone Orthodoxy. He convinced Metr. Georges Tarassoff, who succeeded Metropolitan Vladimir upon the latter's death in 1959, of the need for a new parish that would be entirely French-speaking. In 1964 the archbishop named Fr. Pierre rector of the community that was meeting in the crypt. From this moment on, the parish of the Holy Trinity had a regular liturgical life.

Many of the parishioners were descendants of Russian émigrés, of the same generation as Elisabeth's children. The son of Paul Evdokimov, Michel, became the choir director and contributed to the important task of adapting the liturgical texts to French, a job that had already been undertaken by the parishioners of Our Lady Joy of the Afflicted and with whom those of the Holy Trinity collaborated. The death of Fr. Pierre Struve in an automobile accident in December 1968 was a painful setback for the expanding parish community. Metropolitan Georges named Fr. Boris Bobrinskoy as Fr. Pierre's replacement.

As soon as she settled in Paris, Elisabeth started attending this new parish, alternating with Our Lady Joy of the Afflicted, which she had known since 1936. Although her Paris friends went to this parish of the Moscow patriarchate and it had a well-developed liturgy in French, she felt that she should support the young community that was beginning in the crypt, and she started to go there more often. Shortly after her arrival in Paris, Fr. Boris asked her to take on the functions of lay head. This position became official in 1973, when the community was elevated to the rank of parish. Elisabeth, faithful to her Protestant upbringing, methodically organized the life of the parish, especially its finances, so to ensure an income for the rector. She also participated in the publication of the *Bulletin of the Crypt*, which started to appear in September 1971. Right up to her death, Elisabeth published numerous articles, travel accounts, and summaries of current events in the bulletin.

The creation of this parish corresponded to a generational change in the Orthodox presence in France stemming from the Russian emigration. The generation of Elisabeth's children felt the deep need for a place where the form of worship would be adapted to their culture, which was now principally Francophone. Many French people who had recently discovered Orthodoxy, such as Danielle and Vsévolod Gouseff and Hélène Aristoff, all of Russian descent, joined the core of the founders. Elisabeth, thanks to her spiritual and family kinships with Russia, was able to serve as a link between the different groups within the community. Father Boris Bobrinskoy's calming and conciliatory character contributed greatly to the creation of a convivial parish where different influences were brought into harmony.

The dynamism of the young parish of the Holy Trinity was a sign of the renewal of the Church in the 1970s, when the ecclesial situation was tense due to the divisions among jurisdictions and the temptation for the Orthodox to shut themselves up in their own ethnic communities. In a letter that seemed to reply to the reactions of a group of young people worried about the generally alarming situation of the Orthodox Church in the West, Elisabeth painted the nuanced picture of an Orthodoxy in the midst of changes, which should respond to the challenges of adapting to the times if it wanted to continue to be the messenger of the Gospel:

> The statistics you cite . . . the decreasing number of parishes and priests, the aging of the clergy, etc., . . . are, in fact, sadly eloquent . . . There is no doubt that these statistics are the expression of a serious crisis that affects our ecclesial body. A crisis, as you well know, can lead to death or life. The present crisis could be the beginning of a necessary mutation, of a death in view of a new life. "Unless the grain of wheat that falls on the earth dies, it remains alone; but if it dies, it will bear much fruit."
>
> After having so often taken on the thankless role of Cassandra—which earned me many reproaches[5]—I'm now inclined to be moderately optimistic. The very courage and lucidity with which your group and a whole segment of Orthodox young people strive to look at reality in the face, seems to me to be a healthy and promising reaction. Moreover, I'm convinced that, in the midst of con-

temporary spiritual seeking (very real quests, in spite of scientism and technical, erotic, or other intoxications), Orthodoxy has its own word, perhaps decisive, to say. May we know how to respond to such a vocation!

Before seeking remedies, shouldn't we perhaps try to diagnose our malady? This, moreover, has already been attempted many times. So my thoughts don't pretend to be original. But I think it must be stressed that the crisis we are suffering is within an *overall context* that is affecting all the Christian confessions, even all the religious beliefs, and within a *particular context* special to a sociological entity with which our ecclesial community has been identified for nearly a half century.

Here, I can only rapidly call to mind the radical questioning of the Creed and the ecclesiastical structures that have shaken all the historical Christian communities. You cannot ignore this fact, and some people have had their faith shaken at its very roots. But the fact that Roman Catholics and Protestants are presently experiencing a crisis of priestly and pastoral vocations analogous . . . to ours, cannot be a consolation for us. Yet I think that there are two things that can be said here. On the one hand, it can be seen that Orthodoxy, in spite of the extensive but superficial apostasy of the masses in the Socialist countries, has resisted remarkably well, in its mystical depths, to the scouring (but perhaps, in some cases, salutary) "Death of God" theologies.

On the other hand, Orthodoxy cannot remain a stranger to this crisis, which is shaking up the whole of the Christian West and which must live with and rise above it. Otherwise the historical Orthodox Churches, from which our archdiocese has escaped, run the risk of dropping off into a "dogmatic slumber," and the awakening from such a slumber can only be cruel. But this solidarity demands that we make an effort of expediency, of creative fidelity to our faith, of renewal touching the inner man as well as theological thought and ecclesial structures.

Our Orthodox Churches, and in particular our Orthodox community in France and in Western Europe, although rooted in the Eternal and the Absolute, are nonetheless called to participate in the historical dynamism of our times. If they refuse to do so, do they not risk condemning themselves to withering like the barren fig tree?

But this renewal appears as both particularly urgent and particularly difficult, given the situation of our archdiocese. The dying out of our parishes, the drying up of priestly vocations appear to be linked, in effect, to an inescapable historical process: the disappearance little by little of the Russian émigré community as the sociological base (understood as a microsociety held together by a common language and collective representations) of our ecclesial community.

I don't want to reopen a debate where I have sometimes been accused of sentiments of hostility toward the Russian element; such sentiments are absolutely foreign to me, as belied by my whole life and all my activity.

By the same token, I am not so naïve as to imagine that a massive "frenchifying" of the parochial structures and the liturgical language would be immediately possible and desirable and that it could save the burning building! I believe that in all these matters, one must go forward with a great deal of prudence and charity, while keeping in mind that the most important thing is not the language but the authenticity of the spiritual life, for which the liturgical language is the vehicle.

In her synthetical vision of the situation, Elisabeth's originality resided in the fact that, for thirty-five years, she had lived in the reality of a backwater parish where inertia reigned, and not in the dynamic upheaval of the Paris communities. She painted a clear and uncompromising sociological sketch of these parishes:

In practice, I'm more familiar with the parishes in the provinces, which are all quite similar, than with those in Paris.

The assimilation of the "Russian émigré" element into the overall population is obviously much more complete in the provincial cities than in the capital. Twenty years ago a relatively flourishing *Russian milieu* could still be found in Nancy or Strasbourg or Belfort. Today, this milieu has disappeared, or, more precisely, only its traces survive: the very old people tended to consider the parishes (which they built and maintained) as their private property. In church, for the old lady behind the table where she sells her tapers, this is the last "salon" where she can receive her friends, her last refuge from a world to which she does not want to be assimilated, and, above all, a place where nothing, absolutely nothing, changes. Such a situation is understandable and worthy of respect. But it is a fact: these poignant oldtimers, whose devotion is often admirable, show themselves to be psychologically incapable of accepting someone from the outside—French Orthodox, foreign students from Orthodox countries, even their own children and grandchildren—in the measure in which these henceforth belong to a cultural world different from their own.

Obviously, an aging of the clergy corresponds to this aging of the parishes. How many priests under forty-five or fifty in our jurisdiction serve provincial parishes?

But what young priest would have the inner strength to resist spiritual suffocation in a world apparently without horizons or a future, where he would have to live in solitude and be condemned, unless he has a trade, not only to poverty but also to misery?

And we also still have to be afraid of sliding down a tunnel toward nothingness: the extinction of the last Orthodox spiritual centers in the provinces, at least in the case of our archdiocese. (We shouldn't forget, however, that Mgr. Jean Kovalevsky has founded several parishes in provincial cities.)

A deep revision of mentalities was necessary if Orthodoxy was to continue to witness to the Gospel message within Western society—a task that the younger generations should take upon themselves:

It does not seem to me, however, that this evolution would be fatal. These old parishes, apparently ossified, but where the faithful celebration of the Eucharist keeps a spiritual flame burning, are still hanging on to life. Today, perhaps more than yesterday, they still have some chance of changing for the better. For this to happen, I think that a lot depends on the younger generation and those who are now between thirty-five and forty-five years old.

To be sure, some parishes, which no longer correspond to demographical realities, ought to disappear. But elsewhere, particularly in university cities where the Orthodox population is periodically renewed and enriched by outside elements, parishes could very well awake from their impotent lethargy under two conditions: 1) that younger men replace members who are too old on the parish councils; and 2) that the parishes agree to frankly and effectively play the multinational card according to the principle affirmed by the diocesan assembly of 1966.

In my opinion, it would be the responsibility of our archbishop to incite the parish councils to renew themselves, to open themselves to Orthodox of diverse national origins, to seek contacts with all the Orthodox residing in the same region, in such a way as to arrive at local understandings on a *modus vivendi*, until there is a solution to the prickly and fruitless problem of jurisdictions. It is also up to the Orthodox youth, especially those from Paris who wind up in the provinces and consider this an exile, to take their turn at playing the game by assuming responsibilities in the parishes and showing their dedication!

Moreover, where there is no parish or where the parish seems, for the moment, incapable of reform, more flexible structures of welcome—such as groups of young married couples—could constitute, with the help of a team, little Eucharistic cells, which could also become circles of friendship, for this is something for which the isolated Orthodox feels a need.

The experience of Fr. Boris Bobrinskoy in Normandy with the help of a group of laypeople could serve as an example in this matter. I think that these family communities could also be the source of a new type of priest, which we are already beginning to see in our midst and which the Russian émigrés, to their credit, are endorsing: priests from different professional backgrounds, close to the laity whose culture they share, capable of promoting and coordinating collaboration among the men and women of their parish.

This "nonclerical" clergy, who would be the envy of Catholics and Protestants, should have a theological and liturgical education different from the classical academic studies: correspondence classes, evening classes, sessions of specialized studies—biblical, patristic, liturgical, etc.

All these ideas might appear utopian. And yet, if we only had faith like the grain of mustard seed, rather than consoling beliefs![6]

The renewal of the "old parishes" as well as other changes that Elisabeth advocated—the multiplication of contacts between communities, especially in the provinces, and the possibility of a new way of teaching theology—came about, little by little, during these years when the vast process of ecclesial evolution affirmed itself.

The parish of the Holy Trinity, with its diversified sociological makeup and its constant orientation toward openness, was very much in the line of the transformations that Orthodoxy was experiencing in its efforts to establish itself in France. But the diversity of the parish, even though it enabled people to tend toward the essentials of faith, also caused certain tensions among the members, not all of whom had the same vision of community.

Following a meeting in 1977, where the different factions were in opposition, Elisabeth exchanged letters with a parishioner in which she defended her special status as member of an old Western family and the positions she took because of that:

> We come from different backgrounds. If each one of us clings to the habits of our childhood, then we risk not only of never understanding one another but also—and this is more serious—of obliterating the essential message of the Gospel and of authentic Tradition. If I were a revolutionary or a "horizontalist," as you seem to think, why would I have left Protestantism at the price of very painful separations? Few traditional Orthodox seem to give a thought to what it cost me to tear myself away, as if they were themselves the victims of an undesirable invasion. When I asked to be received into the Orthodox Church, I wanted, in all conscience, to unite myself to the Una Sancta, in continuity with the Apostles and Fathers. This tradition is continuity of faith and continuity of life, but not immobile or paralyzed. When we propose certain changes (that are in the spirit of authentic Tradition or that should at least be examined calmly to see if they are), we should, certainly, be prudent and take into consideration the sensitivities of others. But without wanting to block everything and without reciprocal excommunications, couldn't we try to go forward together, trusting in our rector to guide us in this necessary evolution? . . . We are all asked, like Abraham, the father of believers, to quit the country of our ancestors for the Promised Land.[7]

The split between those Orthodox who wanted to hang on to Tradition, such as their fathers had handed it down to them, and those who, like Elisabeth, advocated for a creative renewal, was especially evident among the descendants of the Russian émigrés, who were attached to certain specific liturgical practices—the use of Slavonic, for example—and those Westerners who had converted to Orthodoxy and were seeking a style of liturgical celebration that would be meaningful.

Elisabeth called for an enlightened vision of the traditions transmitted by the Church, especially concerning the liturgical language, so that these practices might be freed from stagnant ritualism and always be focused on an authentic life in Christ: "I'm not in favor of a 'policy of change.' I love the old conventions (even Slavonic, if it is comprehensible!). I recognize the value of 'being rooted in the ancient formulas, so eloquent and venerable.' But are *all* the ancient formulas—whose ancientness is, moreover, often relative—equally 'eloquent' and 'venerable'? Some of them, introduced during periods of spiritual decadence or as a function of particular historical situations, such as in the Constantinian era, can obliterate the authentic message of the Gospel and Tradition."

Although she was often criticized for positions judged to be too reformist and was sometimes considered as being hostile to the traditions of the Russian Church, Elisabeth continued to call for reflection on liturgical practices so that they might be the expression of a living faith and not dead ritualism. This spirit of openness was in line with the movement of liturgical renewal that accompanied the progressive translation of the Daily Office into French. Father Alexander Schmemann, who had settled in the United States, was one of the instigators of this reflection, calling for making the liturgy the true participation in the Kingdom of God and not simply a codified ritual. All this he set forth in an important book entitled *The Eucharist, Sacrament of the Kingdom,* published in 1988, five years after his death.

At Holy Trinity parish, as soon as he became rector, Fr. Pierre Struve tried to mark the liturgies with this need to improve the way in which the Mysteries were celebrated. It was he who decided to celebrate the office of the Liturgy of the Presanctified in the evening, as was done in the early Church, and not in the morning, as a more recent custom dictated as general practice.[8] The liturgical calendar was adapted so as to take into account the Gregorian reform so that the feast days—notably Christmas—could be celebrated at the same time as other Christians, and not with thirteen days out of phase with the Julian calendar, which was used in most Orthodox Churches.

Within the parish, Elisabeth continued her collaboration with Fr. Boris Bobrinskoy, with whom she had already worked as part of the *Contacts* group. This professor of dogmatic theology at the St. Sergius Institute and his parishioner, who shared the same spirit of openness and conciliation, maintained a privileged and ever-increasing bond of affection. Elisabeth liked to recall the tall, hungry adolescent who used to spend his vacations with the Mojaïskys.

She remained wholly faithful to the Holy Trinity community; until her death, she would come every Sunday and lean against the central pillar of the crypt as though she was supporting its foundations. The ecclesial changes in her parish also found expression in her activities on a broader scale, begun by Elisabeth and her generation during the postwar years within the Confraternity, and which seemed to fully blossom at this time.

The Orthodox Fraternity and the Outcome of the Informal Meetings of the CIMADE

> The danger . . . that threatens the Orthodox diaspora is fragmenta-
> tion: the juxtaposition of dioceses and ethnocentric "jurisdictions,"
> of parishes more preoccupied with their ties to their faraway mother
> country, of the preservation of a tradition where the national-cultural
> element is mixed in with the religious element . . . than with probing
> the essence of the apostolic message for *all* peoples and its radiance
> *here and now* in the countries where we live.[9]

In addition to the evolution of the parish of the crypt, the ecclesial dynamism of the 1970s was expressed by the expansion of the Frater-nity, which began with the core group of *Contacts* and subsequently was enlarged, thanks to the CIMADE meetings centered on Paul Evdo-kimov and Fr. Lev Gillet. The spontaneous growth of the informal

Massy Sundays brought together Parisians and people from the provinces who wanted to live their faith in common. The expectations of this group had already been defined by the by-laws of the Fraternity, which Olivier Clément and Elisabeth had redacted in 1961. The Fraternity wanted to expand from a simple local circle to encompass all those Orthodox of Western Europe who were animated by "a serious and mature vocation: to be an Orthodox believer here and now, according to a conscious and personal act of faith," as stated in Article 1 of the by-laws. The movement brought together people of very different backgrounds, descendants of émigrés or recent arrivals, and those of French descent, who were received into Orthodoxy.

Elisabeth, who had been the youngest member of the first Francophone parish in Paris in the 1930s, was now one of the oldest members of the Fraternity. She thus ensured a continuity of spirit between these two initiatives stemming from the same vocation. However, the Fraternity was not the only group working toward a coming together of the different jurisdictions: the Orthodox youth movements in France had a similar goal, which led to the creation of a coordinating committee.

Coordinating Committee of the Orthodox Youth Movements

> The activities of the Committee, which should always be in the line of a discreet impulsion, are directed toward establishing relations not only between existing youth movements but also between isolated individuals and groups, and toward facilitating the creation of small pan-Orthodox communities.[10]

At the end of 1962, the future writer Gabriel Matzneff, speaking in the name of a new generation of Orthodox, addressed an open letter to the editorial board of *Contacts*. He deplored the ecclesial apportioning among the Orthodox Church in France. This letter appeared in the fortieth issue of the review within a section set aside for exchanges of viewpoints entitled "Open Forum." Elisabeth was careful to introduce this new section as being consistent with the desire of the review to "not separate theological thought from the concrete, historical life of the Church, for which we are all accountable, each in one's own way."[11] She then presented a brief summary of the contemporary situation of the Orthodox Church in order to put into context the burning issues raised by Matzneff's letter.

The step taken by Gabriel Matzneff revealed a widespread desire, especially among the young people, for meetings and exchanges among the different communities so as to break down the ethnic ghettos in which Orthodoxy tended to seek refuge. In the face of this tendency, he envisaged certain solutions:

> Here is what I propose: the creation of an Orthodox committee, which, over and above jurisdictions and nationalities, but without infringing on the prerogatives of the bishops, would have the power to centralize, coordinate, and organize and would be entitled to speak in the name of Orthodoxy in France . . . The existence of such a committee would have many advantages. First of all, it would be a way for the Orthodox leaders in different jurisdictions to get to know one another; moreover, . . . through this committee, non-Orthodox who want to establish contact with us *would henceforth know where to turn.*[12]

Olivier Clément, whose enthusiasm for community had already contributed to the founding of the Fraternity, was sensitive to this aspiration. It was he who had given the impetus that had led to the founding of the Coordinating Committee of Orthodox Youth in 1964. This organization brought together different youth movements such as the ACER, represented by its president, Cyrille Eltchaninoff, and by Michel Sollogoub, and the Russian scouts. The Orthodox Youth of the Midi (JOM), which brought together young people of Greek descent, from the south of France, were also involved with the Committee thanks to the active participation of Fr. Cyrille Argenti.

Father Cyrille, who, in 1979, had founded the first Francophone community in Marseille, the parish of Saint Irenaeus, made the Paris group aware that the hopes of the Orthodox of the Midi were similar to theirs. Elisabeth had very vivid memories of Fr. Cyrille's warm and attracting personality, which enabled him to make known the orientation of the Greek communities, he himself being of Greek descent. Because he was firmly anchored in parochial reality, Fr. Cyrille brought a unique and living testimony to the Paris group.

The Coordinating Committee proved to be very dynamic: along with the Sunday meetings of the Fraternity, it also organized the

Sunday gatherings at Montgeron, centered around the celebration of the Eucharist followed by lectures, as well as pilgrimages in the suburbs of Paris. In addition, it published a bulletin that made known the different youth activities and served as a concrete link among Orthodox of diverse ethnic origins. In 1975 this bulletin was replaced by the *Orthodox Press Service* (SOP), a monthly organ of information founded by Jean Tchékan, another active member of these Orthodox assemblies, and Michel Evdokimov.

Committee members also made numerous trips to provincial parishes to help in adapting the Daily Office to the French language and to establish a network of links among the different communities. Séraphim Rehbinder was one of the organizers of these missionary trips and drove the young people from one parish to another. The committee held local congresses at Grenoble, at Marseille . . . centered on theological, liturgical, and spiritual themes. These activities, supported by the older members of the Fraternity and by Syndesmos, contributed little by little to bringing down the walls erected by the isolated communities that comprised the Orthodox churches.

As president of the Coordinating Committee, Olivier Clément was their contact with the Fraternity and facilitated their cooperation in the pursuit of the same goal. Linked with the Fraternity, the Coordinating Committee became a place of conciliation for the different jurisdictions, especially by bringing their bishops together: "Given the temporary impossibility of the Orthodox Church to apply territorial rules of conduct to Western Europe, the members of the Fraternity engage themselves to favor all forms of cooperation among their respective bishops" (Article 12 of the by-laws).

During the gatherings at Montgeron, Metropolitan Meletios, the exarch of the Ecumenical Patriarchate, showed himself to be very open to the idea of organizing regular meetings between the bishops of all the jurisdictions present in France. The involvement of the Orthodox Church in ecumenical movements manifested the need for an official spokesperson. It was with this view that, thanks to the impetus of the Fraternity and the Coordinating Committee, the Inter-Episcopal Committee was created in 1967. This organization, which brought together the different bishops, also included priests and laypeople as support staff.

Elisabeth was one of these lay observers, taken into confidence by Metropolitan Meletios, who had always impressed her as a very open person, simple and humble. In the meetings of the Inter-Episcopal Committee, where she was proud of being the only woman, Elisabeth's reactions were lively, numerous, and respected. She spoke out on problems common to all the parishes when these were brought up in the discussions: ecumenical relations, catechesis, publications.

Although it constituted a step toward a territorial organization of the Orthodox Church in France, the Inter-Episcopal Committee had no canonical status justifying the use of an executive power. This led, in 1997, to the creation of a more official institution: the Assembly of the Orthodox Bishops of France (AEOF), presided over by the exarch of the patriarchate of Constantinople, where the whole of the local episcopate met on a regular basis. This assembly, which was more formalist and less dynamic, was composed of only the bishops. According to their needs they convoked commissions that included laypeople. Elisabeth would remain a member of the theological commission until her death.

First Congress of the Fraternity, Annecy, 1971

In June 1971, Gabriel Matzneff took a look at the impact of the activities of the Coordinating Committee:

> With the help of the Inter-Episcopal Committee presided over by Metropolitan Meletios, the Coordinating Committee, from its beginning, has tried to convince those who were often hunkered down in their precious little differences, that it is only by working together that we can respond to the hopes of Orthodox youths at this end of the twentieth century. . . . On January 31 and February 1, 1970, . . . we took stock of the six years of the Committee's activities: congresses, catechism by correspondence, missionary work in the provinces, written press, television, etc.[13]

The progressive scope of the activities of the Coordinating Committee led core members of the founding group to organize, in 1971, the first national congress, a step desired by the local assemblies.

This first congress, whose success depends on each one of us, should not be considered a point of arrival, but rather the beginning of a new departure. It should help us to respond to the questions that we are asking ourselves and that come down to only one: how to be worthy of our baptism, how to put on Christ fully, how to live according to the Gospel, how to become beings of light, how to transmit to the world this deposit of truth found in the Orthodox Church and which the world needs so badly?[14]

The organizers decided to hold this assembly at Annecy. The proposed theme was "The Resurrection and Today's Man," and the actuality of faith in a society where religion no longer seemed to have a place. The members of the Fraternity, Elisabeth among them, followed closely all the preparations for the event.

She shared the same anxiety as the organizing team, as they looked at the road that wound up to the house they had rented above the lake, wondering whether there would be any response to their invitation. The number of cars denoted a heavy turnout. Nearly three hundred, mostly young people, took part in a series of lectures and workshops over a period of three days. The participants came from all the jurisdictions in France, notably the Russian Church Outside of Russia and the ECOF.

The very intense atmosphere of communion in which these days were lived, culminated in the celebration of the Sunday liturgy. Gabriel Matzneff described it: "It would be no exaggeration to state that all those who had the grace of participating in this liturgy on October 31 will never forget it. Father Cyrille Argenti's homily made clear his happiness in this extraordinary certainty of unity in faith, praise, and love that came to each one of us, whether priest or layperson, in this Eucharistic celebration."[15] At the end of the congress, the Coordinating Committee issued a general statement, addressed to the bishops, that articulated the aspirations of Orthodox youth. This first major assembly, which, all in all, was a great success, marked the transition of the Paris Fraternity and the local meetings of the Coordinating Committee toward a much larger movement of federation among the Orthodox faithful.

Three years later, the Coordinating Committee organized a second congress at Dijon, where about seven hundred people took part, including a great number of bishops from all the jurisdictions, to reflect together on the Christian meaning of life according to the Gospel. This congress, which Elisabeth attended with keen interest, manifested, by the number of participants and the intensity of the dialogue, the need felt by Western Orthodox to meet among themselves. Jean Tchékan gave a report:

> Dijon represented a discovery and rediscovery of the Church especially in its unity and catholicity. For members of urban communities or of fraternities scattered here and there, often living in their own little worlds, this was an occasion to "sense" the Church, to see the emergence of a local Orthodox reality of which they were a part, a reality nourished by the experience of Greek, Slavic, Arabic, or Athonite Orthodoxy, in communion with universal Orthodoxy, seeking to serve mankind and, in order to do so, seeking its own way in the Western world.[16]

Around 1975, the Coordinating Committee and the Fraternity formally merged to create a unique entity, the Orthodox Fraternity in Western Europe, which sought to maintain the original intentions of both groups. This merger was initiated by Olivier Clément in order to concentrate their forces and preserve the movement from being taken over by one or another of the communitarian tendencies.

Elisabeth, who was involved in all the congresses of the Fraternity, was very disappointed that Fr. Lev wanted to remain on the fringe of all this collective enthusiasm. He refused to go to the congress at Dijon in spite of Elisabeth's pleas. He replied: "A lot of people will be there who are very competent both in the *theoria* and the *praxis* . . . my own call is neither toward doctrine nor toward organization but to be an *evangelizer*."[17]

This refusal was consistent with the character of Fr. Lev, who liked to speak informally, improvising in front of a small group, and had a horror of formal gatherings. Although he had had a central role in the early days of the Fraternity, during the period of Sèvres and Massy, he preferred to keep his distance once the movement had taken wing. In this case, too, he played the role of instigator, of an outside counselor, who withdrew as soon as the enterprise took on a certain amplitude.

The disappearance, little by little, of this first generation, such as Paul Evdokimov and Fr. Lev Gillet, as well as the institutionalization of the structures of the Fraternity, brought about a change of climate within the movement. The openness of the Fraternity had caused a certain dispersal of its original core group, and the Paris meetings were the first to suffer. Other effective activities became more important than local congresses. The trips of the younger members to the provinces contributed to the creation of provincial fraternities and widened the network outside of the capital. Elisabeth occasionally took part in some of these missionary trips to the provinces.

The dynamic spirit that characterized the Fraternity, its desire to live the Tradition of the Church according to the contemporary realities of the diaspora, was not without its detractors. In 1978, as a member of the Fraternity's council, Elisabeth replied to a letter that seemed to criticize the positions of the movement as being excessively open. She recalled the universality toward which Orthodoxy should lean, without any clannishness:

> It goes without saying that we do not pretend to have a monopoly on truth. As Khomiakov used to say, that is only given to those who persevere in fraternal love—a love that does not exclude lucid rationality but rather underlies and envelopes all reflection. The building up of a local Orthodox Church in France should be the task of all the Orthodox who live in this country. This was our conviction when, from 1960 onward, with Paul Evdokimov and the advice of Archimandrite Lev Gillet, we laid the first stones of the Orthodox Fraternity in France . . .
>
> I would like to add a personal testimony: when I entered the Orthodox Church more than forty-five years ago after a decision "in conscience," I never disassociated this choice from an ecumenical commitment. It was through such a commitment that I had discovered Orthodoxy and had been given many opportunities to witness to the fullness I had found in the Church . . . To belong to Christ in the Orthodox Church does not mean having access to a restricted club; it means penetrating ever more deeply into the mystery of the whole Body of Christ, of which all baptized persons are members.[18]

Elisabeth opposed the universal dimension of the Fraternity as a remedy against any tendency toward an elitist withdrawal. If the Fraternity was to be more than a circle of the privileged, then it had to make room for dialogue, accepting believers from different social circles and from diverse cultural levels. She would champion this spirit of openness in the Fraternity until her death, through her very active participation in the different congresses and assemblies in Paris. Elisabeth became the most senior member of the movement, the living memorial of the great era of Sèvres and Massy, of which she always spoke very willingly.

Evolution of the Theologian

Thanks to her multiple ecclesial involvements and her numerous research projects, Elisabeth gradually emerged as an authority on Orthodox theology. In the course of forty-five years of unceasing theological activity, she had acquired a vast erudition due to her curiosity and her intellectual prowess. Her dynamic engagement in the Church, sustained by a spiritual sensitivity constantly in search of God, led her to a profound experience of a life in Christ.

Elisabeth put her increasing fame to the service of transmitting her theological wisdom. Several areas of activity gave her the opportunity to make her voice heard, an unusual feminine voice in an essentially masculine milieu, an often audacious voice in an area of reputedly conservative reflection.

Contacts remained the privileged organ of publication for the expression of her theological thought. She also collaborated with another Francophone review, more Slavophile in its orientation, *Le Messager orthodoxe*, founded in 1958 by Nikita Struve, who is still the director. The coexistence of several publications was a guard against theological uniformity since it permitted the expression of different points of view; this corresponded to Elisabeth's outlook since she was always trying to broaden circles, to establish relations between people and ideas.

Correspondence Courses through Contacts *and the St. Sergius Institute*

Contacts, which was closely linked to the activities of the Fraternity, little by little became a reference source in Francophone Orthodoxy as well as in ecumenical circles. The Enotikon publishing house, with which *Contacts* was paired, answered a request by its subscribers for theological works by offering a sales service by correspondence. Soon, the readership of the review, some of whom had just entered into communion with the Orthodox Church, expressed their desire for basic theological instruction.

In response, the editorial board decided to put into place a correspondence course. The members of the board divided the work of writing and mimeographing theological essays according to each one's special field. This was a purely in-house enterprise. The installments were first handwritten, then typed by Paula Minet, a parishioner of Our Lady Joy of the Afflicted, and mailed out by her husband Jacques.

When asked to write one of the courses, Elisabeth chose a theme with which she was familiar and around which most of her theological research converged: Orthodox spirituality. She then drew up a general presentation of the subject entitled *The Place of the Heart*. In the preface, she wrote: "This introduction to Orthodox spirituality . . . hopes to respond to a request made by adults who are seeking a better understanding of the faith of the Church and who desire to deepen their spiritual lives.[19] . . . I have tried to show how the great, living, and diverse river of Orthodox spirituality flows from a unique source that was and always will be the Gospel of Jesus Christ."[20] The theme of spirituality—the living and breathing theology of the Christian who is permeated by the teaching of his Church—allowed Elisabeth to offer her readers a structured presentation of Orthodoxy and its Tradition as it had been formed in the course of time and through different cultures.

In this historical exposition that sought to describe the identity of the Eastern Church, Elisabeth returned to monasticism as the focus of a spirituality centered on the contemplative life, where the recital of the Jesus Prayer flourished. This prayer, so dear to Elisabeth and the subject of several of her articles in the past, appeared as the very breath of Eastern spirituality. The prayer was not the exclusive domain of monks, and everyone could recite it to approach Christ and create true bonds among people: "The goal of the Jesus Prayer . . . is living, ineffable contact with Christ: it is not dissolution in an impersonal ocean, but a super-personal encounter, an abyss of communion with the supreme Lover who is always the supreme Beloved and who introduces us into the kingdom of love of the Holy Trinity."[21]

The Place of the Heart again bore witness to Elisabeth's historical rigor and her skill at using her data to present a structured exposition of the faith of the Church. The contribution of this work was not simply intellectual; it took on all its meaning in the link that she established with personal experience, summoning the reader to make the Tradition of the Church a theology made incarnate in his life. The historical retrospective concerning the hesychastic movements came across as an invitation to discover, notably through the practice of the Jesus Prayer, this place of the heart where Christ dwells.

This correspondence program set up by *Contacts* turned out to be a heavy burden for the editorial team. A Theological Formation by Correspondence (FTC) program was developed at the St. Sergius Institute beginning in October 1981, under the direction of Fr. John Breck, a specialist in biblical exegesis; and henceforth the review guided those readers desiring a correspondence course in theology toward that program. *The Place of the Heart* was integrated, as mimeographed copies, into an FTC course on introductory ascetic theology. It was later printed in book form in 1989 by the Cerf publishing house.

During the first years of the FTC, the St. Sergius Institute commissioned Elisabeth to give the examinations on ascetic theology to the correspondence-school students. This was her only long-term collaboration with the Institute. Although she was occasionally asked to give lectures, she never taught a real cycle of courses. After defending her thesis on Bukharev in 1977, Elisabeth had hopes of teaching at St. Sergius, but the dean at that time, Fr. Alexis Kniazeff, never made her an offer. She was disappointed by the still-very conservative character of the professorial staff, which, at that time, did not include any women.

Teaching Assignment at the Ecumenical Institute

It was left to an ecumenical organization to offer Elisabeth an opportunity to give a regular theology course. In 1976 the Institute of Ecumenical Studies (ISEO) proposed a first series of classes to her. This department of the Faculty of Theology and Religious Studies at the Catholic Institute of Paris had been created in 1967 to train specialists in ecumenical questions, but it was also open to anyone who wanted to know more about the different Christian confessions. In order to do so, professors from each denomination explained the fundamentals of their tradition. It was in this context that Elisabeth was called upon to present diverse aspects of Orthodox theology.

The themes of these courses recapitulated the favorite topics that she had studied in depth during her many years of research. There was, first of all, Orthodox spirituality in its Russian expression. Elisabeth gave two series of courses on this subject: in the first, "The History of Orthodox Spirituality in Russia," she traced the spiritual characteristics of each period and its important hagiographical figures. This course included a special and significant history of the Jesus Prayer as well as outlines of the lives of Saint Tikhon of Zadonsk and Saint Seraphim of Sarov, two saints she had researched in detail.

The second series of courses on spirituality, given in 1981, was entitled "Russian Holiness." The first and important part treated the general idea of holiness and its scriptural origins; Elisabeth then went on to the specifically Russian manifestation of holiness as it appeared in the hagiographies. These themes were taken directly from her master's thesis but had been enriched by her later investigations.

An important course in which Elisabeth was interested allowed her to explore very varied fields of theological knowledge: it was a general introduction to Orthodox anthropology entitled, "In the Image and Likeness of God." The plan for this course represented themes that were dear to her, and this is why the outline, found in her manuscript notes, is presented here.

1) Introduction
2) Scriptural foundations
3) The theme of the image of God and divinization according to the Eastern Fathers—Gregory of Nyssa, Maxime the Confessor, Evagrius. Monastic asceticism. Monasticism as a path to divinization
4) The anthropological implications of the Christological and pneumatological definitions of trinitarian theology from Nicaea to Chalcedon. Their importance in modern Orthodox Theology. Vladimir Lossky. The anthropological significance of the veneration of icons

5) The paths of deification in Byzantine spirituality and in ancient Russia. Hesychastic spirituality. Nicolas Cabasilas[?]

6) The paths of holiness in ancient Russia: the predominance of an evangelical personalism

7) The divino-humanism of Alexander Bukharev

8) Questions concerning Men and Women in contemporary Orthodox thought—Paul Evdokimov, Olivier Clément, Panayotis Nellas, Elisabeth Behr-Sigel.

In accordance with the Lutheran rigor of her biblical education, Elisabeth was very careful to anchor her reflection in an analysis of the Scriptures. Steeped as she was in the patristic heritage of the first centuries thanks to her neopatristic friends—notably Vladimir Lossky—she linked this heritage to her specialized field (Russian Holiness) after reflecting on the contributions of hesychism and the Jesus Prayer. Elisabeth then arrived at a vision of the divinization of man as Bukharev, her favorite author, had envisaged it at the beginnings of modern theology. She was thus able to open up a contemporary reflection on anthropology that led her to a consideration of the ministry of every Christian and particularly of women. In this way, Elisabeth incorporated into her course all the fields of theological reflection with which she was familiar, those areas where she had acquired a profound expertise through her research.

Far from limiting herself to theories, Elisabeth was careful, at each step of her presentation, to analyze the problem of divinization through concrete examples. For her, the essence of Orthodox anthropology was based on the theology of the person, which called for everyone to become God by participating in the communion of love among the Three Persons of the Trinity.

The question of ministry was taken up again in her course on "The Theology of the Royal Priesthood of the Laity in the Orthodox Church," a theme treated at varying lengths in her notes and that she seemed to have developed according to diverse contexts. This reflection on the place of the laity was at the heart of her concerns and led her to consider the specific ministry of each member of the Church, especially the place of women.

In 1977, Elisabeth's course centered on three theologians of the first half of the twentieth century whom she had known and admired:

Fr. Sergius Bulgakov, Vladimir Lossky, and Paul Evdokimov. She introduced her students to the life and thought of these three great personalities, who were so different in their outlook but who shared the same fundamental concern with living from within the Tradition of the Church and renewing, each in his own field, the theological approach of their times. Thus, the classes given at the ISEO represented an overall panorama of Elisabeth's thought at that time and manifested the perspective she used in her theological reflection: by making the person the center, she showed that the theology of the Church was made incarnate in the lives of men and women who wanted to respond to the call of Christ.

Metropolitan Emilianos Timiadis and the Women of Agapia, 1976

At the time when she began teaching at the ISEO, Elisabeth was led to explore a neglected area of reflection: the place of women in the Orthodox Church, a theme that had already personally concerned her for a long time. There was, first of all, her experience as a pastor. The few months she had spent at Villé-Climont had marked her profoundly: she realized that she was capable of concretely taking on a pastoral ministry in its everyday reality. When she posed the question about the ordination of women, Elisabeth knew what she was talking about.

Even though this prophetic ministry was very brief, it was followed by a permanent commitment within the theological questioning of her times. In an almost exclusively masculine field, she could sense the singularity of her feminine perspective. Moreover, certain aspects of Orthodox parochial reality that Elisabeth had encountered, in Paris as well as on her trips in the provinces or abroad, seemed to constitute an unjustifiable sexual discrimination, which led her to reflect on the status of women in the Church.

True to her critical spirit, she whom Fr. Lev, some years previously, had tenderly described as "a restless child, seeking and questioning, sometimes stubborn and irritating," never stopped examining the theological foundations of the different traditions that defined ecclesial life. Elisabeth's obstinate and independent character was astonished, sometimes indignant, when faced with certain kinds of segregation that Church customs imposed on women:

Having been introduced to Orthodoxy by such great free thinkers as Fr. Sergius Boulgakov and Archimandrite Lev Gillet, I was particularly shocked to find that, in its empirical reality, it was encumbered with archaic prejudices and Old Testament taboos concerning women: shadows that the light of Christ should have dissipated . . . Even more serious was the discrepancy I saw between an ecclesiology of communion and of conciliarity (the *sobornost* of the nineteenth-century Russian Slavophiles)—an ecclesiology that stressed the royal priesthood of the whole Christian people—and a sometimes heavy-handed clericalism that excluded the laity, and women above all, from participation in responsibilities and important decisions.[22]

Until 1976, Elisabeth concentrated on other aspects of Orthodox theology. From this date forward, she dedicated herself more actively to the situation of women, but did so thoughtfully and within a theological context: "I did not feel called to take part personally in the battles of feminism. I followed them at a distance and with a critical perspective."[23] Once again, it was a friend who directed her attention to this vast area of research. About fifteen years previously, Elisabeth had begun to correspond with Metropolitan Emilianos Timiadis concerning the germinal idea of the Fraternity. It was he who proposed that she participate in a meeting of Orthodox women who wanted to reflect on the specificity of their status in the Church. Metropolitan Emilianos, who represented the Ecumenical Patriarchate in the World Council of Churches, wanted this question to be debated in the Orthodox world since it was already of capital importance in the ecumenical dialogue.

Since the 1974 meeting of the Faith and Constitution Commission, a study concerning "the Community of Women and Men in the Church" had been undertaken by the different Christian denominations. Orthodox members of the World Council of Churches, faithful to the spirit of Paul Evdokimov, whose writings already manifested a reflection on the specific status of women, supported a project to consult Orthodox women.

This initiative greatly surprised Elisabeth, whose youthful enthusiasm for adapting Tradition to contemporary concerns had slackened somewhat in the face of the inertia that generally opposed any desire for change in the Orthodox Church: "Incredulous, like old Sarai at the news of the birth of Isaac, I felt like laughing."[24] It was in this state of mind that she received the invitation to participate in the conference of Orthodox women.

Elisabeth was called upon to give the opening lecture. According to her, she was given this responsibility because the organizers of the conference were aware of her long friendship with Paul Evdokimov and also because she was one of those rare Orthodox women who had been able to pursue a course in theology. The patriarch of Romania agreed to host the conference, which took place on September 11–20, 1976, in the Romanian monastery at Agapia.

This journey was another occasion for Elisabeth to experience the reality of a Socialist country where the position of the Church was ambiguous, just as it was in the USSR. She arrived a few days before the meeting began and had the time to immerse herself in the atmosphere of Bucharest, which she described in detail in a draft of a letter to Fr. Lev:

> Bucharest: a city where the past, present, and future become confused. A capital before 1914, a big Balkan town where you wallow in mud when it rains . . . with endless suburbs where hundreds of thousands of inhabitants are packed in. Dreary blocs of concrete, unfinished yet with people living in them, rise up alongside old, single-story houses. The dilapidation of private townhouses where the rich bourgeoisie once lived. You can see a concern for a bit of greenery everywhere. Virginia creeper overruns the balconies. A country that is trying to get its economy on its feet. Factories. Food doesn't seem to be lacking: it is simple, not very tasty to my French palate, but very inexpensive. . . . As for the other things, clothing, housing, medical facilities, above all, the standard is very low. There is no open religious persecution, but strict surveillance of the Church. The people still believe and are very pious. When a streetcar goes by a church, everyone on board makes the sign of the cross. At Bucharest, nearly three hundred churches are open all day. You always find people praying in them. Last Sunday, Metropolitan Hazim celebrated the liturgy at Saint Spiridon. A crowd. It took him nearly forty minutes to leave because so many people were flocking to kiss

his *panaghia* [pectoral image of the Mother of God worn by Orthodox bishops].[25]

After several days spent in exploring the capital by herself, Elisabeth was taken in charge by the organizers of the women's conference:

> The 10th. Departure for Agapia.
>> They tell me at the last minute.
>> Once we embark for Cythere, everything is organized; a few
>> stops along the way, meals, etc.
>> I arrive at Agapia exhausted. Supper at midnight. Very cold
>> rooms. The 11th, I'm not feeling well but I can't call off my lecture. I
>> don't think people understood it. Too bad![26]

The little group of thirty women meeting at Agapia represented
several different nationalities: Indians, Scandinavians, Greeks, Americans. In spite of very great differences in mindset, all of them anchored their thoughts in a shared spirituality and a same desire to
reflect on their role within their home communities. For the first
time, the women were not asked to listen to a speech about them but
were invited to speak up directly and give their opinion. Metropolitan
Emilianos's presence was very low-key, thus enabling the participants
to feel free to express their ideas.

On the margin of the official purpose of this meeting, Elisabeth
sensed that there were political and ecclesiastical maneuverings at
play in this religious conference in a Communist country: "Metropolitan Antoine, the vicar of the patriarchate, is here with us. This
conference is part of the subtle game of Romanian politics, as well as
a chance for the Romanian Church to show itself capable of receiving
and organizing an international conference."

In Romania, Elisabeth again found a Church muzzled by a Communist regime and moving in a permanent atmosphere of suspicion
and deceptive appearances:

> What can I say? The people (Antoine, Justinian [the patriarch]) are
> all compromised with the regime. But they also want to save the
> Romanian Church: that is by no means an insignificant task. A

Treasure of culture, of beauty. The government is hesitant and certainly uses the Church to consolidate the nation. The Church, at least the hierarchy, accepts the Romanian Socialist Republic, but with what reservations?[27]

The program alternated lectures and workshops with numerous visits to monasteries, which gave the participants the opportunity to have more informal contacts with one another. In her notebook, Elisabeth described the day of September 12 as typical of her stay in Agapia:

> 8 AM a radiant sun. A hearty breakfast.
>
> 9 AM meditation and Bible studies. A Romanian woman and a Greek woman. The first is rather conventional, the latter more personable. Photo session with Metropolitans Antoine, Emilianos, and Hazim.
>
> 10 AM a long lecture by Fr. Staniloae read by Professor Grigorios.
>
> 11:30 AM departure for Sekoul. An ancient car. A rattletrap. We ford a river. Then the road disappears. We roll along in a cloud of dust.
>
> 5 PM Sekoul. A very beautiful monastery in the same style as Agapia. When we cross the threshold, all the bells start to peal. The superior and the monks are waiting for us. We then have a hearty snack.
>
> Departure for Sihastria. Once again the bells ring out with all their might. We are received by the former abbot, Fr. Cleopha: a good example of a starets, humble and good. They shove him out of the sanctuary. He gives (or does he recite?) a welcoming address in the course of which he mentions the Jesus Prayer. It's touching, but you can't keep from wondering whether this isn't a bit theatrical and that Antoine is using the starets, making him do his act.
>
> An abundant meal served by the monks.
>
> My neighbor talks to me in a low voice about the ruined peasants, about the hypocrisy of the leaders of the Church . . .
>
> Conversation with Ion Bria: the Romanian Church is surviving thanks to the piety of the people of Moldavia.
>
> Return to Agapia. Group workshops. The magnificent Office of the Exaltation of the Cross in the evening. The same extraordinary piety of the people. The nuns chant admirably well.[28]

Aside from the stunning beauty of the Romanian monasteries, these visits left Elisabeth with mixed feelings: beneath the hypocrisy of a performance designed to give foreigners the impression of affluence, she perceived the distress etched on these "timid, secretive faces"[29] along with the strength of the spiritual resistance that emanated from the people, especially through figures such as the starets Cleophas, who "cited the Fathers of the Church from memory."[30] "More than anything else, this hypocrisy inculcated into the young people is the great sin of totalitarian regimes," wrote Elisabeth at the end of a draft of a letter destined for Fr. Lev. She was painfully aware of the ambiguous attitude of the official Church, which was forced into collaborating with the Communist authorities in order to preserve religious practice.

Over and above the particularities of its context, the Agapia conference marked the beginning of a dynamic reflection on the place of women in the Church. Among the participants, most of whom came from countries with an Orthodox majority, Elisabeth was an original: she was the only woman from France, she was from the Lutheran tradition and of Western culture, she had been determined to study theology, she had had experience as a pastor—and all this gave her a very special freedom.

In her introductory lecture entitled "The Meaning of the Participation of Women in the Life of the Church," Elisabeth opened the dialogue on the role that women could aspire to within their Church: "I think it would be good for Orthodox women to break the silence . . . imposed on them, not by the authentic ecclesial Tradition but by customs and social conventions. I think it would be good if they could dare to express their view of things (which is that of half the Church), that they dare to speak out—not in a spirit of anger or contrariness to bitterly claim their rights but to assume, with the men, their responsibilities as members of the people of God, called by the Holy Spirit to different diaconates."[31]

Elisabeth had been living the ecclesial implications of her baptism for the past fifteen years in the context of the parish of the Crypt and in the different Orthodox manifestations where she was completely free to express herself. She was aware, however, that hers was a privileged situation, since most Orthodox women, especially those in countries where the Orthodox Tradition had been implanted for several centuries, were under the thumb of a clear-cut clericalism.

She then called upon the Church to respond to the questions posed by the modern world, a context where women's liberation movements were changing society's conception of gender differences. For Elisabeth, the claims of these movements, even though they could, at times, be excessive, should find an echo in the Church, which was capable of formulating a response according to the Gospel.

This appeal was followed by an analysis of the Scriptures on which she based her theme: "we find . . . [in the Gospels and in the apostolic communities] the seed of the 'revolution of Jesus' concerning women, a revolution that consists in a change of sense that does not aim to negate femininity but rather to transfigure it by the energies of the Holy Spirit."[32]

Elisabeth continued by tracing a brief historical panorama in which she explained how the question had been put in the background for centuries because of the predominance of a monastic spirituality that tended to transcend gender polarization. "An Orthodox anthropological reflection on the theme of femininity only began in the second half of the nineteenth century with theologians such as Alexander Bukharev and Soloviev."[33] She presented the position of Paul Evdokimov concerning the place of women in the Church, as he had put it in his book *Woman and the Salvation of the World,* where he affirmed that each gender has specific charismas, with women possessing a spiritual sensitivity that makes them attentive to the suffering of others. Elisabeth nuanced this viewpoint that idealized women while confining them to defined social roles. In order to counterbalance the danger of overemphasizing the specific vocations of men and women to the point of completely disassociating them, she recalled the ontological similarity of the two genders: "Man and woman are, above all, persons called to transcend, in the freedom found in Christ, biological and cultural determinisms." Once this ultimate convergence had been reaffirmed, it was necessary to envisage the particularity of charismas on the basis of gender diversity: "Does this difference, received as riches, as a grace, result in different missions, different and complementary vocations, or a different way of fulfilling similar missions?"

After a brief mention of the idea of the royal priesthood of the laity, which summons every Christian to involve himself in his community within the life of the Church, Elisabeth spoke very openly about the ordination of women to the hierarchical priesthood. After recalling the history of the role of deaconesses who were ordained by the Church at certain moments in its history, she advanced prudently along this new path, limiting herself to raising the question. She concluded: "It is not for me to give an answer."

In her presentation, she first exposed the weaknesses of many of the arguments against the priesthood for women, whether physiological, such as menstrual impurity, or psychological, objections rooted in a sexism that idealized women while refusing them any official position, and retained the only argument that seemed valid: the iconic dimension of the priest as representing Christ who, although He took on all of humanity in His human nature, chose to become incarnate as a man in a specific context and place.

This argument in favor of an exclusively male priesthood brought up again the idea of a diversity of tasks whose function was specific to men and to women. By challenging the masculine exclusivity of the priesthood, Elisabeth tried to appeal to the fundamental complementarity among the different ecclesial ministries, united by bonds of interdependence that were urgently in need of revitalization. The lecture given at Agapia contained the seeds of all of Elisabeth's later reflection on the status of women in the Church.

Her preparation for this lecture gave her the opportunity to study the question systematically. To this end, she plunged into feminist literature and took an interest in the social phenomenon of women's emancipation, which had surged to the forefront in the 1960s. In the course of her research, she discovered that there had been no rigorous theological study on the place of women in the Church, that this place had been defined by an ensemble of traditions and customs that had no theological basis.

An untilled field of reflection seemed to open up to her within the context of her principal concern of finding a response to the problems of each era in the Tradition of the Church. This challenge corresponded perfectly to the injunction of Christ to "discern the signs of the times,"[34] a Gospel verse that she liked to cite when justifying the need to renew theological research. Elisabeth thus left Romania convinced that it was necessary to undertake the important work of redefining Orthodox anthropology and harmonizing it with the sociological reality of parish life.

Aftermath of Agapia: A New Field of Research for Elisabeth

In *The Ordination of Women in the Orthodox Church*, Elisabeth had stated: "Among the problems of modern Western civilization, one of the most important concerns the establishment of an authentic partnership, an authentic reciprocity, between men and women, without losing sight of their respective identity."[35] She would not have been able to take on the problem of the place of women in the Church, a problem whose novelty stirred up lively controversies in Orthodoxy, without feeling that she had deep support. Her friend, Metropolitan Anthony of Sourozh, whom she saw every year at the Fellowship meetings, urged her to insist that her voice be heard on this important subject.

Involvement of Women in the Church and the Encouragment of Metropolitan Anthony

Metropolitan Anthony experienced the reality of this problem in the context of the Fellowship of St. Alban and St. Sergius, where the Orthodox found themselves confronted with the first ordinations of women by the Anglicans. He encouraged Elisabeth not to be afraid of stating the urgency of an examination of this question by Orthodoxy. With his support, she became aware that it was up to her, because of her own experiences and her theological training, to engage herself actively in this field of investigation. The backing of Metropolitan Anthony was, for Elisabeth, the official guarantee that allowed her to proceed boldly into a very controversial field without the risk of being condemned by the ecclesiastical authorities.

Prior to Agapia, the awakening to the need for a dialogue in modern times on the status of women could already be found in Elisabeth's writings, especially in her treatment of Juliana Lazarevskaya in

Prayer and Holiness in the Russian Church. The chapter on Juliana revealed Elisabeth's fondness for examples of female holiness outside of the traditional hagiographic stereotypes: "An exceptional figure, animated by an heroic charity, Juliana Lazarevskaya incarnates and brings to their culmination the virtues of thousands of Russian Christian women whom history has ignored."[36] The life of abasement and of the gift of self led by this holy laywoman, entirely devoted to her family and to her countrymen, has similarities with the destiny of Bukharev, who wanted to live in the world in order to face up to the problems of his times.

Elisabeth, faithful to these models whom she had so diligently studied, decided to respond to the needs of her own times by embarking upon an anthropological reflection on the place of women in the Church. Her meditations on the specific status that women had acquired within humankind can be glimpsed in certain brief annotations in her notebook, sandwiched in between two reports on her activities or on her conversations: "The vocation of the woman: the one who inspires . . . who is present in the effacement of self for the sake of another . . . A noble ideal but perhaps also the expression of a sublimated form of sexism and of masculine egoism. *The woman is also a person.*"[37] The whole of her thoughts on this theme, which matured through meetings and congresses, would be set forth several years later in her book *The Ministry of Women in the Church,* with a preface by Metropolitan Anthony. We will return to this work later.

She was always careful to inform her contemporaries of the evolution of her thought on this matter. As soon as she returned from Agapia, she published an article in the *SOP* entitled "Women and Men in the Church," where she called attention to the ecclesial status of women, as it had been defined during the conference. Her aim was to provoke a reflection as broad as possible on the subject of ministries with a view to rethinking the place of women in the Church. In this article, she reaffirmed the need to pose the question of the ordination of women, a question she wanted to raise in order to advance the debate on the subject, but to which she did not want to give a categorical answer. The iconic argument of the male priest representing Christ was again invoked to justify a specificity of charismas: "Mysterious analogies can be found between masculinity and the Word who creates and orders all things—as between femininity and the Holy Spirit who inspires and assists the Incarnate Word. Since these analogies have been confirmed by a long-standing tradition, they cannot be neglected."[38]

Most of the conferences in which Elisabeth took part resulted in reports, signed by her, that appeared in *Contacts*, the *SOP*, or the *Bulletin of the Crypt*. By doing this, she gave an ecclesial dimension to her research, which should touch the conscience of all believers and not hole itself up in academia, where it would appeal only to a handful of intellectuals. Little by little, the theme of the place of women in the Church found an echo in the parish reality of the Orthodox faithful, notably through a group that was formed to respond to a survey by the World Council of Churches, of which Elisabeth was the prime mover.

Involvement in the World Council of Churches: The Study of Communities of Men and Women in the Church, 1977–1981

The World Council of Churches invited its members to make the theme of women "one of the principal topics of theological investigation,"[39] and, in 1977, it undertook a "study on the community of women and men in the Church." Using a very detailed questionnaire, forty pages long, the World Council asked each study group to reflect on the particular status of women within their own Church by defining their sociocultural enrollment and their relationship with the teachings of the Church and its ecclesial structures.

With a group of Orthodox friends, men and women who were parishioners of the two Francophone communities in Paris (the Holy Trinity and Our Lady Joy of the Afflicted Saint Genevieve), Elisabeth set about responding to the questionnaire. This task was the subject of numerous discussions, in the course of regular meetings over a period of nearly four years. At the end of these discussions, Elisabeth prepared a fifteen-page reply in the name of the group. From this summary, it can be seen that most of the participants had not previously felt the need to reflect on their specific status as women. They were satisfied with the role that fell to them within their communities and were conscious of a privileged status that allowed them to function when it suited them. Indeed, Elisabeth's document stated: "In our Francophone Orthodox communities, but also in other Orthodox parishes of the diaspora, women take a very active part in the life of the Church."[40]

Even though the questionnaire did not provoke dramatic debate, it enabled the group to reaffirm the importance of respecting the diversity of charisms in a dynamic of love and openness to one another. The theme of women priests was purposely avoided in order to affirm the need to reflect upon the place of the laywomen, as such, in the Church without necessarily focusing on their ordination. Elisabeth's initiative in engaging a group of Orthodox to reply to the questionnaire on "the community of women and men in the Church" made her the group's spokesperson before the World Council. She went periodically to Geneva, its headquarters, to attend meetings . . .

She also spoke at numerous regional conferences in Alsace, Germany, and Czechoslovakia. At the World Council of Churches consultation on the ordination of women, in August 1979 in Alsace at the Klingenthal chateau, she was one of the few Orthodox representatives.

Elisabeth's involvement in the situation of women went beyond the bounds of the World Council of Churches. She included this theme in her courses at the Advanced Institute of Ecumenical Studies and at the Catholic University of Lyon where in February 1978 she offered a course on women in the Orthodox Church. She took care to spread this theme as widely as possible wherever she lectured, such as those conferences on Sunday held by the Fraternity at Montgeron. There, led to evoke the experience she had at Agapia, she insisted on the foundational significance of that event for introducing the Orthodox world to reflection on the situation of women. She also tried to communicate to the bishops about what was going on in the Orthodox parishes of Paris. For the Inter-Episcopal Committee she wrote an account of the activities of a small group gathered to pursue a World Council of Churches investigation. She wrote: "In keeping with and emphasizing the unique ministry of bishops and priests in the Church, can we not hope for the reviving some of the more charismatic ministries that existed in the early Church?"[41]

Following the line of various conferences on the place of women in the Church, she greatly enlarged her acquaintance with others likewise committed to this issue, such as women from Lebanon and Australia. Little by little an international network emerged, each woman bringing her own singular perspective, rooted in her own distinctive experience. Elisabeth seemed to be the epicenter of the movement, maintaining a significant correspondence, a clearing-house for many articles on the subject of women in the Church.

The series of investigations supported by the World Council of Churches culminated in the major conference held in 1981 in Sheffield. The Catholic Church , though not an official member of the World Council of Churches, participated in the work of Faith and Order and was present at the conference. The impatient, energetic atmosphere at Sheffield witnessed to the dynamism of the reflection on the place of women in the Church. With Protestants and Anglicans in the majority, there was an effort at once both enthusiastic and bold to persuade the Orthodox to support the ordination of women. The final report sent to the World Council of Churches demanding women's access to priestly ordination, appeared to emanate from the consensus of the conference's participants. But in fact it was not representative of or satisfactory to the Orthodox minority who had the feeling of being bullied into agreement. And this declaration encountered suspicion and disagreement from Orthodox bishops to whom it was eventually sent.

Despite the consultation's effervescence, stemming from the intense sharing during its course, Sheffield marked a break in the effort to reach some agreement among the churches. Elisabeth came to believe that the proponents of the ordination of women had acted far too hastily for their position to be capable of reception. Despite her unwillingness to go along with all that came out of Sheffield, she continued to be very active in various international gatherings of the World Council of Churches.

The World Council of Churches center for formation and study at Bossey, Switzerland, long directed by Suzanne de Dietrich, organized international meetings of women, seminars, and study weeks at which Elisabeth became a frequent and familiar presenter. From 1980 onward she was regularly at the biennial gathering at the center, bringing with her others from her own circle to share in these encounters.

In ecumenical and Orthodox circles, Elisabeth was so effective that her name could not become disassociated from the debate on the place of women in the Church. From this point on, she was considered the Orthodox spokesperson, continually attending meetings of the World Council or of some other ecumenical group, always at work writing an article or minutes or a course relating to this topic. A list of her activities during the latter years of her life shows an impressive number of meetings and lectures relative to the place of women—to such an extent that, in her notebook, she expressed a certain weariness with the subject in which she had become a specialist: "At the Christian Writers' Day at Enghien, I spoke about women in the Ortho[dox] Church. This will wind up making me nauseous."[42]

Father Lev: The Continual Presence of a Friend

"I think that you are doing well by orienting yourself toward Paris," Lev Gillet had written to Elisabeth when she was on the point of moving. "I think that it is there that you can receive the most and give the most." In fact, since settling in Epinay and beginning her retirement, Elisabeth's life overflowed with intense activity within the Church but never at the expense of her role in her family as the matriarch of an ever-increasing tribe. An extraordinary vitality animated this frail and stubborn little woman who, at the age of nearly seventy, dedicated her energy to helping the Tradition of the Church evolve along new lines corresponding to the needs of the times.

The special relationship that still linked her to Fr. Lev was a source of strength, guided her in her choices, and gave her the courage to take them on. But this singular complicity, which Elisabeth needed so much, was never attained, insofar as Fr. Lev, for her, remained unpredictable. Sometimes he radiated understanding and affection, sometimes he was an impenetrable wall. Elisabeth suffered from the mood changes of the old man who would shut the doors on their friendship when she was in dire need of his support. Since his serious coma in 1971, following a crisis of uremia, Fr. Lev had aged drastically. He moved about with difficulty, became hard of hearing, wrote with a shaking hand, but still had a lively and witty mind. With Elisabeth, he alternated between tenderness and exasperation. He was sometimes annoyed by the attention she showed him and would oppose her marks of affection with an epistolary silence.

The two still saw each other only rarely. Over the course of time, a routine set in: in the summer, Elisabeth would go to High Leigh for the Fellowship conference in the company of Fr. Lev, whom she would usually meet in London. In the winter, when on the road to Formby to spend Christmas and New Year's with the Greenans, she would stop a few days at St. Basil's House. They would also get together when Fr. Lev came to Paris, once or twice a year, to take part in a Sunday meeting of the Fraternity at Montgeron. The rest of the time they stayed in touch by letter and sometimes by telephone, even though Fr. Lev disliked this means of communication because of his deafness.

After the mutual realization, clearly expressed to each other in 1964, of the privileged nature of the bond between them, both of them made an effort to always live their relationship under the gaze of God. They made the difficult decision to renounce the purely human element in their love, in order to remain faithful to their respective life choices. Father Lev explained to Elisabeth how he envisaged this:

> More than just accepting the fact, it is a question of arriving at a certain detachment, which is really a transformed attachment. That implies a sort of inner and exterior silence, a distance as far as physical proximity goes, an effort to avoid any pressure that might be a source of trouble, any obsessive, burdensome concern. We were thinking of this ultimate goal, considering that our relationship should be directed toward a superior and spiritualized state. I think that these frank steps were enriching instruments of new graces.[43]

This appeal for an evolution in their bond corresponded to a new stage in Fr. Lev's life as a priest and a monk, which was the result of his own reflections on his past experiences:

> Now for what concerns me, I have to respond to—and obey—a very precise call. I must, in the broad sense of the term, *entbehren*.[44] You are more anchored in life than I am, more attached to it by family and work that demand immediate attention. As for me, I ought to be

mainly "alone with the Sole One" and totally given over to the whole Christ. God gives me the painful privilege of living among the suffering, among the lives of others whose destinies cry out and cover me with shame when I regard my relative security, my relative well-being. I wanted to give my life and I missed two white-hot opportunities. The first was to be killed with the brothers of Metropolitan Andrei Sheptytsky, which would have happened had I not been absent from Ukraine. The other was to be deported and killed with Mother Maria Skobtsova, which would have happened had I not been absent from Paris . . . Yes, like [Fr. Dmitri] Klepinine, I could have shared her fate, but I was in a safe place. I don't speak about this, but it is an open wound.[45]

By stressing the disparity between their respective destinies, Fr. Lev reminded Elisabeth how much each of them owed to their particular vocations and of the need to make sure that their affectionate relationship was a support for and not an obstacle to their ministries.

In May 1976, Fr. Lev went to Paris to take part in one of the Sunday gatherings at Montgeron. This turned out to be another chance for Elisabeth to experience the dual nature of their relationship, and she continually fluctuated between unity and opposition. She confided to her notebook:

These meetings are always difficult. Moments of intense communion . . . and then that falls apart and there is only a harsh and rough exterior that takes offense at any little thing. Trifles? Grains of sand to be swept away? Failure?

Nothing is ever assured. Every relationship is always reinvented if it is to be authentic. It seems to me that I am called to *be* with him not because that is delightful—although there are also some delightful aspects—but in order to carry his cross with him.[46]

Elisabeth tried to understand the enigmatic character of her friend, whose reactions as a sick old man—he was eighty-three at the time—sometimes showed the spark of an enormous spiritual strength: "at a deeper level there is the true person: a tremendous capacity for love, a great kindness. Help him to become what he is. And that in spite of the inevitable destruction—destructuration—of old age. Deterioration of his faculties, of his self-control, tics, idiosyncrasies."[47]

A few weeks later, she described another meeting of the Fraternity where Fr. Lev offered a meditation on the chalice and on the drunkenness of Noah: "L[ev]. Marvelous, inspired! The biblical theme of the chalice. Powerful, poetic. The Holy Spirit passed and spoke through 'the little old man' . . . As always, he is full of contradictions: a canonist when you're expecting a charismatic, a scholastic after speaking as one inspired, which he is at times."[48]

Realizing that he was soon going to "cross over to the other side of the river," Elisabeth continually questioned him about his past in an attempt to understand his rich and complex personality, as though she already had the idea of retracing the entire journey of his life:

> It was the shock of the encyclical *Mortalium animos* that made him decide in 1927 to unite himself to the Orthodox Church. Same path as Soloviev but in the opposite direction. A universalist free-thinker.
>
> Like Soloviev, he doesn't arrive at an inner unity.
>
> I ardently desire that he find peace—this poor anguished heart—that he find peace![49]

Because of the complexity of his character, Fr. Lev remained incomprehensible to Elisabeth. In the face of the impasses that sometimes marked their relationship, she could do nothing more than to offer her compassion to her deeply wounded friend.

During the summer of 1976, thanks to the entries in her notebook, we can retrace Elisabeth's itinerary in England. On the road to the Fellowship conference, where she would meet Fr. Lev, she stopped at the Orthodox monastery of Saint John the Baptist, founded by Archimandrite Sophrony Sakharov, a disciple of Saint Silouan of Athos. This monastery, located northeast of London, had a special vocation: the mixed community of monks and nuns of different nationalities was very open to receiving guests. Elisabeth noted her impressions of her stay there:

> A monastery founded by Fr. Sophrony. Eight monks, five nuns. After a sleepless night, the liturgy is celebrated in the church, in Greek,

with a few prayers in English. Struck by the real attention of those present, mostly Cypriot families and their children, and the way Fr. Sophrony celebrated: intense, personal.

A monastery unlike the others, open to the world: on Sunday the children run all over the place. Everybody does the dishes, peels the potatoes, etc. . . . Bearded monks with long hair, serious but smiling. Tea at any hour. Dressed as bricklayers, with hard hats, they're building the monastery's guest house. They are Greeks, English, Romanians, Australians, Russians, etc. A very warm welcome from Fr. Cyrille and Fr. Sophrony.[50]

This monastery, as it expanded, would have a great influence.

After the Fellowship conference, Elisabeth spent several days in London with Fr. Lev and was happy to again sense a full inner communion with him: "With F. L. in London . . . Peace, transparency beneath a few ripples on the surface. All is grace."[51] But this joy was tempered a week later: "I'd have to add: lucidity, getting beyond a certain romanticism . . . It's hard to love others as they are. It is also difficult to realize that you are known and loved in your nakedness. He who has such a great desire for unity, just like his alter-ego Soloviev, is terribly multiplied and compartmentalized . . . And yet, at a level more profound than these diverging lines, there is the unity of an immense impulse that runs through them and magnetizes them."[52]

The relationship between Fr. Lev and Elisabeth, marked by this tension between true unity and total incomprehension, was always dynamic—a source of suffering for her when she felt set aside, but also a source of questions, of confrontations between two different points of view on life that aspired to the same goal. Elisabeth noted a few moments she spent with Fr. Lev in December 1976 before going to Formby:

London. St. Basil's. Reunion with L. . . .

These three days have been an in-depth progression. His aggressive attitude has disappeared. I feel both free and yet attached with an immense tenderness to this old man full of dreams, utopist, visionary.

Conversation on the difficulty in believing. We have different positions. He sees an absolute division between the spheres of knowledge and faith. I cannot keep from trying to reconcile them. He showed me a horrible little statue of the Sacred Heart, worthy of Saint Sulpice, which seems to be the support for his prayer. I found this mediocre symbol more annoying than anything else. But, beyond all that, I sense that he is in communion with the Love that is without limits.

Our final conversation: breakfast at the Kentucky Bar. As was the case at Kenilworth yesterday and in the little Greek restaurant (and the little Indian restaurant) we talked and talked . . . The waiters must have gotten a kick out of this old chatterbox couple.

A moment of great and deep emotion: *consecration* to the reconciliation of Jews and Arabs. I feel weak and powerless before this immense and overwhelming task. *Con-se-cra-tion.* Can faith still move mountains?[53]

The following summer, at the Fellowship meeting, Elisabeth, at the request of Fr. Lev, gave a talk on the Agapia conference and its consequences insofar as it opened up a new field of ecclesial reflection for Orthodoxy. She felt herself supported by Fr. Lev's inspiring presence, which gave her the courage to clearly assert her position: "The best moment: the hour I spent with Fr. Lev in his room to prepare my lectures. He goes right to the most important, to the essential. He gives me the courage to say what I think. He is proud of my success. And there is always that last quarter of an hour before I leave. So much tenderness and love in his eyes. That is *his truth.*"[54]

In her biography of Fr. Lev, Elisabeth pointed out the interest he took in this new question of the place of women in the Church and how much he supported her in her exploration of the topic:

At Fr. Lev's suggestion, I was invited to give a talk on the place of women in the Orthodox Church with reference to the conference at Agapia in which I had taken part a year earlier . . . In order to make people aware of the seriousness and the reality of the problem, he encouraged me to speak at High Leigh, urging me to express myself freely, "without fear." "You must always say what you think," he whispered, before introducing me to an audience who was liable to be surprised, or even shocked, at my ideas.[55]

After such moments of sharing, united in their common ideal, Elisabeth was disconcerted by the way that Fr. Lev distanced himself from her, seldom writing and rarely accepting invitations to participate in meetings in France. Especially painful was his refusal of an invitation to take part in the Third Congress of the Fraternity in November 1977 in Amiens. Elisabeth, bitterly disappointed, mulled over this disappointment:

> The awful sadness of these dialogues of the deaf on the phone. This morning, as has happened so often, it was impossible to communicate. The spiritual deafness of L. He draws back, cuts himself off, or hides behind a smokescreen of meaningless words . . . Refusal to come to Amiens under pretexts that are plausible or ridiculous. Obligation of attending a mundane, political ceremony for war veterans!!! On the other hand, a trip to Switzerland. What is it that attracts him there? A dream or a reality? A dream that sometimes makes him cry out sublimely. But hasn't he missed his true vocation? Amiens, for example, where he could have prevented the break with Blanqui [the ECOF]. After that, it's easy to cover oneself in lofty sentiments and indignation. It would have been better if he came, even at the risk of his life, to try to fend off disaster. It wasn't for nothing that I begged him to come. I sensed disaster approaching. It is because I love him—in spite of everything—that I would like to shout all that at him.
>
> O poet, O miserable man who dreams instead of acts![56]

Elisabeth continued to see in Fr. Lev the man who could have reconciled the different currents in local Orthodoxy and avoided the break at the Congress of Amiens between the members of the ECOF, whose canonical status was challenged, and the rest of the participants, had he chosen to commit himself to this task. But Fr. Lev's vocation seemed to be elsewhere: in accordance with the slogan he liked to repeat—"Small is beautiful"—he preferred informal gatherings, small groups where he would have more opportunities to have those heart-to-heart talks that brought out the best in him.

It was such a small ecumenical group, which had sprung up spontaneously among friendships forged during the 1965 pilgrimage of Syndesmos, that attracted Fr. Lev to Switzerland. At the request of a handful of people, he directed retreats at a place near Geneva, giving meditations on the Gospel, at which he excelled. Elisabeth was jealous of these "trips to Switzerland" to which he gave preference, while she had to practically twist his arm to convince him to go to a Sunday at Montgeron

When she and Fr. Lev got together in London during the winter of 1977, they broached the painful subject of Amiens—which Elisabeth considered symptomatic of her friend's reluctance to be in the same place as she was:

> London. December 22–24. Entirely with L. Arrival on the 22nd, near midnight. L. was waiting for me. He received me warmly . . . He is happy that my book has been published [the thesis on Bukharev]. The following morning there is a difficult conversation about his refusal to come to Amiens and, more generally, to Paris, whereas he went twice to Geneva-Grenoble.
> I wind up close to tears.[57]

Elisabeth, very sensitive when it was a question of Fr. Lev, felt the need to express her frustration over his unpredictable behavior. In her journal, she noted what she had said to him: "What saddens me is that you're sometimes so unlike what is best in you. You write that we should approach every man and every woman invoking the Name of Jesus. But you do not approach others, and when someone comes to you, they run into a wall, a hard surface, impenetrable. L.: 'Yes, that's it. That's my great misfortune.'"[58]

Her stay in London at the end of 1977 seemed to be entirely overshadowed by these mood swings. There was a tense evening when Fr. Lev expressed his concern over the break with the ECOF, in which he saw "a symbol of Russian arrogance" . . .[59] But the next day, when Elisabeth had to leave, the two of them were again in complete agreement:

I leave the next day around 12:30. L. promises to write a review of my book. Very relaxed. His sense of humor has returned. We take leave of one another saying, "I'll see you again soon." I'll see him for a few hours on the way back. This fragile man, secret, full of weaknesses and contradictions but so profound and radiant in the depths of his being—I love him! And I know that he loves me too, in his tortuous way. "You, you're something else," he said to me.

Concerning a message to some young Orthodox people. Me: "What do you want me to say to them on your behalf?" Him: "Just one word: *conversion*." Me: "What do you mean by conversion?" Him: "Communion with Jesus. Find pardon, salvation, life."[60]

After a joyous New Year with her family in Formby, Elisabeth found the time to spend a moment with Fr. Lev when she stopped in London on her way home:

An in-depth meeting with L. on January 4. Four hours together in the waiting room of British Caledonian . . .

The past, my past, I put into God's hands. When the time comes for me to leave, he hugs me and murmurs, "blessed, blessed." How many times have we said goodbye on a train station platform! I remember one day, nearly fifty years ago, when I accompanied him to a train station in Paris—I think it was Montparnasse—I lingered in the street, sad, my eyes closed. Suddenly someone kissed me on the forehead. It was Fr. Lev, who had come back to give me this kiss, and then disappeared again.[61]

When she left her old friend, knowing she would not see him again for several months, Elisabeth could not help thinking of his ultimate departure, something she would soon have to confront: "This new type of separation is a reality I have to envisage. But 'love is as strong as death.' On the train, I was silently weeping with both pain and joy."[62]

This was the beginning of a new period of distance between the two. In spite of Elisabeth's intense activity during the first months of 1978, with the publication of her book on Bukharev, the classes at the ISEO, and her many presentations concerning the role of women in the Church, she kept expecting a sign of life from Fr. Lev to comfort and support her. When she finally telephoned him, she understood that she had to accept the distance that he wanted to maintain between them: "Telephoned L. . . . Another dialogue of the deaf. L. cannot or doesn't want to understand (maybe both at the same time). Better to give up. Yet he told me, 'Sometimes I miss you . . . but God calls me elsewhere.' Masochism, an irresistible attraction of sacrifice? God knows. I surrender all that to Him. I did what I could. Maybe I was wrong. *Put everything into God's hands.*"[63] From this point on, Elisabeth, armed with this resolution, came to accept a little more easily the emotional divide between herself and Fr. Lev after so many years of close proximity. Their meeting at the Fellowship conference in the summer of 1978 reflected this new state of affairs. Elisabeth was less attentive to Fr. Lev, and he was more open and understanding. He agreed to participate in a Fraternity Sunday at Montgeron on October 15.

A few days prior to this event, Elisabeth had to face the death of her mother-in-law, Mariana Borissovna, who had been living in the Russian old-age home at Cormeilles-en-Parisis for several years. The funeral gave Elisabeth the chance to have her children close to her:

> October 8 (the birthday of Nicolas) the death of Babushka. Two days previously, we said goodbye with a great deal of affection. "This isn't anything," she said to me, "I'm just getting old." She died at the Argenteuil hospital, where they had rushed her during the night of 6–7. One of her last words: "Why are you putting me in a room by myself? I like to have company."
>
> Even at the age of eighty-six, death is still something awful. This flesh that I embraced, warm and sweet, had suddenly become glacial. The family is very united. Mariane came. Nicolas was very helpful. The wonderful sweetness of this sunny morning when we entrusted her body to the earth of the Russian cemetery of Saint-Geneviève-des-Bois.[64]

With Fr. Lev arriving from England at almost the same time, it seemed as though communion had been fully restored. "Arrival of L. the day after the burial. A good day at Montgeron. He is clear with me . . . He said . . . 'I felt that this meeting was so profound, so authentic, as never before.' A few moments of reflection together, to give thanks for all that was good, to ask pardon for the bad that was mixed in with it."[65] At Montgeron, Fr. Lev enlivened a day of reflection penetrated by peace, which would be the last time he took part in the Sunday meetings of the Fraternity.

In the course of their final contacts, Elisabeth seemed to have become reconciled to her friend's unpredictable character; she only wanted to see what was best in him, and she excused his moments of harshness as the consequences of his great age, of a certain psychic instability caused by his depression. After her stay in London in December 1978, when Fr. Lev was very understanding and tender with her, Elisabeth was not surprised by his silence after that, or by his hostility on the telephone:

> The other day, Lev spoke of the split personality of Paul Tillich as though it was something that affected him personally. He has the same split personality. The man who wrote *Love without Limits*, the man whose eyes can show so much love, and *the other* who seems to enjoy hurting me.
>
> Let him go his way like a bristling cat. He'll come back . . . or all will become clear in the Kingdom of Heaven . . . Look after him from afar. Try to understand. Curious how a sincere Christian can also be gloomy and hard as a rock. This inhumanity scandalizes me . . . I shouldn't dramatize his beastly character.[66]

There were hardly any contacts between Elisabeth and Fr. Lev in 1979. This was a difficult burden for Elisabeth, who still felt the need for a physical connection with the man who held such an important place in her intellectual, spiritual, and emotional life.

When autumn came, she was not able to endure his silence any longer and decided to join him at the retreat he was giving to his little ecumenical circle of friends on the outskirts of Geneva. She was well aware that this initiative risked being interpreted by Fr. Lev as an unacceptable intrusion into his life:

> Weekend at Geneva, at the Ecumenical Fraternity of Etoy, with L. I decided to make this trip because I could no longer bear his silence

but knowing that I risked provoking a break . . . I was afraid that he would avoid any one-to-one conversation. But, to my great surprise, it was he who took the initiative to speak with me. He had just finished a commentary on the parable of the *Sower*, the grain that had to be crushed underfoot to penetrate into the soil and burst forth. We exchanged very harsh words and separated with the impression of a total and reciprocal misunderstanding. After lunch, he gave the second meditation. The parables that tell us how to find again what had been lost. The drachma. The lamp that is Christ. My heart was heavy. I couldn't keep myself from crying. All the same, I was able to get some sleep . . .

During the liturgy, I felt very cold and critical. At the prayer of absolution, Fr. Lev did not say, May the Lord grant *you* His pardon, but May the Lord grant *us* His pardon. I was able to pray and, suddenly, I heard these words within myself: "The old things have passed, I make all things new." Joy. Peace. After dinner, I knocked on his door, went into his room, and simply repeated these words. He made the sign of the cross over me, saying, "May you be blessed," and we embraced with immense tenderness. Peace, peace. I fear that, being what we are, there will still be clashes, and some mud— which, sad to say, still lies dormant at the bottom of our hearts— will be kicked up. Yet something definite has happened. Under the mud lying in the depths, deeper than the mud, is the granite of a lasting love.

We are a couple of old fools. Preserve this certainty, this remedy against despair: the folly of love. A love that envelops the whole being. He probably loves me through Christ. I love Christ through him. Blasphemy, illusion? Yet this feeling of peace, of inner clarity, is something very real. The same can be said of this experience lived out once again: God is this light that shines in the middle of darkness. The Bridegroom comes in the middle of the night when we are no longer expecting Him.[67]

This encounter, which Elisabeth imagined would be a stormy confrontation, swept away the mutual misunderstandings when she and Fr. Lev again placed their relationship under the light of Christ.

At Etoy, Elisabeth found once more that ineffable experience that had marked her life on so many occasions: when things looked bleakest, when the situation seemed to be without a solution—her emotional dependence vis-à-vis a monk who henceforth refused her the privileged complicity they had had in the past—a joy suddenly sprang up, sweeping away despair. A joy that was the sign of the presence of God at the core of this difficult relationship, as was proven by the feelings "of peace, of inner clarity" that came over Elisabeth. Moments of lucidity also: she realized that "I love Christ through him."

Elisabeth was well aware of the inequality in their relationship. While she had to struggle to place her exclusive human love for Fr. Lev on a spiritual plane, to transfigure it, he seemed, at this period, to have looked on her with affection, which he wanted to do with everyone in order to give his love a universal dimension according to the dynamics of his monastic vocation. The monk, who had never betrayed his pastoral charisma, succeeded in placing Christ at the center of his rapport with Elisabeth and, by so doing, supported her in her own spiritual journey and made their love a means of sanctification. When, several days later, Elisabeth reflected on what she felt for him, she noted in her journal: "I cannot conceive that human love can be foreign to God. But much suffering is necessary before it erupts into its divine reality."

The very moving encounter at Etoy, where the two friends rediscovered their authentic communion, was the last moment given to Elisabeth to be with Fr. Lev. The old and weak monk, who was in his eighty-sixth year, never again left England. From this point on, Elisabeth no longer was put off by the absence of letters from Fr. Lev and no longer tried to telephone him. She understood that she would soon have to face his final departure.

Upon rereading Claudel's play, *Partage de Midi*, which had moved her deeply in the long-ago evenings of the Féde, she copied, on March 21, 1980, the speech of Mesa to Ysé at the end:

Adieu! I have seen you for the last time.
By what long and painful paths
Still distant yet not ceasing to weigh
The one on the other, are we going
To lead our souls in travail?
Remember, remember the sign! . . .
Man, in the splendor of August,
The victorious Spirit in the transfiguration of noon![68]

Several days later, Elisabeth received a telephone call from England informing her of Lev Gillet's death on the afternoon of March 29. This news, far from devastating her, was seen as liberating, and it reinforced the peace that had been growing within her during the last few months. Two days after his death she wrote in her notebook:

> Everything is clear now. Having shed the skin of an old man, he has entered into the kingdom of light and liberty toward which he was reaching with all his soul.
> Like a flash, the feeling that now nothing separates us any more.
> Poor Lev! You were tied, you were chained.
> Now you are free. Your eyes finally see . . .
> Here you are, purified, at peace.[69]

A month after his death, these lines, written to a friend, show the detachment with which she accepted his death:

> The Vigil of Palm Sunday, the Saturday of the Resurrection of Lazarus, my old friend, the "Monk of the Eastern Church" (Archimandrite Lev Gillet)—you certainly have read some of his books—fell asleep in the Lord. He was going on eighty-eight, and I think it was a great grace that he left us when he did, without having to know the deterioration that old age often brings. Pray for him as for an older brother, a precursor on the long and difficult road that leads to Unity, but along which we are already advancing in the Light of the Word.[70]

During the months following the death of her friend, Elisabeth, upon rereading some of his letters, thought about the road they had walked together—a juxtaposition of broken lines. She thought of all the moments of misunderstandings and apparent failures through which this road had to pass, so that their love might take on its true dimension. "I give thanks for this cup that we drank together, a cup of joy and of sorrow. But the sorrow is swallowed up in joy."[71]

With the death of Fr. Lev, Elisabeth experienced all the reality of this passage from the Song of Songs, which she so often had cited in her notebook: "Love is as strong as death."[72] Henceforth, she was clearly aware of his permanent presence near her. She mentioned this a year after his death: "First anniversary of the departure of L., of his 'passing to the other side.' Reassurance and intensity in his presence. A new encounter, cleansed, purified. Encounter in the Lord, through the Holy Spirit. Not happiness, but the first fruits of beatitude when the heart is full and at peace."[73] This experience of the final separation introduced Elisabeth into the mystery of a greater intimacy between persons; her union with Fr. Lev was now founded entirely on the communion of the Holy Spirit, the cement of love among those who seek God.

In her notebook, Elisabeth established an eloquent parallel between her last conversation with Fr. Lev and the Gospel's account of the Ascension: "Our final goodbye, so terrible and marvelous. He was like an old volcano, apparently extinct, whose crater is covered with petrified larva. Then suddenly, suddenly, it erupts—torrents of mud, then of flame. And the final words, with a kiss: 'May you be blessed.'"[74] A few months later, on the feast day of the Ascension, she wrote: "Sermon on the Ascension. 'It was when He was leaving them, at the moment when He was taken up, it was at this moment that He blessed them.' So similar to my experience with L."[75]

This gesture of a last benediction by Fr. Lev, in the image of Christ blessing His Apostles before leaving them, was, for Elisabeth, the supreme sign that her relationship with him had been and still was a road where both of them were advancing toward their meeting with the Living God. It was an unusual and dangerous road—certainly scandalous in the eyes of a certain type of moral conduct—and yet a road of sanctification, lived in the freedom of the Holy Spirit, who transcends all our moralities.

Little by little, the dregs of the difficult tribulations of this love settled to the bottom and left Elisabeth with the better part: "I thank you, Lord of Love, for all that I have received from You through L. I thank You for this marvelous, painful, marvelous life."[76]

The death of Fr. Lev was soon followed by that of several close friends: of Dr. Pierre Châtelain, who had entered a retirement home after giving his large property to the city of Nancy; of Herta, Elisabeth's childhood friend. Elisabeth, now seventy-six years old, asked herself: "When will my turn come? I feel that there is nothing more that interests me."[77] This very human discouragement on the part of a woman worn out by a rich and eventful life did not, however, last long. The experience, acquired over these last few years, of a greater closeness to God gave Elisabeth the energy to continue to work for the ecclesial tasks that had fallen to her. In addition to the many fields in which she was already active, she realized that it was up to her to transmit to new generations the message of Fr. Lev, this "universalist free-thinker,"[78] whose personality and writings could help many people rediscover the path of an authentic Christianity.

chapter 4

THE RADIANCE OF MATURITY, 1980–2005

For Elisabeth, the death of Fr. Lev marked the end of a restless period in her life, which had been dominated by the unpredictable reactions of the monk toward her. His demise led her to experience another kind of relationship, exempt from all the shadows of misunderstandings, thanks to which she felt him close to her.

During the 1980s, Elisabeth seemed to have arrived at that "calm haven" that Fr. Lev had desired for her. Her incisive and prickly personality, sometimes irritating when she was obsessed with defending certain opinions at all cost, seemed to mellow little by little, leaving room for an affability that made her more attentive and open to others.

Although the wrinkles of old age etched themselves on her broad, thoughtful forehead, Elisabeth's piercing blue eyes shone with goodness without losing any of their sparkle and vivacity. Aside from a few warning signs of certain health problems, notably cancer in 1967, the septuagenarian seemed to have an iron constitution, swimming whenever she could, enjoying a cigarette, drinking black coffee in the evening because it gave her, as she explained, "the energy to go to sleep."

With her new youthful enthusiasm, Elisabeth did all she could to transmit the richness of her experience while remaining astonishingly attentive to the changes in the world around her. "I'm a sort of estuary,"[1] she said, indicating with a sweep of her hand the piles of books and magazines that cluttered her little apartment in Épinay. Most of the religious publications of the period found their way to her mailbox and enabled her to keep up to date on what was going on.

She was also kept informed through her voluminous correspondence, which took on a great deal of diversity as she made new friends in the course of her travels. Having acquired an international reputation, Elisabeth was now invited to different points of the globe to give lectures or series of classes, either on the specific theme of the place of women in the Church or on more traditional theological questions. Thanks to her spirit of openness and the solidity of her erudition, she possessed the art of transmitting the fundamental aspects of Orthodox theology through a personal approach that showed that this theology had been integrated into her own life.

From One Continent to Another, 1983–1984

Tantur, 1983, 1984

In 1983, thanks to a proposal to give a new series of classes, Elisabeth was able to return to the Holy Land, for which she had so many dazzling memories after her pilgrimage there in 1965. She agreed to give courses at the Ecumenical Institute of Tantur, situated between Jerusalem and Bethlehem. This center of theological research had been founded in 1972 at the request of Pope Paul VI, who wanted to commemorate his historic meeting with Patriarch Athenagoras at Jerusalem in 1964. Subsidized by the University of Notre Dame, not far from Chicago, the Institute enabled theologians of different denominations to take a common approach to questions of faith. "The concept of the Institute is founded on the conviction that, by living and studying together, a community of men and women of diverse doctrinal and liturgical traditions can contribute to hastening the advent of a full ecclesial communion."[2]

Exegete Oscar Cullman, who had been Elisabeth's professor at the Protestant Faculty of Strasbourg, took part in the creation of the center and doubtless played a part in Elisabeth's invitation. From March to April 1983 she led a weekly seminar on her favorite topic, women in the Church, as well as a public course entitled "Some Aspects of the Theology and of the Experience of the Holy Spirit in the Orthodox Church." This conference drew on recent interventions she had made in ecumenical circles concerning the theology of the Holy Spirit. She retraced the historic evolution of the *Filioque* throughout the stages of the schism and its role in the relations between the Eastern and Western Churches. After she developed aspects of Eastern Trinitarian theology, Elisabeth suggested ways of arriving at an understanding with the West by insisting on the importance of finding a common contemporary language when treating of the *Filioque*.[3] Then, in the spring of 1984, she returned to Tantur for a new series of classes. These visits were marked by a fruitful ecumenical dialogue with English university students.

Her memories of the Tantur center were of a paradise where English comfort went hand in hand with the charm of Israel. In her notebook she wrote: "Tantur = a sort of ecumenical Hilton, a civilized and disinfected Orient." From Tantur, she could go on foot to Bethlehem and by taxi to Jerusalem, only a few kilometers away.

During her stays at Tantur, Elisabeth discovered other corners of the Near East: in the company of a group of Catholic friends from the center, she followed the banks of the Dead Sea and crossed the Negev desert as far as the Sinai Peninsula. There she visited the monastery of Saint Catherine, which impressed her greatly, both because of the warm greeting the monks gave her and also because of the traditional sunrise on Mount Moses after a long, nocturnal ascent by camelback.

Her little trips outside of the center, to Bethlehem and Jerusalem, enabled her to form an opinion of the situation of Christians in Israel.

Elisabeth, always sensitive to injustices, noted the rift between the Greek clergy and the Palestinian faithful:

> The Greeks consider themselves, above all, as the guardians of the holy places. Keep for the Greeks the part that, by tradition, belongs to them. Little or no concern for pastoral work. The Orthodox faithful, who are Arabs, are abandoned to married Arab priests who are considered an inferior class. In fact, they only receive a mediocre theological education. The celibate clergy is recruited among Greeks imported from Greece. They are the ones who constitute the Fraternity of the Holy Sepulcher, which does not include a single Arab. The government of Jordan has asked that there be two Arabs among the bishops. In reality, the only Arab bishop died during the voyage of Patriarch Diodorus to Moscow, so that there is no longer any "indigenous" bishop. Bitterness on the part of the Greeks who cling to their privileges. But even more bitterness on the part of the Arabs. Father B. told me that this explains the attitude of young Orthodox Palestinians who declare themselves Christians but challenge their link with their Church . . . Father B. pointed out the case of young Palestinian Orthodox who did their theological studies at Balamand in Lebanon and whom the patriarch refused to ordain. The ecumenical situation is difficult. These young Orthodox Palestinians are attracted to the Uniate Melkites[4] even though the latter have no intention of proselytizing.
>
> Return trip through the picturesque Arab quarter. I'm struck by the ravaged features of the old women. There is a curfew in the villages around Hebron and Napalouse because people are throwing stones at cars. David against Goliath.[5]

The length of her stay at Tantur enabled Elisabeth to participate in the daily life of the place: "Went up to Bethlehem to buy a few things and get my camera fixed. The person in the camera shop took care of the little problem as I watched. Not only did he refuse to accept payment, but he offered me a cup of coffee. 'This has been a pleasure for me,' he said. 'Pray for me.'"[6] Mixed in with the local people, she was part of the Catholic Palm Sunday procession that retraced Christ's route from the Mount of Olives to Jerusalem. She was surrounded by "a large cosmopolitan crowd, yet most were Arabs and rabble." There, she once again noted the pastoral concern of the Catholic Melkites for the Arab population:

> The strength of the Catholic Church: to be all things for all peoples . . . here for the Arabs whom the Orthodox patriarch of Jerusalem, the "local Church," neglects! . . .
> The Melkite Archbishop . . . an extraordinary personage, intelligent, charismatic perhaps, concerned at any rate about being a shepherd for his people. I was tired when I got back, but not exhausted and above all, happy. I walked with the Arabs the whole length of the way.[7]

Consistent with her character, Elisabeth naturally sided with the weakest, with the common people, neglected by the Orthodox clergy and supported by Eastern Rite Catholics whose actions, even if they were sometimes hegemonic, at least had the merit of being attentive to each person. She returned many times to Tantur. The construction of the wall sealing off the occupied West Bank territories placed the Ecumenical Institute at one of the Israeli checkpoints, thus making her little trips to Bethlehem much more difficult.

Ottawa, 1984

The reputation of the frail little lady with penetrating eyes crossed the Atlantic. Through the mediation of some Canadian friends she had met at the Sheffield conference, Elisabeth was invited in October 1984 by the Dominican College of Ottawa for a colloquium celebrating its seventy-fifth anniversary. Every year, this Francophone institution of philosophy and theology invited a European scholar to teach within its walls. Elisabeth had established herself as a solid Orthodox speaker on the place of women in the Church, and her field of expertise fitted in very well with the theme of the congress, "Otherness: To Live Together While Being Different." In the *Bulletin of the Crypt*, Elisabeth wrote about this experience: "As a woman and as an Orthodox, I made incarnate, for my hosts, some aspects of this *difference* with which we have to learn to live."

Elisabeth spent a month at the college. After the colloquium, she gave two series of classes over a period of three weeks. She felt at ease in this university milieu where the people, mostly French-speaking, were very attentive to what she had to say. In the *Bulletin of the Crypt*, she wrote: "I was impressed by the open minds of my audience and their great desire to be informed on what was happening around them."

At the end of her stay, she shared with her children, as was her custom through the many letters she sent them, her impressions of the college:

> It is with sadness that I'm leaving my new Dominican friends whose exquisite and simple hospitality I greatly appreciated. Preparing my classes was hard work but the audience—both theology students and those who were just sitting in—was very sympathetic . . . I spent the final weekend in Montreal at the invitation of the rector of a tiny but lively Orthodox Francophone parish. There I gave a lecture on the controversial topic of the place of women in the Church! I was also interviewed on television and radio. The problem of women is here the order of the day. This evening, I'm invited to a reception that will bring together partisans of women's rights, including some bishops and theology professors.[8]

At the beginning of November, Elisabeth left Canada for the United States, where she stayed with Fr. John Meyendorff, the new rector of the Orthodox seminary of Saint Vladimir, near New York. The seminary, where Elisabeth had, quite naturally, the opportunity to talk with some women, impressed her by its dynamism and influence.

The Place of Women in the Church

Elisabeth had now established herself as the Orthodox theologian specializing in the place of women in the Church, a theme that the Eastern Tradition had never treated in a systematic manner. Aware of the importance of the question in contemporary Western debates, she played the role of an interface between ecumenical and Orthodox circles, confronting their often divergent positions with a positive dialogue that would lead to greater clarity. In meetings of the World Council of Churches, she had the opportunity to meet proponents for the ordination of women and transmitted their point of view to the Orthodox.

For the Eastern Church, the question of the place of women came from without: it was not an inherent need that pushed the Orthodox Church to consider this situation, but rather the influence of the surrounding Western society where women's emancipation made equality a right in all fields, including religion. It was a delicate undertaking to introduce this demand within the ecclesial community. Should not the assembly of believers realize, already and here below, the Kingdom of Heaven, the communion of love between God and mankind, where each person realizes his or her personal identity, with its own specificities and charismas? By militating for an interchange of ministries, is there not the risk of allowing, within the Church, a negation of the particularities of each gender, such as our daily life proposes more and more and which, in many aspects, seems to be opposed to the meaning of God's design for His creature?

The caricature that men give of the Church, often disfigured by personal power struggles, justifies the introduction of such a consideration. Even if we are still not capable of fully living in the harmonious communion that Christ proposed for us when he taught us to "love one another, and by this shall all men know that you are my disciples,"[9] we must be attentive to the distortions and abuses that we commit within our communities and try to remedy them.

To think about the particular place given to women can contribute to reestablishing a certain balance in fields where, too often, the female had been treated as inferior, impure, unworthy. With her characteristic open-mindedness, Elisabeth began this reflection with an audacious question posed to the Church's Tradition, which obliged it to rethink all the theology of each person's respective role: Why cannot women have access to ordination? This central question oriented the debates of a new group of meetings that Elisabeth brought to life.

"Women and Men in the Church": A Pan-Orthodox Dialogue

The "Study on the Community of Women and Men in the Church," undertaken by the World Council of Churches in the 1980s, enabled

Elisabeth to bring together, on a regular basis, a group of Orthodox Parisians to reflect on the place of women. Following the World Council conference, which culminated in the great meeting at Sheffield, it was thought necessary to pursue exchanges on this theme on a less official level.

Biennial meetings were then organized. The first meetings gave certain women the opportunity to vent the frustrations they had felt in their parishes. Elisabeth and the other organizers decided to use a more rigorous format in these meetings to avoid their becoming a place where people would go merely to rehash their bitterness. Henceforth the meetings would begin with a lecture on a specific theme, then open up to questions and to an exchange of opinions.

This interjurisdictional group was sometimes joined by representatives of other denominations, notably Catholics. All sorts of problems were discussed. Certain questions were recurrently raised as new people joined the group: the monthly impurity of women as set forth in Deuteronomy;[10] the prohibition, in most communities, of women entering the sanctuary; the baptismal procession for a baby girl that generally halts before the holy doors of the church . . . As the meetings continued, the reflections on the place of women were followed by real effects in the life of certain parishes. The debates invited all men and woman to find their place in the community where they could realize their Christian vocation according to their own charismas.

On a theological level, the group's reflections led to a distinction between diaconal ministry and priestly ministry. The ordination of deaconesses, practiced in the first Christian communities and then sporadically in certain Churches, did not provoke any theological reservations. This question enabled the consideration of the need for a general remodeling of the diaconate, which, over these last centuries, had become limited to a liturgical service.

In 2000 this group wrote a collective letter addressed to the Ecumenical Patriarch and sent to representatives of the different Orthodox Churches, in which it requested the reestablishment of this ministry for women, citing its necessity in the contemporary world:

In our modern societies, where, more and more, men and women share the same activities and responsibilities—each in his or her own manner—the deaconess should be at the service of the whole of the ecclesial community, . . . imploring the guidance of the Holy Spirit . . .

In order to make our parish communities both assemblies for liturgical prayer and places of community life, it is fitting to appeal to those men and women whose backgrounds, talents, and personal charismas predispose them to become the helpers and colleagues of a priest who, given the conditions of contemporary life, is often over-worked and overwhelmed.[11]

To define the tasks of deaconesses, the letter suggested that it was necessary to rethink those of deacons so as not to limit them to the liturgical service, as was the case nowadays: "The profound bond that unites the sacrament of the altar to what Saint John Chrysostom calls the 'sacrament of the brother' is forgotten, or at least we have lost sight of it. The restoration of a female diaconate might help us to re-member it."[12]

The group stressed the importance of a formal ministry that would assure the legitimacy of the person who exercised it and confer the divine support necessary to do the job: "Today, within our commu-nities, women are taking on numerous responsibilities, and some are, in fact, exercising a ministry that is quasi-diaconal. Authentification, recognition of their vocation by the Church, the invocation of the gifts of the Holy Spirit over them, the epiclesis of diaconal ordination would assure and fortify these women in the exercise of their min-istry."[13] This appeal received no response; there was no action on the part of the hierarchy.

Although it met every two years at the beginning, the "Women and Men," whose high point seems to have been the composition of the unanswered letter, later came together more sporadically. At the beginning of the twenty-first century, the group had a fruitful collabo-ration with a Catholic movement of the same name directed by Fr. Hervé Legrand, whom Elisabeth had kept close to at several ecumeni-cal meetings. Each group was able to share questions regarding the other's ministry and offered another chance for a deeper knowledge of the other's Tradition.

Elisabeth also found herself leading the reflections on the place of women in the workshops that were held every three years at the congresses of the Orthodox Fraternity. Since Amiens in 1977, each subsequent congress systematically held a workshop on the place of women in the Church prompted by Elisabeth, who was later joined by her daughter Nadine as well as by Véronique Lossky, a Slavic scholar who was a specialist in the Russian poet Marina Tsvetaeva. In the course of these meetings, Elisabeth was able to develop personal responses in women who often had inherited a more traditional view of the ecclesial community.

Congress of Rhodes, 1988

In the wake of the ecumenical gatherings where ordination of women was discussed, and thanks to Elisabeth's efforts to make people aware of it, the Orthodox Church began to feel the need for an internal dialogue on this question. Father Alexander Schmemann and Fr. John Meyendorff, conscious of the importance of reflecting on the place of women in the Church, succeeded in interesting the Ecumenical Patriarch. And thanks to their mediation, a pan-Orthodox conference was organized. It took place on the island of Rhodes from October 30 to November 7, 1988. This meeting, which assembled members from all jurisdictions, both laypeople and clerics, denoted a general realization of the problem by the Orthodox. Women constituted one third of the attendees, and Elisabeth found among them some who had been at Agapia. During the conference, she acutely sensed the deep divide between the representatives of Western Orthodoxy and those of the more ancient Churches, especially those of Russia and Greece.

The very purpose of the conference already oriented the result of the debates: it was convened, from the outset, to reflect on the arguments against women acceding to ordination. All the same, the participants felt the need to broaden the debate to include the overall role of women in the Church. Thus, three positions were taken: some participants were very clearly opposed to any sort of change in the status of women in the ecclesial communities; others were attached to an idealized and disincarnate view of women, inherited from the controversial opinions of Paul Evdokimov on the matter, where women were associated with the Holy Spirit and therefore could not assume a priestly ministry that would make them belong to Christ. A minority, headed by Elisabeth, tried to propose a frank discussion on the question of women priests.

Just before the congress, Metropolitan Anthony wrote to Elisabeth to explain his anthropological view of women and the priesthood, which he lifted from Paul Evdokimov:

> Although we speak of Christ as the Second Adam, we obviously do not do so in terms of the fallen Adam. He is the Adam of the Beginning, containing in Himself all that is masculine and all that is feminine, in their fullness and their perfection, inseparably united, like the Three Persons of the Trinity, in a perfect Union without confusion, in a perfect diversity without separation.
>
> The old adage that says that what Christ did not assume, He has not saved is dramatically true in this case: if He has not assumed all that is feminine, then Woman is excluded from the Mystery of Salvation; but He is the Whole Man, like the first Adam, but with a fullness and perfection that surpasses the Adam of Genesis, and enables his coexistence with Eve in Him. So it is that what is true of Him is not only true of man (*vir*), but also of woman (*mulier*). The man and the woman are, therefore, equally in the Image of Christ, but, both of them, imperfectly, while He is their Prototype, perfectly. Both are icons in the (imperfect) sense where a painted icon is and is not the Object it represents. The priest celebrates "*in Christo*" but is not Christ substantially, no more than a portrait that reveals its subject is, nonetheless, a reflection and not the thing itself. The only celebrant of the Mysteries in the Church is Christ, the High Priest of all Creation, and the only power that performs the sacramental miracle is the Holy Spirit. Apostolic succession cannot give any power over matter . . . nor, still less, over God . . . (by the simple repetition of a sacred formula, be that even the very Word of God). The priesthood is, then, the prerogative of God alone, who alone can sanctify everything, while we can only present Him with our offering, already made holy (in the sense that it belongs to God alone by the fact of our act of faith); that is the mystery of the Annunciation: "Behold, the handmaiden of the Lord"; and in the Eucharist: "Of Thine own we offer unto Thee . . ."[14]

Metropolitan Anthony encouraged Elisabeth to voice her positions very clearly: "*Dare!* Don't speak 'in the name of the Church' but in the name of the Truth!"[15] However, every time she tried to speak, she was cut off and was unable to explain the whole of her thoughts during the lecture.

Even though the conclusions at Rhodes against the ordination of women seemed categorical, the final document urged the reestablishment of an authentic female diaconate. The document also proposed several possible paths for considering the ministries that would enable women to enter into:

> a diaconate of support, as a complementary pastoral dimension, in harmony with the specifically sacerdotal ministry of the clergy: a) Christian education at all levels, from parish schools to advanced theological teaching in the seminaries; b) spiritual direction for married couples and for families, preparation for marriage, preparation for baptism and help for those in difficulty; c) ecclesiastical administration, participation in decision-making at the levels of the parish, the diocese, and the national Church; d) social services, including activity on behalf of the aged, of those in hospitals, of the oppressed and the forgotten; e) work with young people; f) representation in the different sectors of the ecumenical movement; and g) publications and communications.[16]

Although this resolution was approved unanimously by all the participants, no bishop took the initiative afterward to make it effective by ordaining a deaconess, once again proving the difficulty of transforming ecclesial decisions into concrete acts in the life of the parishes.

Writings on the Theme of Women in the Church

The maturing of Elisabeth's reflections on the place of women in the Church led to the publication by the Cerf publishing house, in 1987, of *The Ministry of Women in the Church*. This book was the first of its kind on the subject. It combined articles and lectures with previously unpublished chapters in order to give an overall view of her thinking on the matter.

In her introduction, Elisabeth—who was usually reticent about speaking about herself except to answer interviewers—gave a rapid summary of how she had become interested in the theme of the place of women in the Church and explained the reasons that had made her particularly sensitive about it. She showed how her own unusual experiences, notably her pastorate, had predisposed her to reflect on such a topic, but it was more through outside circumstances, such as Agapia, rather than her own initiative that had led her to become involved.

The first chapter was the text of the lecture she had given at the Dominican College of Ottawa in 1984 concerning "The Gender Difference in the Context of a Christian Civilization." Beginning with a sociological analysis of the place of women in our modern world, Elisabeth then shifted to an evangelical and patristic approach to situate the condition of women in the course of the Church's history. She concluded with the exhortation, which kept recurring in her writings, to return to the sources of the Church's Tradition to search for the solutions to contemporary problems: "To try to make . . . Scripture relevant, doesn't mean trying to make it say what we want it to say. It means listening humbly to the Divine Word that reverberates in it in order to discern the will of God in our own day."[17]

The second chapter, written especially for the book, summarized what Elisabeth thought should be the place of women in Tradition and served as a transition to introduce her intervention at the World Council of Churches' congress at Sheffield, "Toward a New Community." In this document, she outlined the Orthodox vision of the ecclesial community, illustrating it by Rubliev's icon of the Trinity and that of the Deisis,[18] where the Virgin and John the Baptist can be said to represent, respectively, the feminine and masculine parts of humanity in their journey toward God. The contemplation of the mystery of Trinitarian and ecclesial unity, depicted in these icons, can lead each one of us, man and woman, to find our place in the Church community. "This 'heavenly vision' should lead to action," Elisabeth wrote.[19]

The counterpart to this heavenly vision was the reality of the facts, and this is what Elisabeth developed in the following chapter, "Women in the Orthodox Church: The Heavenly Vision and History," which she had already published in *Contacts* shortly after Agapia. Next was a more synthetic chapter, written for the book, which again took up "The Place of Women in the Church," from the assertions of Saint Paul, which Elisabeth situated in their context, to contemporary questions that the ecumenical movement had introduced into the Orthodox Church.

Through her evangelical and patristic approach, Elisabeth stressed the complete equality of the nature and vocation of women with men. She then pointed out the capital role played by women in the life of Orthodox parishes where they had taken on a number of material and spiritual functions. These observations led to the questioning of a certain number of ecclesial practices—or the lack of practices—that were not in conformity with what theology had to say about women.

A chapter devoted to "Mary, Mother of God," taken from her lecture given during a Marian colloquium at Strasbourg in 1985, analyzed the role of the Virgin as a specific feminine model. Elisabeth insisted on the broader exemplarity of the Mother of God who, above all, was an exemplar of holiness for every Christian. The appendix contained a text published in the *SOP* as a result of the meetings of "Women and Men in the Church" and signed by thirty-six of its participants. Entitled "Questions on Man and Woman in the People of God," it made known the state of their thoughts on the place of women in the Orthodox Church as well as the developments that the group expected. Overall, Elisabeth's book left an impression of an abundance of ideas where one could find a great deal of new information. It invited the reader to modify his perspective and consider the question from a different angle, rather than simply appealing to Tradition blindly, without making the effort to render it intelligible.

The collection of articles that made up *The Ministry of Women in the Church* accounted for its unsystematic and often repetitive approach; the same analyses were sometimes found in different chapters. Although it was not a clear reference work on the question, the book gave insights into Elisabeth's thinking on all fronts, ecumenical as well as pan-Orthodox, and treated the sociological aspect of the problem as well as its theological one. Thanks to this approach, which sought to be as global as possible, Elisabeth succeeded in conveying the complexity of the problem. The choice of such an approach was at the expense of a certain linear rigor that doubtlessly would have given the book more coherence.

The Ministry of Women in the Church also reflected Elisabeth's many contributions, in colloquiums and review articles and within very different contexts, on this theme. In 1991 an international periodical of Orthodox women was founded in Australia. Entitled *Mary Martha*, it mostly published articles in English with occasional texts in French. Elisabeth made numerous contributions, most of them adaptations of interventions she had made at different meetings on the subject of women.

Several years later, in 1998, together with her friend Metropolitan Kallistos Ware, she would publish another book on the same theme, *The Ordination of Women in the Orthodox Church*. This one manifested a deeper and more settled reflection than *The Ministry of Women in the Church*. It was more synthetic, more directly focused on the essential questions and employed a rigorous historical approach.

Elisabeth made much of the indefinite article and the broader ministry of women as well as of men in the title of this book. Ordination, whether to diaconal or priestly service, concerned only a small number of Christians and had to be placed in the context of reflection about the wider issue of the ministry of all members of the Church.

The book compared Elisabeth's viewpoint with that of Metropolitan Kallistos, which he set forth in a text entitled, "Man, Woman, and the Priesthood of Christ." This twofold approach proposed two readings that sometimes diverged and sometimes superimposed themselves on one another. The authors analyzed, each in his or her own way, the three approaches to the question of the ordination of women. There was, first of all, the tradition of the Church that, for two millenniums, had only ordained men: while both theologians agreed about its fundamentally dynamic character, which evolved according to circumstances, Elisabeth saw this as a possible opening for the ordination of women, whereas Metropolitan Kallistos invited more prudence: "If something has never been done in the Church for two thousand years, then we must have very precise and necessary reasons for starting to do it now. Perhaps there is no conclusive argument against the ordination of women, but is there such an argument *in favor of it?*"[20]

The second, or anthropological, approach focused on the significance of a humanity divided into two genders. Elisabeth, going back to the patristic analysis of the American theologian Verna Harrison, showed that, according to the Fathers of the Church, gender differentiation was subordinate to the unique character of the vocation of every human being. For Metropolitan Kallistos, this did not diminish the importance of the differentiation: "For my part, I believe very strongly that masculinity and femininity, as gifts of God, have dimensions that are not only biological but also spiritual."[21] The two theologians concluded that the anthropological definitions, such as they were expressed in the Church at present, were unable to resolve the question of the ordination of women and needed to be studied more in depth.

There remained the third approach, traditionally called "the iconic argument": the priest, representing Christ, should be a man in order to respect the liturgical symbolism. Elisabeth redefined the priest's representative dimension in these terms: "It is by repeating the words of Christ at the Last Supper and making the same gestures with which the Priest indicates the invisible, spiritual presence—*in and by the Holy Spirit*—of the unique High Priest, Christ . . . Why cannot these hands and this tongue be those of a Christian woman, baptized, chrismated, *christified* . . . by her communion with He who is the supreme Anointed of the Holy Spirit, Christ Himself?"[22] Metropolitan Kallistos replied with another question: "Is the exclusively masculine character of the priesthood an integral element of a symbolism revealed and given by God, which we can touch only at our risk and peril?"[23]

This collaborative study, which recapitulated the contemporary arguments on the question of the ordination of women, brought to light the still embryonic character of theological thought in this field. Both theologians called for a more profound investigation, inspired by the Holy Spirit, to determine whether it was possible and necessary, in our day, to ordain women to the priesthood. Elisabeth's voice would open the debate within the Orthodox Church on a tone that was both audacious and respectful of tradition.

Ecumenical and Social Activity

Elisabeth's personal destiny was intimately linked to the surge of the ecumenical movement throughout the twentieth century. It was this movement that had brought her to Orthodoxy and, in the course of her work, established her reputation as a woman of dialogue, at the axis of the different Christian traditions. When she spoke of her participation in the ecumenical movement, Elisabeth always referred back to the little circle in Nancy during the war years, the first fruits of a rewarding collaboration with other Christians, as her most intense ecumenical experience. She wrote in a letter to a friend: "For me, the experience of the first ecumenical group in Nancy, which was started in 1942 and which brought us together both in view of Unity and the 'Resistance,' remains one of the most profound of my life."[24] Through the hardships they took on together during those days of German occupation, and despite their denominational divergences, they sensed their unity of faith in Christ above and beyond its different dogmatic, liturgical, and spiritual expressions.

From this experience, Elisabeth retained a desire to live an ecumenism expressed by deeds, where Christians committed themselves to act together in the face of the needs of the world around them. She felt a certain sadness when confronted with the one-sided Monophysitism[25] too often found in an Orthodoxy lost in the contemplation of spiritual beauty to the detriment of the reality of human suffering. Collaboration with the Western Churches could help to avoid the pitfall of introversion, a survival reflex in view of conserving one's identity, a temptation to which the Orthodox in France were particularly susceptible due to their small numbers.

Elisabeth, who was always involved in multiple projects and tried to not separate the different aspects of her life—profession, family, and theology—but rather live them as a whole before God, did not want to cloister herself in purely intellectual theological activity in her retirement. On the contrary, she put herself at the service of an intensified ecumenical and social commitment.

Vice President of the ACAT, 1981–1993

A new opportunity enabled Elisabeth to become involved in concrete actions. In 1981, Deacon Michael Evdokimov, at Saint Nicholas parish in Boulogne, no longer had the the time to carry out his duties as vice president of the Christian Action for the Abolition of Torture (ACAT). Elisabeth was elected to replace him. The ACAT had been founded less than ten years previously, following an appeal by Amnesty International for a reaction against the rise of torture in the world. A handful of Christians mobilized to create an association dedicated to respecting Article 5 of the 1948 Universal Declaration of Human Rights, which stated that no human being should be subjected to torture.

This Christian humanitarian movement acted on a material as well as a spiritual level: it informed and sensitized public opinion about the contemporary reality of torture; led campaigns of appeal, of petitions to be signed; organized prayer vigils; and helped to set up a network of intercession. Since it was interdenominational, the ACAT enabled all Christians to work together for a cause that transcended their divisions.

Elisabeth had followed the emergence of this association from its beginnings and was one of the co-signers of a letter addressed to Pope Paul VI in 1976 concerning the victims of torture. Some Orthodox who were actively engaged in the ACAT, such as Frs. Cyrille Argenti and Michael Evdokimov, were her close friends. She thus had the background to take the place of Fr. Michael when he withdrew. What Elisabeth liked in the ACAT was its concern for taking into account the sufferings of the world and reacting, in the world, as Christians. She thought that an Orthodox presence within the association was essential: "From their Catholic and Protestant brothers and sisters, the Orthodox receive the impetus of a more active spirituality that is present in the world without being of the world. The Orthodox know how to sing the joy of Christ's Resurrection perhaps better than others do. But they have to learn—and adherence to the ACAT could facilitate this—to pose acts that bear witness to their faith *here and now.*"[26]

This new responsibility multiplied the number of Elisabeth's activities and meant participating in numerous meetings as well as maintaining a voluminous correspondence. She became the relay person in the exchange of information between the ACAT and Orthodox circles. *Le Courrier de l'ACAT* circulated information and also included serious theological articles on each denomination "in order to promote better awareness and better reciprocal understanding, the conditions for an authentic progress toward unity in regard to a fraternal love that respects our differences."[27]

In June 1986, Elisabeth went to Rome with an ACAT delegation that included Guy Aurenche, the Catholic president of the FIACAT, the international association of the ACAT; Jacqueline Westercamp, the Protestant president of the ACAT; and Fr. Pierre Toulat, its Catholic vice president. The object of this trip was to encourage Pope John Paul II to take a clear public stand against capital punishment. Elisabeth was impressed by the way the Holy Father listened to them, and she offered him a copy of the review *Irénikon*, where she had written an article on the Mother of God. The pope took time to question them with kindness. Nonetheless, this initiative of the ACAT did not lead to an official declaration by the Holy Father.

In *Le Courrier de l'ACAT*, Elisabeth published a number of articles in which, most often, she developed a theological theme from her Orthodox perspective. Most notably, she gave an overall view of the dogmatic points on which Eastern and Western Christians disagreed in an article entitled, "Orthodoxy and Catholicism (Some Points of Doctrinal Divergence)."[28] She began by explaining why intercommunion was not possible for the two Churches, coming back to the significance of the Eucharist: "from the Orthodox point of view, sacramental Communion, participation in a common Eucharistic Liturgy, is the expression, actualization, and crown of the communion in the same faith in a One God in Three Persons—Father, Son, and Holy Spirit. In spite of the progress that has already been made in this direction, thanks to the ecumenical dialogue, the [Orthodox] Churches doubt that this unity of faith has already been fully realized between them and the other denominations or Christian Churches."[29]

She then developed the points that were obstacles to this unity of faith and especially noted the dogmatic implications that had pushed the Orthodox to oppose the *Filioque* formula[30] adopted by the Western Churches: "It is a question of maintaining the balance (of which the Orthodox Church is, according to its vocation, the guardian) between the Christic and institutional aspect of the Church and, inseparable from this last, its 'pneumatic,' spiritual reality that comes from the freedom of the Holy Spirit who breathes wherever it pleases . . . The problem concerning the theology of the Holy Spirit and the ecclesiological problem are intimately linked."[31]

Elisabeth then treated the consequences of this divergence in Trinitarian theology on the organization of each Church. As opposed to Roman primacy, which gave the pope immediate authority over all Catholics, Orthodoxy had a whole group of patriarchal jurisdictions: "The Orthodox Church sees itself as a communion of local-subject Churches, in the image of the communion of the Persons in the Divine Tri-Unity. The grandeur of its vocation resides in this heavenly vision, which is also, perhaps, one of the causes of its empirical weakness. To maintain unity while respecting the freedom of the persons of the Sister Churches is a humanly impossible task that can only be envisaged by confiding in the presence and aid of the Holy Spirit."[32]

Elisabeth also contributed to *Documents ACAT*, a publication whose goal was to help people to deepen both their faith and the social commitment inspired by this faith. At the ACAT, she held the position of vice president until 1993, organizing different congresses both in France and within FIACAT, which coordinated the associations around the world. She spoke at the meetings of the movement, notably at Basle for the FIACAT congress, which treated the theme of "The Tortured, the Torturers, and Christian Hope." In her address, she cited the importance of prayer for those who suffer. Her lecture, "The Prayer of Intercession in the Struggle against Torture," showed how an act of love, expressing itself in supplicating God on behalf of the tormented, possessed a mysterious but undeniable efficacy. Prayer was presented as an effective means of helping those who were being tortured.

After she left her position as vice president, Elisabeth continued as a member of the ACAT's theological committee until her death. The team, who were responsible for the preparation of theological colloquiums and the publication of in-depth documents, were very appreciative of Elisabeth's freedom of expression; she was not afraid to state her positions with audacity and humor. Her status as an Orthodox who was immersed in Western sensitivity was a precious asset: she was able to make the Catholic and Protestant members understand the point of view of Eastern spirituality in a language they could grasp.

In March 1999 she wrote *Watch and Pray*, a document on Orthodoxy destined for the different Christian confessions so that they might know one another better. Elisabeth impressed the members of the theological committee by her radiant personality and by her unfailing fidelity: in spite of her great age, she stubbornly persisted in taking the Metro to get to meetings. She was also a member of the humanitarian branch of the CIMADE and made numerous contacts there. From 1983 to 1985, she represented the archdiocese of the parishes of Russian tradition in Western Europe.

An Abundance of Ecumenical Activities

The modern context, marked by a certain universalism of Western culture, once again favors, as in the Hellenistic period, contacts and exchanges. Among Christians of different theological and spiritual traditions, it seems that it is possible to find a common language, by trying to understand the other's language and speaking one's own in a way that is comprehensible to the other. This effort demands both sympathy—"become all things to all people," like Saint Paul—and firmness of faith in the enthusiasm of a renewal of Pentecost.[33]

Elisabeth, who was always ready to jump at new opportunities, was aware of the ecumenical possibilities in the rapid development of modern communications, which could broaden encounters and dialogue. Having inherited the optimistic perspective of the period of postwar ecumenism, when interdenominational contacts took place in an atmosphere of enthusiasm that inspired the hope of an imminent communion, Elisabeth wanted to transmit this momentum, in spite of the subsequent weakening of the movement toward Christian unity. In the ecumenical context of the end of the twentieth century, she was regarded as the spokeswoman of an Orthodoxy rooted in its Tradition, but desirous of going as far as possible in its dialogue with other Churches, in order to confront contemporary problems together.

It is difficult to retrace her calendar of ecumenical activities during the 1990s with any accuracy because she was always traveling to different congresses, colloquiums, seminars, and study groups. Although Elisabeth was nearly ninety, she was not afraid to use any means of transportation whatsoever in order to respond to an invitation to give a lecture. Thus, she went frequently to the ecumenical center sponsored by the World Council of Churches at Bossey, in Switzerland; she also regularly spent a week at Lyon, where Fr. Michalon invited her to give lectures at the Catholic Faculty. It was there that she took part, in 1996, in a Marian colloquium on "Mary and Women," where she asserted the Orthodox position vis-à-vis the Mother of God. She had earlier written to Mother Eliane: "I'm critical of a certain type of feminism that would make the Theotokos the prototype of femininity and of a specifically feminine spirituality. That seems to me to be theologically senseless and humiliating for Mary, who represents not only women but also humanity."[34] Far from being a simple model for women, the Virgin is an example for all the faithful who, whether men or women, are called to carry Christ, to give birth to Him spiritually with the same realism with which the Mother of God carried Him physically.

Most of the colloquiums in which she took part—at Assisi, Palermo, the Escorial in Spain, in Greece—were sponsored by the World Council of Churches, within which Elisabeth was very active. She also remained close to the Benedictine monastery of Chevetogne, an offshoot of the convent of Amay-sur-Meuse, where Fr. Lev had been one of the founders and which brought together monks of the Western and Byzantine rites. She was a regular contributor to *Irénikon*, the monastery's prestigious review, which began to publish her articles as early as 1935. Father Emmanuel Lanne, the Benedictine theologian engaged in ecumenical questions, was one of her regular correspondents. On August 23–27, 1982, Elisabeth took part in the annual week of theological studies dedicated to bilateral and multilateral ecumenical dialogues. Her lecture assessed the state of interdenominational relations and then asked what could be done to advance the cause of Christian unity:

It can be said that two different approaches to unity divide those who are in charge of the ecumenical dialogue . . . For some, unity, culminating in sacramental Communion, should be conditioned by total doctrinal agreement. This "all or nothing" method relegates unity to a distant and unforeseeable future. The other more pragmatic approach proposes to proceed "step by step" and with "progressive sympathies," taking into consideration the sensitivities concerned, local situations, and a history that has not been the same for everyone. In the empirical reality, the two approaches coexist and intermingle.[35]

Elisabeth's deep friendship with the Chevetogne community lasted all her life, and she stayed there many times. "I'm part of the furniture there," she would say.[36] The former Lutheran also participated in the Orthodox-Protestant dialogue committee for the Paris region. She faithfully attended the two annual conferences organized by the Protestant Federation of France.

It was through the ecumenical group in Nancy that Elisabeth, when she was in Paris, happened to become involved in a very original project: the founding of an Eastern-rite Carmelite monastery. Through Fr. Berthélemy, who frequented the ecumenical circle, Elisabeth, in 1964, had met the Carmelite sisters of Nancy, where he was the chaplain. Ten years later, she ran across two of these sisters in the parish of the Crypt: Sister Teresa and Sister Eliane. They spoke to her of their plan to found an Eastern-rite Carmelite monastery, in line with the ecumenical openness inaugurated by Vatican II. Elisabeth advised them to contact Fr. Lev Gillet, thinking that his particular vocation would make him sensitive to their project.

Four nuns then went to Saint-Remy, in Burgundy, to found the monastery of Saint Elias. Elisabeth actively supported this new undertaking in the direction of Christian unity through her letters and counsels to her friend, Mother Eliane.

Like you, I don't believe that, in general, individuals going from one denomination to another hasten the hour of Unity. They hurt those whom we have left behind while we have kept the best of them. Sometimes, however, it is impossible to do otherwise because inward honesty is at stake. I would most certainly never dream of inviting you to go over to Orthodoxy! In this field, each person should simply follow his conscience and ask the Holy Spirit for light. Your prayer is certainly good and agreeable to the Lord. But, above all, we must pray for our common conversion to a life in Christ ever more true and profound.[37]

Elisabeth visited the new Carmelite monastery for the first time in 1980. She was invited to give a lecture in the context of the Week of Christian Unity and allowed to choose the theme herself. She proposed two possibilities to Mother Eliane: "*Kenosis* (abasement) and Resurrection in Orthodox Spirituality," or "Renunciation of the World and of Social Service in Orthodox Monastic Spirituality, in Ancient Russia and Today." The two themes represented Elisabeth's ongoing concern: to make known Orthodox spirituality in the Western world by presenting it as able to respond to the questions posed to it—in this case, those of a monastic community who had chosen to withdraw from the world.

To the Carmelites, she developed the first theme, on *kenosis* and resurrection, a subject she had treated at Assisi a few months earlier. She presented the two aspects of the incarnation of Christ: the battered body of the One who humbled Himself to accept the torture of the Cross had its counterpart in the resplendent face of the Resurrected One, the vanquisher of death. These two inseparable visions recapitulated the meaning of the whole work of humanity's salvation by God.

Elisabeth applied these two aspects to the separation between Eastern mysticism, which, with its emphasis on the Resurrection, tended to be blind to the difficulties of the present day, and a Western spirituality, which was more attentive to human suffering but often lost sight of the transcendental dimension of existence. Even though she was aware that this separation corresponded to a reality, Elisabeth warned against the simplistic and reductive character of the stereotype that opposed a Western Church given over to action and an Eastern Church dedicated to contemplation. Both Churches should strive to live the mystery of the Incarnation in its fullness: "The Christian message—and this is the supreme folly, the folly of the Cross—proclaims inseparably the humanity and divinity of Christ, His Cross and His Resurrection, the victory, in apparent weakness, of the Son of God who is also the Son of Man."[38]

The vocation of the Christian was one and the same, whatever might be the tradition he had inherited or the position he occupied in society, whether monk or layman. After reaffirming this principle, Elisabeth returned to her central theme: "In the face of a culture that is deeply secular, where large sectors are hostile or indifferent to the Gospel, in the face of a world threatened by a tidal wave of nihilism where the 'death of God' seems to lead to the death of humanity, what should be, in this day and age, the principal axis of the testimony of a Church both stripped and glorious, in distress but yet strong in its faith in the Risen One?"[39] It is by reconciling the two natures of the Person of Christ—His suffering humanity and His radiant divinity—and it is by taking part actively in the struggle against the sorrows of His time while drawing strength in the contemplation of the Risen Christ, that the reductive vision that defines the Churches as opposites can be overcome. Elisabeth tried to embody the image of a Christian who has integrated *kenosis* and resurrection by taking a stand within a broken world through the strength she derived from her prayer life.

This first visit to the monastery of Saint Elias inaugurated the tradition of annual conferences at Saint-Remy during the Week of Christian Unity. Elisabeth spoke there on other occasions, notably in 1986, the year when the monastery was officially recognized as an Eastern-rite Carmelite convent, when she gave a talk on "The Mother of God in the Orthodox Church." The text was published in *Irénikon* later and then inserted in *The Ministry of Women in the Church*. Another event also brought Elisabeth to Saint-Remy on a regular basis—the feast day of the prophet Elijah on July 20, the eve of her birthday. Whenever she could, she would celebrate this day with the community.

She wholeheartedly supported the project of the Eastern-rite Carmelites, maintaining a correspondence with Mother Eliane for more than thirty years. When, in the 1990s, there was talk of creating a fraternity of Christians associated with the monastery, Elisabeth gave some advice to Mother Eliane:

> Could the Fellowship of St. Alban and St. Sergius serve as a model for the "fraternity" you dream of? The circumstances and the milieu are not quite the same. I have a little brochure in English, which gives a brief history of the Fellowship from 1928 to 1978. I'd like to bring it or even mail it to you. Have you consulted the monks of Chevetogne? As you know, I'm a militant feminist (!), but sometimes men can be useful!

In my opinion, you shouldn't try anything spectacular for the time being: pray, act together as far as this is possible, *speak truthfully*, and do all you can to clear up misunderstandings.[40]

The Saint Elias Fraternity saw the light of day on December 14, 1991, during a round-table discussion in which Elisabeth participated. It defined the objectives of the interdenominational group, which included laypeople and clerics, monks and secular delegates: "The members commit themselves to work for Christian unity through prayer, in charity and evangelical truth, according to their state of life, wherever they find themselves. Every day they are united in the cry of the prophet Elijah: 'You are the Living Lord, O God of Israel, before Whom I stand!'"[41]

Elisabeth was enthused about this initiative, which she saw as a new framework of reconciliation among the Churches in line with the Fellowship of St. Alban and St. Sergius and of the monastery of Chevetogne. After leaving the round-table meeting, she gave Mother Eliane her impressions: "How have you lived this day? I think that it was witness to a fact: your community, as it responds to needs. The needs may be different, but they are real. Persevere in your openness to what God might ask. It is important, *among other things*, that Catholics of the Byzantine rite and Orthodox find a meeting place in your house, a place where they can converse in clarity and charity."[42] The Fraternity began publishing a bulletin entitled *Mikhtav*, to which Elisabeth contributed.

In 1994, contacts established in Romania led to the founding of a daughter house in that country, the Skite of the Holy Cross at Stänceni. Mother Eliane, who had succeeded Mother Elisabeth as the superior of the Saint-Remy convent in 1978, went to live in Romania.

In 2003 the friendship between Elisabeth and the Eastern-rite Carmelites was reinforced by an initiative on the part of the Saint Elias Fraternity: to offer Elisabeth a volume of original essays for her ninety-sixth birthday. A large delegation of the Behr family as well as many friends, such as Fr. Boris Bobrinskoy and Metropolitan Daniel Ciobotea, gathered at Saint-Remy for the event, which took place on July 19–21. Elisabeth was presented with *And You, Follow Me*, a collection of forty articles written in her honor by members of the Saint Elias Fraternity and edited by the Carmelites of Saint-Remy-

Stänceni.[43] And it would be at Saint-Remy that Elisabeth would celebrate her ninety-eighth birthday, a few months before her death.

Even though her very active participation in the ecumenical movement took on an "official" character during the last third of her life, it continued to be the expression of a desire for spontaneous unity, lived in a spirit of camaraderie such as she had experienced within the ecumenical group in Nancy during the war. For Elisabeth, working together was every bit as important as reflecting in common on theological questions.

Her most original denominational route, representative of a whole century marked by the reciprocal rediscovery of the divided Christian traditions, raised the question of what exactly constituted the essence of Christian unity. Having discovered Orthodoxy through the historical circumstances of the Russian émigrés, Elisabeth felt the need to integrate a Tradition that was foreign to her upbringing without, however, rejecting what was positive in Lutheranism.

But she who sometimes defined herself as an "Orthodox Protestant" was not inclined toward syncretism: she was well aware of the points of divergence between the Christian Traditions but, by an intellectual and spiritual effort, she assimilated the heritage of the Eastern Church while remaining open to aspects of other confessions that seemed consistent with what she believed. Since the dilemma of her pastoral experience, which she undertook shortly after she embraced Orthodoxy, Elisabeth had been able to clarify and deepen her own identity to the point of promoting an unequivocal and more lucid Orthodoxy. The youthful idealization of the Eastern Church that she had discovered through the heirs [Russian émigrés] of the Silver Age was succeeded by a realistic vision of the problems confronting contemporary Orthodoxy. In her openness toward other denominations, Elisabeth was ready to pose acts of unity as long as they did not compromise the truth of her faith.

To pray together seemed to her to be one of the principal paths toward true communion, even if this prayer was not without obstacles, as she described when she wrote of her ecumenical experience at Tantur:

> There is a difficulty that is common to all of us: that of putting our own prayer into forms with which we are unfamiliar, which

appear foreign to us. This calls for self-renunciation, a real asceticism. But the effort is worth it. It enables us to discover what is deepest in the *other*, to perceive this word through which God has touched the other's heart; and it is a matter, from our Orthodox point of view, of reformulating it within the totality of *catholic* ecclesial truth.

It is true that I have met Orthodox, especially in Jerusalem, who, in the name of truth and with reference to the ancient canons,[44] hesitate to pray with those whom they consider schismatics or heretics. Such an attitude has the advantage of a certain coherence. But is it not the result of the mechanical application of a rule that might have been justified during determined historical circumstances to a new and very different situation?

We no longer live in the Christian empire. Together we are facing the nihilism of a civilization of non-sense, of despair and of self-destruction. Faced with an apocalyptic threat, should we not take seriously the prayer that Christ addresses to the Father but which is also addressed to us: 'That they all may be one; as You, Father, are in me, and I am in You, that they also may be one in us so that the world may believe that You have sent me" (John 17:21).[45]

This historical urgency of Christian unity, which led to questioning the ancient canons in the light of contemporary needs, was something Elisabeth made incarnate in her life—she who was always at the pivot point of the different traditions in a spirit of understanding and firmness. She was well aware of the obstacles that still needed to be overcome to arrive at communion among all Christians, and she never watered down the reality of differences of faith. If she sometimes participated in a Catholic or Lutheran Eucharist,[46] it was always in a very specific situation where she felt herself called to do so.

In a parish catechetical instruction, Elisabeth explained that "intercommunion cannot be an easy recipe for Church unity. But could it not be envisaged *in certain cases* as a prophetic sign in view of the reconciliation of our Churches, which have become so tragically separated? . . . Without making intercommunion an easy general rule, I could see, in a country such as France, the possibility of practicing intercommunion *in certain circumstances,* if it is done responsibly and in communion with the hierarchy of the Churches, as a gesture of hope."[47]

In another ecumenical event, Elisabeth gave us the example of a Christian who was aware of the consequences of her actions, who took on the specificity of her confessional commitment to the point of dedicating her life to going deeply into its Tradition. Solidly anchored in her own Church, she conversed and acted with other denominations as much as her Orthodoxy would allow her to do so. In this dialogue, she expressed herself with all her customary frankness, sometimes very critically, especially in regard to Roman authority: "Another thing that disturbs me and frustrates me: these interventions of the Vatican on ethical problems such as contraception. According to Orthodox Tradition, the priesthood of the faithful is very important; each Christian judges according to his conscience, with the help of a spiritual director, if necessary, but not according to orders that always come from above."[48] Instead of taking refuge in the comfortable assurance of having discovered the truth in the Eastern Tradition, Elisabeth spared no effort in trying to reconcile the litigious points among the different Christian denominations. She experienced very personally the hopes and blows of the century of ecumenism, and she remains one of the principal figures in this movement.

A Pen in the Service of the Faith

In addition to being a talented speaker, with so much to say that it was sometimes difficult to restrain her, Elisabeth was also very gifted in expressing her theological thoughts in writing. Although her first books and articles established her more as a historian of Russian spirituality, her subsequent works extended her reputation as an authority in other fields besides that of the question of women in the Church. The keen interest she had always taken in the dialogue between the Tradition of the Church and the contemporary world led her to take positions about the political and religious realities of our times through her articles. Her extraordinary longevity gave her a unique historical perspective with which she kept alive the heritage left by numerous religious figures of the twentieth century whom she had known personally.

For an Orthodoxy Engaged in
the Contemporary World

As an Orthodox Christian and a member of French society, Elisabeth felt personally called upon by every interrogation to find an answer that had metaphysical implications. She was well informed on current events and, with the wisdom accumulated in the course of the years, she never lost her temerity, never hesitated to react, to take sides openly in the name of the Gospel. Many of her articles and letters are the result of her taking a stand on a contemporary event. She was especially sensitive to the fate of the Church in Russia, which had helped her so much on her spiritual journey. In 1985 she reacted to an article published by Georges Nivat in the review *Réforme* concerning the situation of the Orthodox Church in the Soviet Union. She tried to complement the perspectives of this Slavicist by adding historical details that nuanced his vision. More specifically, she analyzed the idea of a "religion of the Russian people,"[49] such as had been forged in the course of centuries, and warned against the dangers of this concept that "could just as easily be at the service of a religious nationalism, still very much alive in Russia today."[50]

The celebration of the millennium of the baptism of Russia led Elisabeth to return to the theme of the religious significance of the Russian emigration in an article in *Contacts*, "The Presence of Russian Orthodoxy in the West." She retraced the evolution of the Western conception of Orthodoxy, from the prejudices that had characterized the nineteenth century because of the lack of contacts, to the encounter with Orthodoxy in exile after the Russian Revolution of 1917. Elisabeth then developed the ecclesial consequences of this exile for the Orthodox faithful: awareness of the fundamental nature of Faith, which could not be lived as a mere cultural component, the jurisdictional divisions between the different tendencies, but, above all, the impact of Orthodoxy on Western religious thought. Here, she herself was an example. In her conclusion, she wrote: "Although the Russian emigration, historically speaking, had to die, it brought forth a great deal of fruit, like the grain of wheat in the Gospel. It was the catalyst that brought forth the seed of that Orthodoxy of Western culture that is bursting forth in Europe and America."[51]

Elisabeth did not hesitate to write letters to *Le Monde* when she felt that the newspaper was not giving a correct vision of Orthodox reality; these correctives were sometimes published. In 1992 she exchanged letters with the journalist Henri Tincq, after he published an article concerning the crisis between Orthodox and Catholics over the problem of proselytism.

Three principal areas of religious actuality, related to her specific concerns, occasioned Elisabeth's articles on theology: the question of women, ecumenical relations, and the events of Orthodox life in the West. She was an untiring chronicler of the many meetings in which she participated. With a great deal of assurance, she excelled in summarizing the major themes treated in these meetings as well as in giving her own point of view on the questions being debated. She transmitted news to the Orthodox media of ecumenical events, notably the activities of the World Council of Churches, the CIMADE, and the ACAT, three organizations where she was considered the spokeswoman of Orthodoxy.

Through her writings, she continued to exercise her role as the intermediary between the Eastern and Western Traditions. She contributed many articles to both Catholic and Protestant reviews. Disposed to dialogue and yet rigorous in her positions, she represented, for these reviews, the point of view of the Eastern Tradition of the Church. These writings were characterized by the careful journalistic precision in the information she gave to the reader. She took care to collect the data that would permit her to analyze a problem in its entirety. This scruple about being exhaustive and truthful led her to produce complex articles, sometimes overly meticulous, but she never succumbed to a certain simplification that would have made them more easily readable.

An avid reader herself, she shared her curiosity for the theological publications of her time through numerous lecture notes and critical reviews, most of which appeared in *Contacts*. From the key work of Fr. Lev Gillet, *Orthodox Spirituality*, published in 1946, to the 2003 study of Fr. Boris Bobrinskoy, *The Mystery of the Church*, Elisabeth reviewed about 115 books. In each case, she tried to show what the author contributed to contemporary theological reflection while maintaining the right to express certain reservations of her own.

The whole of her articles and reviews constitutes a vision of the events of religious life in Western Europe during the second half of the twentieth century that is both analytical and engaged. She combined the objectivity of her scholarship with her own particular way of seeing things, not as a simple spectator but as a party to the life of the Church. Far from regarding religious thought as a science, Elisabeth bore witness in her reactions to a Christianity that took on all aspects of human existence, even its most banal daily reality.

Her contributions went beyond the religious field. She participated in a colloquium of the Paul Claudel Society, where she spoke about *Partage de Midi*, a play by Claudel that had marked her profoundly. She analyzed "the transcendent experience of human love," showing a great deal of rigor in her literary approach and, at the same time, an understanding based on what she herself had lived. The theme of the play was, in fact, somewhat similar to the complex relationship between herself and Fr. Lev. Referring to the characters in *Partage de Midi*, Elisabeth asked:

> Is the fulfillment of the human *eros* impossible during our earthly pilgrimage? In regard to this question, Claudel, who was obsessed with the Beyond and lived in constant eschatological tension, would seem, more often than not, to reply "yes" . . . The object of human love appears as a bait used by the Divine Fisherman. But here we have the transfiguration of *Partage de Midi*, where Ysé and Mesa go from death to life, *here and now*. "Lord Love" (as the Monk of the Eastern Church calls Him) grants them, at the end of an earthly banquet that leaves them thirsty, a foretaste of the new wine that they will drink forever in the Kingdom of God. What is impossible for man is possible for the Spirit of God when, breathing upon a man and a woman, He lifts them up toward one another and toward God, in the midst of purifying tears, in a mutual exaltation.[52]

Elisabeth gave us a reading of Claudel that was rooted in her knowledge of the literature of his time and enriched by her theological vision as well as by her personal experience. In her writings, art appeared as the expression of the tension between the failings of life and one's aspiration toward a fullness of existence—a fullness, she again recalled, that could be found in God.

"So many deaths these last few months," Elisabeth lamented in her notebook entry on January 6, 1983. Then, the following summer: "Death of Pierre Pascal on July 1. This death adds to the long list of those who have died over the last months. Paul Fidler also." As the years began to make themselves felt in her frail body, Elisabeth witnessed the passing of many of her mentors and then of her friends. Rather than letting herself be depressed by the sadness of so many deaths, Elisabeth took in hand the longevity that had been given her. Far from treating old age as a burden, she took it on as a radiant grace.

As one of the rare witnesses to an era already consigned to history, she was aware of the treasure that she held in trust. Her precise memory of facts and persons enabled her to hand on her recollections so that future generations might build on the base of a past known to them, open to them as a source of learning. Elisabeth assumed her role of spiritual doyenne with an astonishing enthusiasm. She published many obituary notices, most of them in *Contacts*, where she brought out the personality and message of deceased friends: Paul Fidler and Pierre Pascal in 1983, Dom Olivier Rousseau in 1984, Nadezhda Gorodetsky, a friend from the first Francophile parish, in 1985 . . .

For a long time, Elisabeth had wanted to make known the message of one of the major personalities of the Orthodox Church of the twentieth century, Mother Maria Skobtsova, whom she had known personally. Beginning in 1965, when she published an article in *Contacts*, "For the 20th Anniversary of the Death of Mother Maria Skobtsova," Elisabeth kept adding to her testimonies concerning this nun, who had died in a concentration camp and whose dramatic destiny, which assimilated her to the kenotic Christ, touched her in more ways than one. The desire to work in the world was a preoccupation shared by both women, although through two different ways of life— the one through monasticism, the other through marriage.

Elisabeth found similarities between Mother Maria's attentiveness to her era and Bukharev's choice, even though the historical circumstances did not permit the latter to become "a monk in the city" in the same way that Mother Maria was able to realize this vocation. The exceptional manner in which Mother Maria became involved in the events of her times even led her to the gas chambers of Ravensbrücke, a tragic end that touched Elisabeth deeply, since her maternal family had suffered the same fate.

For Elisabeth, Mother Maria's social work was a diaconal ministry, endorsed de facto by the Church, even if it was not officially recognized as such. It was this ministry of assistance, of counseling, and of support that Elisabeth herself had carried out in her little village in the Vosges. The absence of official ordination was of little importance to her ministry and did not prevent Mother Maria from being inscribed on the list of saints venerated in the Orthodox Church. Elisabeth was very moved when, on Sunday, May 2, 2004, in the cathedral of Saint Alexander Nevsky, she took part in the celebration of the canonization of Saint Maria of Paris and of four of her contemporaries.

Of all those deceased friends whom Elisabeth had known, it was the memory of Fr. Lev that, quite naturally, she cherished most. He was also the one she knew best. She was aware that she was the privileged trustee of her friend's spiritual message. Immediately after his death, she published articles in Orthodox reviews recapitulating Fr. Lev's rich life. She received requests from all sides to give her testimony: "Letter from Fr. Stephanos asking me to prepare a broadcast on L. with Olivier Clément and Michel Evdo[kimov]."[53] She immediately sensed the difficulty in such a testimony insofar as it reawakened in her the memory of their relationship both spiritual and emotional, one difficult to explain: "But how to speak of him without betraying him? And, all of a sudden, the miracle happened. I reread *Time-Bound Ladder*, *Love without Limits*, some pages of this diary. Everything became clear, luminous. The wonderful vision that dwelt within you . . . The flame that burned so much in you . . . Jesus between the two of us, poor sinners, putting His hand on our heads, forgiving, blessing. Love = the ordeal that pierces, that opens to Love without limits. To let one's self be carried, be carried away by an immense wave with the confidence of a little child."[54]

In addition to the numerous references to Fr. Lev that she had noted in her diary, Elisabeth had in her possession a voluminous correspondence as well as unique documents written in the monk's own hand. Above all, she had the memory of more than a half century when her path was never far from that of Fr. Lev, of so many moments of closeness during which she acquired a very intimate knowledge of the strange destiny of her friend. Finally, above and beyond all that was memory, Elisabeth, through her faith in the Risen Christ, could draw upon the experience of a relationship that would endure beyond physical death:

> A dream. L[ev] appearing to me, radiant with joy, holding out his arms. "So it's true. You're not dead?" "Of course . . . but didn't you know?"[55]
>
> A dream. But a dream so intense, bringing a presence, bringing joy, peace, reconciliation. We are, we will be together, fraternally, in the light of God . . . Now all has been overcome. "The old order has passed. Behold, I make all things new."
>
> Powerful words that make the walls of Jericho crumble around our hearts. The earthquake that moves the stone.
>
> Cry out unceasingly: Christ is risen from the dead. *By death* He has conquered death.[56]

It is this message of joy, which transcends all affliction of loss, that Elisabeth wanted to express by retracing Fr. Lev's complex journey.

Thus began a long and meticulous task as she followed the track of her memories. It was a task of research, questioning those who had known Fr. Lev well, going through his archives and correspondence. The fact that there were segments of his life when he was very isolated did not make it easy. Elisabeth visited milieus very different from one another, from Dauphiné, where he was born, to England and Lebanon. Little by little she reconstructed the different stages in her friend's life, notably his younger years, before they met.

In her diary, Elisabeth noted her visit to Fr. Léonide Chrol's sister. Both had known Fr. Lev when he was a young monk who had just entered into communion with the Orthodox Church:

> Searching for time long past: a visit to Olga Chrol, the sister of Fr. Léonide, at Montauban. The example of a life totally dedicated with the greatest simplicity. A life given to God, given to her brother, with

him, so that he might accomplish the task to which he felt himself called . . .

Olga also piously retains her memories of Fr. Lev, the years she lived with him at Saint-Cloud, in the house of Count Ignatieff. In her photo album, I saw the pictures Fr. Lev had given her, others that Léonide probably took at B [?], Antibes, when both were staying at the château of Clauzonnes.[57]

Olga Chrol also had photographs that Fr. Lev had entrusted to her of his younger days:

Louis Gillet, a little boy in a dress like a little girl. Long dark ringlets framing a little face where one sees only the eyes: immense eyes, extraordinarily sparkling, serious, questioning.

Louis as a slender student, wearing glasses. The grandmother in the garden of the old house with the crumbling walls at Valence. At Clauzonnes, in the midst of children, telling a story; at Antibes, with Olga, on the rocks overlooking the sea."[58]

Elisabeth profited from her visits to Mariane and Tony at Formby to reconstruct Fr. Lev's life in England. To the Greenans' dining room, she invited all sorts of different people to share their memories of the monk. The biography also took shape through her many conversations with her daughter and her son-in-law, where she shared with them her questions and doubts and listened to their advice.

Little by little, she began to put some order into the massive quantity of information that she had collected during five years of research, before attacking the writing part. This job, which required isolation and stability, was constantly interrupted by the many theological activities in which she was involved. Nonetheless, she was able to put aside segments of time entirely devoted to the biography: "After a year when I traveled more than usual, I plan to remain quietly at Epinal during July and August so as to make some headway with the biography of Fr. Lev."

Her work over the course of that summer seems to have been fruitful. A month later, she wrote to a friend: "I hope to finish the biography of Fr. Lev within the next few months. In September, as usual, I plan to spend two or three weeks on the Var coast." It was in her refuge on the Mediterranean that Elisabeth found the most favorable conditions for writing. Halfway up a slope, on the road between Saint-Tropez and Gassin, there was a cabin that belonged to some wine-growing friends and that was furnished with a table, a bed, and camping gas [propane]. Elisabeth went there every year. She would install herself under a cork oak tree to work, in spite of the heat. In the afternoon she would pack her towel and sun umbrella into her little car and go down to the beach at Gigaro to swim.

Until her nineties, Elisabeth spent the month of September at Gassin in solitude, which was a time both of study and of vacation and had something to do with her longevity, as she explained to Mother Eliane: "I'm writing from Gassin, a fortified town on the Côte des Maures, where, every year, before winter sets in, I take a little treatment of sun and sea, and this enables me to face winter a bit better."[59]

In spite of her best efforts, her biography of Fr. Lev did not advance as rapidly as she wanted. Summer was really the only time propitious for writing, since the rest of the year was taken up by lectures, trips, and colloquiums. In November 1991 she seemed to have resumed her work on the book with better results: "After a period of stagnation, the biography of Fr. Lev is coming along well and I'm beginning to see the end."[60]

Several years would still pass, however, before this imposing memorial would see the light of day. Elisabeth was constantly called upon: "After a week dedicated to ecumenism (Saturday I gave a talk at the Church of the Holy Spirit [Cath.], on the boulevard Daumesnil), I'm back to the biography of Fr. Lev, which demands a lot of meticulous research and takes up a lot of time."[61] And other, more intimate motives also slowed her down. Elisabeth had moments of doubt and discouragement in the face of the difficulty of the work to be done and its relative unimportance alongside the dramas that were unfolding around her: "In spite of a few problems, my biography is well advanced. But is it good for anything? I ask myself sometimes. The world's absurdity is overwhelming."[62]

Another event pushed the biography into the background: the celebration of the centenary of the birth of Fr. Lev, a task that required a great deal of organizing and that occupied Elisabeth's attention a year in advance. On November 7, 1992, she wrote to Mother Eliane: "The biography is coming along. Some news that might interest you: for the hundredth anniversary of the birth of the 'Monk of the Eastern Church' we are planning a colloquium on Lev Gillet for October 2–3, 1993. We = a little group of friends: Fr. Boris B., Fr. Michel Evdokimov, Olivier and Monique Clément, Nicolas Lossky, myself, etc. We want this celebration to be ecumenical. Chevetogne will be represented. We would be delighted to have you! Organizing all this scares me. But I trust in God's grace."

During the summer of 1993, Elisabeth finally finished. Several months before the colloquium, she started reading the galley proofs, and this allowed her to take an overall, critical view of her work: "I'm afraid of having given birth to a monster: the book is way too long. More than 530 pages plus the illustrations. But whatever might be the deficiencies that I'm aware of, it depicts this great adventure (which is not yet over) of the meeting between Eastern Orthodoxy and Western Christianity during the twentieth century. This is told through the destiny of an exceptional, difficult, somewhat enigmatic and genial man: 'a universalist free-thinker, evangelical and mystical.' That's the subtitle. I'm leaving now for the Midi so as to *finally* get some rest."[63]

The colloquium dedicated to the memory of Fr. Lev took place a few days before the publication of the biography. It presented a first general survey of the important spiritual heritage of Fr. Lev, especially in its pastoral and ecumenical aspects. Elisabeth seemed very satisfied: "The atmosphere at the colloquium was one of great conviviality, spiritual communion, and clarity. The lectures were all on a very high level. We will try to publish them in *Contacts*."[64]

When *A Monk of the Eastern Church* appeared in bookstores a short time later, its thoroughness justified the ten years of work that Elisabeth had put into it. Through the life story of her friend, she introduced the reader to a whole section of the history of the Orthodox Church in the West by making Fr. Lev the incarnation of the mutual rediscovery of the traditions of the East and the West thanks to the Russian émigrés. This volume of more than 600 pages was a reference book on the history of Orthodoxy as well as on that of the ecumenical movement. Elisabeth's precise and polished style gave a very human vision of Fr. Lev, where one could see both her immense admiration for her friend and her lucidity concerning the difficulties of his character.

The biography presented a gallery of the key personalities of the twentieth-century Church and a detailed picture of the interplay of the major events of Western religious history during this period: the founding of Chevetogne, the encyclical *Mortalium animos*, the dialogue between French intellectuals and the Russian émigrés, the beginnings of the ECOF and the Orthodox Fraternity . . . The book was also Elisabeth's own story, which can be read between the lines— something she liked to point out when people suggested that she write her autobiography. The lives of the two friends, in fact, had many similarities, from their discovery of Orthodoxy through the Russian émigrés to their role as intermediaries at the crossroads of two Traditions and their joint efforts to fashion a French expression of the Orthodox Church. Elisabeth's biography of Fr. Lev was, without doubt, her major work, a masterpiece of historical rigor as well as a lively tribute to the friend with whom she had shared so many hopes and hurts.

A Theological and Spiritual Ministry:
The Grande Dame of Western Orthodoxy

On Elisabeth's eightieth birthday in 1987, Olivier Clément had addressed his friend: "Ah, Elisabeth, we have lived the same dream, we have searched for the same nuggets of gold. What counts is that we still have in our hands, held out to others, a few unmerited grains of the precious ore."[65] These two heirs of the exciting postwar period when the Western Orthodox Church was so productive, notably through *Contacts* and the emergence of the Orthodox Fraternity, were very aware of the need to transmit the treasure they had drawn from the great river of Church Tradition to future generations.

With the passage of time, Elisabeth, like Olivier Clément, was led to assume her role of intermediary in a new perspective: that of being a bridge between two different generations, so that the younger ones might benefit from the experience of their elders in their involvement in the Church. As a voice that was recognized and respected, Elisabeth accepted, in spite of her growing fatigue, the role of doyenne, so that she might continue to contribute to making Western Orthodoxy a place where Christ could be found, a task to which she had dedicated her whole life.

A Theological Point of Reference

As an untiring missionary of the Good News, Elisabeth always had her suitcase packed, ready to respond to the requests of the Orthodox and ecumenical worlds when they needed her testimony. In her talks, she would return to the key events in the history of the Church in the West, events in which she had taken part. She most frequently invoked her memories of the time of the founding of the first Francophone parish, in 1929, along with the figure of Fr. Lev Gillet. Two themes corresponded to Elisabeth's fundamental concerns: an Orthodoxy articulated within the framework of Western life, and the need for maximal openness to dialogue, such as practiced by Fr. Lev.

It was especially in the congresses and the meetings organized by the Orthodox Fraternity, of which she remained an active member, that Elisabeth gave her testimony concerning the history of the Orthodox Church in France. Once, in a gathering of the Orthodox Fraternity, where the participants were asked to introduce themselves, Elisabeth seemed to be dozing in her chair. When her turn came, she briskly opened her eyes, surveyed the group with a lively glance, and identified herself: "Elisabeth Behr-Sigel, dinosaur." She then relapsed into her meditative torpor.

As the last witness of the first Orthodox Francophone community in Paris, she was very conscious of her unique position. She found it amusing to see herself still active in a milieu that she had entered seventy-five years ago and where she now collaborated with the grandchildren of her deceased friends. Elisabeth's bent figure, leaning on a cane because of a loss of equilibrium due to a hearing problem, was a familiar sight at all the pan-Orthodox and ecumenical assemblies, where her vitality was legendary. But she felt the weight of her years, which prevented her from being as effective as before. She lamented to Mother Eliane: "I am getting old, I tire more quickly. It takes more effort and much more time now for me to respond to all the requests for articles and lectures. On March 21, I'm going to have a cataract operation."[66] Yet she did not spare herself, aware of her responsibility toward the new generations. This headstrong lady, who was one of the first women in France to study theology at a university, was very sensitive to the importance of a theological education, which she supported.

Elisabeth was still a familiar sight on the hill of the St. Sergius Institute with its tall chestnut trees, even though she no longer had to pass exams there. The professors of St. Sergius were among her closest friends: Fr. Boris Bobrinskoy, who became dean after the death of Fr. Alexis Kniazeff in 1991, Nicolas Lossky, Olivier Clément . . . She took an active part in some of the events there, notably the traditional round table organized by the Paris Fraternity, which was held each year at St. Sergius, on the Sunday of Orthodoxy. In 1995 the theme of the round table was "The Christian in the City." It was an occasion on which to evoke three major figures of twentieth-century Orthodoxy: Elisabeth once again spoke of Fr. Lev Gillet. Hélène Arjakovsky-Klépinine, the daughter of Fr. Dimitri Klepinine, who had replaced Fr. Lev as chaplain of the shelter on the rue de Lourmel and who would be canonized several years later, revived the memory of Mother Maria Skobtsova. Simone Boullenger, a parishioner of Saint Irenaeus at Marseille, spoke on the still-real presence of Fr. Cyrille Argenti, who had died the previous year. Three luminous figures, who, each in his and her own way, spread the power of the love of the Gospel in the heart of urban agitation.

Elisabeth continued to have an international influence, notably through the translation of her works into numerous languages. The St. Andrew Institute in Moscow undertook the Russian translation of her books on the status of women in the Church. These translations had a certain success in Russia.

More and more, however, she felt the effects of her unceasing activity, as she confided to Mother Eliane early in 1998: "Recently I had an 'attack of old age.' My memory is failing. I get tired very quickly. Pray for me: that I may accept getting old. I think of what Jesus said to Peter: "fasten a belt around you and take you where you do not wish to go" (John 21:18). Although without any aspirations to martyrdom, I abandon myself to He who will carry me."[67]

Her minor health problems were a source of anguish because she saw her strength declining to a point where she would no longer be able to continue her activities. The following year, much to her chagrin, she had to give up her car: "I'm doing relatively well but feel the weight of my years. I had a stupid accident with my car, which led to its being taken away from me, most likely for good."[68]

Her little car, racing recklessly across the place de l'Etoile en route to the cathedral on the rue Daru, was well known in Orthodox circles. Elisabeth's small stature hardly allowed her to see the road over the dashboard, and, to passersby, it looked as though the car was without a driver. Her children worried about her successive fender-benders, and it was only with great difficulty that they persuaded her not to drive anymore. Elisabeth wrote to Mother Eliane: "I'm not sick. But I'm growing old, and that's normal: a sickness for which there is no cure. I'm ninety-four years old. Getting around is becoming difficult, even in and around Paris. To obey my children, I no longer drive, and that's a big handicap when you live in the suburbs."[69]

The end of her independence was difficult to accept; she now had to depend on public transportation, which, in Épinay, was not very convenient. Until her death, a couple of devoted friends from the parish, Olga and Jean-Paul Dard, gave her a ride to church on Sunday mornings. Now her letters to Mother Eliane would show her growing concern with her old age: the progressive loss of her independence to the point of becoming totally dependent on others. Her final battle was resigning herself to her physical decline.

Little by little, Elisabeth's family provided more active and indispensable support. Nadine, the only one of her children who lived in the Paris area, came to assist her mother as often as her own numerous grandchildren allowed her to do so. She looked after Elisabeth with great care, attention, and discretion, arranging her trips and the practical details of her life. This task was complicated by the fact that it was not easy to get to Épinay-sur-Seine. Nadine also had to contend with her mother's independent character, which made it difficult for her to accept help. The attempts of her children to persuade her to move some place nearer to them met with a categorical refusal. Nicolas took care of his mother's administrative obligations, while the Greenans accompanied her on her annual vacations and welcomed her at Formby whenever she could go there.

When she felt that a task was beyond her, Elisabeth would sigh wearily: "I wonder why God still keeps me in this life." Nonetheless, she never lost her absolute confidence in Christ, having been tested and fortified through numerous trials. She enjoined Mother Eliane: "Save all your energy. The grace of God works in our weakness."[70]

Far from dedicating herself only to the memories of the past, Elisabeth invested her efforts into supporting new projects that testified to the vitality of the Orthodox Church in the West and had faith in its future. In December 1998 she was invited to give a lecture on the occasion of the inauguration of an institute of theological education in the university city of Cambridge. There, she stressed that "if the multiethnic Orthodox communities that are taking root in the United Kingdom are to remain as sources of spiritual life, then they need clergy and laymen with a solid theological background."[71] This event gave her the opportunity to examine the mission of theological education in the contemporary world. The encounter between the Churches of the East and of the West, through the ecumenical movement characteristic of the twentieth century, implied a new vision of the patristic tradition, a process of dynamic integration that would enable the formulation of a Christian response to the questions of our time.

Elisabeth dwelt on one of the major characteristics of our era: globalization. It was the duty of a believer to promote, on the worldwide scale in which our activities now were taking place, a mode of human relations founded on communion in Christ. A great spiritual master of the twentieth century, Saint Silouan of Athos, called Christ the "total Adam" in order to point out that He recapitulates all of humanity in His person. When the Christian sees the misery of the world on his television screen, he knows that the suffering of each person, which is made so real that it takes an effort to become truly aware of it, is carried by Christ to all the corners of the Earth. This phrase "the total Adam," at once new and inherited from the Church Fathers, with all the theological development it implies, shows that it is possible and necessary to rephrase the patristic definitions so that they might become meaningful for our time.

She also wholeheartedly supported another innovation in the transmission of the Orthodox faith in the West. In Belgium, in 1998, a course in Orthodox religion was added to the official philosophy curriculum offered to the students. In May 2005, at the request of the inspector of Orthodox religion, Christophe D'Aloysio, who was in charge of the country's Francophone schools, Elisabeth went to Belgium to attend a day of teachers' training. This would be one of her last conferences. At the age of nearly ninety-eight, she was not afraid to travel to Brussels to speak to the teachers. She encouraged the participants to ask her questions on anything whatsoever and knew how to put herself at the level of her audience.

The theme of the role of women was a major part of her work there. Even though she had not sought the "reputation as a feminist" that had been given her, as she often indicated in her talks, Elisabeth never hesitated to take a woman's point of view when that was called for. And, going from one colloquium to another, she met many Orthodox women who shared her concerns. Elisabeth was considered a pioneer and a reference point. She maintained very close links with American, Australian, and Lebanese women and supported them in their theological efforts. She was notably in contact with Saint Nina's Quarterly, a group of American Orthodox theologians, as well as with Saint Catherine's Vision, a group founded by Kiriaki FitzGerald, which organized lectures by women and supported publications on this subject. In Elisabeth's wake, these people wanted to reflect upon the ways that women are called today to put their charismas at the service of the Church.

At the end of the spring of 2003, Elisabeth made another trip, this time to the United States. This one took her from New York to Boston to give two lectures on the role of women and also was the occasion to meet Orthodox on the other side of the Atlantic: first at St. Vladimir's Seminary in the context of the annual meeting of the Orthodox Theological Society of America, and then at the Holy Cross Greek Orthodox school of theology in Boston. Her two lectures were very successful and were an opportunity for fruitful exchanges on the role of women.

At St. Vladimir's Seminary, Elisabeth gave the Georges Florovsky Lecture, a yearly highlight of the meeting of the Orthodox Theological Society of America. In memory of the great Russian theologian who had been involved in the dawn of the ecumenical movement, she chose as the theme, "The Problem of the Ordination of Women to a Sacramental Ministry: A Crucial Point in the Ecumenical Dialogue."

This lecture, read with emotion by the president of the Association of American Orthodox Theologians, Susan Ashbrook Harvey, who had translated it prior to the talk, aroused a wave of enthusiasm in the audience.

Elisabeth was very much in demand for exchanges and interviews during her stay in America. Her grandson, Cyril Arnould, discreetly organized the details of her travels, also serving as interpreter and making sure that his grandmother did not wear herself out with all the requests made on her time. It was during this trip that she received a copy of her last book, *Discerning the Signs of the Times.* Published through the instigation of Philip Tamoush, at that time the director of Oakwood Press, it included several of Elisabeth's articles that were key to giving a global vision of her thought. Since, in the meanwhile, Oakwood had been bought by St. Vladimir's Press, the book appeared under the imprint of the American seminary. The choice of texts for the English version and some of the translations were made by Fr. Michael Plekon, a priest of the Orthodox Church in America and a professor at Baruch College, City University of New York, and Elisabeth's friend and longtime correspondent. In the following year, the Cerf publishing house took over the plan of this collection, with the exception of a few chapters, to put out a French equivalent, *Discerner les signes du temps,* which included the original of the texts translated in the American edition.

The preface, written with the help of Lyn Breck, who also translated several of the articles into English, constituted the longest autobiographical sketch that Elisabeth had published during her lifetime. There, she gave a summary of her early years and the route she had followed to arrive at Orthodoxy. The articles that followed were arranged in four parts and could be read as the continuation of her journey in the Orthodox Church. These articles brought together all the essential themes of her thought: first, there was the foundation, the analysis of Scripture and the Tradition of the Church, as it discovers a specifically Russian expression in the theme of the *kenosis,* or emptying of Christ in His incarnation. Next, the great hagiographic figures on whom Elisabeth had focused, such as Alexander Bukharev and Mother Maria Skobtsova. After that, there was the vision of the Church as the place where the message of Christ is constantly made relevant to our contemporary reality. Finally, there was a reflection on the place of women in the Church, the cause with which Elisabeth had become associated.

Discerning the Signs of the Times can be read as a condensed version of Elisabeth's message insofar as it expresses, according to her own specific outlook and according to themes that the reader can easily identify, her concern with the dialogue between Tradition and modernity, as the title of the book indicates. Elisabeth Lacelle, a Canadian theologian, wrote a critical study of this compilation for *Science et Esprit*, the review of the Dominican College of Ottawa.[72] There, she analyzed the themes of the articles with precision, situating them in the evolution of the thinking and life of Elisabeth in order to show how much the book mirrored her vocation of being "a meeting place between the West and the East and an example of ecumenical ecclesial communion."[73]

This collection of Elisabeth's writings allows us to make a few observations on her specific theological method. In spite of her philosophical training, she rarely used a purely speculative approach. She stressed the historical and factual angle and was more interested in ideas made incarnate in the particular destiny of a person or the effective impact of an event than in having recourse to a theoretical construction. She did not give us an abstract vision of the Russian spirituality she cherished so much but rather presented a gallery of personalities, from Saint Seraphim of Sarov to Bukharev, to illustrate the kenotic aspect of this spirituality. Likewise, when she dealt with women in the Church, even though she brought in certain analytical developments, the strength of her argument was in the examples she gave, whether Juliana Lazarevskaya or Mother Maria Skobtsova. Elisabeth's goal was not to formulate new sociological diagrams for modern times, but to make people think about how women could serve the Church in the present day within their parish communities.

Elisabeth did not pretend to put forth innovative theology. Her approach was rather than of a permeation, a deep assimilation of the Tradition of the Church in order to put this tradition into practice in the modern world. She was, above all, a theologian of the Incarnation, centered on the possibility that we might encounter Christ in the midst of our fallen lives. She never ceased to draw the consequences of what Scripture and Tradition tell us about the coming of Christ into our own time and space: each person's capacity to become, here and now, like Christ, to become one Body and one Spirit with Him without losing one's own identity, to become a receptacle of the All-Present One who accepts, through love, the paradoxical limitation that our freedom imposes on Him.

A Look at the Present Situation of Western Orthodoxy

On November 9, 1989, Elisabeth watched the fall of the Berlin Wall on her television screen. She wrote in her notebook:

> Profound emotion: the Berlin wall—the wall of shame—has symbolically crumbled. On television the touching faces of the East Berliners clearing the frontier guard posts. Freedom, freedom . . .
>
> For myself, this represents the end of this long nightmare I've been living since my stay in Berlin in the winter of 1931–32, with the appearance of the Vile Beast [Satan], the assassination of the Germany of philosophers and poets, the assassination of Europe, *my native land.*
>
> Perhaps this will be a new beginning: a Europe extending from the Atlantic to the Ural Mountains . . . I can't keep from crying when I think of everything that has happened, of so many victims . . . and now, hope![74]

This event, which changed the face of Europe, enabled Elisabeth to better realize how much history had happened since her childhood.

The Alsatian girl of Jewish descent, whom the vagaries of life had successively made German, French, and Russian through marriage and sympathies, had developed a sensitivity that was, above all, European, and that was in line with her spirit of openness. The fall of the totalitarian regimes that she had known most of her life and that had caused so much suffering for her family and friends, marked, in her mind, the birth of a new era, which, she hoped, would be characterized by freedom of thought and of faith.

These historical changes affected the life of the Church: a new era had also begun for Orthodoxy. The end of Communism in Eastern

Europe made it possible for religion to be practiced freely in these countries, but, at the same time, the opening of the Iron Curtain brought a new wave of immigrants to the West, who joined the first important communities formed by the Russians who had been driven out by the Bolshevik Revolution, and by the Greeks who had fled the Turkish yoke in Asia Minor or the precarious state of the economy.

This population shift had its effects on the sociological makeup of the Orthodox communities in Western Europe: the newly arrived immigrants sought a liturgical and parish life that corresponded to their own language and their own culture. New parishes of Russians, Serbs, Romanians, and Bulgarians had sprung up, stifling the already existing communities. This intermixture was not without its difficulties. The Orthodox who had become rooted in French culture sometimes considered that the need to start all over again the inculturation process, initiated by their forebears in the 1920s, represented a regression. And not all of them felt that inculturation was necessary: if some of the new emigrants wanted to adapt their religious practices to the realities of the country where they had chosen to settle, then others saw the parish as a haven where they could find once more the culture of their country of origin.

Further, the fact that the Orthodox of Eastern Europe were now free implied a new type of relationship between the emigrants or the descendants of emigrants—Russians, Romanians, Serbs, Bulgarians, etc.—and the Church of their home country. The rapport of affiliation was complex: some Churches reclaimed their status as Mother Church for those Orthodox who had left their native country and were installed in Western Europe, whether they depended on their jurisdiction or not. In the face of multiple dioceses within the same territory, which occasioned struggles for influence, even for power, within the Church, the need for a local Orthodox jurisdiction became acutely evident.

In April 2003 the patriarch of Moscow addressed a letter to the Orthodox of the West. His Holiness Alexis II called for the formation of a local metropolis, under his authority, in order to bring the three branches issued from the Russian émigrés under a sole jurisdiction: the diocese of the parishes of Russian Tradition in Western Europe, which Metropolitan Evlogy had placed, in 1931, under the jurisdiction of the patriarchate of Constantinople; the Russian Church Outside of Russia, which came out of the split of Karlovtsy; and the parishes that had remained under the authority of Moscow during the Communist era.

This letter, made public on the eve of the election of a new archbishop for the exarchate of the Ecumenical Patriarchate, at a moment when this diocese was without a leader, aroused a lot of controversy. An association that called itself Local Orthodoxy of the Russian Tradition (OLTR) was formed in France to support the project. It organized round tables and sent out communiqués aimed at the creation of a local metropolis. But the diocesan council—under the newly elected archbishop, Mgr. Gabriel de Vylder, a Flemish convert from Catholicism—chose to ignore the letter from Moscow and to continue to remain dependent on the Ecumenical Patriarchate. It considered that the appeal of His Holiness Alexis II did not take into account all the grassroots work over the years that tried to integrate Orthodoxy into Western Europe so that it might become a local Church. The discussions were the rage within the Paris circles and on the Internet.

Elisabeth, who had contacts on both sides of the dispute, followed the jurisdictional quarrels very closely. She was alarmed: it seemed to her that the hardening of positions according to ethnic rather than ecclesial perspectives was endangering the work of the preceding generations, who had patiently built up a network among the different communities, united in the same faith to the Risen Christ. She took a firm stand against the patriarch's appeal, which seemed to her to be an attempt to recover the Orthodox living in Western Europe for reasons that were more political than spiritual. In November 2004 she wrote an open letter to the president of the OLTR, Séraphim Rehbinder, expressing her consternation:

> The spokesmen of the OLTR present themselves as the defenders of the ecclesial Tradition through fidelity to their "fathers," who . . . were Russian. But aren't they deluding themselves? By treating as dangerous innovators those who are working for the emergence of Orthodox communities of Western culture, by their petty criticisms, without any kindness or competence, of the liturgical celebrations of Orthodox Francophile parishes . . . are they not confusing the

authentic Tradition—the living transmission of the Word of the Living God—with a paralyzed, repetitive, fearful, and obscurantist traditionalism? By so doing, are they not showing themselves unfaithful to the spirit of those whom we call the Fathers of the Church, the founders of Orthodox theology, as well as to the spirit of these other "fathers" represented, for us, by the great theologians of the Russian first émigrés?[75]

For Elisabeth, the letter from the patriarch of Moscow showed her to what extent the reality of Orthodoxy was lived very differently in Russia and in the West after seventy-five years of evolution on both sides:

> What is striking in this text is the misreading it shows concerning both the sociological and spiritual reality of our local Church, a reality fashioned through a specific historical experience very different from that of the Mother Church: an experience—paid at the price of its poverty—of freedom with respect to the State, of a free and respectful dialogue with Christians from other denominations, of encounters with Orthodox brothers and sisters of different nationalities and cultures, and, in this context, the experience and renewed awareness of the catholicity of the Church. Catholicity understood as unity, as communion of faith, the work of the Holy Spirit, among the diversity of nationalities, languages, and cultures.[76]

The patriarch's project of founding a metropolis in the West under his authority was, in Elisabeth's eyes, unacceptable for reasons that touched on the very definition of the Church:

> It is in the perspective of a Eucharistic ecclesiology, recently rediscovered underneath the dross of scholastic ecclesiologies marked by Western influences, that the plan for a Russian metropolis in Western Europe seems to me to be non-Orthodox, not in conformity with the catholicity of the Church as it is confessed in the symbol of the faith. The Russian patriarch sees the Church as an ecclesial entity unified not by a communion in the faith of the Church but according to an ethnic factor that is becoming weaker as the years pass.[77]

Elisabeth was very worried about the situation of the Church. She participated in some round tables sponsored by the OLTR in order to make known her vision of a local Church, a vision formed through the experiences of her life from her important discovery of Russian spirituality to her promotion of an Orthodoxy of French expression, open to contemporary realities.

She reacted in the same spirit to a crisis in London in 2002 that opposed Metropolitan Anthony of Sourozh to his auxiliary bishop, Hilarion Alfeyev, who had recently arrived from Moscow. The latter had shown a marked preference for the newly arrived Russian émigrés, to the detriment of those Orthodox who had adapted themselves to English culture thanks to a lifelong work of integration on the part of Metropolitan Anthony. Elisabeth followed this conflict through the Greenans, who were active in the parish of Manchester. She gave her opinion in a letter to them:

> I think we should support Metropolitan Anthony's stand. It is he who, over a period of more than fifty years, has built up the diocese of Souroge while maintaining a balance between an unwavering fidelity to the patriarchate of Moscow and the freedom of conscience and adaptation that is indispensable for the Western context. It's not a question of belittling the Russian Church, which has produced saints and continues to do so. It's a matter of inciting its *hierarchy* to recognize and respect the *difference* of a Church of the Diaspora whose vocation is not to be an ethnic ghetto or a "colony" of the patriarchate of Moscow, but rather to become, *little by little*—one must be patient—a local Orthodox Church that unites believers of different ethnic origins and cultures in a same faith. By acting with *intelligence* and *generosity* toward this local Church, the Mother Church does honor to herself. I hope she understands that.[78]

When she spoke of the jurisdictional disputes, Elisabeth's sparkling gaze became veiled over with disappointment; her voice, high-pitched and quavery for lack of breath, took on a tragic tone. The attitude of the Russian Church, which she interpreted as hegemonic, seemed incomprehensible to her. Curled up in her armchair in her apartment in Épinay, she challenged the patriarch of Moscow: "Be proud of this new Orthodoxy that is emerging from the Russian Tradition! Let this child you have begotten grow up!"[79]

She saw Western Orthodoxy as a young plant with its roots deep in the soil of multiple emigrations, which should now blossom, according to its species, under local skies. Elisabeth unceasingly called for the convocation of a great pan-Orthodox meeting to decide the future of the diaspora while hoping that, in the meanwhile, the many conflicts would not become irreparable.

She deplored the institutionalization of the structures of reconciliation that she had seen come into existence: the lack of dynamism in the Orthodox Fraternity, the very insignificant role played by the Assembly of Bishops since it had assumed an official status. She who had been part of the great creative movements of the 1970s sometimes thought that what her generation had accomplished had been swept away by a regressive attitude on the part of the different Orthodox communities. What had happened to this conciliarity, this communion of love among the Churches, which had aroused such enthusiasm in the young Elisabeth when she first read Khomiakov?

A Pastoral Role

Although she was now bent over a cane and no longer perched on a bicycle, as she had been during her days at Villé-Climont, it was still the same ministry that Elisabeth continued to exercise, whether as an auxiliary pastor or as a lay member of an Orthodox community. The style was the same. To visit people in need or open one's door to them, give advice, suggest readings, make recommendations, provide support, encourage: although she needed a hearing aid, she still turned an attentive ear to anyone's problems.

Many members of the Holy Trinity parish sought her opinion. She also exercised her ministry through her letters. She maintained an extensive personal correspondence with people the world over. She would take an interest in the concerns of her correspondents, suggest solutions to their problems, and encourage them to persevere in the faith and to place their entire lives in God's hands.

If, at times, she seemed lost in intellectual spheres and was not very accessible, she nonetheless remained sensitive to life's practical details. When the members of a family within the Orthodox Fraternity had to move, for business reasons, to a city where they did not know anyone, Elisabeth, who was not particularly close to the family, phoned them on Christmas Day to wish them a joyous feast and to tell them that she was supporting them during this period of change.

Elisabeth was present to others in a way that was discreet, loving, and also direct. Her vivacity did not diminish as time went on. She remained frank and incisive in her opinions; she always said what she thought. Often this tireless speaker would focus on a subject and from there branch off into many digressions in a breathless voice; then, suddenly, in the middle of a flood of words, she would come out, forcefully and rapidly, with a phrase that resonated as if it were a personal appeal to the listener. She would sometimes get lost in the meanderings of her own reflections, but she would always return to the person whom she was addressing. She took an interest, asked questions, and gave her opinions with disconcerting accuracy.

The pastoral and spiritual responsibility that Elisabeth assumed quite naturally illustrated the fundamental intuition that oriented her overall theological thoughts and her life: the royal priesthood of each Christian. The apostle Peter spoke of this when he affirmed, "You are a chosen people, a royal priesthood, a holy nation."[80] This reminds us that all believers have the same responsibility, whatever might be their personality or role within the ecclesial community: become receptive to Christ. The concept of the royal priesthood for each baptized Christian is sometimes overshadowed by a clericalized vision of the Church, which tends to compartmentalize ecclesial functions, often centering them in the hands of the priest and making the laity simple observers of a law. Elisabeth rose up against such a concept of the Church, which generated tensions and struggles for power.

As a woman of dialogue, conciliatory to an extreme, sometimes trying to unite, at any cost, two diametrically opposed realities, Elisabeth worked throughout her life to narrow the split between clergy and laity. She also endeavored to reconcile monks and secular priests by emphasizing their fundamental complementarity, whereas the tendency was to oppose them according to a hierarchy that implied that one path of sanctification was superior to the other. She asked that the originality of the ministry of each person, man or woman, be

recognized in our common journey toward a unique goal, the Kingdom of God. As Saint Paul put it, "For you are all the children of God
through faith in Christ Jesus, for as many of you as have been baptized into Christ have put on Christ. There is neither Jew nor Greek,
neither slave nor free, neither male nor female, for you are all one in
Christ Jesus."[81]

Babou and Her Cosmopolitan Descendants

The stately and solemn demeanor of a speaker at international theological congresses was hardly characteristic of Elisabeth in her daily
life. When one pushed open the door of her little apartment in
Épinay—usually out of breath after climbing ten flights of stairs because the elevator was not working—Elisabeth showed herself to be,
above all, a grandmother or Babou, as she was affectionately called by
her family. She was, in fact, very attentive to each one of her descendants. She liked nothing better than to talk about her grandchildren
and great-grandchildren, while commenting on the photographs of
family events that hung on the walls. Unless someone turned the
conversation to an important ecclesial topic, she would go on and on
about her family.

She was very proud of the cosmopolitan character that her nine
grandsons and one granddaughter had brought to the family by mar-
rying people of other nationalities: English, German, American,
Guinean, Armenian-Russian. The palette of colors and the variety of
languages represented by her twenty-five great-grandchildren was her
greatest satisfaction and was very much in line with the atmosphere
of openness in which she herself had been raised.

Elisabeth's personality had not predisposed her to be a doting
grandmother. She maintained a relationship with her descendants
that was both affectionate and exacting. She asked them about their
activities, their surroundings, their aspirations. She exhorted and encouraged them. She supported each one of them with unbending
firmness.

Even in her extreme old age, she was particularly attentive to her
grandson Marc, who suffered from mental problems. The moments

of anxiety that she herself had experienced made her a counselor and confidante for the Greenans in their times of difficulty. When she was at Formby, Elisabeth, one of the few persons whom Marc would receive, spent long hours with her grandson. When every other relationship in the outside world became unbearable for him, Marc would call for his Babou. On several occasions, he stayed with her at Épinay. During her last years, her correspondence was marked by her constant concern for her grandson, whom she entrusted to the prayers of her friends. Earlier, in a letter to Mother Eliane, she had written: "I continue to commend Marc and his parents to your prayers. He's doing better but has his ups and downs. People like him have a very hard time finding a place in our society, which is so competitive and cruel to the weak."[82]

Babou carried the weight of the infirmities and troubles of her numerous descendants on her fragile shoulders. For them, she was an ancestor, both venerable and close, who knew how to share their joys and support them in times of adversity. Nothing made her eyes shine more brightly than to talk about the performance of Richard Strauss's *Arabella* at the Châtelet theatre, where she saw her grandson Andrew Greenan, who had become an international soloist.

Not all of Elisabeth's frequent trips were related to theology. She visited her grandchildren often—even those far away, such as Etienne Arnould and his family, whom Babou went to see when they were living in the Ivory Coast. One or another of her grandchildren accompanied her during her summer outings, notably to Gassin and Alsace. For many years she spent Christmas with the Greenans at Formby, where she made friends among their English neighbors. She could often be found on the dunes surrounded by a crowd of children whom she was taking on a walk. When great-grandchildren began to arrive, Elisabeth stayed with the Arnoulds and the Behrs in Paris during the winter holidays. She liked nothing better than to combine a conference with a family reunion; the itineraries of her trips were planned in such a way as to integrate the different interests that constituted her life.

Her trip to Cambridge in 1998 for the inaugural conference of the institute of theology was an example of the way in which the family cooperated to allow her to continue her activities while she visited them. Nadine packed her suitcase and drove her to the airport. The Greenans picked her up at Manchester, and Elisabeth was able to relax at their home in Formby for several days before they drove her to Cambridge. After the conference, which Mariane and Tony attended, they took Elisabeth to Lewes where, to her great delight, she found herself with her English great-grandchildren. The theologian who, several hours previously, had spoken of what was at stake in twentieth-century theological education, became once more the affectionate Babou.

For Elisabeth's ninetieth birthday, a big family reunion was organized at Saint-Prix, at a parish in the suburbs of Paris. She had the joy of being surrounded by nearly all of her descendants as well as her close friends. A photograph of this event shows a radiant great-grandmother, enthroned in the middle of a crowd of children, one of whom she holds in her frail arms. For this birthday, the family had offered her a trip to a place of her own choosing. She opted for Russia. She went the following year, in 1998, accompanied by the Greenans, for an emotional visit during which she got to know some of André's family. This was her way of reaffirming her attachment to her husband's country, which had given her so much on both the ecclesial and spiritual levels.

Elisabeth always maintained a link between the different aspects of her life, without establishing boundaries between her theological activities and her family responsibilities. Her work and thinking were elaborated in the course of a permanent dialogue with her family, especially during her stays at Formby when she was working on the biography of Fr. Lev or when she had to give a lecture in English. She was glad to see her daughter Nadine take on the organization of women's meetings, and her son Nicolas participate in the Orthodox Fraternity and the life of Our Lady Joy of the Afflicted parish, while Mariane and her husband played an essential role in their parish in Manchester. The grandsons took up the torch: Antoine Arnould was the warden of Our-Lady Joy of the Afflicted for nearly fifteen years, and Gabriel Behr was very active in the Orthodox youth movement in France.

Elisabeth was the model of a complete woman who lived her convictions down to the smallest details of her professional or family life.

Her personal integrity was manifested in her availability to others in her daily life, in the way she addressed every person along her way, without prejudice and with a genuine interest, whether that person was a bishop or a next-door neighbor.

The Calm Haven

"And the same day, when evening came, Jesus said to them, 'Let us go over to the other side'" (Mark 4:35). If Elisabeth's intellectual lucidity remained intact, her body began to feel the wear and tear of a life that had been long and intense. "I suffer from a cardiac deficiency," she wrote in a letter to Mother Eliane, near the end of 2004. "After almost a century of good and loyal service, my old heart is tired."[83]

On the evening of December 31, Elisabeth was hospitalized after blood tests aroused fears of a pulmonary embolism. She very angrily went through an battery of tests that did not reveal anything abnormal. When she returned home, she continued to climb up and down the ten flights of stairs to get her mail when the elevator was out of service. These breakdowns accentuated Elisabeth's feelings of being isolated. She compared her life at Épinay when the elevator was not working to that of Saint Simeon the Stylite! It made her realize how physically weak she had become.

In her work too, she felt the weight of her years: she was frustrated when she could not complete on time promised texts, confused by the different versions of articles when she reread them, and overwhelmed by her too-numerous archives. This did not prevent her from organizing, in March 2005, a round table at the St. Sergius Institute on the twenty-fifth anniversary of the death of Fr. Lev. At the age of ninety-eight, she brought together different theologians and asked them to witness to the heritage of "the Monk of the Eastern Church." For her part, she spoke of the founding of the first Francophone parish in Paris in the 1930s and its prophetic character. During this event, she gave an impressive show of energy and vitality in her desire to transmit Fr. Lev's message, which seemed to her, and rightly so, to be very relevant to the contemporary Church.

The doyenne of Orthodoxy in France went through her usual routine during the summer of 2005. She was faithful to her annual visits: the Eastern-rite Carmelites for the feast day of Saint Elias and, in August, Mayenne, where she was reunited with a part of her family on the grand estate of the Bornants.

In September, Elisabeth went with Mariane and Tony to the Peloponnesus, where she was still able to go for a swim. The summer of 1997 was the last she spent at Gassin. Thereafter, the Greenans took her to Greece with them every year in place of her usual solitary stay on the Var coast, which had become too risky due to her advanced age. After stays at Parga, in Epireus, and then on the isle of Kos, Elisabeth settled in the little village of Stupa, on the southern tip of the Peloponnesus, where she was affectionately received and soon became a familiar sight. She frequented the *gelateria* on the harbor, not far from the studio, which she had to herself. The Greenans were lodged in the building next door. In the mornings, Elisabeth and her daughter would go to the beach, where the vacationers would keep a watchful eye on the nearly hundred-year-old lady when she decided to head for the water. Every evening, she and her children enjoyed their customary Nescafé on the terrace of the studio looking out into the Greek night.

In the month of September, Elisabeth returned to Épinay, radiant and refreshed, even though she complained about no longer being able to swim more than a few strokes in the Mediterranean. Her work awaited her: she had to write an article on the relationship between Fr. Lev and the St. Sergius Institute. She still hoped to finish a study she had promised to the Carmelites of Saint Elias for a compilation in honor of Metropolitan Emilianos Timiadis. She also had to prepare for a lecture on Fr. Lev to be given at Oxford in early November for the anniversary of the Fellowship of St. Alban and St. Sergius. This last event was to take place at almost the same time as the twelfth congress of the Orthodox Fraternity, which had as its theme the passage from the Apocalypse, "Behold, I make all things new"—a passage that was decisive in the relationship between Elisabeth and Fr. Lev. She did not attend this congress, which was to take place in Belgium, because of her commitment to the event in England.

At the beginning of November, she arrived, tired and anxious, at the Greenans' place in Formby: always so conscientious, she still had not prepared her talk on the bonds of Fr. Lev with the Fellowship. The

Greenans reassured her that she would have no trouble speaking on a subject with which she was so familiar. Then, one morning, Elisabeth, who was hard of hearing, leaned over the staircase in the cottage, trying to understand what her daughter was saying. She lost her balance, toppled down the stairs, and landed unconscious on the floor. Mariane rushed to take her mother in her arms, fearing the worst and already wondering how to break the news to Nadine and Nicolas. But Elisabeth opened one eye and declared, "I could do with a glass of port to help me get over this." She knew that she had fallen but really did not know what had happened to her. She complained of dull pains in her chest and arms. A physician was called, who said that there were no internal injuries, only some little bruises and contusions. However, she had to have complete rest. It was with great chagrin that she was obliged to give up her lecture on Fr. Lev and stay in bed at the Greenans.

Even while confined to bed, Elisabeth continued to be active: first, she wrote a text on Fr. Lev to be read in her name at the Fellowship congress. She insisted on the profound spiritual communion between the monk and Metropolitan Anthony Bloom, something she seemed anxious to express during these final days at Formby. Through the Internet, her son-in-law found a copy of Fr. Lev's out-of-print book on Christian-Jewish dialogue, *Communion in the Messiah*. Elisabeth was so enthused that she immediately began to write a review of it for *Contacts* in her shaky handwriting, which stretched out over the pages of her stack of white paper without taking the time to form letters. She ardently desired to make this work of Fr. Lev known and hoped to see it translated into French.

She also spent long hours in discussions with her daughter, especially about an Iranian couple from the Manchester parish, threatened with expulsion, who risked the death penalty if they returned to their native country because they had converted to Orthodoxy. Mariane went to court to testify that they were members of her parish. Elisabeth took their situation very much to heart and wrote a list of arguments that she hoped would convince the judges. The couple was eventually allowed to stay in England.

During her stays at Formby, Elisabeth had become a familiar figure in the neighborhood, and she spent some of her convalescence with an English friend who would come to visit her. Amid all the pillows, she always remained attentive to others. She occasionally left her room to take her meals with Mariane and Tony along with her grandson André, who had come to Formby for three days to see his grandmother. In the evening she lingered to carry on long discussions over her cup of Nescafé.

On Sunday, the Greenans went, as usual, to their parish in Manchester where they were in charge of the choir. Elisabeth promised to stay in bed. Mariane carefully put everything her mother would need within her reach so that she would have to move as little as possible. When her daughter returned, Elisabeth sheepishly told her: "I have something to confess. You forgot the bread. I went downstairs to go to the kitchen . . ." But there was a spark of pride in the old lady's eyes, for her spunk had gotten the better of those dangerous stairs.

"It's time for me to pass over to the other side, as my friend Fr. Lev used to say," was a phrase she kept repeating during those days of forced immobility. She told Mariane to "telephone Nadine and Nicolas and tell them that I don't want to die in England." After ten days of complete rest, it was decided that Elisabeth would return to Épinay.

A few days before her departure, on Monday, November 21, Mariane took her for a walk at Southport, a seaside resort a few miles from Formby. "This dear old Southport," as Elisabeth called it, was on the sea, its avenues lined with awnings harboring kiosks and galleries, giving it a quaint charm. The atmosphere reminded her of the thermal spas of Central Europe and brought back memories of her trips as a child through the spas of Bohemia when she went to visit her family. On the following Wednesday, Mariane, encouraged by this little excursion, took her to the airport.

The day after Elisabeth returned to Épinay, Nadine came accompanied by two visitors, who wanted to question her about her memories of Metropolitan Anthony Bloom. She answered the telephone, spoke to her son Nicolas, planned some meetings, and went to bed, taking the newspaper *La Croix,* which had just arrived in her mailbox, for her customary bedtime reading.

Two days later, on the morning of Saturday, November 26, the Kabuli cleaning woman, whom Elisabeth appreciated both because of her devotion and because she was aware of Saint Augustine's Carthaginian origins, found her still in bed, with the newspaper lying at its foot. Her body was already cold. Since there had been no sign of life in the apartment during the day on Friday, the twenty-fifth, the physician concluded that she had died during the night of November 24–25. Nevertheless, her death was officially registered as having taken place on Saturday, the twenty-sixth. The news quickly spread among her three children.

When Mariane arrived at Épinay, one of the first objects that Nadine showed her was a little lacquered Russian box on which was painted a scene of a river flowing among silver birch trees. On the bank were two boats tied up at the foot of a golden-domed church. Elisabeth, too, had finally passed over to the other bank, to the calm haven, where so many friends had already preceded her.

Her body remained in the Épinay apartment for several days, watched over by those who had been close to her, until it was placed in a coffin during a ceremony celebrated by Fr. Boris Bobrinskoy on the following Tuesday. The coffin was then taken to the Holy Trinity parish. The next day, family and friends crowded into the cathedral to take part in the funeral service in the Crypt on November 30, the feast day of Saint Andrew.

Her grandchildren then carried the frail remains of the doyenne of Western Orthodoxy along the paths of the Russian cemetery of Sainte-Geneviève-des-Bois, accompanied by the Trisagion hymn, "Holy God, Holy Mighty, Holy Immortal, have mercy on us" and the wisps of breath from the singers on that cold day.

A crowd of children accompanied the cortege, picking their way among the tombstones in order to escort their Babou to the open grave. The youngest held the hands of the older ones. With them all intertwined in front of the coffin, which soon disappeared into the depths of the earth, a passage of Péguy came to mind, of which Elisabeth and Fr. Lev had been very fond—where Hope is depicted as a little girl holding the hand of her two older sisters, Faith and Charity. Father Lev often alluded to this passage in his letters, and Elisabeth underlined it in her copy of *The Porch of the Mystery of the Second Virtue*:

What astonishes me the most, says God, is Hope.
And I still can't quite get over it.

This little Hope that seems to be nothing at all.
This little girl Hope.
Immortal.

For my three virtues, says God,
The three virtues my creatures,
My daughters, my children,
Are themselves like my other creatures,
Of the race of men.

Faith is a faithful spouse,
Charity is a mother,
An ardent mother, all heart,
Or like an older sister who is like a mother.
Hope is an insignificant little girl

Born on Christmas day of last year . . .
But it is this little girl who will cavort across the worlds,
This insignificant little girl,
She alone, carrying the others, will cross the worlds of yore

As the star that led the Three Kings from the depths of the East
Toward the cradle of my son,
Thus like a trembling flame
Will she alone lead the virtues and the worlds.
A flame will pierce the eternal shadows.

This was the flame of hope, kindled at the dawn of the Resurrection, when three women hastened in the cold of the soon-ending night toward the empty tomb.

Epilogue

As the elevator goes up to the tenth floor, I feel a knot in my throat. I'm recalling all those Saturdays when Elisabeth would greet me at the door of her apartment, with a twinkle in her eye and with her arms wide open: "Oh, there you are! Come in, come in!" I'm thinking of that very first Saturday when I timidly entered her apartment in Épinay and was impressed by the bookshelves and the photographs and the porcelain from Alsace. Above all, I was fascinated by the diminutive mistress of the house, who went toddling off to the kitchen to pour me a glass of port.

Elisabeth's high-pitched voice, a bit shaky from breathing difficulties, transports me far from Épinay to the suburb of Strasbourg, where she was born nearly a century ago. "I remember my childhood very well." Thus did she begin on that first Saturday, while I struggled

Editor's note: Olga Lossky presented these reminiscences of her Saturday lunches with Elisabeth at a conference in her memory at the St. Sergius Theological Institute in Paris on June 23, 2007. On July 21, Elisabeth would have been one hundred years old. With Olga Lossky's permission, her talk, which pulls together this whole biography, serves as an epilogue here. It appeared in the French Orthodox journal *Contacts*, no. 220 (October–December 2007): 498–502.

to grasp the fact that this fragile old lady, who barely occupied half of her armchair, had heard the declaration of the outbreak of hostilities in the First World War. Figures long since disappeared lit up her sparkling eyes: her grandfather, Eugene, who had left his studies to become a pastor and instead became an officer: "he had lost his faith..."; her mother, Emma, who died when Elisabeth was only twenty years old; her father, Charles, with whom she had a very tender relationship. And then the encounter with the "young Russians" of Paris, her immersion in the exciting intellectual circles of the 1930s...

During these lunches, Elisabeth would evoke the different stages of her life, some exhilarating, some painful. She often lingered on the period of the Second World War, on her daily struggle for survival, in Nancy, in the company of her husband. She returned several times to the episode of the roundup of the Jews and seemed to relive it each time she spoke of it; the little grocery store at the end of the street, the German truck parked in front of it, the passersby gathering around it, the family dragged out of the shop and Elisabeth's question on seeing an old man molested by the soldiers—a question that expressed all her anguish in the face of the tragedy she was witnessing: "Should I throw myself under the truck?"

In the small apartment in Épinay, time marched on. Sometimes, Elisabeth, exasperated by her awkwardness when she tried to pull out the papers she was seeking, would rise to dig up a file in a cupboard. From her stack of archives she would come up with an article scribbled in her impulsive handwriting, a photograph accompanied by a commentary on the people therein, sometimes a dog-eared review or book with a dedication by the author. Often, with a weary wave of her hand, she would point to the piles of paper and the shelves sagging under their weight: "All that should be sorted out. I'm no longer up to it." Every time I proposed that the two of us tackle the job, she would shrug: "Some other day..."

Between Saturdays, I would listen to the tapes I had recorded, sort out her recollections, take note of topics that should be explored more in depth. Elisabeth turned out to be an inexhaustible mine of information. Pastor Marc Boegner, Nicolas Berdiaev, Fr. Sergius Bulgakov, Mother Maria Skobtsova, Fr. Lev Gillet, Vladimir Lossky, Paul Evdokimov—she had vivid memories of all these personalities, peppered with anecdotes that made them very human and accessible. The Fédé, the first Francophone parish in Paris, the Fellowship of St. Alban and St. Sergius, the Word Council of Churches, the ACAT—so many enterprises in which she participated, lived out her faith, and communicated it to the world! The "grande dame of Western Orthodoxy" was also anchored in the present and liked to evoke current political and religious matters, but always with the underlying question: "What can be done *today* to bear witness to the reality of our faith?" She was saddened by the dissensions within the Church, enthusiastic about new initiatives that she wanted to support wholeheartedly, and emotional when she talked about her numerous descendants. Sometimes a cloud passed over her face when she spoke of friends who were no longer of this earth: "I really ask myself why God still keeps me here. My passage to the other side is long overdue." The fact that she was the friend of my great-great-grandfather caused her to laugh, but it was a laugh tinged with melancholy.

When I left Elisabeth, at the end of the afternoon, with my head filled with images of bygone times and my heart warmed by our friendship, it seemed clear to me why, at the age of ninety-eight, she still remained so attentive to the contemporary world. Just a single look from those sparkling eyes was enough to make you believe in life. She would accompany me to the landing and give me a warm hug: "Don't wait too long before you come back!" When the elevator doors closed, I would carry away the image of her frail frame leaning against her door—an image of both fragility and energy.

This Saturday, when the elevator stops at the tenth floor, the doors open onto an empty landing. Elisabeth is not waiting for me on the threshold of her apartment. Gabriel, her grandson, had phoned that morning while I was getting my tape recorder and my notes ready before leaving to have lunch with her: "Babou has died." This news, although foreseen, astonishes me. We all had become so accustomed to see time sparing Elisabeth Behr-Sigel that we would not have been surprised to see her reach the age of the Old Testament patriarchs. And here it is that she has left us suddenly, without any signs of sickness or decline.

I'm apprehensive as I enter the little room where the members of her family have gathered. Elisabeth is lying in the next room. I cast an incredulous glance at her body wrapped up in a green bedspread, at her face wearing a severe expression, her eyes closed, her hair bundled up behind her. When I kiss her, her forehead is as cold as a piece of stone. I cannot bring myself to believe that this is the same perky little lady who, two weeks ago, was chatting with so much feeling.

After a snack, accompanied by a bottle of rosé that Elisabeth had put aside, we organize the night vigil. Four of us will remain in the apartment. In a cupboard, Gabriel finds the folding cot he had slept on as a child when he came to see his Babou. Mattresses are stretched along the shelves with their venerable books.

We take turns reading psalms in the presence of Elisabeth's body, frozen in death. As the night is getting on, a strong odor of candle wax pervades the room. The flame of the candle throws long shadows on the furniture. A few hours earlier, Fr. Alexis Struve had told us that "it is very important to accompany the deceased. I don't know why, but it is very important to be there."

I softly recite the verses of a psalm, often looking over to the bed to convince myself of the reality of her death. More and more, I feel the weight of fatigue, my eyelids are heavy; heavy, too, is the odor, my unease at those large fantastic shadows, my companions sleeping in the next room. As I try to focus my benumbed mind on the words of the psalm, which I'm beginning to recite more and more indistinctly, it dawns on me that these words are the very expression of Elisabeth's soul, a cry to God. I've lost track of the hours and psalms. I focus on Psalm 119, where the psalmist pours forth his thirst for the path that leads to God. "The law of your mouth is better to me than thousands of gold and silver pieces . . . My soul clings to the dust, revive me according to your word" (vv. 72, 25)

Before this flesh that is slowly returning to dust, there can no longer exist any doubt. Faith is a hope that goes against all appearances. In spite of this body, already a mere shadow of itself, I'm certain that Elisabeth continues to exist somewhere, that she is near to Christ, there where the fullness of life is found. Faith in the resurrection might seem to be a foolish wager, yet without it the sight of a dead person would be hard to bear.

A while later, rummaging through Elisabeth's papers, I will find this account of a dream she had when her friend, Fr. Lev Gillet, died:

A dream. L[ev] appearing to me, radiant with joy, holding out his arms. "So it's true. You're not dead?" "Of course . . . but didn't you know?" A dream. But a dream so intense, conveying a presence, conveying joy, peace, reconciliation. We are, we will be together, fraternally, in the light of God.

The psalm is finished, and I grope my way into the adjoining room to shake the shoulder of my replacement at the vigil before collapsing on the mattress myself. Early Sunday morning, while the light of dawn floods through its large windows, I leave the apartment without any nostalgia for its walls lined with memories. I am going to the liturgy certain of Elisabeth's continual presence and knowing that she is alive in the glorious vision of the Risen Christ.

Notes

Chapter 1. The Encounters of the Formative Years, 1907–1932

1. Elisabeth Behr-Sigel (hereafter EBS), unpublished autobiographical fragments found in her archives.

2. Ibid.

3. Ibid.

4. Ibid.

5. EBS, "Comment je suis rentrée dans la communion de l'Eglise orthodoxe," 1992.

6. EBS, authobiographical fragments.

7. For an account of the history of FUACE, see Suzanne de Dietrich, *Cinquante ans d'histoires, la Fédération universelle des Associations chrétiennes d'étudiants (1895–1945)* (Paris: Ed. du Semeur, 1946).

8. EBS, autobiographical fragments.

9. Ibid.

10. Letter of E. Levinas to EBS, March 3, 1931.

11. EBS, autobiographical fragments.

12. Ibid.

13. This painting is reproduced in the gallery of this volume.

14. A. S. Khomiakov, quoted by Antoine Gratieux in *Khomiakov et le mouvement slavophile* (Paris: Éd. du Cerf, 1939), 112.

15. Ibid.

16. Ibid., 118.

17. EBS, "Comment je suis rentrée."

18. Ibid.

19. Ibid.

20. EBS, interview on January 15, 2005.

21. "Grands témoins: Elisabeth Behr-Sigel," interview with Catherine Aubé-Elie, *Unité des chrétiens* 137 (January 2003): 32.

22. EBS, *Discerning the Signs of the Times* (Crestwood, NY: St. Vladimir's Seminary Press, 2001), 6.

23. EBS, *Discerner les signes du temps* (Paris: Éd. du Cerf, 2002), 15.

24. EBS, *Lev Gillet, "A Monk of the Eastern Church"* (London: Fellowship of St. Alban and St. Sergius, 1999), 16.

25. Metropolitan Evlogy, *Le Chemin de ma vie* (Paris: Presses Saint-Serge, 2005), 445.

26. On the Confraternity of St. Photius, see *A Monk of the Eastern Church*, 146ff.

27. Metropolitan Evlogy, *Le Chemin de ma vie*, 445.

28. A. Arjakovsky, *La Genération des penseurs religieux de l'émigration russe* (Kiev and Paris: L'Esprit et la Lettre, 2002), 195.

29. EBS, autobiographical fragments.

30. "Grands Témoins: Elisabeth Behr-Sigel," 32.

31. The reasons for this crisis and its development can be found in *Un moine de l'église d'Orient, Le père Lev Gillet* (Paris: Éd. du Cerf, 1993), 206. See also Arjakovsky, *La Genération*, 265ff.; and Metropolitan Evlogy, *Le Chemin de ma vie*, 499-521.

32. Letter of Fr. Lev Gillet to EBS, June 5, 1931, cited by EBS in *Un moine*, 159.

33. Ibid., May 7, 1931.

34. EBS, *Un moine*, 160.

35. Letter of Fr. Lev Gillet to EBS, October 12, 1931.

36. Letter of EBS to Mariana Behr, September 21, 1931.

37. Letter of EBS to André Behr, November 10, 1931.

38. Letter of Fr. Lev Gillet to EBS, 1931, no precise date.

39. Later published as EBS, *Prière et sainteté dans l'Eglise russe* (Paris: Éd. du Cerf, 1950), 20.

40. Ibid., 38.

41. Ibid., 21.

42. Letter of EBS to André Behr, February 4, 1932.

43. Ibid., February 11, 1932.

44. "Ecclesial," as it is used here, signifies that which concerns the Church as a whole.

45. Letter of EBS to André Behr, February 18, 1932.

46. Ibid.

47. EBS, "Rapport sur mon séjour en Allemagne. Novembre 1931–février 1932," unedited archives.

48. Letter of EBS to André Behr, November 10, 1931.

49. EBS, "Rapport sur mon séjour en Allemagne."

50. Letter of EBS to André Behr, February 23, 1932.

51. Ibid., February 11, 1932.

52. *Schutzpolizei*, literally "protection police."

53. EBS, "Rapport sur mon séjour en Allemagne."

54. EBS, interview on January 15, 2005.

55. Letter of EBS to André Behr, January 10, 1932.

56. Ibid., December 21, 1931.

57. Ibid., February 23, 1932.

58. Ibid., February 28, 1932.

59. Ibid., February 25, 1932.

60. "Grands Témoins: Elisabeth Behr-Sigel," 32.

61. Letter of EBS to André Behr, July 1, 1932.

62. Ibid., August 3, 1932.

63. Ibid., August 10, 1932.

64. Ibid., August 20, 1932.

65. Ibid., August 28, 1932.

66. Ibid., August 24, 1932.

67. Fr. Nicolas Behr, who had emigrated to London.

Chapter 2. The Years in Nancy, 1933–1969

1. "Vie et pensée de la jeunness protestante," *La Vie intellectuelle* 38/7 (October 10, 1935): 36.

2. Ibid., 41.

3. Ibid., 42.

4. Ibid., 43.

5. Letter of Fr. Lev to EBS, September 1938. The root of the name Nadine signifies hope.

6. Letter of EBS to Mariana Behr, October 3, 1934.

7. Letter of Fr. Lev to EBS, July 24, 1933.

8. For more on the shelter on the rue de Lourmel, see *Un moine*, part II, chap. 7, 210ff. See also Mother Marie Skobtsova, *Le Sacrament du frère*, coll. "Le Sel de la Terre" (Paris: Éd. du Cerf, 1995), 43ff.

9. "La Sophiologie du père Serge Boulgakov," in *Revue d'histoire et de philosophie religieuses* 2 (1939). Reprinted in *Le Messager orthodoxe* 57 (1972).

10. *Le Messager orthodoxe*, 22.

11. Ibid., 29.

12. Letter of Fr. Lev to EBS, August 1937.

13. EBS, wartime notebook no. 1, end of August 1939.

14. Ibid., August 28, 1939.

15. Ibid., August 29, 1939.

16. Ibid., August 30, 1939.
17. Ibid., September 2, 1939.
18. Ibid., Sunday, September 3, 1939.
19. Ibid., November 18, 1939.
20. Letter of EBS to Mariana Behr, December 26, 1939.
21. Ibid., December 27, 1939
22. Ibid., January 7, 1940.
23. Ibid., January 18, 1940.
24. Ibid., June 16, 1940.
25. The Reynaud government, which had been in place since March 21, 1940, and had retreated to Bordeaux, wanted to continue the war against Germany. On June 16, Paul Reynaud, the premier, faced with a majority in favor of an armistice with Germany, resigned. Field Marshal Pétain was then named head of the French government.
26. EBS, wartime notebook no. 1, June 21, 1940.
27. Ibid.
28. Ibid.
29. Ibid., June 28, 1940.
30. Ibid.
31. Ibid., August 30, 1940.
32. Ibid., September 22, 1940.
33. Ibid., October 25, 1940.
34. Ibid.
35. Letter of EBS to Mariana Behr, November 28, 1940.
36. Ibid., June 25, 1942.
37. Ibid., March 21, 1941.
38. Ibid.
39. Ibid., November 18, 1941. On October 12, 1941, the members of the Legion of French Volunteers against Bolshevism (LVF) swore obedience to Hitler.
40. Letter of EBS to Mariana Behr, December 21, 1941.
41. EBS, wartime notebook no. 1, January 11, 1942.
42. Ibid., April 22, 1942.
43. Ibid., August 12, 1942.
44. Father Sergius is alluding to Florovsky's principal work, *The Paths of Russian Theology*, published in 1937. The two theologians had divergent views and Florovsky considered Bulgakov's Wisdom theology as a deviant form of Gnosticism, which he expressed in his book.
45. Letter of Fr. Sergius Bulgakov to EBS, Easter Day 1942.
46. Letter of EBS to Mariana Behr, May 3, 1942.
47. Ibid., February 28, 1944.
48. See Skobtsova, *Le Sacrament du frère*, 50–55.
49. Letter of Fr. Sergius Bulgakov to EBS, May 26, 1942.

50. Ibid., December 19, 1942.

51. EBS, wartime notebook no. 1, September 23, 1942.

52. Letter of Fr. Sergius Bulgakov to EBS, June 12, 1943 (in Russian).

53. EBS, wartime notebook no. 1, August 8, 1943.

54. Ibid., January 1, 1944.

55. Letter of EBS to Mariana Behr, May 11, 1944.

56. Ibid., June 14, 1944.

57. Ibid., May 11, 1944.

58. Ibid., August 27, 1944.

59. Ibid., September 1, 1944.

60. Ibid., September 3, 1944.

61. Ibid., September 6, 1944

62. Ibid., September 9, 1944.

63. Ibid., September 13, 1944.

64. Ibid., September 15, 1944.

65. EBS, wartime notebook no. 2, November 23, 1944.

66. Letter of EBS to Mariana Behr, May 20, 1945.

67. Ibid., July 9, 1944.

68. Ibid., June 21, 1946.

69. Pierre Pascal became a friend of Elisabeth and the director of her thesis.

70. Letter of EBS to Mariana Behr, December 14, 1946.

71. Quoted by EBS, *La Douloureuse Joie*, Bellefontaine Abbey, "Spiritualité orientale," no. 14, 1993, p. 117.

72. Ibid., 93.

73. Ibid., 117.

74. Letter of Fr. Lev Gillet to EBS, June 2, 1947.

75. On the founding of the Fellowship and Father Lev's role, see *Un moine*, 263ff; also 270 for a description of the camp conferences. See also Metropolitan Evlogy, *Le Chemin de ma vie*, 492ff.

76. Letter of EBS to Mariana Behr, August 4, 1947.

77. Ibid., August 8, 1947. As for the "jurisdictional quarrels": when Metropolitan Evlogy died in 1946, the Moscow patriarchate wanted to dissolve the archdiocese of Russian Orthodox Churches that had been founded in Western Europe in 1931. The successor to Metropolitan Evlogy, Metropolitan Vladimir, was opposed to this decision and maintained the dependence of the diocese on the patriarchate of Constantinople.

78. Letter of EBS to Mariana Behr, no date (between September 1946 and October 1949).

79. Letter of Fr. Lev Gillet to EBS, December 29, 1947.

80. Letter of EBS to Mariana Behr, September 27, 1948.

81. Letter of Fr. Lev Gillet to EBS, August 19, 1949.

82. Letter of EBS to Mariana Behr, February 12, 1950.

83. EBS, wartime notebook no. 2, February 2, 1953.

84. EBS, *Prière et sainteté dans l'Eglise russe*, 14.

85. Ibid., 15.

86. Ibid., 178.

87. This is the title of the article by EBS on Bukharev, which appeared in the *Revue de l'histoire et de spiritualité* 52 (1976): reprinted in EBS, *Discerning the Signs of the Times*, 55–81.

88. Letter of Fr. Anthony Bloom to EBS, December 30, 1951.

89. See Paul Evdokimov, *Ages of the Spiritual Life*, rev. trans. Michael Plekon and Alexis Vinogradov (Crestwood, NY: St. Vladimir's Seminary Press, 1998), 135–56.

90. Letter of Father Lev to EBS, 1952, no precise date.

91. Alexander Bukharev, cited by EBS, *Alexandre Boukharev, un théologien de l'Eglise orthodoxe russe en dialogue avec le monde moderne* (Paris, Beauchesne, 1977), 71.

92. Letter of Alexander Bukharev to Father Valerian and Alexandra Lavrski, in ibid., 122.

93. Ibid.

94. Letter of Fr. Lev Gillet to EBS, January 30, 1954.

95. Basil Zenkovsky, *Histoire de la philosophie russe* (Paris: Gallimard, 1953), 352.

96. More recently there was the work in English of Paul Valliere, *Modern Russian Theology: Buhkarev, Soloviev. Bulgakov; Orthodox Theology in a New Key* (Grand Rapids, MI: Eerdmans, 2000).

97. Alexander Bukharev, cited by EBS, *Alexandre Boukharev*, 97.

98. The term comes from the Greek word *ekenosen*, used by Saint Paul in his letter to the Philippians to evoke the self-emptying of Christ become man: "He who, being in very nature God, did not consider equality with God as something to be grasped, but made Himself nothing (*ekenosen*), taking on the nature of a slave" (Phil. 2:6–7).

99. Letter of Fr. Lev to EBS, February 12, 1975.

100. EBS, *Un moine*, 423.

101. Ibid., 69.

102. Letter of Fr. Lev Gillet to EBS, December 2, 1951.

103. Ibid., August 3, 1954.

104. EBS, *Un moine*, 352.

105. EBS deals with the "Winnaert affair" in *Un moine*, 249ff, 270ff.

106. For Fr. Alexis Van den Mensbrugghe, see Gabriel Matzneff, *Boulevard Saint-Germain* (Paris: Ed. de la Table Ronde, 2006), 112.

107. EBS, *A Monk of the Eastern Church*, 362ff.

108. Letter of Fr. Lev to EBS, March 28, 1955.

109. Ibid., April 18, 1956.

110. EBS, *A Monk of the Eastern Church*, 364.

111. This action group had been founded in 1939 by Suzanne de Dietrich to help those Alsatians who were evacuated toward the interior of France. The movement then widened its scope to include all displaced persons, notably Jews and refugees from Eastern Europe.

112. Letter of EBS to Metropolitan Vladimir, May 8, 1956.

113. Letter of Fr. Lev to EBS, May 30, 1956.

114. Ibid.

115. Ibid., June 14, 1956.

116. Letter of Fr. Anthony Bloom to EBS, August 20, 1957.

117. Letter of Fr. Lev Gillet to EBS, January 10, 1958.

118. Ibid.

119. Ibid., September 11, 1958.

120. Ibid., August 31, 1959.

121. *Contacts*, no. 173 (1996): 198.

122. Ibid., no. 25 (1959): 1.

123. Ibid., 8.

124. John Meyendorff, *Introduction à l'étude de Grégoire Palamas* (Paris: Ed. du Seuil, 1959).

125. Fr. Lev Gillet, quoted by EBS, *Un moine*, 508.

126. That is to say, depending directly on the patriarch, in this case the patriarch of Constantinople.

127. In Latin, *pallium*, an ornament, worn by the bishop on his shoulders, which signifies his responsibility for his flock. "Take under his omophor" thus means that a bishop "accepts his ecclesial responsibility."

128. Letter of EBS to Metr. Emilianos Timiadis, August 18, 1959.

129. *Contacts*, no.55 (1966): 199.

130. Letter of Metr. Emilianos Timiadis to EBS, October 6, 1959.

131. Letter of Fr. Lev Gillet to EBS, June 27,1960.

132. Ibid., November 18, 1960.

133. EBS describes these Sundays in *A Monk of the Eastern Church*, 360ff.

134. Letter of Fr. Lev Gillet to EBS, October 16, 1963.

135. "La Fraternité orthodoxe en Europe occidentale," *Contacts* 18/55 (1966), 201.

136. Letter of Fr. Lev Gillet to EBS, July 1965.

137. Ibid., February 24, 1963.

138. Letter of Marcel Roubault to M. Voisin, inspector general of Secondary Education, June 8, 1959.

139. Letter of Fr. Lev Gillet to EBS, September 23, 1958.

140. EBS, wartime notebook no. 2, March 10, 1957.

141. Ibid., February 12, 1959, the only entry on that date.

142. Ibid., April 8, 1961, Holy Saturday.

143. Ibid., October 24, 1964.

144. Ibid., December 18, 1961.

145. Ibid., February 5, 1962

146. EBS, notebook no. 3, June 7, 1964.

147. Letter of Fr. Lev Gillet to EBS, 1959, no precise date.

148. Ibid., June 27, 1960.

149. Ibid., October 24, 1959.

150. Ibid., November 18, 1960.

151. Draft of a letter of EBS to Fr. Lev Gillet, no date.

152. Letter of Fr. Lev Gillet to EBS, August 15, 1962.

153. Ibid., November 9, 1962.

154. Ibid., November 18, 1960.

155. Ibid., August 13, 1964.

156. Ibid., December 9, 1959

157. Ibid., August 15, 1962.

158. Ibid., June 7, 1960.

159. Two twentieth-century proponents of nonviolence—the first an Indian disciple of Mahatma Gandhi, the second an Italian poet who opposed Fascism.

160. Letter of Fr. Lev Gillet to EBS, November 18, 1960.

161. Ibid., January 30, 1962.

162. Ibid., October 26, 1967.

163. Ibid., March 24, 1960.

164. Ibid., October 26, 1962.

165. Ibid., September 25, 1965.

166. Ibid., Palm Sunday, 1964.

167. EBS, notebook no. 3, April 16, 1964.

168. Letter of Fr. Lev to EBS, June 24, 1964.

169. Ibid., July 27, 1964.

170. Ibid., July 4, 1964.

171. Ibid., beginning of 1965, no precise date.

172. Ibid., January 18, 1965.

173. Ibid., February 13, 1967.

174. Ibid., January 17, 1968.

175. Ibid., January 18, 1965.

176. Ibid., February 13, 1965.

177. Ibid., July 1965.

178. EBS, draft of a letter to Fr. Lev Gillet, July 1965.

179. Letter of Fr. Lev Gillet to EBS, November 21, 1965.

180. Ibid., March 31, 1967.

181. Ibid., October 22, 1968.

182. Ibid., March 11, 1965.

183. Ibid., May 31, 1967.

184. Ibid., August 2, 1963.

185. EBS published an account of this pilgrimage in *Contacts* 17/49 (1965): 73. She also mentioned it in *Un moine*, 387–89.

186. Letter of Fr. Lev Gillet to EBS, July 1965, no precise date.

187. EBS, notebook no. 4, August 12, 1965.

188. Ibid., August 14–16, 1965.

189. Ibid., August 20, 1965.

190. Ibid., August 23, 1965.

191. Ibid., August 25-28, 1965.

192. Father Lev, cited by EBS, *Un moine*, 389. Concerning the Broumana reunion, see 388ff.

193. EBS, notebook no. 3, July 15, 1967.

194. Ibid.

195. "There's nothing here."

196. EBS, notebook no. 3, August 2, 1967.

197. Ibid.

198. Ibid.

199. Letter of Fr. Lev Gillet to EBS, November 9, 1965.

200. Ibid., May 24, 1967.

201. Ibid., September 29, 1967.

202. EBS, notebook no. 3, May 29, 1968.

203. Ibid.

204. Ibid.

205. Letter of Fr. Lev Gillet to EBS, July 12, 1968.

206. Ibid., February 15, 1969.

207. Ibid., 1969, no precise date.

Chapter 3. Paris as a Turning Point, 1969–1980

1. Letter of Fr. Lev Gillet to EBS, August 24, 1969.

2. Ibid., December 10, 1969.

3. Ibid., March 21, 1970.

4. Ibid., May 25, 1970.

5. See *Contacts*, 16/45 and 16/48 (note of EBS).

6. EBS, draft of a letter, undated, 1970s.

7. Letter of EBS to a parishioner of the Crypt, September 4, 1977.

8. The Typicon of the Great Church, a tenth-century work that regulated the celebration of the Daily Office at the Church of Holy Wisdom (Saint Sophia) in Constantinople, specified that the Presanctified Liturgy be celebrated during Vespers, hence in the evening. In his work *Great Lent*, Fr. Alexander Schmemann expanded on the theological meaning of the hour when this liturgy is celebrated.

9. EBS, "The Fraternity in France and Western Europe," the bulletin *Kaire*, around 1985.

10. Charter of the Coordinating Committee, 1971.

11. EBS, "Introduction à la Tribune libre," *Contacts*, 14/40 (1962): 265.

12. Gabriel Matzneff, "Le jeunesse orthodoxe en France et ses problèmes," *Contacts*," 14/40 (1962): 278.

13. Gabriel Matzneff, "Ensemble, tout est plus vrai," *Témoinage et pensée orthodoxes* #2 (June 1971), reprinted in *C'est la gloire, Pierre-François!* (Paris: Ed. de la Table ronde, 2002), 60.

14. *C'est la gloire, Pierre-François!* 61.

15. Gabriel Matzneff, "Le Congrès d'Annecy," *Bulletin d'information du Comite de coordination de la jeunesse orthodoxe* (November 1971), reprinted in *C'est la gloire Pierre François!* 62–63.

16. Jean Tchékan, "Préambule," *Contacts* 26/89 (1974): 4.

17. Letter of Fr. Lev Gillet to EBS, October 23, 1974.

18. EBS, reply to a letter addressed to Olivier Clément in the cadre of *Contacts*, 1978.

19. EBS, *Le Lieu du coeur* (Paris: Éd. du Cerf, 1989), 9.

20. Ibid., 9.

21. Ibid., 120.

22. EBS, *Le Ministère de la femme dans l'Eglise* (Paris, Éd. du Cerf, 1987), 14, 15.

23. Ibid., 16.

24. Ibid., 11.

25. Letter of EBS to Fr. Lev Gillet, September 22, 1976.

26. EBS, notebook no. 3, September 11, 1976.

27. Ibid.

28. Ibid., September 12, 1976.

29. Ibid., September 15, 1976.

30. Ibid.

31. EBS, "Le sens de la participation des femmes à la vie de l'Eglise," Orthodox Women Conference, Background Paper, World Council of Churches, 1.

32. Ibid., 7 & 8.

33. Ibid., 8.

34. See Matt. 16:3.

35. EBS, *L'Ordination des femmes dans l'Église orthodoxe* (Paris: Éd. du Cerf, 1998), 48, 49.

36. *Prière et sainteté dans l'Eglise russe, Spiritualité orientale* 33 (1982): 109.

37. EBS, plaid notebook, June 3, 1977.

38. EBS, "Femmes et hommes dans l'Eglise," *SOP* 12 (November, 1976): 10.

39. *Etude sur la communauté des femmes et des hommes dans l'Eglise*, document of the World Council of Churches, 1978, 7.

40. "Réponse à l'enquête du COE," edited by EBS, 6.

41. EBS, draft of a letter to the members of the Inter-Episcopal Committee, no date.

42. EBS, notebook no. 3, February 15, 1978.

43. Letter of Fr. Lev Gillet to EBS, September 11, 1973.

44. That is, "do without, deprive one's self of."

45. Letter of Fr. Lev Gillet to EBS, September 11, 1973.

46. EBS, notebook no. 3, June 3, 1976.

47. Ibid.

48. Ibid., June 27, 1976.

49. Ibid.

50. Ibid., July 31–August 2, 1976.

51. Ibid., August 9–12, 1976.

52. Ibid., August 19, 1976.

53. Ibid., December 15–17, 1976.

54. Ibid., August 28, 1977.

55. *Un Moine*, 434–35.

56. EBS, notebook no. 3, December 1, 1977.

57. Ibid., December 22–24, 1977.

58. Ibid.

59. Ibid.

60. Ibid.

61. Ibid.

62. Ibid.

63. Ibid., February 15, 1978.

64. Ibid., October 25, 1978.

65. Ibid.

66. Ibid., February 16, 1979.

67. Ibid., September 15, 1979.

68. Paul Claudel, *Partage de Midi*, coll. "Bibliothèque de la Pléiade" (Paris: Gallimard, 1956), 1061, 1062.

69. EBS, notebook no. 3, March 31, 1980.

70. Letter of EBS to Mother Eliane, May 1, 1980.

71. EBS, notebook no. 3, August 8, 1980.

72. See Song of Sol. 8:6.

73. EBS, notebook no. 3, March 29, 1981.

74. Ibid., November 21, 1980.

75. Ibid., May 12, 1981.

76. Ibid., January 6, 1983.

77. Ibid.

78. These words, which Fr. Lev used to describe Soloviev, were adoped by Elisabeth to describe her friend.

Chapter 4. The Radiance of Maturity, 1980–2005

1. EBS, interview on March 12, 2005.

2. Unpublished text concerning the future of the Ecumenical Center in Tantur (in English), 1985.

3. EBS, "Quelques aspects de la théologie et de l'expérience de l'Esprit saint dans l'Eglise orthodoxe aujourd'hui," lecture given at Tantur on April 21, 1983, Tantur Yearbook, 1982–1983, 129–50.

4. The Uniate Melkites are Eastern Christians who have been under the authority of Rome since the eighteenth century but who preserve the Byzantine rite.

5. EBS, loose notes, March 25, 1984.

6. Ibid., March 27, 1984.

7. Ibid.

8. Letter of EBS to Mariane and Tony Greenan, October 25, 1984.

9. John 13:34–35.

10. The prohibition against taking Communion during menstruation also has another interpretation: since the communicant participates in the Body and Blood of Christ by this act, our own blood becomes the Blood of Christ, of precious value, and this would be immediately emptied out by the menstrual flow.

11. *Letter to His Holiness the Ecumenical Patriarch Bartholomy I*, dated July 9, 2000, and signed by thirteen personages of the Orthodox world, published in *Contacts* 53/195 (2001): 254–58.

12. Ibid.

13. Ibid.

14. Letter of Metropolitan Anthony Bloom to EBS, no precise date.

15. Ibid., letter received July 18, 1988.

16. Collective, "The Place of the Woman in the Orthodox Church and the Ordination of Women," conclusions of the Inter-Orthodox Theological Congress, published in *Contacts* 41/146 (1989): 90.

17. EBS, *Le Ministère de la femme dans l'Eglise*, 80.

18. An icon that shows Christ seated with the Virgin Mary at His right and John the Baptist at His left, both turned toward Jesus in a gesture of supplicant veneration.

19. EBS, *Le Ministère de la femme dans l'Eglise*.

20. Metropolitan Kallistos Ware, "Man, Woman, and the Priesthood of Christ," in EBS, *The Ordination of Women in the Orthodox Church* (Paris: Éd. du Cerf, 1998), 77.

21. Ibid., 83.

22. Ibid., 47.

23. Ibid., 95.

24. Letter of EBS to Mother Eliane, March 7, 1995.

25. A heresy that affirms that Christ had only one, divine nature. This means that, as a man, he really did not experience suffering and death. The Fourth Ecumenical Council, in 451, proclaimed the two natures of Christ, united in one Person.

26. EBS, "Etre plus efficacement présent au monde," draft of an article published under the title "Spiritualité plus active," in *Le Courrier de l'ACAT* 100–101 (1989): 27.

27. EBS, "Orthodoxie et Catholicisme," *Le Courier de l'ACAT* 109 (1990): 22.

28. Ibid.

29. Ibid., 23.

30. The quarrel over the *Filioque* was one of the major causes of the schism of 1054 between Eastern and Western Christians. The East reproached the West for having introduced a formula that they thought heretical into the Symbol of faith, according to which the Holy Spirit proceeded both from the Father and the Son *(Filioque)* and not from the Father alone, as was stated in the original text. The *Filioque* had been first introduced in order to combat an Arian heresy in Spain.

31. EBS, "Etre plus efficacement présent au monde."

32. Ibid.

33. EBS, "Quelques aspects," 132.

34. Letter of EBS to Mother Eliane, December 30, 1996.

35. EBS, "Colloque de Chevetogne—August 23–27, 1982," *Contacts* 34/120 (1982): 354.

36. EBS, interview of February 26, 2005.

37. Letter of EBS to Mother Eliane, October 29, 1979.

38. EBS, "Kénose et résurrection dans la spiritualité orthodoxe," unpublished archives.

39. Ibid.

40. Letter of EBS to Mother Eliane, November 8, 1991.

41. Mother Eliane OCD, *Toi, suis-moi, Mélanges offerts à EBS*, foreword, 19.

42. Letter of EBS to Mother Eliane, December 15, 1991.

43. This book was issued by Trinitas, the publishing house of the Orthodox diocese of Moldavia and Bucovina. It contained a very detailed bibliography of Elisabeth's books and articles.

44. Canon 65 of the Holy Apostles: "If a cleric or layperson enters a synagogue of Jews or heretics to pray there, may he be deposed if a cleric, and excommunicated if a layperson." This canon, found in the *Apostolic Constitutions*, and thus prior to the fourth century, was probably stated in a context where the Judaic influence was very strong. Today, some defend a literal application, while others want to reinterpret its meaning in a new context.

45. "De retour de Jérusalem, un entretien avec EBS," *SOP* 80 (July–August 1983): 16.

46. "Etapes d'un itinéraire spirituel."

47. EBS, "Le problème de l'intercommunion," catechetical instruction given on January 10, 1985, at the parish of Saint John the Theologian, Issy-les-Moulineaux.

48. Extract from the article,"Elisabeth Behr-Sigel: Une voix libre et la connaissance d'une identité," in *L'Alsace*, May 3, 1987.

49. See Pierre Pascal, *Le Réligion du peuple russe*, Lausanne, 1973.

50. EBS, "A propos de la situation de l'Eglise orthodoxe dans l'Etat sovietique," *Contacts* 37/130 (1985): 147.

51. EBS, "Présence de l'Orthodoxie russe en Occident," *Contacts* 40/143 (1988): 239.

52. EBS, "Mort et transfiguration: L'expérience transcendée de l'amour humain (Partage de Midi)," *Bulletin de la société Paul Claudel*, 1981.

53. EBS, notebook no. 3, January 6, 1983.

54. Ibid.

55. This dream was very similar to one experienced by Father Lev shortly after the death of Mother Maria, when the nun appeared to him in a field of wheat. He was astonished to see her since he had been told that she was dead. Mother Maria answered him, with a mischievous sparkle in her eye: "People tell all sorts of stories . . . You can see for yourself that I am alive!" (see *Discerner les signes du temps*, 52).

56. EBS, notebook no. 3, April 14, 1985.

57. Ibid., May 7, 1985.

58. Ibid.

59. Letter of EBS to Mother Eliane, September 1, 1992.

60. Ibid., November 8, 1991.

61. Ibid., January 28, 1992.

62. Ibid., September 1, 1992.

63. Ibid., August 22, 1993

64. Ibid., October 21, 1993.

65. Letter of Olivier Clément to EBS, July 29, 1987.

66. Letter of EBS to Mother Eliane, March 6, 1996.

67. Ibid., January 14, 1998.

68. Ibid., June 11, 1999.

69. Ibid., January 25, 2002.

70. Ibid., January 14, 1998.

71. EBS, *Discerning the Signs of the Times*, 11.

72. Elisabeth Lacelle, "Elisabeth Behr-Sigel, *Discerner les signes du temps*," review, *Science et Esprit* 56/1 (January–April 2004): 121–30.

73. Ibid., 130.

74. EBS, notebook no. 3, November 9–10, 1989.

75. Letter of EBS to Séraphim Rehbinder, November 8, 2004.

76. Ibid.

77. Ibid.

78. Letter of EBS to Mariane and Tony Greenan, July 11, 2002.

79. EBS, interview on January 15, 2005.

80. 1 Pet. 2:9.

81. Gal. 3:26–28.

82. Letter of EBS to Mother Eliane, October 7, 1981.

83. Ibid., November 18, 2004.

Bibliography of Works by Elisabeth Behr-Sigel

Prewar, 1931–1939

Articles

"La vie estudiantine à Berlin: Impressions d'Allemagne." *Les Dernières Nouvelles*, Alsace-Lorraine, December 2, 1931, signed L. S. and reprinted in *Le Petit Marseillais*.

Theological Works

"Notes sur l'idée russe de sainteté d'après les saints canonisés de l'Église russe." *Revue d'histoire et de philosophie religieuses*, Strasbourg, November–December 1933, pp. 537–54.

"Le Temps pascal dans l'Église orthodoxe d'Orient." *La Quinzaine protestante*, May 16, 1935.

"Vie et pensée de la jeunesse protestante." *La Vie intellectuelle*, October 10, 1935.

"Études d'hagiographie russe." *Irénikon*, Amay-sur-Meuse, vol. 12, 1935, pp. 242–54 and 571–98; vol. 13, 1936, pp. 25–37 and 297–306; vol. 14, 1937, pp. 363–77; vol. 15, 1939, pp. 554–65.

"La Sophiologie du père Serge Boulgakov." *Revue d'histoire et de philosophie religieuses*, Strasbourg, 1939, pp. 130–58. Reprinted in *Le Messager orthodoxe*, no. 57, 1972, pp. 21–48.

After the War, in Nancy, 1945–1969

Books

Prière et sainteté dans l'Église russe. Paris, Éd. du Cerf, 1950. Revised and expanded edition in the collection "Spiritualité orientale," no. 33, Abbaye de Bellefontaine, 1982; Portuguese translation, *Oraçao e santidade na igreja russa.* Saõ Paulo, Éd. Paulinas, 1993.

Essays

"La prière de Jésus ou le mystère de la spiritualité monastique orthodoxe." *Dieu vivant*, Paris, no. 8, 1947. English translation in *Eastern Churches Quarterly*, 1947; Reprinted in *Pages de spiritualité orthodoxe*, Paris, Éd. Enotikon, 1957, pp. 27–39; Reprinted in *Contacts*, no. 17, pp. 1–13. Reprinted and expanded in *La Douloureuse Joie*, "Spiritualité orientale," no. 14, 1974, pp. 81–129; new edition 1981, pp. 77–118. Romanian translation in *Fericita întristare*, Bucharest, 1997, pp. 83–129.
"Monachisme et contemplation dans l'Église orthodoxe." *Bulletin du Cercle Saint-Jean-Baptiste*, Paris, 1953.

Articles and Reports

1957
Le Messager ecclésial
 "L'Orthodoxie universelle et la vocation spirituelle de la Russie," May–December, pp. 25–28.

1958
Le Messager orthodoxe
 "'Orthodoxie occidentale.' Réflexions sur la brochure de L. Zander," pp. 12–17.

1959
Contacts, vol. 11
 "Vers l'Unité chrétienne," no. 26, pp. 121–26.
 "Du Phanar au Vatican," no. 28, pp. 121–26.
 "Le message spirituel de Gogol I," no. 28, pp. 233–56.

1960
Contacts, vol. 12
"Le message spirituel de Gogol II," no. 29, pp. 22–37.
"Réflexions sur la doctrine de Grégoire Palamas," no. 30, pp. 118–24.
"Réflexions sur l'iconostase," no. 32, pp. 309–12.

1961
Contacts, vol. 13
"Un philosophe en quête de l'Église: Brice Parain," no. 33, pp. 15–27.

1962
Contacts, vol. 14
"La vie religieuse en URSS," no. 37, pp. 62–65.
"Introduction à la Tribune libre," no. 40, pp. 265–68.

1963
Contacts, vol.15
"Aspects majeurs de la spiritualité russe du XIVe au XVIe siècle," no. 41, pp. 34–40.
"À la mémoire du père Basile Zenkovsky," no. 41, pp. 65–66.
"Réponses reçues à 'Contacts'—Un mot de Mme Behr-Sigel," no. 42, pp. 127–29.
Le Messager orthodoxe
"Les orthodoxes et le pèlerinage de Paul VI," nos. 24 and 25, pp. 31–33.

1964
Contacts, vol. 16
"Perspectives de l'Orthodoxie en France," no. 45, pp. 42–55.
"Rencontre avec la Grèce chrétienne," no. 45, pp. 56–62.
"Repenser la théologie du mariage," no. 48, pp. 291–301.
"À propos de la présence orthodoxe en France," no. 48, pp. 311–12.

1965
Contacts, vol. 17
"Le Centre œcuménique de Strasbourg," no. 49, p. 73.
"Réponse à Panayotis Nellas," no. 49, p. 80.
"Pèlerinage de la Jeunesse orthodoxe à Jérusalem et Conférence de Syndesmos à Broumana (Liban)," no. 49, pp. 327–34.
"Pour le 20e anniversaire de la mort de mère Marie Skobtsoff," no. 51, p. 178ff.
Le Messager orthodoxe
"Les conférences de Rhodes: bilan et vœux," nos. 29 and 30, pp. 18–23.

1966

Contacts, vol. 18

"La Fraternité orthodoxe en Europe occidentale," no. 55, pp. 198–203.
"À propos de 'La Quête d'Irénée Winnaert,'" no. 56, pp. 315–19.

1967

Contacts, vol. 19

"Un essai de spiritualité contemporaine: le combat de Jacob," no. 58, pp. 167–75.

1968

La Table ronde

"Le Christ kénotique dans la spiritualité russe," no. 250, pp. 204–17; new edition in *Cahiers Saint-Dominique*, no. 170, 1977. Reprinted in *Prière et sainteté dans l'Église russe,* "Spiritualité orientale," no. 33, 1982, pp. 219–36.

Concilium, Revue internationale de théologie

"Les startsy russes," no. 37, pp. 55–69. English translation: "The Russian Startsy: The Monks of 'Holy Russia,'" *Concilium, International Journal for Theology,* no. 7, pp. 30–40.

1969

Contacts, vol. 21

"Un Origène moderne: à propos d'une initiation à Paul Tillich," no. 65, pp. 70–85.

Literary Criticism

Listed beneath each journal are the author and title of the work reviewed by EBS.

Contacts

A Monk of the Eastern Church, *Orthodox Spirituality*, 1957, pp. 47–54.
H. Schütte, *Um die Wiedervereinungen im Glauben*, 1960, p. 222.
Un moine de l'Église d'Orient, *Simples regards sur le Sauveur*, 1960, p. 145.
H. D. Teuffen, *Der Rebell von Kamtchatke*, 1960, pp. 151 and 152.
Vincent de Lérins, *Commonitorium*, 1961, pp. 76–80.
L. Bouyer, *Introduction à la vie spirituelle*, 1961, pp. 68 and 69.
V. Zenkovsky, *N. B. Gogol* [in Russian], 1962, pp. 68 and 69.
K. Barth, *La Proclamation de l'Évangile*, 1962, pp. 283–87.
D. H. Teuffen, *Die ostliche Welt*, 1963, pp. 71 and 72.
Un moine de l'Église d'Orient, *Sois mon prêtre*, 1963, pp. 69–71.
L. Bouyer, *Dictionnaire théologique*, 1964, pp. 150–55.

"Le Messager orthodoxe," nos. 24 and 25, 1964, pp. 237–40.
S. Hackel, *One of Great Price: The Life of Mother Maria Skobstova*, 1965, pp. 260 and 261.
Un moine de l'Église d'Orient, *Le Visage de lumière*, 1967, p. 93.
L. Bouyer, *La Spiritualité orthodoxe et la Spiritualité protestante et anglicane*, 1967, pp. 93–96.
J. Hermel, *Les Sources de la foi*, 1967, p. 184.
A. Perchenet, *Renouveau communautaire et unité chrétienne*, 1967, pp. 330–33.
G. Matzneff, *Comme le feu mêlé d'aromates*, 1969, pp. 342–44.

Dieu Vivant
Arch. Spiridon, *Mes missions en Sibérie*, intro. and trans. P. Pascal, no. 19, 1951.
N. Gorodetsky, *Saint Tikhon de Zadonsk*, no. 22, 1952.

In Paris, 1970–2005

Books

Alexandre Boukharev, un théologien de l'Église orthodoxe russe en dialogue avec le monde moderne, Paris, Beauchesne, 1977.
Le Ministère de la femme dans l'Église, Paris, Éd. du Cerf, 1987. English translation: *The Ministry of Women in the Church*, Redondo Beach, CA, Oakwood Publications, 1991; Greek translation: Athens, Éd. Bonne Presse, undated; Russian translation: Moscow, Saint-André Institute, 2002.
Le Lieu du cœur, Initiation à la spiritualité orthodoxe, Paris, Éd. du Cerf, 1989. English translation: *The Place of the Heart: An Introduction to Orthodox Spirituality*, Torrance, CA, Oakwood Publications, 1992; Italian translation: *Il Luogo del Cuore. Iniziazione alle spiritualità ortodossa*, Milan, Éd. Paoline, 1993.
Lev Gillet, "un moine de l'Église d'Orient," Paris, Éd. du Cerf, 1993. English translation: *Lev Gillet, "A Monk of the Eastern Church,"* Oxford, Fellowship of St. Alban and St. Sergius, 1999.
L'Ordination des femmes dans l'Église orthodoxe, Paris, Éd. du Cerf, 1998. English translation: *The Ordination of Women in the Orthodox Church*, World Council of Churches Publications, 2000; Russian translation, Moscow, Saint-André Institute, 1998; Bulgarian translation, Silistra, 2002.
Discerning the Signs of the Times: The Vision of Elisabeth Behr-Sigel, Crestwood, NY, St. Vladimir's Seminary Press, 2001.
Discerner les signes du temps, Paris, Éd. du Cerf, 2002.

Articles and Reports

1970
Contacts, vol. 22
    "À propos du débat sur le célibat sacerdotal dans l'Église latine," no. 69, pp. 54–60.

1971
Contacts, vol. 23
    "Témoignage sur Paul Evdokimov," nos. 73 and 74, pp. 237–40.
Unité des Chrétiens
    "La prière de Jésus," 1971, pp. 17–19.

1972
Contacts, vol. 24
    "Charles Westphal (1896–1972)," nos. 78 and 79, p. 214.
Vers l'Unité chrétienne
    "Impressions du congrès de la jeunesse orthodoxe. Annecy 1971," 1972/2, pp. 30–32.

1973
Contacts, vol. 25
    "Un prophète orthodoxe: Alexandre Boukharev (1822–1871)," no. 82, pp. 93–111.
Bulletin de la Crypte
    "Question à propos d'une célébration œcuménique," no. 13, p. 8.
    "Dimanche de l'Orthodoxie," no. 15, p. 14.

1974
Contacts, vol. 26
    "Tikhon de Zadonsk," no. 85, pp. 35–65.
SOP (*Service orthodoxe de presse*)
    "Femmes et hommes dans l'Église," no 12, pp. 8–11; reprinted and expanded in *Vers l'Unité chrétienne*, no. 46, pp. 40–45.
Bulletin de la Crypte
    "Retraite de la Fraternité orthodoxe de la région parisienne à Montgeron," no. 29, pp. 14 and 15.
    "Deuxième congrès de la jeunesse orthodoxe—Dijon 1er–3 novembre 1974," no. 30, pp. 5–7.

1975
Contacts, vol. 27
    "Des orthodoxes œuvrent au sein de la CIMADE," no. 90, pp. 209–11.

Bulletin de la Crypte

"Éditorial (Semaine de prière pour l'Unité)," no. 32, pp. 1 and 2.

"Rassemblement panorthodoxe du 9 mars 1975," no. 34, pp. 24 and 25.

"Fraternité orthodoxe en Europe occidentale," no. 36, p. 17; reprinted in *Contacts*, no. 90, pp. 228–30.

1976

Contacts, vol. 28

"Des voix sous les décombres," no. 93, pp. 60–69.

"Un colloque Vladimir Soloviev à Paris," no. 93, pp. 70–72.

Bulletin de la Crypte

"Éditorial (le Carême)," no. 42, pp. 1 and 2.

"Fraternité orthodoxe de la région parisienne," no. 45, pp. 13 and 14.

"Consultation des femmes orthodoxes à Agapia," no. 47, pp. 11–13.

Revue de l'histoire de la spiritualité

"Le moine dans la ville: Alexandre Boukharev (1822–1871)," vol. 52, pp. 49–88; reprinted in *Discerner les signes des temps*, pp. 65–97.

World Council of Churches Document

"The Meaning of the Participation of Women in the Life of the Church," in *Orthodox Women: Their Role and Participation in the Orthodox Church*, Agapia, pp. 17–29.

SOP

"Chrétiens face au drame libanais et au destin de Jérusalem," no. 6, pp. 7–11.

"Après la semaine de prière pour l'unité des chrétiens," no. 15, p. 7.

Réforme

"Orthodoxie et Protestantisme," 8 May 1976; reprinted in *SOP* no. 9, pp. 8 and 9.

1977

Contacts, vol. 29

"La femme dans l'Église orthodoxe, vision céleste et histoire," no. 100, pp. 285–326; reprinted and expanded in *Unité chrétienne*, nos. 53 and 54, 1976, pp. 7–43.

Bulletin de la Crypte

"Rencontre œcuménique féminine (Kairé)," no. 55, pp. 18 and 19.

"Conférence jubilaire du *Fellowship of St. Alban and St. Sergius*," no. 57, pp. 11 and 12.

1978

Contacts, vol. 30

"Atelier sur la place de la femme dans l'Église orthodoxe," no. 104, pp. 391 and 392.

Bulletin de la Crypte
　　"Éditorial. Roi du ciel, Consolateur . . . ," no. 64, p. 1.
　　"Témoignage sur Irène Tchesnakoff," no. 64, p. 12.

1979
Contacts, vol. 31
　　In memoriam: Archevêque Paul (1914–1979), no. 105, p. 78; reprinted
　　　　in *Bulletin de la Crypte*, no. 70.
Bulletin de la Crypte
　　"Consultation de Klingenthal," no. 76, p. 23.
SOP
　　"Après le colloque sur la diaconie," no. 24, pp. 7–11.

1980
Contacts, vol. 32
　　"Consultation de COE à Strasbourg-Klingenthal sur l'ordination des
　　　　femmes," no. 109, pp. 68–70.
　　"In memoriam: Archimandrite Lev Gillet (1892–1980)," no. 110, pp. 186
　　　　and 187.
　　"Réponse à l'enquête du COE sur 'Hommes et femmes dans l'Église,'"
　　　　no. 111, pp. 246–55.
　　"L'œcuménisme au féminin," no. 112, pp. 337–41.
　　"In memoriam: pasteur Henri Roser, Suzanne de Dietrich," no. 112,
　　　　p. 342.
Bulletin de la Crypte
　　"Dimanche de l'Orthodoxie," no. 82, p. 9.
　　"In memoriam: archimandrite Lev Gillet (1892–1980)," no. 83, pp.
　　　　11–16.
　　"La CIMADE fête son 40e anniversaire," no. 87, p. 12.
　　Unité des chrétiens
　　"Les droits de l'homme chez les orthodoxes," no. 37, pp. 6–8; excerpts
　　　　published in *Bulletin de la Crypte*, no. 81, pp. 5–7.
SOP
　　"À propos de l'affaire Kung: un crise, mais l'espérance est indéfectible,"
　　　　no. 45, pp. 9–11.
　　"Le père Lev Gillet (1892–1980)," no. 48, pp. 17–20.

1981
Contacts, vol. 33
　　"Débat sur un rite orthodoxe occidental (New York)," no. 114, p. 163.
　　"In memoriam: Annie Jaubet (1912–1980)," no. 114, p. 164.
　　"Rencontre œcuménique de Chantilly (6–8 juin 1981)," no. 115, pp. 235
　　　　and 236.

"Vers une communauté nouvelle (Sheffield 1981)," no. 115, pp. 236–40.
"Jalons pour une biographie du père Lev," no. 116, pp. 263–305.
"Bibliographie des œuvres du père Lev," no. 116, pp. 359–61.

Bulletin de la société Paul Claudel

"Mort et transfiguration. L'expérience transcendée de l'amour humain (*Partage de Midi*)," no. 83, pp. 33–38.

Réforme

"Offert à tous, le triple sacrement," 6 June 1981; reprinted in *Bulletin de la Crypte*, no. 97, pp. 23 and 24.

1982

Contacts, vol. 34

"Vers une communauté nouvelle," no. 119, pp. 270–77. English translation in *Orthodox Tradition as Resource for the Renewal of Community*, C. Parvey, *The Community of Women and Men in the Church*, World Council of Churches, 1983.
"Colloque de Chevetogne, 23–27 août 1982," no. 120, pp. 343–46.

Mid-Stream

"Woman Too in the Likeness of God," vol. 21, no. 3, pp. 369–75.

HOKMA

"Théologie et contemplation. Introduction à quelques textes de Vladimir Lossky," no. 20, pp. 17–22.

Unité des chrétiens

"Le Christ, vie du monde. Méditation sur 1 Jean 1:1–4," no. 48, pp. 6 and 7.

Bulletin de la Crypte

"Fête de la Transfiguration," no. 105, pp. 7 and 8.

Tantur Yearbook

"Quelques aspects de la théologie et de l'expérience de l'Esprit saint dans l'Église orthodoxe aujourd'hui," pp. 129–50; reprinted in *Contacts* no. 127, 1984, pp. 261–84.

SOP

"L'Athos et le dialogue avec Rome," no. 66, pp. 12–14.

1983

Contacts, vol. 35

"La femme aussi est à l'Image de Dieu," no. 121, pp. 62–70.
"In memoriam: Paul Fidler (1900–1983)," no. 121, pp. 75–77.
"In memoriam: Pierre Pascal (1890–1983)," no. 124, pp. 361 and 362.
"Chronique anglo-russe: Julia de Beausobre, Sunset Years," no. 124, pp. 363–65.

Irénikon

"La place de la femme dans l'Église," vol. 58, pp. 46–53 and pp. 194–214.

SOP

"De retour de Jérusalem," no. 80, pp. 14–19.

1984

Contacts, vol. 36

"Quelques aspects de la théologie et de l'expérience de l'Espirit saint dans l'Église orthodoxe aujourd'hui," no. 127, pp. 261–84.

"Women and the Priesthood," no. 127, pp. 207–14.

"In memoriam: dom Olivier Rousseau (1898–1984)," no. 128, pp. 377 and 378.

Bulletin de la Crypte

"Passion du Christ, passion des hommes, colloque de l'ACAT, 1984," no. 125, p. 23.

SOP

"Le schisme de 1054: origines, conséquences et perspectives," suppl. 86-A; excerpts in *SOP* no. 86, pp. 17–20.

"Passion du Christ, passion des hommes," suppl. 89-A; excerpts in *SOP* no. 89, pp. 12–16.

"Les oubliés de la visite de Monsieur Gorbatchev," no. 102, p. 14.

1985

Contacts, vol. 37

"À propos de la situation de l'Église orthodoxe dans l'État soviétique," no. 130, pp. 145–47.

"In memoriam: Nadejda Gorodetzky (1901–1985)," no. 130, pp. 147 and 148.

Unité des chrétiens

"Une religieuse chrétienne à Paris. Mère Maria Skobstov (1891–1945)," no. 58, pp. 21–23.

Irénikon

"Marie, Mère de Dieu. Mariologie traditionnelle et questions nouvelles," no. 4, pp. 451–70.

Le Supplément

"Passion du Christ et passion des hommes," no. 152, Paris, Éd. du Cerf, pp. 31–43.

Courrier de l'ACAT

"Que Ta volonté soit faite," no. 55, pp. 20 and 21.

SOP

"Les lendemains du BEM," suppl. 102-B.

1986

Contacts, vol. 38

"L'Église d'Orient est-elle patriarcaliste?," no. 135, pp. 235–37.

Irénikon
"Marie, Mère de Dieu. Mariologie traditionnelle et questions nouvelles (suite)," no. 1, pp. 20–31.
L'Altérité, vivre ensemble différents
"L'altérité homme-femme dans le contexte d'une civilisation chrétienne," M. Gourgues and G. D. Mailhiot (eds.), Paris, Bellarmin-Éd. du Cerf, pp. 389–426.
Unité des chrétiens
"Une créature nouvelle, réconciliée avec Dieu en Jésus-Christ (2 Cor. 5:17)," no. 64, pp. 2 and 3.
Monachisme d'Orient et d'Occident
"Nil Sorsky, un hésychaste lettré," Éd. Les amis de Sénanque, pp. 35–54.
SOP
"Semaine de l'Unité: faire l'effort d'aller vers l'autre," no. 104, pp. 12 and 13.

1987
Courrier de l'ACAT
"L'hospitalité eucharistique," no. 75, pp. 7 and 8.
SOP
"Assemblée générale de l'ACAT: briser sans cesse les mécanismes qui dégradent l'homme," no. 118, pp. 14–18.
"Roi du ciel, Consolateur . . ." (allocution d'ouverture à l'Assemblée générale de l'ACAT), no. 118, pp. 21 and 22.

1988
Contacts, vol. 40
"Présence de l'Orthodoxie russe en Occident," no. 143, pp. 226–39.
Unité des chrétiens
"Marie, visage de l'humanité nouvelle," no. 69, pp. 20 and 21; reprinted in part in *Unité des chrétiens*, no. 95, 1994, p. 37.
Courrier de l'ACAT
"Le baptême de la Russie," no. 84, pp. 7 and 8; reprinted in *Bulletin de la Crypte*, no. 164, pp. 16–18.
Irénikon
"Les orthodoxes s'interrogent sur la place de la femme dans l'Église," no. 4, pp. 523–29.
SOP
"Développement de la théologie orthodoxe en Europe occidentale," suppl. 131-C.

1989
Contacts, vol. 41
"La consultation interorthodoxe de Rhodes," no. 146, pp. 81–93.

Le Messager orthodoxe

"Mère Marie Skobtsov," no. 111, pp. 56–70; excerpts in *Bulletin de la Crypte*, no. 171, 1989, pp. 14 and 15, then in no. 224, pp. 6–11; reprinted in *Discerner les signes du temps*, pp. 51–64.

Courrier de l'ACAT

"L'Église orthodoxe et l'ACAT," nos. 100 and 101, pp. 25–27.

Mille ans de christianisme russe

"La folie en Christ dans la Russie ancienne," Paris, YMCA Press, pp. 141–52.

Spirituality III

"Hesychasm and the Western impact in Russia: St. Tikhon of Zadonsk (1724–1783)," New York, Crossroad, pp. 432–46.

1990

Contacts, vol. 42

"L'ordination des femmes, un problème œcuménique," no. 150, pp. 101–27; reprinted in *Discerner les signes du temps*, pp. 131–52.

"À propos de la femme dans l'Église (Réponse à M. Monsaingeon)," no. 152, pp. 299–303.

Courrier de l'ACAT

"Orthodoxie et Catholicisme (quelques points de divergences doctrinales)," no. 109, pp. 22 and 23.

SOP

"La prière d'intercession dans la lutte contre la torture," no. 152, pp. 16–21; reprinted in *Torturés, tortionnaires, espérance chrétienne*, Paris, Éd. FIACAT-Éd. du Cerf, pp. 73–88; reprinted in *La Feu sur la Terre, Mélanges offerts au père Boris Bobrinskoy à l'occasion de son 80e anniversaire*, Paris, Presses Saint-Serge, 2005.

1991

Bulletin de la Crypte

"VIIe assemblée du COE," no. 190, p. 24

1992

Bulletin de la Crypte

"Images féminines et spiritualité orthodoxe, Bossey, 24 mai–3 juin," no. 205, p. 17.

"Rencontres orthodoxes-protestants," no. 207, p. 23.

Le donne secondo Wojtyla

"Ci si puo fermare qui?," M. A. Macciocchi (ed.), Milan, Éd. Paoline, pp. 137–59.

Courrier de l'ACAT

"Le Dieu de l'espérance," no. 123, p. 7; reprinted in *SOP*, no. 166, pp. 21–23.

Tychique
"Le baptême dans l'Esprit chez Syméon le Nouveau Théologien," no. 97, pp. 67–75.
Trajets (Cahiers universitaires catholiques)
"Réflexion sur le ministère et les ministères dans l'Église. Une voix orthodoxe," no. 2, pp. 53–57.

1993
Contacts, vol. 45
Un colloque "Lev Gillet," no. 161, pp. 4 and 5.
Bulletin de la Crypte
"Colloque 'Levi Gillet,' 2–3 October 1993," no. 211, p. 21.

1994
Contacts, vol. 46
"Le concélébrant de Clamart et la fondation de la première paroisse orthodoxe française," no. 165, pp. 4–21.
Bulletin de la Crypte
"Le 30e anniversaire de la rencontre Paul VI-Athénagoras," no. 220, p. 24.
"Célébration parisienne du Dimanche de l'Orthodoxie," no. 222, p. 26.
"La Fraternité Saint-Élie," no. 227, p. 22.
Mary Martha
"Les femmes prêtres vues par les orthodoxes," pp. 24 and 25.
Trajets
"Réflexion sur le ministère et les ministères dans l'Église. Une voix orthodoxe," no. 2, pp. 53–57.

1995
Lien des contemplations
"Aux sources de la spiritualité orthodoxe," no. 120, pp. 1–18.
Courrier de l'ACAT
"Père Cyrille Argenti," nos. 151/152, p. 3.
SOP
"L'Église orthodoxe et la paix," suppl. 204; English translation in *In Communion*, Orthodox Peace Fellowship, 1995/3.
Communion et réunion
"L'ordination des femmes, une question posée aussi aux Églises orthodoxes," Leuven.
Mary Martha
"The Orthodox Women in United Europe," vol. 4/1, pp. 15 and 16.

1996

Contacts, vol. 48

"L'Orthodoxie et la paix," no. 173, pp. 5–13; reprinted in *Discerner les signes du temps*, pp. 121–27.

Bulletin de la Crypte

"Milan, Bose, Sylvanès . . . Expériences d'unité spirituelle," no. 245, pp. 23 and 24.

"9e congrès orthodoxe en Europe occidentale," no. 248, pp. 18 and 19.

Courrier de l'ACAT

"Madeleine Barot (1909–1995)," no. 163, pp. 26 and 27.

Mary Martha

"The Life of Elisabeth Skobstov," vol. 4/2, pp. 16–21.

"The Community of Women and Men: What Does This Mean for a Prophetic and Sacramental Church?," vol. 4/2, pp. 22–30.

Maschio e femmina li créo

"Anche la Donna è a immagine di Dio," Bose, Qiqajon, coll. "Spiritualità ortodossa" 16, pp. 19–28.

1997

Contacts, vol. 49

"Un moine de l'Église d'Orient, sur sa conversion à l'Orthodoxie," no. 180, pp. 294–99.

Théologie, histoire et piété mariale

"Marie et les femmes," colloque de la faculté de Lyon, Profac, pp. 309–24; reprinted in *Discerner les signes du temps*, pp. 21–33.

Œcuménisme et information

"Au tournant de l'histoire, chrétiens et chrétiennes vivent de nouvelles alliances. Lyon, 7–8 mars 1997," no. 274, p. 7.

Unité des Chrétiens

"L'ordination des femmes: la consultation de Rhodes," no. 107, pp. 12 and 13.

Mary Martha

"Entretien avec Lyn Breck," vol. 5/2, pp. 13 and 14.

1998

Contacts, vol. 50

"La Bible, la Tradition, les sacrements, source de l'autorité dans l'Église," no. 183, pp. 204–14; reprinted in *Discerner les signes du temps,* pp. 111–19.

Œcuménisme et information

"La place des orthodoxes dans le mouvement œcuménique," no. 287, pp. 20 and 21.

Mary Martha

"Jesus and Women," vol. 6/1, pp. 35–56.

1999

Contacts, vol. 51

"Les tâches de la formation théologique orthodoxe au XXIe s.," no. 185, pp. 76–88; reprinted in *Discerner les signes du temps*, pp. 101–9; text reviewed for *Unité des chrétiens*, no. 116, pp. 21–25, excerpt in *SOP*, no. 235, pp. 19–28.

SOP

"La création de la première paroisse orthodoxe de langue française (fin 1928–début 1929)," Institut Saint-Serge, 28 February 1999, suppl. 237-B.

Orthodox Women Speak

"Women and Jesus Earthly Life," Geneva, World Council of Churches Publications, pp. 51–55; reprinted in *Discerner les signes du temps*, pp. 15–19.

"The Meaning of Ministry," pp. 93–97.

Veillez et priez

"L'Église orthodoxe," *Document ACAT*, pp. 93–105.

Diakonia

"What Are the Tasks of Theological Education for the Twenty-First Century?," vol. 32/3, Scranton (PA), pp. 223–32.

Strantsi

"The Ordination of Women: A Question Also for Orthodox Churches" (in Russian), Moscow, Saint-André Institute, vol. 4/1, pp. 24–32.

"The Ordination of Women Is Being Discussed in the Orthodox Church As Well" (in Russian), vol. 4/2, pp. 190–200.

2000

Contacts, vol. 52

"Pour un témoignage chrétien renouvelé," no. 189, pp. 35–45; reprinted in suppl. *SOP* 243-B.

"La place de l'Église orthodoxe dans la construction européenne," no. 190, pp. 157–69; reprinted in *Œcuménisme et information*, no. 307, pp. 9–16.

"Vingtième anniversaire de la mort du 'moine de l'Église d'Orient,'" no. 191, pp. 242 and 243.

Bulletin de la Crypte

"Pour le 20e anniversaire de la mort du père Lev Gillet," no. 281, pp. 18 and 19.

Œcuménisme et information

"Regard orthodoxe sur le protestantisme," no. 301, pp. 12–16 and no. 302, pp. 13–16.

"20e anniversaire de la mort du père Lev Gillet," no. 306, p. 12.

2001

Contacts, vol. 53

"L'ordination des femmes: un point chaud du dialogue œcuménique,"
no. 190, pp. 236–52; reprinted in *Discerner les signes du temps*,
pp. 153–66.

"Vers une restauration créative du diaconat féminin?," no. 195, pp.
253–58.

Courrier de l'ACAT

"Christianisme et droits de l'homme," no. 218, pp. 30–32 and no. 219,
pp. 32 and 33; reprinted in *Œcuménisme et information*, no. 320,
pp. 13–15 and no. 321, pp. 10–12.

Œcuménisme et information

"Dixième anniversaire de la Fraternité Saint-Élie," no. 320, pp. 5 and 6.

2002

Contacts, vol. 54

"Contacts 1949–2002: retour sur les origines de la 'Revue française
de l'Orthodoxie': un entretien avec Élisabeth Behr-Sigel," no. 200,
pp. 351–76.

Bulletin de la Crypte

"Un anniversaire," no. 299, pp. 19 and 20.

Réforme

"Porteurs de valeurs," no. 3000, p. 11.

SOP

"Le 75e anniversaire de Chevetogne," no. 265, pp. 27–29.

Mikthav

"Célébration œcuménique de la fête du prophète Élie," no. 34, pp. 3 and
4; reprinted in *Bulletin de la Crypte*, no. 306, p. 21, and in *Œcuménisme et information*, no. 328, pp. 11 and 12.

2003

Contacts, vol. 55

"Au métropolite Antoine de Souroge, mémoire éternelle," no. 204,
p. 456.

Bulletin de la Crypte

"Rencontre orthodoxes-protestants en région parisienne," no. 309,
pp. 20 and 21.

Œcuménisme et information

"La rencontre annuelle orthodoxes-protestants," no. 331, p. 68.

"L'œcuménisme au féminin," no. 334, pp. 8 and 9.

2004

Contacts, vol. 56

"Mère Marie Skobtsov et le père Lev Gillet," no. 208, p. 361; reprinted
with minor changes in *Contacts*, vol. 57, no. 212, 2005, p. 315.

Contacts

Collectif, *Le Diaconat. Le peuple de Dieu*. 1970, pp. 165–67.

A Monk of the Eastern Church, *The Burning Bush*, 1972, pp. 73–75.

A. Bloom, *God and Man*, 1972, pp. 233–35.

Un moine de l'Église d'Orient, *Amour sans limites*, 1972, pp. 316–19.

N. Psaroudakis, *Christianisme social et socialisme scientifique*, 1972, pp. 68–70.

A. Lequeux, *Concert spirituel*, 1972, pp. 234 and 235.

Fr. Marie-Félix, *Recherches et réflexions à propos de l'habit monastique*, 1973, p. 64.

Un moine de l'Église d'Orient, *La Prière de Jésus*, 1974, pp. 368–70; reprinted in *Bulletin de la Crypte*, no. 29, 1974, pp. 15 and 16.

Mgr. Antoine [Bloom], *Voyage spirituel*, 1974, p. 373.

Un moine de l'Église d'Orient, *L'An de grâce du Seigneur*, 1974, p. 96.

Reldif-Filderlski [P. Fidler], *Âges qui passent et demeurent*, 1974, p. 192.

Un moine de l'Église d'Orient, *Ils regarderont vers lui*, 1975, p. 248; reprinted in *Bulletin de la Crypte*, no. 36, 1975, p. 19.

La Prière des heures, 1976, p. 171.

O. Clément, *L'Autre Soleil*, 1976, pp. 168–71.

E. Schmidt, *J'étais pasteur en Algérie*, 1976, p. 172.

N. Afanassief, *L'Église du Saint-Esprit*, 1976, pp. 263–69.

A Monk of the Eastern Church, *Orthodox Spirituality*, 1976, pp. 351 and 352.

M. D. Molinié, *Le Courage d'avoir peur*, 1977, pp. 160–64.

D. Doudko, *L'espérance qui est en nous: entretiens de Moscou*, 1977, pp. 160–64.

E. Simonod, *La Prière de Jésus suivant l'évêque Ignace Briantchaninoff*, 1977, pp. 250 and 251.

F. Quéré, *La Femme avenir*, 1977, pp. 348–51.

J. Dunphy, *Paul Tillich et le symbole religieux*, 1978, pp. 80–82.

L. Bouer, *Mystère et ministères de la femme*, 1978, pp. 181–84.

S. Knecht, *Un pape, un jour*, 1978, pp. 184–87.

O. Clément, *Le Visage intérieur*, 1978, pp. 410 and 411.

J. Serr, O. Clément, *La Prière du cœur*, 1978, pp. 410 and 411.

M. A. Costa de Beauregard, I. Bria, T. de Foucauld, *L'Orthodoxie hier-demain*, 1979, pp. 439–43.

M. Neusch, B. Chenu, *Au pays de la théologie*, 1979, p. 444.

J. Borella, *La Charité profanée*, 1980, pp. 174 and 175.

J. Goettmann, *Approches de la Bible*, 1980, p. 179.

P. Dabosville, *Foi et culture dans l'Église aujourd'hui*, 1980, pp. 352 and 353.

P. Evdokimov, *Le Buisson ardent*, 1981, pp. 241 and 242.

S. Hackel (ed.), *The Byzantine Saint*, 1981, pp. 362 and 363.

P. Dumitriu, *Zéro ou le point de départ*, 1982, pp. 92 and 93.

Das Gebet der Orthodoxen Kirche, 1982, pp. 193 and 194.

É. Fouilloux, *Les Catholiques et l'Unité chrétienne*, 1982, pp. 373–77.

T. Goritcheva, *Nous, convertis d'Union soviétique*, 1983, pp. 380 and 381.

R. Girault, *L'Œcuménisme, où vont les Églises?*, 1983, pp. 94 and 95.

Un moine de l'Église d'Orient, *Introduction à la spiritualité orthodoxe*, 1984, pp. 145–47.

S. Hausammann, S. Heitz, *Christus in euch Hoffnung auf Herrlichkeit*, 1984, p. 227.

B. Frost, *Living in the Tension between East and West*, 1985, p. 73.

M. Hébrard, *Les Femmes dans l'Église*, 1985, pp. 74–76.

O. Clément, *Orient-Occident—Deux passeurs: Vladimir Lossky et Paul Evdokimov*, 1985, pp. 317–20.

R. Mehl, *Essai sur la fidélité*, 1986, pp. 72–75.

Les Fêtes et la Vie de Jésus-Christ. I. L'Incarnation, 1986, pp. 77 and 78.

Vocabulaire théologique orthodoxe, 1986, pp. 77 and 78.

La Divine Liturgie de saint Jean Chrysostome, 1986, pp. 157 and 158.

R. Girault, A. Nicolas, *Sans tricher ni trahir sur la grand-route œcuménique*, 1986, pp. 161–63.

R. Albrecht, *Das Leben der heiligen Makrina auf dem Hintergrund de Thekla-Traditionen*, 1987, pp. 77–79.

P. Jérôme, *Car toujours dure longtemps*, 1987, pp. 79 and 80.

C. Aslanoff, P. Minet, *Le "Credo" de Nicée-Constantinople*, 1987, pp. 310–13.

V. Rochcau, *Saint Séraphin—Sarov et Diveyevo*, 1987, pp. 310–13.

M.-J. Aubert, *Des femmes diacres. Un nouveau chemin pour l'Église*, 1987, pp. 316–19.

A. Jensen, *Die Zukunft der Orthodoxie*, 1987, pp. 319 and 320.

F. Quéré, *Une lecture de l'Évangile de Jean*, 1987, p. 321; reprinted in 1988, p. 134.

V. Vodoff, *Naissance de la chrétienté russe*, 1988, pp. 136–39.

O. Cullmann, *L'Unité par la diversité*, 1988, pp. 139–43; coll. "Catéchèse orthodoxe," 1989, pp. 299–302.

P. Hocken, *Rassemblés par l'Esprit: la grâce œcuménique du renouveau*, 1989, pp. 317 and 318.

O. Clément, *Anachroniques*, 1991, pp. 69–73.

J. Beaude, *La Mystique, la prière du cœur*, 1991, pp. 73–75.

J. Becher, *Women, Religion, and Sexuality*, 1991, pp. 76 and 77.

O. Clément, *Berdiaev. Un philosophe russe en France*, 1992, pp. 68–70.

O. Cullmann, *Les Voies de l'unité chrétienne*, 1992, pp. 147–49.

Nouvelle petite philocalie, 1992, pp. 233 and 234.

A. Jensen, *Gottes selbstbewusste Tochter, Fauen-Emmanzipation im Fruhen Christentum?*, 1993, pp. 153–56; "Passé et présent religieux en Russie," *Revue d'études comparatives Est-Ouest*, 1994, p. 26

R. Bichelberger, *L'Unité maintenant*, 1994, pp. 151–53.

Mère Marie (1891–1945). *Le Sacrement du frère*, 1995, pp. 239 and 240.

Pont entre l'Orient et l'Occident, 1996, pp. 149 and 150; reprinted in *Bulletin de la Crypte*, no. 242, 1996, p. 28.

J. Meyendorff, *L'Église orthodoxe hier et aujourd'hui*, 1996, pp. 60–63.

E. J. Lacelle, *L'Incontournable Échange*, 1996, pp. 63–65.

Vivre l'amour de la Trinité, 1997, pp. 188–90.

N. Struve, *Soixante-dix ans d'émigration russe*, 1997, pp. 196–99; reprinted in *Bulletin de la Crypte*, no. 254, 1997, pp. 22 and 23.

P. Païssios, *Le Vénérable Georges, moine de l'Athos (1809–1886), saint Arsène de Cappadoce (1840–1924)*, 1997, pp. 282–84.

P. Gabriel, *Foi de prêtre (1923–1988)*, 1997, pp. 365 and 366.

D. M. Debuisson, *L'Œuvre du sixième jour. Création de l'homme*, 1997, pp. 365 and 366.

Un moine de l'Église d'Orient, *Au cœur de la fournaise*, 1998, pp. 183 and 184; reprinted in *Œcuménisme et information*, no. 289, 1998, p. 20.

M. Evdokimov, *Une voix chez les orthodoxes*, 1998, pp. 184–86.

Bild Christi und Geschlecht, 1999, pp. 179–81.

J.-C. Larchet, *Pour une éthique de la procréation*, 1999, pp. 185–87.

B. Bobrinskoy, *La Compassion du Père*, 2000, pp. 266–68.

I. Séménoff-Tian-Chiansky, *Printemps de la Foi en Russie*, 2000, pp. 269–71.

K. K. Fitzgerald, *Orthodox Women Speak*, 2000, pp. 271–74; reprinted in *Bulletin de la Crypte*, no. 286, 2000, pp. 21 and 22.

O. Clément, *Christ est ressuscité. Propos sur les fêtes chrétiennes*, 2000, pp. 350 and 351.

M. I. Tataryn, *Augustine and Russian Orthodoxy: Russian Orthodox Theologians and Augustine of Hippo: A Twentieth-Century Dialogue*, 2002, pp. 107–11; reprinted in *Œcuménisme et information*, no. 327, p. 19.

X. Iouriev, *L'Église et les Femmes*, 2003, pp. 136–41.

B. Bobrinskoy, *Le Mystère de l'Église, cours de théologie dogmatique*, 2004, no. 208, p. 377.

SOP

E. Moberly, *Suffering, Innocent and Guilty*, 1979, p. 10.

Bulletin de la Crypte

P. Florensky, *La Colonne et le Fondement de la vérité*, no. 36, 1975, p. 19.

Le Mystère de l'Église et de l'Eucharistie à la lumière du mystère de la Sainte Trinité, no. 231, 1995, p. 23.

M. Evdokimov, *Le Christ dans la tradition et la littérature russes*, no. 246, 1996, pp. 27 and 28.

Veillez et priez, no. 273, 1999, p. 21.

L. Varaut, *Mère Marie*, no. 289, 2001, p. 26.

M. Evdokimov, *Les Chrétiens orthodoxes*, no. 290, 2001, p. 26; reprinted in *Œcuménisme et information*, no. 311, 2001, pp. 20 and 21.

Works about Elisabeth Behr-Sigel

Collectif, *Toi, suis-moi, Mélanges offerts à EBS*, Éd. Trinitas, 2003, Saint-Remy-Stânceni.

E. Lacelle, "Élisabeth Behr-Sigel: *Discerner les signes du temps*," review, *Science et Esprit*, vol. 56, fasc. 1, January–April, 2004, pp. 121–30.

"Élisabeth Behr-Sigel (1907–2005), Une grande figure de l'orthodoxie en France," *Contacts* no. 220, October–December, 2007.

Index

Beauvoir, Simone de, 150
Behr, Alexis, 99, 100
Behr, André (husband of EBS)
    alcoholism, 68–69, 77, 103, 105,
      148
    background, 29–31
    career, 50, 53–54, 76–77, 102, 103,
      145–46
    death, 176–77
    Gillet, Lev and, 152–53, 154, 174–75
    health, 67, 68–69, 102–6, 107,
      145–47, 148, 174–75
    letters from EBS, subject of:
    —communion of the Church, 37
    —desire to serve the Church, 37,
      45
    —fear of the "other," 41
    —Germany, pre-WWII, 40, 41, 42,
      43
    —her link to spiritual figures of
      the Church, 36–37
    —ideological propaganda of
      political agitators, 40
    —making preserves, 50–51
    —master's thesis, 34–35, 50
    —ministry in the Reformed
      Church, 48
    —Orthodox Church, calling of, 49
    —Protestantism, break from, 49
    —Protestantism, criticism of, 50
    —Shahovskoy, John, 44, 45
    mentioned, 27, 58, 86, 92
    military service, 33, 46, 50, 51, 63,
      67, 74, 75
    philatelist, 148
    relationship with EBS:
    —beginnings, 31
    —engagement, 33, 46
    —marriage, 50, 51, 53
    —post-WW II, 102
Behr, Gabriel, 288, 297–98
Behr, Maria Alexandrovna (née
    Lanceray), 29, 53

Behr, Mariana Borissovna (née
    Soukhanoff-Podkolzine), 30–31,
    33, 44, 47, 58, 68, 71–72, 76, 78,
    89, 95, 100, 102–3, 105, 108, 146,
    148, 226
Behr, Mariane, 58, 64–65, 67–68, 71,
    76, 77, 83, 85, 88, 91–93, 94, 95,
    99, 103, 107, 108, 146, 147, 148.
    See also Greenan, Mariane
    (née Behr)
Behr, Michel Alexeevitch, 29–30, 59,
    71, 148
Behr, Nadezhda (née Nicolaievna),
    29–30, 59
Behr, Nadia (née Vorontsov-
    Veliaminov), 176
Behr, Nadine, 58, 64–65, 67–68, 72,
    76, 77–78, 80, 83, 85, 88, 91–93,
    99, 103, 107, 108, 115, 135, 147,
    148. See also Arnould, Nadine
    (née Behr)
Behr, Nicolas (son of EBS), 94–95,
    99, 100, 101, 103, 107, 108,
    115–16, 146, 147, 148, 166, 167,
    174, 176, 226, 288, 291, 292
Behr, Nicolas (uncle of EBS), 44, 53
Behr, Tatiana, 99
Behr, Viktor, 30
Behr family, 287
Behr-Sigel, Elisabeth. See also career;
    characteristics; education; faith;
    Gillet, Lev, relationship with;
    travel; works
    adolescence, 10–11
    birth, 1, 4
    birthday celebrations, 257–58,
      288
    childhood, 4–10
    children. See individual children
    cultural identity, 9–10, 34, 72, 78
    death, 182, 292–94, 297–99
    Epinay-sur-Seine apartment,
      181–82

Hitler, Adolph, 42, 43, 53, 63, 70, 78
Husserl, Edmund, 14

Ignatieff, Count, 268

Jaggi, Mme. (painter), 16
Jaggi, M. (musician), 16
Jean, Bishop. *See* Kovalevsky, Evgraf
Jeanne (childhood friend of EBS), 5
John of San Francisco, Saint, 126
John Paul II, 250–51
Joseph of Volokohlamsk, Saint, 34,
    114–15
Jost, M., 64–65
Jost family, 54, 82, 84
Jouanny, Fr., 122
Juárez, Benito, 3

Kedroff family, 22
Khodr, Georges, 169
Khomiakov, Alexis, 16–17, 22, 27, 38,
    198, 284
Klepinine, Saint Dimitri, 83, 87, 219,
    273
Kniazeff, Alexis, 108, 201, 273
Knutz, Mr., 50
Koppel, Pierre, 183
Kovalevsky, Evgraf, 21–23, 27, 29, 31,
    60, 122–26, 177, 180
Kovalevsky, Maxime, 123
Kovalevsky brothers, 22, 31, 60

Lacelle, Elisabeth, 278
Lanceray, Eugene, 29
Lanceray, Maria Alexandrovna.
    See Behr, Maria Alexandrovna
    (née Lanceray)
Lanne, Emmanuel, 254
Lavrski, Alexandra, 118
Lazarevskaya, Saint Juliana, 212–13,
    278
Legrand, Hervé, 241
Le Hire, M., 65

Lenin, 113
Lev, Fr. *See* Gillet, Lev
Levinas, Emmanuel, 13–14
Lialine, Don Clement, 95
Lossky, Madeleine, 60, 99, 108, 122
Lossky, Nicolas, 123, 124, 135, 270,
    273
Lossky, Olga, 295
Lossky, Véronique, 242
Lossky, Vladimir, 22, 23, 31, 60, 96,
    101, 123–24, 130, 133, 135, 202,
    203, 204, 296

Maria of Paris, Saint, 266. *See also*
    Skobtsova, Saint Maria
Maritain, Jacques, 25–26
Marrou, Henri Irénée, 57–58
Mathiot, Pastor, 46, 54, 68, 82, 83,
    96
Matzneff, Gabriel, 192–93, 195–96
Maury, Pierre, 12
Maximovitch, John, 126
Meletios, Metr., 194–95
Mélia, Elie, 82, 90, 94
Meyendorff, John, 127, 129, 132, 135,
    137, 167, 238, 242
Meyendorff, Marie (née Mojaïsky),
    132
Michalon, Fr., 254
Minet, Jacques, 200
Minet, Paula, 200
Mojaïsky, Marie, 95, 132
Mojaïsky, Olga, 82, 107
Mojaïsky family, 82, 83, 96, 135, 191
Monod, Wilfred, 26
Mott, John R., 11
Mounier, Emmanuel, 25, 57
Mussolini, 70

Napoleon III, 3
Nellas, Panayotis, 203
Nil of Sora, Saint, 34, 87
Nivat, Georges, 262

Odette (the maid), 70
Ouspensky, Leonide, 60

Palmer, William, 17
Pascal, Pierre, 96, 113–15, 117–18, 126, 265
Paskevitch, Boris Ivanovitch, 30
Patton, George, 91, 94–95
Paul, Saint, 163, 286
Paul VI, 234, 250
Péguy, Charles, 12, 293
Péguy, Marcel, 25
Pétain, Philippe, 70
Peter the apostle, 285
Plekon, Michael, 277
Popov, Eugene, 106

Rabey (Rabbinovitch), Mme., 83
Rabey (Rabbinovtch) Yvonne, 83
Rehbinder, Séraphim, 194, 281
Renan, Ernest, 3
Revault d'Allones, Germaine, 134, 135, 136
Reynaud, Paul, 70
Rousseau, Oliver, 265

Sartre, Jean-Paul, 150
Schakovskoy, John, 48
Schmemann, Alexander, 100, 190, 242
Schneider, Jean, 82–83, 95–96, 106
Séménoff Tian-Chansky, Fr., 100
Seraphim of Sarov, Saint, 49, 97, 101, 202, 278
Serikoff, Georges, 16, 17, 19
Shahovskoy, John, 44–46
Sigel, Anne-Marie (second wife of Charles), 51, 67, 73, 147
Sigel, Catherine (née Stressinger), (grandmother of EBS), 3–4, 8
Sigel, Charles (father of EBS), 1–2, 26, 29, 51, 54, 67, 73, 75, 78, 104, 107, 147, 296

Sigel, Emma (née Altschul), (mother of EBS), 1–2, 4, 6–7, 9–11, 14–15, 29, 147, 296
Sigel, Eugene (grandfather of EBS), 2–4, 5, 8, 296
Silouan of Athos, Saint, 150, 220, 275
Simeon the Stylite, 289
Skobtsova, Saint Maria, 59, 83, 87, 109–10, 113, 219, 265–66, 273, 277, 278, 296
Skobtsova, Yur, 87
Sollogoub, Michel, 193
Soloviev, Vladimir, 62, 210
Sophrony (Sakharov), 220, 221
Soukhanoff-Podkolzine, Mariana Borissovna. See Behr, Mariana Borissovna (née Soukhanoff-Podkolzine)
Spiller, Vsevolod, 174
Spiridon, Archimandrite, 113
Stalin, 131
Staniloae, Fr., 208
Stark, Boris, 172, 174
Stephanos, Fr., 266
Strauss, David Friedrich, 3
Strauss, Richard, 287
Stressinger family, 3
Struve, Alexis, 298
Struve, Nikita, 199
Struve, Pierre, 168, 169, 183, 190, 199
Struve, Tatiana, 168
Sylvester, Fr., 90

Tamouch, Philip, 277
Tarassoff, Georges, 183
Tchékan, Jean, 194, 197
Teresa, Sister, 255
Teresa of Avila, Saint, 150
Theodore de Beza, 47
Theophane the Recluse, Saint, 89, 115
Thomas à Kempis, 121

Tikhon of Zadonsk, 113, 202
Tillich, Paul, 227
Timiadis, Emilianos, 138, 139, 205,
  290
Tincq, Henri, 263
Toulat, Pierre, 251
travel of EBS
  Cambridge, 287–88
  Gassin, summers at, 107–8, 269,
    287, 290
  to Greece, 165–67
  Holy Land, 167–71, 234–37
  Ottawa, 237–38
  Romania, 206–17
  Russia, 288
  Tantur, 234–37
  United States, 276–77
  the USSR, 171–74

Valerian, Fr., 118
Van den Mensbrugghen, Alexis, 123,
  141
Velitchkovsky, Saint Paissius, 115
Villot, Cardinal, 137
Vivin, Liliane, 85
Vivin, Mme., 54, 84, 85
Vladimir, Grand Prince, 18
Vladimir, Metr., 127, 129, 183
Vogt, Vsevolod de, 25
Volkringer family, 107
Vorontsov-Veliaminov, Nadia (Behr),
  176
Vylder, Gabriel de, 281

Walters family, 64
Ware, Kallistos, 101, 247–48
Westercamp, Jacqueline, 251
Westphal, Charles, 12
Whitman, Walt, 161
Winnaert, Bishop, 123
works of EBS
  1931–1939, 315–16
  1945–1969, Nancy, 316–19

1970–2005, Paris, 319–34
Alexander Bukharev, 118
Discerning the Signs of the Times,
  277–78
"Easter in the Eastern Orthodox
  Church," 55–56
"Eastern Monasticism and Its
  Role as Guardian of the Essence
  of the Orthodox Spiritual
  Tradition," 89
"An Essay on the Role of Monasti-
  cism in the Spiritual Life of the
  Russian People," 109
"For the 20th Anniversary of the
  Death of Mother Maria
  Skobtsova," 265–66
"The Gender Difference in the
  Context of a Christian Civili-
  zation," 245
"In the Image and Likeness of
  God" (course), 202–3
"The Jesus Prayer, or the Mystery
  of Orthodox Monastic
  Spirituality," 96–98
"Life and Thought of Protestant
  Youth," 56
"Mary, Mother of God," 245
"The Meaning of the Participation
  of Women in the Life of the
  Church" (lecture), 209
*The Ministry of Women in the
  Church*, 213, 244–47
A Monk of the Eastern Church,
  266–71
"Notes on the Russian Idea of
  Holiness as Exemplified by the
  Saints Canonized by the
  Russian Church," 35, 37, 55
*The Ordination of Women in the
  Orthodox Church*, 212, 247
"Orthodoxy and Catholicism
  (Some Points of Doctrinal
  Divergence)," 251

OLGA LOSSKY is the author of a novel *Requiem pour un Clou,* many articles, and a play *Lourmel, 26 octobre 1936.* She is the great-granddaughter of the Orthodox theologian Vladimir Lossky.